GENERAL INTERNATIONAL ORGANIZATION

VAN NOSTRAND POLITICAL SCIENCE SERIES

Editor

FRANKLIN L. BURDETTE
University of Maryland

GODSHALL, W. L. (Editor) —*Principles and Functions of Government in the United States*

LONDON, K.—*How Foreign Policy Is Made*

PLISCHKE, E.—*Conduct of American Diplomacy*

DIXON, R. G., JR. and PLISCHKE, ELMER—*American Government: Basic Documents and Materials*

SPROUT, HAROLD and MARGARET—*Foundations of National Power,* 2nd Ed.

LANCASTER, LANE W.—*Government in Rural America,* 2nd Ed.

JORRIN, M.—*Governments of Latin America*

TORPEY, WILLIAM G.—*Public Personnel Management*

PLISCHKE, ELMER—*International Relations: Basic Documents*

GOODMAN, WILLIAM—*The Two-Party System in the United States*

WATKINS, J. T., IV and ROBINSON, J. W.—*General International Organization: A Source Book*

GENERAL
INTERNATIONAL
ORGANIZATION

A Source Book

JAMES T. WATKINS, IV

Executive Head and Professor of Political Science
Stanford University
Stanford, California

AND

J. WILLIAM ROBINSON

Chairman, Department of Political Science
and International Relations
Whittier College
Whittier, California

D. VAN NOSTRAND COMPANY, INC.

PRINCETON, NEW JERSEY
TORONTO · LONDON
NEW YORK

D. VAN NOSTRAND COMPANY, INC.

120 Alexander St., Princeton, New Jersey
257 Fourth Avenue, New York 10, New York
25 Hollinger Rd., Toronto 16, Canada
Macmillan Co., Ltd., St. Martin's St., London, W.C. 2, England

*All correspondence should be addressed to the
principal office of the company at Princeton, N. J.*

Contents

Introduction

THE wisdom of confronting students of history and politics with the documents that belong to the raw materials out of which these disciplines are wrought is not disputed. It may be unimportant that a distinguished professor of public law should refer his students to the Treaty of Chaumont as the first multipartite treaty *document* of its kind or that the textbooks should continue repeating that Wilson and Lloyd George in *a treaty* with Clemenceau bound their two countries to aid the defense of France under given circumstances. Such may perhaps be dismissed as minor faults which familiarity with the instruments themselves will correct. More valuable, however, is the new dimension, a representation in the round, so to speak, which the subject matter takes on once the student goes to the documents which lie behind his textbook.

A growing list of books collecting in one volume the significant documents relating to a subject or a field of study reflects the inconvenience which faces the student who would pursue his studies among the sources, and the professor who would send his class to them and the harassed librarian. Assuming here that the object is not also to acquaint the student with the great multivolume collections, such as the *United States Statutes at Large* or the *British Foreign and State Papers* or the League of Nations *Official Journal,* there is no loss to the student who finds a treaty or despatch or committee report in an anthology rather than in a government publication. For the student it is the document, and not the publication, which gives a higher relief to the event in which he is interested. Especially in the case of classes in institutions where the library is without official publications in which the students can find their sources if they will, we shall make the students familiar with the great state papers or those which are otherwise important only by providing for them such volumes of "selected documents" as this one.

Ours has been compiled with a view to the convenience of our own students and in the hope that others will also find it useful. It has grown out of our own practice. We introduce the students in our international organization courses to the more significant documents which illuminate the subject. For want of a suitable publication we have been faced with the necessity of resorting extensively to the mimeographing machine, and we have been hampered by the consequent limitation upon the number of documents which can be put into students' hands. Because of the undue wear and tear upon collections and curators alike, it is not feasible to turn large undergraduate classes loose in the library's document room. This is our solution.

The organization of the volume reflects the organization of the introductory courses it is designed to serve. We believe that the student comes best to the subject by an approach which brings home to him both the deep roots which it has in history and the recentness with which it has flowered in general international organization, first, under the name of the League of Nations and, now, under that of the United Nations. Any other approach tends to leave in the student's mind an impression of rigidity in institutions, whereas in fact they are fluid. Moreover—and this is especially true of Americans, who tend to reason by analogy with the Federal Union—any other approach leaves the student with the conviction that, by the adoption of the Charter, the United Nations sprang into existence full grown and, like Athena of old, armed and helmeted for war.   •

Contemporary international organization represents only the growing edge of a long evolutionary process. The process has not been steady: deviations and overlappings occur; there have been long periods during which little or nothing was added to international institutional life; and in the last century and a half (with which the present collection is concerned) more has occurred in the development of international organization than during the several millennia of recorded history preceding the Congress of Vienna. Nevertheless, the nineteenth and twentieth centuries—"centuries of action"—continue an old process at an accelerated rate. These centuries are marked by the development of international institutions from relatively simple to more complex forms. If the student can gain an appreciation of the evolutionary character of international organization within the framework of the multistate system, he will more readily understand why the future of both may not lie in one particular organization, even one so important as the United Nations.

Our choice of documents for inclusion in what is a collection of modest scope represents a compromise imposed by reasons of space. Like all such collections it is open to criticism for what others will see as errors of judgment. Nevertheless, both the criteria adopted and the exceptions made are thought to be defensible.

Out of the mass of documents assembled, in number too great either for student consumption or for the volume we contemplated, we have made our selection by a procedure as simple as it has proved satisfactory. We began by asking: What are the ten most important documents in the field? These selected, we went on through successive decades until we reached the number, 65 in all, whose combined length gave us a volume of the size desired.

But what makes a document important? Some, like the Charter of the Organization of American States or the Statute of the Council of Europe, are the organic acts of institutions with a large role in contemporary international relations. Others, like the Holy Alliance or the Red Cross Convention or the Declaration of Human Rights, have become classroom words among students. Still others, such as the first Mouravieff circular, the Balfour report on the Secretariat of the League of Nations, and the draft "Charter of the United Nations" of 1943, remain as the springs from which have started developments of lasting consequence. That there is difficulty in weighing such criteria we are the first to admit.

A glance at our list and through the book will show that we have not been altogether consistent. Although we have strong views as to the value of presenting the whole document for the student to see, in some cases we have included only excerpts. These few are important; the excerpts show what makes the document significant, and the remainder is too lengthy for inclusion. In the interest of space, too, we have omitted from treaty texts the names of diplomatic agents as well as their signatures; but here again, for the purpose of emphasizing shifting fashions we have, for example, given both in the Chaumont treaties and the Locarno Pact. We have been inconsistent even to the point of including two that are not documents at all, but readings. They are here only because we want no student of the subject to miss them.

In conclusion, acknowledgment is gratefully made to Sarah E. Nielsen King of Whittier College and Eugene Lindstrom of Stanford University for their help in typing, photographing and checking texts.

Part One

DOCUMENTS OF THE

NINETEENTH CENTURY

Chapter 1

The Vienna System

1. THE TREATY OF CHAUMONT, 1 MARCH 1814 [1]

Proposed by Castlereagh for the purpose of holding together the coalition if Napoleon should refuse the surrender terms offered him, this "Treaty of Union, Concert and Subsidy," which was a group of three bilateral agreements between Great Britain and Austria, Prussia and Russia, was signed at Chaumont-en-Bassigny, 1 March 1814, and published on the ninth of the same month. The Treaty of Chaumont brought the four powers into a twenty-year alliance, the so-called Quadruple Alliance, which by the later addition of Bourbon France became the Quintuple Alliance.[2]

IN THE NAME OF THE MOST HOLY AND UNDIVIDED TRINITY

His Majesty the King of the United Kingdom of Great Britain and Ireland, His Imperial and Royal Apostolic Majesty the Emperor of Austria, King of Hungary and Bohemia, His Majesty the Emperor of All the Russias, and His Majesty the King of Prussia, having transmitted to the French Government proposals for concluding a General Peace, and being desirous, should France refuse the Conditions therein contained, to draw closer the ties which unite them for the vigorous prosecution of a War undertaken for the salutary purpose of putting an end to the miseries of Europe, of securing its future repose, by re-establishing a just balance of Power, and being at the same time desirous, should the Almighty bless their pacific intentions, to fix the means of maintaining against every attempt the order of things which shall have been the happy consequence of their efforts, have agreed to sanction by a solemn Treaty, signed separately by each of the 4 Powers with the 3 others, this twofold engagement.

In consequence, His Majesty the King of the United Kingdom of Great Britain and Ireland has named to discuss, settle, and sign the Conditions of the present Treaty, with His Imperial and Royal Apostolic Majesty, the Right Honourable Robert Stewart, Viscount Castlereagh, one of His said Majesty's Most Honourable Privy Council, Member of Parliament, Colonel of the Londonderry Regiment of Militia, and his Principal Secretary of State for Foreign Affairs, &c., sic, sic., and His Imperial and Royal Apostolic Majesty having named, on his part, the Sieur Clement Wenceslaus Lothaire, Prince Metternich Winneburgh Ochseuhausen, Knight of the Golden Fleece, Grand Cross of the Order of St. Stephen, Knight of the Russian Orders of St. Andrew, of St. Alexander Newsky, and of St. Anne, of the First Class,

[1] *British and Foreign State Papers*, I, pp. 121-129.
[2] Consecrating the principle of concerted action by the Great Powers in international affairs of general concern, the Treaty of Chaumont and the supplementary agreement of 20 November 1814 (see Doc. 3) laid the basis for the Vienna system and for the Concert of Europe, which followed.

Knight of the Prussian Orders of the Black and Red Eagles, Grand Cross of the Order of St. Joseph of Wurtzburg, Knight of the Order of St. Hubert of Bavaria, of the Golden Eagle of Wurtemburg, and of several others, his Chamberlain, Privy Councillor, Minister of State, of Conferences, and of Foreign Affairs;

The said Plenipotentiaries, after having exchanged their Full Powers, found to be in due and proper form, have agreed upon the following Articles:

Art. I. The High Contracting Parties above named solemnly engage by the present Treaty, and in the event of France refusing to accede to the Conditions of Peace now proposed, to apply all the means of their respective States to the vigorous prosecution of the War against that Power, and to employ them in perfect concert, in order to obtain for themselves and for Europe a General Peace, under the protection of which the rights and liberties of all Nations may be established and secured.

This engagement shall in no respect affect the Stipulations which the several Powers have already contracted relative to the number of Troops to be kept against the Enemy; and it is understood that the Courts of England, Austria, Russia, and Prussia, engage by the present Treaty to keep in the field, each of them, 150,000 effective men, exclusive of garrisons, to be employed in active service against the common Enemy.

II. The High Contracting Parties reciprocally engage not to negotiate separately with the common Enemy, nor to sign Peace, Truce, nor Convention, but with common consent. They, moreover, engage not to lay down their Arms until the object of the War, mutually understood and agreed upon, shall have been attained.

III. In order to contribute in the most prompt and decisive manner to fulfil this great object, His Britannic Majesty engages to furnish a Subsidy of £5,000,000 for the service of the year 1814, to be divided in equal proportions amongst the 3 Powers; and His said Majesty promises moreover to arrange, before the 1st of January in each year, with Their Imperial and Royal Majesties, the further Succours to be furnished during the subsequent year, if (which God forbid) the War should so long continue.

The Subsidy above stipulated of £5,000,000 shall be paid in London, by monthly instalments, and in equal proportions, to the Ministers of the respective Powers duly authorized to receive the same.

In case Peace should be signed between the Allied Powers and France before the expiration of the year, the Subsidy, calculated upon the scale of £5,000,000, shall be paid up to the end of the month in which the Definitive Treaty shall have been signed; and His Britannic Majesty promises, in addition, to pay to Austria and to Prussia 2 months, and to Russia 4 months, over and above the stipulated Subsidy, to cover the expenses of the return of their Troops within their own Frontiers.

IV. The High Contracting Parties will be entitled respectively to accredit to the Generals commanding their Armies, Officers, who will be allowed to correspond with their Governments, for the purpose of informing them of the Military events and of everything which relates to the operations of the Armies.

V. The High Contracting Parties, reserving to themselves to concert together, on the conclusion of a Peace with France, as to the means best adapted to guarantee to Europe, and to themselves reciprocally, the continuance of the Peace, have also determined to enter, without delay, into defensive engagements for the protection of their respective States in Europe against every attempt which France might make to infringe the order of things resulting from such Pacification.

VI. To effect this, they agree that in the event of one of the High Contracting Parties being threatened with an attack on the part of France, the others shall employ their most strenuous efforts to prevent it, by friendly interposition.

VII. In the case of these endeavours proving ineffectual, the High Contracting Parties promise to come to the immediate assistance of the Power attacked, each with a body of 60,000 men.

VIII. Such Auxiliary Corps shall respectively consist of 50,000 Infantry and 10,000 Cavalry, with a train of Artillery, and ammunition in proportion to the number of Troops: the Auxiliary Corps shall be ready to take the field in the most effective manner, for the safety of the Power attacked or threatened, within 2 months at latest after the requisition shall have been made.

IX. As the situation of the seat of War, or other circumstances, might render it difficult for Great Britain to furnish the stipulated Succours in English Troops within the term prescribed, and to maintain the same on a War establishment, His Britannic Majesty reserves the right of furnishing his Contingent to the requiring Power in Foreign Troops in his pay, or to pay annually to that Power a sum of money, at the rate of £20 per each man for Infantry, and of £30 for Cavalry, until the stipulated Succour shall be complete.

The mode of furnishing this Succour by Great Britain shall be settled amicably, in each particular case, between His Britannic Majesty and the Power threatened or attacked, as soon as the requisition shall be made: the same principle shall be adopted with regard to the Forces which His Britannic Majesty engages to furnish by the Ist Article of the present Treaty.

X. The Auxiliary Army shall be under the orders of the Commander-in-Chief of the Army of the requiring Power; it shall be commanded by its own General, and employed in all military operations according to the rules of War. The pay of the Auxiliary Army shall be defrayed by the requiring Power; the rations and portions of provisions and forage, &c., as well as quarters, shall be furnished by the requiring Power as soon as the Auxiliary Army shall have passed its own Frontier; and that upon the same footing as the said Power maintains, or shall maintain, its own Troops in the field or in quarters.

XI. The discipline and administration of the Troops shall solely depend upon their own Commander; they shall not be separated. The trophies and booty taken from the Enemy shall belong to the Troops who take them.

XII. Whenever the amount of the stipulated Succours shall be found inadequate to the exigency of the case, the High Contracting Parties reserve to themselves to make, without loss of time, an ulterior arrangement as to the additional Succours which it may be deemed necessary to furnish.

XIII. The High Contracting Parties mutually promise, that in case they shall be reciprocally engaged in Hostilities, in consequence of furnishing the stipulated Succours, the Party requiring and the Parties called upon, and acting as Auxiliaries in the War, shall not make Peace but by common consent.

XIV. The Engagements contracted by the present Treaty, shall not prejudice those which the High Contracting Parties may have entered into with other Powers, nor prevent them from forming new engagements with other States, with a view of obtaining the same salutary result.

XV. In order to render more effectual the Defensive Engagements above stipulated, by uniting for their common defence the Powers the most exposed to a French invasion, the High Contracting Parties engage to invite those Powers to accede to the present Treaty of Defensive Alliance.

XVI. The present Treaty of Defensive Alliance having for its object to maintain the equilibrium of Europe, to secure the repose and independence of its States, and to prevent the invasions which during so many years have desolated the World, the High Contracting Parties have agreed to extend the duration of it to 20 years, to take date from the day of its Signature; and they reserve to themselves,

to concert upon its ulterior prolongation, 3 years before its expiration, should circumstances require it.

XVII. The present Treaty shall be ratified, and the Ratifications exchanged within 2 months, or sooner if possible.

In witness whereof, the respective Plenipotentiaries have signed the same, and affixed thereto the Seal of their Arms.

2. THE HOLY ALLIANCE, 26 SEPTEMBER 1815 [1]

As early as 1804, Czar Alexander I had proposed that, as soon as Europe should overthrow Napoleon, a League of European States be established. After the close of the Congress of Vienna, Alexander renewed his proposal in the form that comes down to us as the Holy Alliance. Animated by apparently sincere if confused motives, the Czar met with a mixed reception at the hands of his allies, who now feared Russia only less than they had feared France. This "Holy Alliance of Sovereigns," a league of rulers, was signed, however, by the Czar, Francis I, of Austria, and Frederick William III, of Prussia; it was subsequently assented to by all the Christian European rulers except the British (ostensibly for constitutional reasons), who "concurred," and the Pope, who was not included.

IN THE NAME OF THE MOST HOLY AND
INDIVISIBLE TRINITY

Holy Alliance of Sovereigns of Austria, Prussia, and Russia

Their Majesties the Emperor of Austria, the King of Prussia, and the Emperor of Russia, having, in consequence of the great events which have marked the course of the three last years in Europe, and especially of the blessings which it has pleased Divine Providence to shower down upon those States which place their confidence and their hope on it alone, acquired the intimate conviction of the necessity of settling the steps to be observed by the Powers, in their reciprocal relations, upon the

sublime truths which the Holy Religion of our Saviour teaches;

GOVERNMENT AND POLITICAL RELATIONS

They solemnly declare that the present Act has no other object than to publish, in the face of the whole world, their fixed resolution, both in the administration of their respective States, and in their political relations with every other Government, to take for their sole guide the precepts of that Holy Religion, namely, the precepts of Justice, Christian Charity, and Peace, which, far from being applicable only to private concerns, must have an immediate influence on the councils of Princes, and guide all their steps, as being the only means of consolidating human institutions and remedying their imperfections. In consequence, their Majesties have agreed on the following Articles:—

PRINCIPLES OF THE CHRISTIAN RELIGION

ART. I. Conformably to the words of the Holy Scriptures, which command all men to consider each other as brethren, the Three contracting Monarchs will remain united by the bonds of a true and indissoluble fraternity, and considering each other as fellow countrymen, they will, on all occasions

[1] For the French text, see *British and Foreign State Papers*, III, pp. 211 f. This English translation is taken from Edward Hertslet, *The Map of Europe by Treaty*, III, p. 317.

and in all places, lend each other aid and assistance; and, regarding themselves towards their subjects and armies as fathers of families, they will lead them, in the same spirit of fraternity with which they are animated, to protect Religion, Peace, and Justice.

FRATERNITY AND AFFECTION

ART. II. In consequence, the sole principle of force, whether between the said Governments or between their Subjects, shall be that of doing each other reciprocal service, and of testifying by unalterable good will the mutual affection with which they ought to be animated, to consider themselves all as members of one and the same Christian nation; the three allied Princes looking on themselves as merely delegated by Providence to govern three branches of the One family, namely, Austria, Prussia, and Russia, thus confessing that the Christian world, of which they and their people form a part, has in reality no other Sovereign than Him to whom alone power really belongs, because in Him alone are found all the treasures of love, science, and infinite wisdom, that

is to say, God, our Divine Saviour, the Word of the Most High, the Word of Life. Their Majesties consequently recommend to their people, with the most tender solicitude, as the sole means of enjoying that Peace which arises from a good conscience, and which alone is durable, to strengthen themselves every day more and more in the principles and exercise of the duties which the Divine Saviour has taught to mankind.

ACCESSION OF FOREIGN POWERS

ART. III. All the Powers who shall choose solemnly to avow the sacred principles which have dictated the present Acts, and shall acknowledge how important it is for the happiness of nations, too long agitated, that these truths should henceforth exercise over the destinies of mankind all the influence which belongs to them, will be received with equal ardour and affection into this Holy Alliance.

Done in triplicate, and signed at Paris, the year of Grace 1815, 14/26th September.

(L.S.) FRANCIS.
(L.S.) FREDERICK WILLIAM.
(L.S.) ALEXANDER.

3. SUPPLEMENTARY AGREEMENT TO THE TREATY OF CHAUMONT, 20 NOVEMBER 1815 [1]

Although the Napoleonic wars had been concluded by a "General Treaty of Peace," the so-called first Treaty of Paris,[2] between France and the coalition powers, Napoleon's attempted return in the ill-fated "Hundred Days" led to a revision of the peace agreement in the so-called Second Treaty of Paris [3] along much harsher lines, including the stationing in France of an army of occupation.

On the same day the signatories of the Treaty of Chaumont signed a "Treaty of Alliance and Friendship" in the form of three bilateral agreements, which provided, inter

alia, for future conferences at fixed periods. The treaty provides the basis for the subsequent congresses of the Vienna system.

IN THE NAME OF THE MOST HOLY AND UNDIVIDED TRINITY

The purpose of the Alliance concluded at Vienna the 25th day of March, 1815, having been happily attained by the re-establishment in France of the order of things which

[1] British and Foreign State Papers, III, pp. 273-280.
[2] A group of seven bilateral agreements between France and each of the four powers of the Quadruple Alliance as well as Spain, Portugal and Sweden, signed 30 May 1814.

Article XXXIII provided for the calling of the Congress of Vienna.
[3] A group of four bilateral agreements between France and each of the members of the Quadruple Alliance, signed 20 November 1815.

the last criminal attempt of Napoleon Bonaparte had momentarily subverted; their Majesties the King of the United Kingdom of Great Britain and Ireland, the Emperor of Austria, King of Hungary and Bohemia, the Emperor of all the Russias, and the King of Prussia, considering that the repose of Europe is essentially interwoven with the confirmation of the order of things founded on the maintenance of the Royal Authority and of the Constitutional Charter, and wishing to employ all their means to prevent the general tranquillity, (the object of the wishes of mankind and the constant end of their efforts) from being again disturbed; desirous moreover to draw closer the ties which unite them for the common interests of their People, have resolved to give to the principles solemnly laid down in the Treaties of Chaumont of the 1st of March, 1814, and of Vienna of the 25th of March, 1815, the application, the most analogous to the present state of affairs, and to fix beforehand by a solemn Treaty the principles which they propose to follow, in order to guaranty Europe from the dangers by which she may still be manaced (sic.);

For which purpose the High Contracting Parties have named, to discuss, settle and sign the conditions of this Treaty, namely: . . . .

Who, after having exchanged their Full Powers, found to be in good and due form, have agreed upon the following Articles:

ART. I. The High Contracting Parties reciprocally promise to maintain, in its force and vigour, the Treaty signed this day with His Most Christian Majesty, and to see that the Stipulations of the said Treaty, as well as those of the Particular Conventions which have reference thereto, shall be strictly and faithfully executed in their fullest extent.

II. The High Contracting Parties, having engaged in the War which is just terminated, for the purpose of maintaining inviolably the arrangements settled at Paris last year, for the safety and interest of Europe, have judged it advisable to renew the said engagements by the present Act, and to confirm them as mutually obligatory,—subject to the modifications contained in the Treaty signed this day with the Plenipotentiaries of His Most Christian Majesty,—and particularly those by which Napoleon Bonaparte and his Family, in pursuance of the Treaty of the 11th of April, 1814, have been for ever excluded from the Supreme Power in France, which exclusion the Contracting Powers bind themselves, by the present Act, to maintain in full vigour, and, should it be necessary, with the whole of their Forces. And as the same Revolutionary principles which upheld the last criminal usurpation, might again, under other forms, convulse France, and thereby endanger the repose of other States; under these circumstances, the High Contracting Parties, solemnly admitting it to be their duty to redouble their watchfulness for the tranquillity and interests of their People, engage, in case so unfortunate an event should again occur, to concert amongst themselves, and with His Most Christian Majesty, the measures which they may judge necessary to be pursued for the safety of their respective States, and for the general tranquillity of Europe.

III. The High Contracting Parties, in agreeing with His Most Christian Majesty that a Line of Military Positions in France should be occupied by a Corps of Allied Troops, during a certain number of years, had in view to secure, as far as lay in their power, the effect of the Stipulations contained in Articles I and II of the present Treaty; and, uniformly disposed to adopt every salutary measure calculated to secure the tranquillity of Europe by maintaining the order of things re-established in France, they engage that, in case the said Body of Troops should be attacked or menaced with an attack on the part of France, the said Powers should be again obliged to place themselves on a War Establishment against that Power, in order to maintain either of the said Stipulations, or to secure and support the great interests to which they relate, each of the High Contracting Parties shall furnish, without delay, according to the Stipulations of the Treaty of Chaumont, and especially in pursuance of the VIIth and VIIIth Articles of this Treaty, its full Contingent of 60,000 men, in addition to the Forces left in France, or such part of the said Contingent as the exigency of the case may require, should be put in motion.

IV. If, unfortunately, the Forces stipulated in the preceding Articles should be found insufficient, the High Contracting Parties will concert together, without loss of time, as to the additional number of Troops to be furnished by each for the support of the Common Cause; and they engage to employ, in case of need, the whole of their Forces, in order to bring the War to a speedy and successful termination; reserving to themselves the right to prescribe, by common consent, such conditions of Peace as shall hold out to Europe a sufficient guarantee against the recurrence of a similar calamity.

V. The High Contracting Parties, having agreed to the dispositions laid down in the preceding Articles, for the purpose of securing the effect of their engagements during the period of the Temporary Occupation, declare, moreover, that even after the expiration of this measure, the said Engagements shall still remain in full force and vigour, for the purpose of carrying into effect such measures as may be deemed necessary for the maintenance of the Stipulations contained in the Articles I. and II. of the present Act.

VI. To facilitate and to secure the execution of the present Treaty, and to consolidate the connections, which at the present moment so closely unite the 4 Sovereigns for the happiness of the World, the High Contracting Parties have agreed to renew their Meetings at fixed periods, either under the immediate auspices of the Sovereigns themselves, or by their respective Ministers, for the purpose of consulting upon their common interests, and for the consideration of the measures which at each of those periods shall be considered the most salutary, for the repose and prosperity of Nations, and for the maintenance of the Peace of Europe.

VII. The present Treaty shall be ratified, and the Ratifications shall be exchanged within 2 months, or sooner, if possible.

In faith of which, the respective Plenipotentiaries have signed it, and affixed thereto the Seal of their Arms.

Done at Paris, the 20th of November in the year of our Lord, 1815.

(L.S.) CASTLEREAGH.
(L.S.) WELLINGTON.
(L.S.) METTERNICH.
(L.S.) WESSENBERG.

Chapter 2

The Concert of Europe

4. EDWARD GREY'S ACCOUNT OF THE LAST MEETING OF THE CONCERT, 1913 [1]

The Great Alliance and the Vienna system, both fatally weakened by the British return to isolationism, gave way to the "Concert of Europe," intermittent conferences among the leading European powers for the purpose of interposing settlements in the interest of maintaining the general peace. Little more than a tacit agreement that the Powers would consult together and that each had a right to suggest a conference at a time of crisis, the Concert was the measure of Britain's concession to the principle of European unity. Much as in the case of the United States after her rejection of the League of Nations, Britain was represented only at conferences of her choosing.

However, the Concert, although in later decades effective chiefly in connection with the "Eastern question," preserved the principle of the Vienna system that all the Great Powers, as guardians of the European order resting on the post-Napoleonic treaties, had an interest in any situation threatening the general peace. This was a great step forward by comparison with the anarchical practices of the 18th century, but the simple machinery of the Concert offers a striking contrast to the institutions developed after World War I.

[In 1912] The victory of the Balkan Allies over Turkey opened the Balkan question, and the risk of consequent trouble between the Great Powers most concerned became appreciable. . . . The point of friction and danger was Albania. Turkish rule in Albania was smashed by the war; the Balkan Allies were flushed with victory; Serbia wanted access to the Adriatic on com-

mercial ground, and she and Montenegro might regard portions of Albania as part of the prize and spoil of war.

Austria was determined that if Albania ceased to be Turkish territory it should not pass into the hands and form part of the aggrandizement of Serbia. Serbia, borne on the tide of her own victories, might easily reach the point of inevitable conflict with Austria. If this happened, and if Russia felt that she was required to support Serbia, European war was inevitable. To prepare in advance against this danger, and to avoid catastrophe, I proposed a Conference of the Powers. German and Austria agreed, and Russia was willing; this being so, the consent of France and Italy was assured. I did not press for London to be the meeting place; personally I was inclined to Paris. The French would be pleased by the choice of Paris, and the Conference would start with that asset of good-will. Also I was not anxious to have the great addition to work, already heavy, of sitting in the Conference personally. London, however, was chosen, and early in December the Conference met.

There were six of us: Lichnowsky, Mensdorff, and Imperiali, the Ambassadors respectively of Germany, Austria and Italy; Cambon and Benken-

[1] Viscount Grey, *Twenty-Five Years* (New York, 1925), I, pp. 254-256, 262 f., 266 f.

dorff, the Ambassadors of France and Russia; and myself for Britain. Such responsibility as there was of presiding fell to me, but we made the proceedings as informal as those of a committee of friends, which in fact we were. We met in the afternoons, generally about four o'clock, and, with a short adjournment to an adjoining room for tea, we continued till six or seven o'clock.

The Conference did not have its last meeting till August 1913, and during all that time we remained in being as a Conference though we only met when occasion required. The friendly relations between us could not prevent our proceedings from being protracted and sometimes intolerably wearisome. It was said after the first weeks that, Cambon, when asked about the progress of the Conference, had replied that it would continue till there were skeletons sitting around the table. . . .

The question of greatest difficulty, and even danger, was the determination of the boundary on the north and northeast of Albania, where Serbia claimed more than Austria was willing to allow. . . .

After August 1913 the Conference did not meet again. There was no formal finish; we were not photographed in a group; we had no votes of thanks; no valedictory speeches; we just left off meeting. We had not settled anything, not even all the details of the Albanian boundaries; but we had served a useful purpose. We had been something to which point after point could be referred; we had been a means of keeping all the six powers in direct and friendly touch. The mere fact that we were in existence, and that we should have to be broken up before peace was broken, was in itself an appreciable barrier against war. We were a means of gaining time, and the longer we remained in being the more reluctance was there for us to disperse. The Governments concerned got used to us, and to the habit of making us useful. When we ceased to meet, the present danger to the peace of Europe was over; the things that we did not settle were not threatening that peace; the things that had threatened the relations between the Great Powers in 1912-13 we had deprived of their dangerous features.

My own part in this Conference seems very drab and humdrum in recollection. British interests were not affected by the destiny of Djakova or Scutari, and my part was not to initiate or to shape a policy, but to serve as a useful and patient mediator between Russia and Austria, to be diligent in finding the point of conciliation, and burying the point of difference. . . .

It did not occur to any of us to suggest that we should be kept in existence as a Conference, as a body ready to be called together at any moment, to which future Balkan, or indeed any troubles between the Great Powers, might be referred. We could not have suggested this officially ourselves: it was not for us as a body to magnify our own importance. Still less could the British Secretary of State for Foreign Affairs have proposed that there should be a permanent body in London, with himself as President, to settle continental troubles. . . . So far as I know, the good faith, the good-will, the single-mindedness, the freedom from all egotism and personal rivalries that had been characteristic of this Conference, of all its members individually and collectively made no impression, or none but a passing impression, upon the Governments in Europe. These qualities were of little value before the war, not because they did not exist, but because hardly anybody believed in their existence.

The members of the Ambassadors' Conference of 1912-13 were all alive, available and at their posts in 1914; but no one in Berlin or Vienna seems to have remembered the past or found in the recollection of 1912-13 any hope for the future. So, when the crisis came in 1914, although the suggestion of settling by the same machinery as in

1912 was made, it was dismissed peremptorily by Germany and Austria. . . . In 1912-13, the current of European affairs was settling towards war. Austria and Russia were drifting with it, and dragging the other Powers in the same fatal direction. In agreeing to a Conference, and forming one in 1912, it was as if we all put out anchors to prevent ourselves from being swept away. The anchors held. Then the current seemed to slacken and the anchors were pulled up. The Conference was allowed to dissolve. We seemed to be safe. In reality it was not so; the set of the current was the same, and in a year's time we were all swept into the cataract of war.

5. EDWARD GREY'S COLLECTIVE SECURITY OFFER TO GERMANY, 30 JULY 1914 [1]

As Europe slid toward the brink of war during July 1914, Sir Edward Grey, the British Foreign Minister, sought desperately to find some means whereby the catastrophe might be averted. The sands had all but run out when he made what he regarded as a supreme effort [2] by offering Germany, should the crisis be safely passed, British support for some scheme of collective security. The offer reveals how far short of a general international organization on the scale of the League of Nations the imagination of practical statesmen fell only five years before.

Foreign Office, July 30, 1914
(Telegraphic.)

Your telegram of 29th July.

His Majesty's Government cannot for a moment entertain the Chancellor's proposal that they should bind themselves to neutrality on such terms.

What he asks us in effect is to engage to stand by while French colonies are taken and France is beaten so long as Germany does not take French territory as distinct from the colonies.

From the material point of view such a proposal is unacceptable, for France, without further territory in Europe being taken from her, could be so crushed as to lose her position as a Great Power, and become subordinate to German policy.

Altogether, apart from that, it would be a disgrace for us to make this bargain with Germany at the expense of France, a disgrace from which the good name of this country would never recover.

The Chancellor also in effect asks us to bargain away whatever obligation or interest we have as regards the neutrality of Belgium. We could not entertain that bargain either.

Having said so much it is unnecessary to examine whether the prospect of a future general neutrality agreement between England and Germany offered positive advantages sufficient to compensate us for tying our hands now. We must preserve our full freedom to act as circumstances may seem to us to require in any such unfavourable and regrettable development of the present crisis as the Chancellor contemplates.

You should speak to the Chancellor in the above sense, and add most earnestly that the one way of maintaining the good relations between England and Germany is that they should continue to work together to preserve the peace of Europe; if we succeed in this object, the mutual relations of Germany and England will, I believe, be *ipso facto* improved and strengthened. For that object His Majesty's Government will work in that way with all sincerity and good-will.

And I will say this: If the peace of Europe can be preserved, and the pres-

[1] Sir Edward Grey to Sir F. Goschen, 30 July 1914, *British and Foreign State Papers,* CVIII, 754.

[2] "Every thought in the telegram (from the British minister in Berlin) pointed to despair. But while there is still time one does not sit down under despair; only the effort to lift it must be big and the appeal must be big." (Viscount Grey, *op. cit.,* I, p. 317.)

ent crisis safely passed, my own endeavour will be to promote some arrangement to which Germany could be a party, by which she could be assured that no aggressive or hostile policy would be pursued against her or her allies by France, Russia, and ourselves, jointly or separately. I have desired this and worked for it, as far as I could, through the last Balkan crisis, and, Germany having a corresponding object, our relations sensibly improved. The idea has hitherto been too Utopian to form the subject of definite proposals, but if this present crisis, so much more acute than any that Europe has gone through for generations, be safely passed, I am hopeful that the relief and reaction which will follow may make possible some more definite rapprochement between the Powers than has been possible hitherto.

Chapter 3

The Public International Unions

6. THE INTERNATIONAL POSTAL CONVENTION, 9 OCTOBER 1874[1]

Half a century of intolerable confusion in international postal communications led finally in 1874 to the Congress of Berne, at which twenty-two states, including the United States, signed this international postal convention, the "Treaty concerning the formation of a General Postal Union." Under the terms of the convention was established what is known today as the Universal Postal Union, probably the most successful public international union prior to the 20th century. Although many times revised by subsequent "congresses," the original convention created the international postal service substantially in the form that it has today.

Treaty concerning the formation of a General Postal Union, concluded between Germany, Austria-Hungary, Belgium, Denmark, Egypt, Spain, the United States of America, France, Great Britain, Greece, Italy, Luxemburg, Norway, the Netherlands, Portugal, Roumania, Russia, Servia, Sweden, Switzerland, and Turkey.

The undersigned, plenipotentiaries of the Governments of the countries above enumerated, have by common consent, and subject to ratification, agreed upon the following Convention:

ART. I. The countries between which the present treaty is concluded shall form, under the title of *General Postal Union,* a single postal territory for the reciprocal exchange of correspondence between their post-offices.

ART. II. The stipulations of this treaty shall extend to letters, post-cards, books, newspapers, and other printed papers, patterns of merchandise, and legal and commercial documents originating in one of the countries of the Union and intended for another of those countries. They shall also apply to the exchange by post of the articles above mentioned between the countries of the Union and countries foreign to the Union whenever such exchange takes place over the territory of two at least of the contracting parties.

ART. III. The general Union rate of postage is fixed at 25 centimes for a single prepaid letter.

Nevertheless, as a measure of conversion, the option is reserved to each country, in order to suit its monetary or other requirements, of levying a rate higher or lower than this charge, provided that it does not exceed 32 centimes or go below 20 centimes.

Every letter which does not exceed 15 grammes in weight shall be considered a single letter. The charge upon letters exceeding that weight shall be a single rate for every 15 grammes or fraction of 15 grammes.

The charge on unpaid letters shall be double the rate levied in the country of destination on prepaid letters.

The prepayment of post-cards is compulsory. The postage to be charged

[1] *United States Statutes at Large,* XIX, pp. 577-587.

upon them is fixed at one-half of that on paid letters, with power to round off the fractions.

For all conveyance by sea of more than 300 nautical miles within the district of the Union, there may be added to the ordinary postage an additional charge which shall not exceed the half of the general Union rate fixed for a paid letter.

ART. IV. The general Union rate for legal and commercial documents, patterns of merchandise, newspapers, stitched or bound books, pamphlets, music, visiting cards, catalogues, prospectuses, announcements and notices of various kinds, whether printed, engraved, lithographed, or autographed, as well as for photographs, is fixed at 7 centimes for each single packet.

Nevertheless, as a measure of conversion, the option is reserved to each country, in order to suit its monetary or other requirements, of levying a rate higher or lower than this charge, provided that it does not exceed 11 centimes or go below 5 centimes.

Every packet which does not exceed 50 grammes in weight shall be considered a single packet. The charge upon packets exceeding that weight shall be a single rate for every 50 grammes or fraction of 50 grammes.

For all conveyance by sea of more than 300 nautical miles within the district of the Union, there may be added to the ordinary postage an additional charge which shall not exceed the half of the general Union rate fixed for articles of this class.

The maximum weight of the articles mentioned above is fixed at 250 grammes for patterns of merchandise, and at 1000 grammes for all the others.

There is reserved to the Government of each country of the Union the right to refuse to convey over its territory or to deliver articles specified in the present Article with regard to which the laws, orders, and decrees which regulate the conditions of their publication and circulation have not been observed.

ART. V. The articles specified in Article 2 may be registered.

Every registered packet must be prepaid.

The postage payable on registered articles is the same as that on articles not registered.

The charge to be made for registration and for return receipts must not exceed that made in the interior service of the country of origin.

In case of the loss of a registered article, except in the case of *vis major*, there shall be paid an indemnity of 50 francs to the sender, or, at his request, to the addressee, by the Administration of the country in the territory or in the maritime service of which the loss has occurred—that is to say, where the trace of the article has been lost,—unless, according to the legislation of such country, the Administration is not responsible for the loss of registered articles sent through its interior post.

The payment of this indemnity shall be effected with the least possible delay, and, at the latest, within a year from the date of application.

All claim for an indemnity is excluded if it be not made within one year, counting from the date on which the registered article was posted.

ART. VI. Prepayment of postage on every description of article can be effected only by means of postage-stamps or stamped envelopes valid in the country of origin.

Newspapers and other printed papers unpaid or insufficiently paid shall not be forwarded. Other articles when unpaid or insufficiently paid shall be charged as unpaid letters, after deducting the value of the stamped envelopes or postage-stamps (if any) employed.

ART. VII. No additional postage shall be charged for the re-transmission of postal articles within the interior of the Union.

But in case an article which has only passed through the interior service of one of the countries of the Union should, by being re-directed, enter into the service of another country of the Union, the Administration of the country of destination shall add its interior rate.

ART. VIII. Official correspondence relative to the postal service is exempt from postage. With this exception, no franking or reduction of postage is allowed.

ART. IX. Each Administration shall keep the whole of the sums which it collects by virtue of the foregoing Articles 3, 4, 5, 6, and 7. Consequently, there will be no necessity on this head for any accounts between the several Administrations of the Union.

Neither the senders nor the addressees of letters and other postal packets shall be called upon to pay, either in the country of origin or in that of destination, any tax or postal duty other than those contemplated by the Articles above mentioned.

ART. X. The right of transit is guaranteed throughout the entire territory of the Union.

Consequently, there shall be full and entire liberty of exchange, the several Postal Administrations of the Union being able to send reciprocally, in transit through intermediate countries, closed mails as well as correspondence in open mails, according to the requirements of trade and the exigencies of the postal service.

Closed mails and correspondence sent in open mails must always be forwarded by the most rapid routes at the command of the Postal Administrations concerned.

When several routes offer the same advantages of speed, the despatching Administration shall have the right of choosing the route to be adopted.

It is obligatory to make up closed mails whenever the number of letters and other postal packets is of a nature to hinder the operations of the re-forwarding office, according to the declaration of the Administration interested.

The despatching Office shall pay to the Administration of the territory providing the transit, the sum of 2 francs per kilogramme for letters and 25 centimes per kilogramme for the several articles specified in Article 4, net weight, whether the transit takes place in closed mails or in open mails.

This payment may be increased to 4 francs for letters and to 50 centimes for the articles specified in Article 4, when a transit is provided of more than 750 kilometers in length over the territory of one Administration.

It is understood, however, that in any case in which the transit is already actually gratuitous or subject to lower rates, those conditions shall be maintained.

Whenever a transit shall take place *by sea* over a distance exceeding 300 nautical miles within the district of the Union, the Administration by or at the expense of which this sea-service is performed shall have the right to a payment of the expenses attending this transport.

The members of the Union engage to reduce those expenses as much as possible. The payment which the Office providing the sea-conveyance may claim on this account from the despatching Office shall not exceed 6 francs 50 centimes per kilogramme for letters, and 50 centimes per kilogramme for the articles specified in Article 4, (net weight.)

In no case shall these expenses be higher than those now paid. Consequently, no payment shall be made upon the postal sea routes on which nothing is paid at the present time.

In order to ascertain the weight of the correspondence forwarded in transit, whether in closed mails or in open mails, there shall be taken, at periods which shall be determined upon by common consent, the statistics of such correspondence during two weeks. Until revised, the result of that labor shall serve as the basis of the accounts of the Administrations between themselves.

Each Office may demand a revision,—

1st. In case of any important modification in the direction of the correspondence;

2d. At the expiration of a year after the date of the last account.

The provisions of the present Article are not applicable to the Indian mail, nor to the mails conveyed across the territory of the United States of America by the railways between New York and San Francisco. Those services shall continue to form the object of special arrangements between the Administrations concerned.

ART. XI. The relations of the countries of the Union with countries foreign to the Union shall be regulated by the separate conventions which now exist or which may be concluded between them.

The rates of postage chargeable for the conveyance beyond the limits of the Union shall be determined by those conventions; they shall be added, in such case, to the Union rate.

In conformity with the stipulations of Article 9, the Union rate shall be apportioned in the following manner:

1st. The despatching Office of the Union shall keep the whole of the Union rate for the prepaid correspondence addressed to foreign countries.

2d. The receiving Office of the Union shall keep the whole of the Union rate for the unpaid correspondence originating in foreign countries.

3d. The Office of the Union which exchanges closed mails with foreign countries shall keep the whole of the Union rate for the paid correspondence originating in foreign countries and for the unpaid correspondence addressed to foreign countries.

In the cases mentioned under the Nos. 1, 2, and 3, the Office which exchanges the mails is not entitled to any payment for transit. In all the other cases the transit rates shall be paid according to the stipulations of Article 10.

ART. XII. The exchange of letters with value declared and of Post Office money orders shall form the subject of ulterior arrangements between the various countries or groups of countries composing the Union.

ART. XIII. The Postal Administrations of the various countries composing the Union are competent to draw up, by common consent, in the form of detailed regulations, all the measures of order and detail necessary with a view to the execution of the present treaty. It is understood that the stipulations of these detailed regulations may always be modified by the common consent of the Administrations of the Union.

The several Administrations may make amongst themselves the necessary arrangements on the subject of questions which do not concern the Union generally; such as the regulations of exchange at the frontier, the determination of radii in adjacent countries within which a lower rate of postage may be taken, the conditions of the exchange of Post Office money orders, and of letters with declared value, etc., etc.

ART. XIV. The stipulations of the present treaty do not involve any alteration in the interior postal legislation of any country, nor any restriction of the right of the contracting parties to maintain and to conclude treaties, as well as to maintain and establish more restricted unions with a view to a progressive improvement of postal relations.

ART. XV. There shall be organized, under the name of the International Office of the General Postal Union, a central office, which shall be conducted under the surveillance of a Postal Administration to be chosen by the Congress, and the expenses of which shall be borne by all the Administrations of the contracting States.

This office shall be charged with the duty of collecting, publishing, and distributing information of every kind which concerns the international postal service; of giving, at the request of the parties concerned, an opinion upon questions in dispute; of making known proposals for modifying the detailed regulations; of giving notice of alterations adopted; of facilitating operations relating to international accounts, especially in the cases referred to in Article 10 foregoing; and in general of considering and working out all questions in the interest of the Postal Union.

ART. XVI. In case of disagreement between two or more members of the Union as to the interpretation of the present treaty, the question in dispute shall be decided by arbitration. To that end, each of the Administrations concerned shall choose another member of the Union not interested in the affair.

The decision of the arbitrators shall be given by an absolute majority of votes.

In case of an equality of votes the arbitrators shall choose, with the view of settling the difference, another Administration equally disinterested in the question in dispute.

ART. XVII. The entry into the Union of countries beyond sea not yet forming part of it, shall be effected on the following conditions:—

1st. They shall make their application to the Administration charged with the management of the International Office of the Union.

2d. They shall submit to the stipulations of the treaty of the Union, subject to an ulterior understanding on the subject of the cost of sea conveyance.

3d. Their adhesion to the Union must be preceded by an understanding between the Administrations having postal conventions or direct relations with them.

4th. In order to bring about this understanding, the managing Administration shall convene, if there be occasion, a meeting of the Administrations interested, and of the Administration desiring admission.

5th. When the understanding has been arrived at, the managing Administration shall give notice of the same to all the members of the General Postal Union.

6th. If in a period of six weeks, counting from the date of that communication, no objections are presented, the adhesion shall be considered as accomplished, and notice thereof shall be given by the managing Administration to the Administration joining the Union. The definitive adhesion shall be completed by a diplomatic act between the Government of the managing Administration and the Government of the Administration admitted into the Union.

ART. XVIII. Every three years at least, a Congress of plenipotentiaries of the countries participating in the treaty shall be held with a view of perfecting the system of the Union, of introducing into it improvements found necessary, and of discussing common affairs.

Each country has one vote.

Each country may be represented either by one or several delegates, or by the delegation of another country. Nevertheless, it is understood that the delegate or delegates of one country can be charged with the representation of two countries only, including the one they represent.

The next meeting shall take place at Paris, in 1877.

Nevertheless, this meeting may be held sooner, if a request to that effect be made by one-third at least of the members of the Union.

ART. XIX. The present treaty shall come into force on the 1st of July, 1875.

It is concluded for three years from that date. When that term shall have passed, it shall be considered as indefinitely prolonged, but each contracting party shall have the right to withdraw from the Union on giving notice one year in advance.

ART. XX. After the date on which the present treaty comes into effect, all the stipulations of the special treaties concluded between the various countries and Administrations, in so far as they may be at variance with the terms of the present treaty, and without prejudice to the stipulations of Article 14, are abrogated.

The present treaty shall be ratified as soon as possible, and, at the latest, three months previous to the date on which it is to come into force. The acts of ratification shall be exchanged at Berne.

Chapter 4

The Amelioration of War Movement

7. THE GENEVA RED CROSS CONVENTION, 22 AUGUST 1864 [1]

On 24 June 1859 the battle of Solferino took place between the Austrians under Franz Joseph and the French and Sardinians under Napoleon III. The dead and wounded numbered 37,000 with no facilities provided for their care. Happening by in the course of a holiday trip, a Swiss, Henry Dunant, outraged by the carnage, dragooned the local peasantry and some visiting Englishmen into improvising first aid and rescue work. Dunant returned to Switzerland, where he wrote his *Un Souvenir de Solferino*,[2] a masterpiece of reporting which served as a clarion call to humanitarian action. Under the pressure of public opinion aroused by Dunant and his fellow workers, the Swiss Government called an international conference at Geneva in 1864. The conference concluded this "Convention for the Amelioration of the Condition of Soldiers wounded in Armies in the Field," setting up the International Red Cross.

The Swiss Confederation; His Royal Highness the Grand Duke of Baden; His Majesty the King of the Belgians; His Majesty the King of Denmark; Her Majesty the Queen of Spain; His Majesty the Emperor of the French; His Royal Highness the Grand Duke of Hesse; His Majesty the King of Italy; His Majesty the King of the Netherlands; His Majesty the King of Portugal and of the Algarves; His Majesty the King of Prussia; His Majesty the King of Würtemberg, being equally animated with the desire to soften, as much as depends on them, the evils of warfare, to suppress its useless hardships and improve the fate of wounded soldiers on the field of battle, have resolved to conclude a convention to that effect, and have named for their plenipotentiaries, viz: [3]

Who, after having exchanged their powers, and found them in good and due form, agree to the following articles:

ART. I. Ambulances and military hospitals shall be acknowledged to be neuter, and, as such, shall be protected and respected by belligerents so long as any sick or wounded may be therein.

Such neutrality shall cease if the ambulances or hospitals should be held by a military force.

ART. II. Persons employed in hospitals and ambulances, comprising the staff for superintendence, medical service, administration, transport of wounded, as well as chaplains, shall participate in the benefit of neutrality, whilst so employed, and so long as there remain any wounded to bring in or to succor.

ART. III. The persons designated in the preceding article may, even after occupation by the enemy, continue to fulfil their duties in the hospital or

---

[1] *United States Statutes at Large*, XXII, pp. 940-945.

[2] J. Henry Dunant, *Un Souvenir de Solfe-rino* (Geneva, Switzerland, 1862).

[3] Omitted.

ambulance which they serve, or may withdraw in order to rejoin the corps to which they belong.

Under such circumstances, when these persons shall cease from their functions, they shall be delivered by the occupying army to the outposts of the enemy.

ART. IV. As the equipment of military hospitals remains subject to the laws of war, persons attached to such hospitals cannot, in withdrawing, carry away any articles but such as are their private property.

Under the same circumstances an ambulance shall, on the contrary, retain its equipment.

ART. V. Inhabitants of the country who may bring help to the wounded shall be respected, and shall remain free. The generals of the belligerent Powers shall make it their care to inform the inhabitants of the appeal addressed to their humanity, and of the neutrality which will be the consequence of it.

Any wounded man entertained and taken care of in a house shall be considered as a protection thereto. Any inhabitant who shall have entertained wounded men in his house shall be exempted from the quartering of troops, as well as from a part of the contributions of war which may be imposed.

ART. VI. Wounded or sick soldiers shall be entertained and taken care of, to whatever nation they may belong.

Commanders-in-chief shall have the power to deliver immediately to the outposts of the enemy soldiers who have been wounded in an engagement, when circumstances permit this to be done, and with the consent of both parties.

Those who are recognized, after their wounds are healed, as incapable of serving, shall be sent back to their country.

The others may also be sent back, on condition of not again bearing arms during the continuance of the war.

Evacuations, together with the persons under whose directions they take place, shall be protected by an absolute neutrality.

ART. VII. A distinctive and uniform flag shall be adopted for hospitals, ambulances and evacuations. It must, on every occasion, be accompanied by the national flag. An arm-badge (brassard) shall also be allowed for individuals neutralized, but the delivery thereof shall be left to military authority.

The flag and the arm-badge shall bear a red cross on a white ground.

ART. VIII. The details of execution of the present convention shall be regulated by the commanders-in-chief of belligerent armies, according to the instructions of their respective governments, and in conformity with the general principles laid down in this convention.

ART. IX. The high contracting Powers have agreed to communicate the present convention to those Governments which have not found it convenient to send plenipotentiaries to the International Conference at Geneva, with an invitation to accede thereto; the protocol is for that purpose left open.

ART. X. The present convention shall be ratified, and the ratifications shall be exchanged at Berne, in four months, or sooner, if possible.

In faith whereof the respective Plenipotentiaries have signed it and have affixed their seals thereto.

Done at Geneva, the twenty second day of the month of August of the year one thousand eight hundred and sixty-four.

Chapter 5

The Hague System

8. THE FIRST MURAVIËV CIRCULAR, 24 AUGUST 1898 [1]

Several times during the last decades of the 19th century, Russia, which had not been represented at the Red Cross Conference of 1864, took the initiative in another direction —namely, that of seeking restrictions on the use of war weapons. In 1868, at the invitation of Alexander II, seventeen states sent representatives to the so-called Military Commission of St. Petersburg, which produced the abortive Declaration of St. Petersburg [2] outlawing the use of dumdum bullets. In 1874, again at the invitation of Alexander II, fourteen states met in a conference at Bruxelles to consider the conduct of war. They drew up the equally ill-starred Bruxelles Declaration Concerning the Laws and Customs of War. [3] Then in the summer of 1898 the youthful Nicholas II authorized his Foreign Minister, Muraviëv, to sound out the powers represented at St. Petersburg on the acceptability of a disarmament conference. [4] At his weekly reception for the diplomatic corps the Foreign Minister, without preliminary warning, handed the diplomats present a note proposing such a conference.

The maintenance of general peace and a possible reaction of the excessive armaments which weigh down upon all nations present themselves, in the actual present situation of the world, as the ideal toward which should tend the efforts of all governments.

The magnanimous and humanitarian views of His Majesty the Emperor, my august master, are entirely in accord with this sentiment.

In the conviction that this lofty object agrees entirely with the most essential interests and the most rightful desires of all the powers, the Imperial Government believes that the present time is very favorable for seeking, through the method of an international conference, the most effective means of assuring to all nations the benefits of a real and lasting peace, and of placing before all the question of ending the progressive development of existing armaments.

In the course of the last twenty years the aspirations for a general pacification have become strongly impressed upon the minds of civilized nations. The preservation of peace has been set up as the end of international politics; it is in its name that the great powers have formed powerful alliances with one another; it is for the better guarantee of peace that they have developed, to proportions hitherto un-

---

[1] *Papers Relating to the Foreign Relations of the United States, 1898*, pp. 541 f.

[2] *British and Foreign State Papers*, LVIII (1867-1868), p. 16; also Cmd. 4164 in Britain, *Accounts* and Papers, LXIV (1868-1869), for the English version.

[3] *Parliamentary Papers 1875*, LXXXII (c. 1120); reproduced in A. Pearce Higgins, *The Hague Peace Conferences* (Cambridge, England, 1909), pp. 273-280. The Bruxelles conference provided a number of precedents

which helped set the patter of the first Hague Conference in 1899.

[4] In his decision the Czar was influenced partly by the example of his forebears, Alexander I and Alexander II, partly by the teachings of a Russian banker and writer, Ivan Bloch, and partly by the alarm of those of his ministers who were faced with reconciling the Russian budget and the current arms race.

known, their military forces, and that they shall continue to augment them without hesitating on account of any sacrifice whatever.

All these efforts have not, however, yet accomplished the beneficent results of the much-wished-for pacification.

The ever-increasing financial expense touches public prosperity at its very source; the intellectual and physical powers of the people, labor and capital, are, in a great measure, turned aside from their natural functions and consumed unproductively. Hundreds of millions are used in acquiring fearful engines of destruction, which, to-day considered as the highest triumph of science, are destined to-morrow to lose all their value because of some new discovery in this sphere.

It is true also that as the armaments of each power increase in size they succeed less and less in accomplishing the result which is aimed at by the governments. Economic crises, due in great part to the existence of excessive armaments, and the constant dangers which result from this accumulation of war material, makes of the armed peace of our day an overwhelming burden which it is more and more difficult for the people to bear. It therefore seems evident that, if this state of af-

fairs continues it will inevitably lead to that very cataclysm which we are trying to avoid, and the horrors of which are fearful to human thought.

To put an end to these increasing armaments, and to find means for avoiding the calamities which menace the entire world, that is the supreme duty which to-day lies upon all nations.

Impressed with this sentiment, His Majesty the Emperor has deigned to command me to propose to all the governments who have duly accredited representatives at the Imperial Court the holding of a conference to consider this grave problem.

This conference will be, with the help of God, a happy augury for the century which is about to open. It will gather together into a powerful unit the efforts of all the powers which are sincerely desirous of making triumphant the conception of a universal peace. It will at the same time strengthen their mutual harmony by a common consideration of the principles of equity and right, upon which rest the security of States and the well-being of nations.

Cte. MOURAVIEFF.

ST. PETERSBURG, *August 12, 1898.*
(New style August 24.)

9. THE SECOND MURAVIËV CIRCULAR, 30 DECEMBER 1898 [1]

Suspicious of the double-headed eagle lurking behind the dove of peace, the chancellories of the powers received the Czar's manifesto with distinct coolness. After touring the capitals of Europe to learn at first hand the response to his Imperial Master's proposal, Muraviëv circularized the powers with a second note in an effort to meet the objections they had raised.

ST. PETERSBURG, *December 30, 1898.*

MR. AMBASSADOR: When, during the month of August last, my August Master ordered me to propose to the governments who had accredited repre-

sentatives in St. Petersburg the meeting of a conference for the purpose of seeking the most efficient means of assuring to all peoples the benefits of a real and lasting peace, and above all to place a limit upon the progressive development of existing armaments, nothing seemed opposed to the realization in the comparatively near future of this humanitarian project.

The welcome reception accorded to the measure of the Imperial Government by almost all the powers can but

[1] *Papers Relating to the Foreign Relations   of the United States,* 1898, pp. 551 f.

justify this hope. Appreciating fully the sympathetic manner in which the adhesion of almost all the governments has been expressed, the Imperial Cabinet has at the same time received with the liveliest satisfaction the evidences of hearty assent which have been addressed to it, and which do not cease to arrive from all classes of society of the different parts of the world.

Notwithstanding the great current of opinion which has been produced in favor of a general pacification, the political horizon has sensibly changed in its aspect recently. Several powers have proceeded with new armaments, enforcing additional increase of their military forces, and in the presence of this uncertain situation one might be led to ask whether the present moment is opportune for an international discussion of the ideas set forth in the circular of August 12–24.

Hoping, however, that the elements of trouble which agitate the political world will soon give place to a calmer order of things and one of a nature to encourage the success of the proposed conference, the Imperial Government for its part is of the opinion that it will be possible to proceed at once with a preliminary exchange of ideas among the powers with a view—

(a) Of seeking without delay for means of placing a limit upon the progressive increase of land and naval armaments, a question which plainly is becoming more and more urgent in view of the new increase of these armaments; and

(b) To prepare the way for a discussion of the questions relating to the possibility of preventing armed conflicts by the pacific means at the disposition of international diplomacy.

In case the powers consider the present moment favorable for the meeting of a conference on these bases, it certainly will be useful for the cabinets to agree among themselves upon the subject of a programme of its work.

The themes to submit to an international discussion at the actual conference might generally be summed up in the following manner:

1. An understanding stipulating the nonincrease for a fixed term of the present effectives of land and naval forces, as well as of the war budgets relating thereto; a preliminary study of the manner in which there might be even realized in the future a reduction of the effectives and the budgets above mentioned.

2. Interdiction of the putting into use in armies and navies of any new firearms whatever, and of new explosives, as well as more powerful powders than those now adopted, as well for guns as for cannon.

3. Limitation of the use in land campaigns of explosives of great power already in existence, and the prohibition against the throwing of all projectiles and explosives from balloons, or by similar means.

4. The interdiction of the use in naval warfare of submarine torpedo boats or plungers, or other engines of destruction of the same nature; engagement not to build in the future war vessels with rams.

5. The adaptation to naval warfare of the stipulations of the Geneva Convention of 1864, upon the basis of the additional articles of 1868.

6. Revision of the declaration in regard to the laws and customs of war, elaborated in 1874 by the Brussels conference and still remaining unratified.

7. The acceptance in principle of the usage of good offices, of mediation, and of optional arbitration for such cases as lend themselves to it, with a view of preventing armed conflicts between nations; an understanding upon the subject of their mode of application, and the establishment of a uniform code of practice in their use.

It is clearly understood that all questions concerning the political relations of states, and of the established order of things by treaty, as, in general, all questions which do not enter directly into the programme adopted by the cabinets ought to be absolutely excluded from the deliberations of the conference.

In addressing to you, Mr. Ambassador, the request to have the goodness to obtain the instructions of your Government upon the subject of my present communication, I would ask you at the same time to bring to its notice that in the interest of the great cause which lies so near the heart of my August Master, His Imperial Majesty considers that it would be well for the conference not to meet in the capital of one of the great powers, where there are concentrated so many political interests, which might perhaps react against the progress of a work in which are interested in a like degree all the countries of the world.

Accept, etc., COUNT MOURAVIEFF.

10. THE FINAL ACT OF THE FIRST HAGUE CONFERENCE, 22 JULY 1899 [1]

Following the failure of the Vienna system, the practical developments of the 19th century—namely, the Concert of Europe, the public international unions and the many-sided peace movement—were climaxed in the last year of the century by a great power conference called not to make peace but to preserve peace and attended by the representatives of twenty-six powers. Known to contemporaries officially as the "Conference de la Paix," or the "Peace Conference," it is known to history as the first Hague Conference. The accomplishments of the Conference were recapitulated in this Final Act, which was signed by the delegates as an authentic record but not as a convention so as to avoid the commitment to all the conventions, declarations and *voeux*.[2]

The International Peace Conference, convoked in the best interests of humanity by His Majesty the Emperor of All the Russias, assembled, on the invitation of the Government of Her Majesty the Queen of the Netherlands, in the Royal House in the Wood at The Hague on the 18th May, 1899.

In a series of meetings, between the 18th May and the 29th July, 1899, in which the constant desire of the delegates above-mentioned has been to realize, in the fullest manner possible, the generous views of the august initiator of the Conference and the intentions of their Governments, the Conference has agreed, for submission for signature by the plenipotentiaries, on the text of the Conventions and Declarations enumerated below and annexed to the present Act:

I. Convention for the peaceful adjustment of international differences.

II. Convention regarding the laws and customs of war on land.

III. Convention for the adaptation to maritime warfare of the principles of the Geneva Convention of the 22d August, 1864.

IV. Three Declarations:

1. To prohibit the launching of projectiles and explosives from balloons or by other similar new methods.

2. To prohibit the use of projectiles, the only object of which is the diffusion of asphyxiating or deleterious gases.

3. To prohibit the use of bullets which expand or flatten easily in the human body, such as bullets with a hard envelope, of which the envelope does not entirely cover the core or is pierced with incisions.

These Conventions and Declarations

---

[1] *British and Foreign State Papers,* XCI, pp. 963-969; the English translation is taken from James Brown Scott, ed., Texts of the Peace Conference at the Hague 1899 and 1907 (Boston, 1908), pp. 6-21.

[2] Inaugurating what may be called the Hague system by analogy with the Vienna system, which preceded it and the Geneva system of the League of Nations, which followed, the conference marks the transition between the partial organization of the 19th century and the general organization of the 20th. No action looking to a future conference, however, was taken at the first conference.

shall form so many separate Acts. These Acts shall be dated this day, and may be signed up to the 31st December, 1899, by the plenipotentiaries of the Powers represented at the International Peace Conference at The Hague.

Guided by the same sentiments, the Conference has adopted unanimously the following Resolution:

The Conference is of opinion that the restriction of military charges, which are at present a heavy burden on the world, is extremely desirable for the increase of the material and moral welfare of mankind.

It has besides formulated the following *Vœux:*

1. The Conference, taking into consideration the preliminary step taken by the Swiss Federal Government for the revision of the Geneva Convention, expresses the wish that steps may be shortly taken for the assembly of a special Conference having for its object the revision of that Convention.

This wish was voted unanimously.

2. The Conference expresses the wish that the questions of the rights and duties of neutrals may be inserted in the program of a Conference in the near future.

3. The Conference expresses the wish that the questions with regard to rifles and naval guns, as considered by it, may be studied by the Governments with the object of coming to an agreement respecting the employment of new types and calibers.

4. The Conference expresses the wish that the Governments, taking into consideration the proposals made at the Conference, may examine the possibility of an agreement as to the limitation of armed forces by land and sea, and of war budgets.

5. The Conference expresses the wish that the proposal, which contemplates the declaration of the inviolability of private property in naval warfare, may be referred to a subsequent Conference for consideration.

6. The Conference expresses the wish that the proposal to settle the question of the bombardment of ports, towns, and villages by a naval force may be referred to a subsequent Conference for consideration.

The last five wishes were voted unanimously, saving some abstentions.

In faith of which, the plenipotentiaries have signed the present Act, and have affixed their seals thereto.

Done at The Hague, 29th July, 1899, in one copy only, which shall be deposited in the Ministry for Foreign Affairs, and of which copies, duly certified, shall be delivered to all the Powers represented at the Conference.

[Here follow signatures.]

11. THE CONVENTION FOR THE PACIFIC SETTLEMENT OF INTERNATIONAL DISPUTES, 28 JULY 1899, REVISED 18 OCTOBER 1907 [1]

The crowning accomplishment of the first Hague Conference was the "Convention for the Pacific Settlement of International Disputes," which provides, *inter alia,* for the establishment of a "permanent Court of Arbitration," properly known as the Hague Court.[2] The provisions of the convention were amplified at the second Hague Conference in 1907.

PART I. THE MAINTENANCE OF GENERAL PEACE

ART. 1. With a view to obviating as far as possible recourse to force in the relations between States, the *contracting* Powers agree to use their best ef-

[1] *United States Statutes at Large,* XXXVI, pp. 2199-2239.
[2] In preparation for the first Hague Conference, the Americans, the Russians and the

British drafted plans for an international tribunal (for the texts of the drafts as submitted to the conference, see Scott, *op. cit.,* pp. 166 f., 178-183, 188 f.) The most far-

forts to insure the pacific settlement of international differences.

PART II. GOOD OFFICES AND MEDIATION

ART. 2. In case of serious disagreement or dispute, before an appeal to arms, the *contracting* Powers agree to have recourse, as far as circumstances may allow, to the good offices or mediation of one or more friendly Powers.

ART. 3. Independently of this recourse, the contracting Powers deem it expedient *and desirable* that one or more Powers, strangers to the dispute, should, on their own initiative and as far as circumstances may allow, offer their good offices or mediation to the States at variance.

Powers strangers to the dispute have the right to offer good offices or mediation even during the course of hostilities.

The exercise of this right can never be regarded by either of the parties in dispute as an unfriendly act.

ART. 4. The part of the mediator consists in reconciling the opposing claims and appeasing the feelings of resentment which may have arisen between the States at variance.

ART. 5. The functions of the mediator are at an end when once it is declared, either by one of the parties to the dispute or by the mediator himself, that the means of reconciliation proposed by him are not accepted.

ART. 6. Good offices and mediation undertaken either at the request of the parties in dispute or on the initiative of Powers strangers to the dispute have exclusively the character of advice, and never have binding force.

ART. 7. The acceptance of mediation can not, unless there be an agreement to the contrary, have the effect of interrupting, delaying, or hindering mobilization or other measures of preparation for war.

If it takes place after the commencement of hostilities, the military operations in progress are not interrupted in the absence of an agreement to the contrary.

ART. 8. The *contracting* Powers are agreed in recommending the application, when circumstances allow, of special mediation in the following form:

In case of a serious difference endangering peace, the States at variance choose respectively a Power, to which they intrust the mission of entering into direct communication with the Power chosen on the other side, with the object of preventing the rupture of pacific relations.

For the period of this mandate, the term of which, unless otherwise stipulated, can not exceed thirty days, the States in dispute cease from all direct communication on the subject of the dispute, which is regarded as referred exclusively to the mediating Powers, which must use their best efforts to settle it.

In case of a definite rupture of pacific relations, these Powers are charged with the joint task of taking advantage of any opportunity to restore peace.

ART. 9. In disputes of an international nature involving neither honor nor vital interests, and arising from a difference of opinion on points of fact, the *contracting* Powers deem it expedient *and* desirable that the parties who have not been able to come to an agreement by means of diplomacy, should, as far as circumstances allow, institute

---

reaching plan was that of the Americans who proposed an international court modeled upon the United States Supreme Court. The longest draft was that of the Russians, who, however, proposed the least organization: commissions of inquiry (which now enter international practice as a formal procedure for pacific settlement) and a bureau of correspondence. The Russian draft also provided that the expenses of the bureau be met in accordance with the Universal Postal Union's scale of payment; the Russian scheme, adopted by the conference, set the precedent for a similar provision in the Covenant of the League of Nations which was destined to cause the latter great difficulties. The British draft proposed what, in substance, was finally adopted by the conference as the so-called Hague Court.

an international commission of inquiry, to facilitate a solution of these disputes by elucidating the facts by means of an impartial and conscientious investigation.

Art. 10. International commissions of inquiry are constituted by special agreement between the parties in dispute.

The inquiry convention defines the facts to be examined; *it determines the mode and time in which the commission is to be formed* and the extent of the powers of the commissioners.

It also determines, if there is need, where the commission is to sit, and whether it may remove to another place, the language the commission shall use and the language the use of which shall be authorized before it, as well as the date on which each party must deposit its statement of facts, and, generally speaking, all the conditions upon which the parties have agreed.

If the parties consider it necessary to appoint assessors, the convention of inquiry shall determine the mode of their selection and the extent of their powers.

Art. 11. *If the inquiry convention has not determined where the commission is to sit, it will sit at The Hague.*

The place of meeting, once fixed, can not be altered by the commission except with the assent of the parties.

If the inquiry convention has not determined what languages are to be employed, the question shall be decided by the commission.

Art. 12. Unless an undertaking is made to the contrary, commissions of inquiry shall be formed in the manner determined by Articles *45 and 57* of the present Convention.

Art. 13. *Should one of the commissioners or one of the assessors, should there be any, either die, or resign, or be unable for any reason whatever to discharge his functions, the same procedure is followed for filling the vacancy as was followed for appointing him.*

Art. 14. *The parties are entitled to appoint special agents to attend the commission of inquiry, whose duty it is to represent them and to act as intermediaries between them and the commission.*

They are further authorized to engage counsel or advocates, appointed by themselves, to state their case and uphold their interests before the commission.

Art. 15. *The International Bureau of the Permanent Court of Arbitration acts as registry for the commissions which sit at The Hague, and shall place its offices and staff at the disposal of the contracting Powers for the use of the commission of inquiry.*

Art. 16. *If the commission meets elsewhere than at The Hague, it appoints a secretary general, whose office serves as registry.*

It is the function of the registry, under the control of the president, to make the necessary arrangements for the sittings of the commission, the preparation of the minutes, and, while the inquiry lasts, for the charge of the archives which shall subsequently be transferred to the International Bureau at The Hague.

Art. 17. *In order to facilitate the constitution and working of commissions of inquiry, the contracting Powers recommend the following rules, which shall be applicable to the inquiry procedure in so far as the parties do not adopt other rules.*

Art. 18. *The commission shall settle the details of the procedure not covered by the special inquiry convention or the present Convention, and shall arrange all the formalities required for dealing with the evidence.*

Art. 19. On the inquiry both sides must be heard.

At the dates fixed, each party communicates to the commission and to the other party the statements of facts, if any, and, in all cases, the instrument papers, and documents which it considers useful for ascertaining the truth as well as the list of witnesses and ex-

perts whose evidence it wishes to be heard.

ART. 20. *The commission is entitled, with the assent of the Powers, to move temporarily to any place where it considers it may be useful to have recourse to this means of inquiry or to send one or more of its members. Permission may be obtained from the State on whose territory it is proposed to hold the inquiry.*

ART. 21. *Every investigation, and every examination of a locality, must be made in the presence of the agents and counsel of the parties or after they have been duly summoned.*

ART. 22. *The commission is entitled to ask from either party for such explanations and information as it considers necessary.*

ART. 23. The *parties* undertake to supply the commission of inquiry, as fully as they may think possible, with all means and facilities necessary to enable it to become completely acquainted with, and to accurately understand, the facts in question.

They undertake to make use of the means at their disposal, under their municipal law, to insure the appearance of the witnesses or experts who are in their territory and have been summoned before the commission.

If the witnesses or experts are unable to appear before the commission, the parties will arrange for their evidence to be taken before the qualified officials of their own country.

ART. 24. *For all notices to be served by the commission in the territory of a third contracting Power, the commission shall apply direct to the Government of the said Power. The same rule applies in the case of steps being taken on the spot to procure evidence.*

The requests for this purpose are to be executed so far as the means at the disposal of the Power applied to under its municipal law allow. They can not be rejected unless the Power in question considers they are calculated to impair its sovereign rights or its safety.

The commission will equally be al- ways entitled to act through the Power on whose territory it sits.

ART. 25. *The witnesses and experts are summoned on the request of the parties or by the commission of its own motion, and, in every case, through the Government of the State in whose territory they are.*

The witnesses are heard in succession and separately, in the presence of the agents and counsel, and in the order fixed by the commission.

ART. 26. *The examination of witnesses is conducted by the president.*

The members of the commission may however put to each witness questions which they consider likely to throw light on and complete his evidence, or get information on any point concerning the witness within the limits of what is necessary in order to get at the truth.

The agents and counsel of the parties may not interrupt the witness when he is making his statement, nor put any direct question to him, but they may ask the president to put such additional questions to the witness as they think expedient.

ART. 27. *The witness must give his evidence without being allowed to read any written draft. He may, however, be permitted by the president to consult notes or documents if the nature of the facts referred to necessitates their employment.*

ART. 28. *A minute of the evidence of the witness is drawn up forthwith and read to the witness. The latter may make such alterations and additions as he thinks necessary, which will be recorded at the end of his statement.*

When the whole of his statement has been read to the witness, he is asked to sign it.

ART. 29. *The agents are authorized, in the course of or at the close of the inquiry, to present in writing to the commission and to the other party such statements, requisitions, or summaries of the facts as they consider useful for ascertaining the truth.*

ART. 30. *The commission considers*

its decisions in private and the proceedings are secret.

All questions are decided by a majority of the members of the commission.

If a member declines to vote, the fact must be recorded in the minutes.

ART. 31. *The sittings of the commission are not public, nor the minutes and documents connected with the inquiry published except in virtue of a decision of the commission taken with the consent of the parties.*

ART. 32. *After the parties have presented all the explanations and evidence and the witnesses have all been heard, the president declares the inquiry terminated, and the commission adjourns to deliberate and to draw up its report.*

ART. 33. The report is signed by all the members of the commission.

If one of the members refuses to sign, the fact is mentioned; but the validity of the report is not affected.

ART. 34. *The report of the commission is read at a public sitting, the agents and counsel of the parties being present or duly summoned.*

A copy of the report is given to each party.

ART. 35. The report of the commission is limited to a statement of facts, and has in no way the character of an award. It leaves to the parties entire freedom as to the effect to be given to the statement.

ART. 36. *Each party pays its own expenses and an equal share of the expenses incurred by the commission.*

PART IV. INTERNATIONAL ARBITRATION

Chapter I. The System of Arbitration

ART. 37. International arbitration has for its object the settlement of disputes between States by judges of their own choice and on the basis of respect for law.

Recourse to arbitration implies an engagement to submit in good faith to the award.

ART. 38. In questions of a legal nature, and especially in the interpretation or application of international conventions, arbitration is recognized by the *contracting* Powers as the most effective, and, at the same time, the most equitable means of settling disputes which diplomacy has failed to settle.

Consequently, it would be desirable that, in disputes about the above-mentioned questions, the contracting Powers should, if the case arose, have recourse to arbitration, in so far as circumstances permit.

ART. 39. The arbitration convention is concluded for questions already existing or for questions which may arise eventually.

It may embrace any dispute or only disputes of a certain category.

ART. 40. Independently of general or private treaties expressly stipulating recourse to arbitration as obligatory on the *contracting* Powers, the said Powers reserve to themselves the right of concluding new agreements, general or particular, with a view to extending compulsory arbitration to all cases which they may consider it possible to submit to it.

Chapter II. The Permanent Court of Arbitration

ART. 41. With the object of facilitating an immediate recourse to arbitration for international differences, which it has not been possible to settle by diplomacy, the *contracting* Powers undertake to *maintain the* Permanent Court of Arbitration, *as established by the First Peace Conference,* accessible at all times, and operating, unless otherwise stipulated by the parties, in accordance with the rules of procedure inserted in the present Convention.

ART. 42. The Permanent Court *is* competent for all arbitration cases, unless the parties agree to institute a special tribunal.

ART. 43. The Permanent Court sits at The Hague.

An International Bureau serves as

registry for the Court. It is the channel for communications relative to the meetings of the Court; it has charge of the archives and conducts all the administrative business.

The *contracting* Powers undertake to communicate to the Bureau, *as soon as possible,* a certified copy of any conditions of arbitration arrived at between them and of any award concerning them delivered by a special tribunal.

They likewise undertake to communicate to the Bureau the laws, regulations, and documents eventually showing the execution of the awards given by the Court.

ART. 44. Each *contracting* Power *selects* four persons at the most, of known competency in questions of international law, of the highest moral reputation, and disposed to accept the duties of arbitrator.

The persons thus selected *are* inscribed, as members of the Court, in a list which shall be notified to all the *contracting* Powers by the Bureau.

Any alteration in the list of arbitrators is brought by the Bureau to the knowledge of the *contracting* Powers.

Two or more Powers may agree on the selection in common of one or more members.

The same person can be selected by different Powers.

The members of the Court are appointed for a term of six years. These appointments are renewable.

Should a member of the Court die or resign, the same procedure is followed for filling the vacancy as was followed for appointing him. *In this case the appointment is made for a fresh period of six years.*

ART. 45. When the *contracting* Powers wish to have recourse to the Permanent Court for the settlement of a difference which has arisen between them, the arbitrators called upon to form the tribunal with jurisdiction to decide this difference must be chosen from the general list of members of the Court.

Failing the direct agreement of the parties on the composition of the arbitration tribunal, the following course shall be pursued:

Each party appoints two arbitrators, *of whom one only can be its national or chosen from among the persons selected by it as members of the Permanent Court.* These arbitrators together choose an umpire.

If the votes are equally divided, the choice of the umpire is intrusted to a third Power, selected by the parties by common accord.

If an agreement is not arrived at on this subject each party selects a different Power, and the choice of the umpire is made in concert by the Powers thus selected.

If, within two months' time, these two Powers can not come to an agreement, each of them presents two candidates taken from the list of members of the Permanent Court, exclusive of the members selected by the parties and not being nationals of either of them. Drawing lots determines which of the candidates thus presented shall be umpire.

ART. 46. The tribunal being thus composed, the parties notify to the Bureau their determination to have recourse to the Court, *the text of their compromis,* and the names of the arbitrators.

The Bureau communicates without delay to each arbitrator the compromis, and the names of the other members of the tribunal.

The tribunal assembles at the date fixed by the parties. *The Bureau makes the necessary arrangements for the meeting.*

The members of the *tribunal,* in the exercise of their duties and out of their own country, enjoy diplomatic privileges and immunities.

ART. 47. The Bureau is authorized to place its offices and staff at the disposal of the *contracting* Powers for the use of any special board of arbitration.

The jurisdiction of the Permanent Court may, within the conditions laid down in the regulations, be extended to disputes between *non-contracting* Powers or between *contracting* Powers and *non-contracting* Powers, if the parties are agreed on recourse to this tribunal.

ART. 48. The *contracting* Powers consider it their duty, if a serious dispute threatens to break out between two or more of them, to remind these latter that the Permanant Court is open to them.

Consequently, they declare that the fact of reminding the parties at variance of the provisions of the present Convention, and the advice given to them, in the highest interests of peace, to have recourse to the Permanent Court, can only be regarded as friendly actions.

In case of dispute between two Powers, one of them can always address to the International Bureau a note containing a declaration that it would be ready to submit the dispute to arbitration.

The Bureau must at once inform the other Power of the declaration.

ART. 49. *The* Permanent Administrative Council, composed of the diplomatic representatives of the *contracting* Powers accredited to The Hague and of the Netherland Minister for Foreign Affairs, who will act as president, is charged with the direction and control of the International Bureau.

The Council *settles* its rules of procedure and all other necessary regulations.

It *decides* all questions of administration which may arise with regard to the operations of the Court.

It *has* entire control over the appointment, suspension, or dismissal of the officials and employees of the Bureau.

It *fixes* the payments and salaries, and controls the general expenditure.

At meetings duly summoned the presence of *nine* members is sufficient to render valid the discussions of the Council. The decisions are taken by a majority of votes.

The Council communicates to the *contracting* Powers without delay the regulations adopted by it. It furnishes them with an annual report on the labors of the Court, the working of the administration, and the expenditure. *The report likewise contains a résumé of what is important in the documents communicated to the Bureau by the Powers in virtue of Article 43, paragraphs 3 and 4.*

ART. 50. The expenses of the Bureau shall be borne by the *contracting* Powers in the proportion fixed for the International Bureau of the Universal Postal Union.

The expenses to be charged to the adhering Powers shall be reckoned from the date on which their adhesion comes into force.

Chapter III. Arbitration Procedure

ART. 51. With a view to encouraging the development of arbitration, the *contracting* Powers have agreed on the following rules, which are applicable to arbitration procedure, unless other rules have been agreed on by the parties.

ART. 52. The Powers which have recourse to arbitration sign a compromis, in which the subject of the dispute is clearly defined, *the time allowed for appointing arbitrators, the form, order, and time in which the communication referred to in Article 63 must be made, and the amount of the sum which each party must deposit in advance to defray the expenses.*

The compromis likewise defines, if there is occasion, the manner of appointing arbitrators, any special powers which may eventually belong to the tribunal, where it shall meet, the language it shall use, and the languages the employment of which shall be authorized before it, and, generally speaking, all the conditions on which the parties are agreed.

ART. 53. *The Permanent Court is*

competent to settle the compromis, if the parties are agreed to have recourse to it for the purpose.

It is similarly competent, even if the request is only made by one of the parties, when all attempts to reach an understanding through the diplomatic channel have failed in the case of—

1. A dispute covered by a general treaty of arbitration concluded or renewed after the present Convention has come into force, and providing for a compromis in all disputes and not either explicitly or implicitly excluding the settlement of the compromis from the competence of the Court Recourse can not, however, be had to the Court if the other party declares that in its opinion the dispute does not belong to the category of disputes which will be submitted to compulsory arbitration, unless the treaty of arbitration confers upon the arbitration tribunal the power of deciding this preliminary question.

2. A dispute arising from contract debts claimed from one Power by another Power is due to its nationals, and for the settlement of which the offer of arbitration has been accepted. This arrangement is not applicable if acceptance is subject to the condition that the compromis should be settled in some other way.

Art. 54. *In the cases contemplated in the preceding article, the compromis shall be settled by a commission consisting of five members selected in the manner arranged for in Article 45, paragraphs 3 to 6.*

The fifth member is president of the commission ex officio.

Art. 55. The duties of arbitrator may be conferred on one arbitrator alone or on several arbitrators selected by the parties as they please, or chosen by them from the members of the Permanent Court of Arbitration established by the present Convention.

Failing the constitution of the tribunal by direct agreement between the parties, the course *referred to in Article 45, paragraphs 3 to 6, is followed.*

Art. 56. When a sovereign or the chief of a State is chosen as arbitrator, the arbitration procedure is settled by him.

Art. 57. The umpire is president of the tribunal ex officio.

When the tribunal does not include an umpire, it appoints its own president.

Art. 58. *When the compromise is settled by a commission, as contemplated in Article 54, and in the absence of an agreement to the contrary, the commission itself shall form the arbitration tribunal.*

Art. 59. Should one of the arbitrators either die, retire, or be unable for any reason whatever to discharge his functions the same procedure is followed for filling the vacancy as was followed for appointing him.

Art. 60. The tribunal sits at The Hague unless some other place is selected by the parties.

The tribunal can only sit in the territory of a third Party with the latter's consent.

The place of meeting once fixed can not be altered by the tribunal except with the consent of the parties.

Art. 61. If the question as to what languages are to be used has not been settled by the compromis, it shall be decided by the tribunal.

Art. 62. The parties are entitled to appoint special agents to attend the tribunal to act as intermediaries between themselves and the tribunal.

They are further authorized to retain for the defense of their rights and interests before the tribunal counsel or advocate appointed by themselves for the purpose.

The members of the Permanent Court may not act as agents, counsel, or advocates except on behalf of the Power which appointed them members of the Court.

Art. 63. As a general rule, arbitration procedure comprises two distinct phases: pleadings and oral discussions.

The pleadings consist in the communication by the respective agents to the members of the tribunal and the opposite party of cases, counter cases, and, if necessary, of replies; the parties annex thereto all papers and documents called for in the case. This communication shall be made either directly or through the intermediary of the International Bureau, in the order and within the time fixed by the compromis.

The time fixed by the compromis may be extended by mutual agreement by the parties, or by the tribunal when the latter considers it necessary for the purpose of reaching a just decision.

The discussions consist in the usual development before the tribunal of the arguments of the parties.

ART. 64. A *certified copy* of every document produced by one party must be communicated to the other party.

ART. 65. *Unless special circumstances arise, the tribunal does not meet until the pleadings are closed.*

ART. 66. The discussions are under the control of the president.

They are only public if it be so decided by the tribunal, with the assent of the parties.

They are recorded in minutes drawn up by the secretaries appointed by the president. These minutes *are signed by the president and by one of the secretaries and* alone have an authentic character.

ART. 67. After the close of the pleadings, the tribunal is entitled to refuse discussion of all new papers or documents which one of the parties may wish to submit to it without the consent of the other party.

ART. 68. The tribunal is free to take into consideration new papers or documents to which its attention may be drawn by the agents or counsel of the parties.

In this case, the tribunal has the right to require the production of these papers or documents, but is obliged to make them known to the opposite party.

ART. 69. The tribunal can, besides, require from the agents of the parties the production of all papers, and can demand all necessary explanations. In case of refusal the tribunal takes note of it.

ART. 70. The agents and the counsel of the parties are authorized to present orally to the tribunal all the arguments they may consider expedient in defense of their case.

ART. 71. They are entitled to raise objections and points. The decisions of the tribunal on these points are final and can not form the subject of any subsequent discussion.

ART. 72. The members of the tribunal are entitled to put questions to the agents and counsel of the parties, and to ask them for explanations on doubtful points.

Neither the questions put, nor the remarks made by members of the tribunal in the course of the discussions, can be regarded as an expression of opinion by the tribunal in general or by its members in particular.

ART. 73. The tribunal is authorized to declare its competence in interpreting the compromis, as well as the other papers and documents which may be invoked, and in applying the principles of law.

ART. 74. The tribunal is entitled to issue rules of procedure for the conduct of the case, to decide the forms, *order,* and time in which each party must conclude its arguments, and to arrange all the formalities required for dealing with the evidence.

ART. 75. *The parties undertake to supply the tribunal, as fully as they consider possible, with all the information required for deciding the case.*

ART. 76. *For all notices which the tribunal has to serve in the territory of a third contracting Power, the tribunal shall apply direct to the Government of that Power. The same rule applies in the case of steps being taken to procure evidence on the spot.*

The requests for this purpose are to be executed as far as the means at the disposal of the Power applied to under its municipal law allow. They can not be rejected unless the Power in question considers them calculated to impair its own sovereign rights or its safety.

The Court will equally be always entitled to act through the Power on whose territory it sits.

ART. 77. When the agents and counsel of the parties have submitted all the explanations and evidence in support of their case the president shall declare the discussion closed.

ART. 78. The tribunal considers its decisions in private and *the proceedings* remain *secret.*

All questions are decided by a majority of the members of the tribunal.

ART. 79. The award must give the reasons on which it is based. *It contains the names of the arbitrators; it is signed by the president and registrar or by the Secretary acting as registrar.*

ART. 80. The award is read out in public sitting, the agents and counsel of the parties being present or duly summoned to attend.

ART. 81. The award duly pronounced and notified to the agents of the parties, settles the dispute definitively and without appeal.

ART. 82. Any dispute arising between the parties as to the interpretation and execution of the award shall, in the absence of an agreement to the contrary, be submitted to the tribunal which pronounced it.

ART. 83. The parties can reserve in the compromis the right to demand the revision of the award.

In this case and unless there be an agreement to the contrary, the demand must be addressed to the tribunal which pronounced the award. It can only be made on the ground of the discovery of some new fact calculated to exercise a decisive influence upon the award and which was unknown to the tribunal and to the party which demanded the revision at the time the discussion was closed.

Proceedings for revision can only be instituted by a decision of the tribunal

expressly recording the existence of the new fact, recognizing in it the character described in the preceding paragraph, and declaring the demand admissible on this ground.

The compromis fixes the period within which the demand for revision must be made.

ART. 84. The award is not binding except on the parties *in dispute.*

When it concerns the interpretation of a Convention to which Powers other than those in dispute are parties, they shall inform all the signatory Powers *in good time.* Each of these Powers is entitled to intervene in the case. If one or more avail themselves of this right, the interpretation contained in the award is equally binding on them.

ART. 85. Each party pays its own expenses and an equal share of the expenses of the tribunal.

Chapter IV. Arbitration by Summary Procedure

ART. 86. *With a view to facilitating the working of the system of arbitration in disputes admitting of a summary procedure, the contracting Powers adopt the following rules, which shall be observed in the absence of other arrangements and subject to the reservation that the provisions of Chapter III apply so far as may be.*

ART. 87. *Each of the parties in dispute appoints an arbitrator. The two arbitrators thus selected choose an umpire. If they do not agree on this point, each of them proposes two candidates taken from the general list of the members of the Permanent Court exclusive of the members appointed by either of the parties and not being nationals of either of them; which of the candidates thus proposed shall be the umpire is determined by lot.*

The umpire presides over the tribunal, which gives its decisions by a majority of votes.

ART. 88. *In the absence of any previous agreement the tribunal, as soon as it is formed, settles the time within which the two parties must submit their respective cases to it.*

Art. 89. *Each party is represented before the tribunal by an agent, who serves as intermediary between the tribunal and the Government who appointed him.*

Art. 90. *The proceedings are conducted exclusively in writing. Each party, however, is entitled to ask that witnesses and experts should be called. The tribunal has, for its part, the right to demand oral explanations from the agents of the two parties, as well as from the experts and witnesses whose appearance in Court it may consider useful.*

PART V. FINAL PROVISIONS

Art. 91. *The present Convention, duly ratified, shall replace, as between the contracting Powers, the Convention for the pacific settlement of international disputes of the 29th July, 1899.*

Art. 92. The present Convention shall be ratified as soon as possible.

The ratifications shall be deposited at The Hague.

The first deposit of ratifications shall be recorded in a procès-verbal signed by the representatives of the Powers which take part therein and by the Netherland Minister for Foreign Affairs.

The subsequent deposits of ratifications shall be made by means of a written notification, addressed to the Netherland Government and accompanied by the instrument of ratification.

*A duly certified copy of the procès-verbal relative to the first deposit of ratifications, of the notifications mentioned in the preceding paragraph, and of the instruments of ratification, shall be immediately sent by the Netherland Government, through the diplomatic channel, to the Powers invited to the Second Peace Conference, as well as to those Powers which have adhered to the Convention. In the cases contem-*plated in the preceding paragraph, the said Government shall at the same time inform the Powers of the date on which it received the notification.

Art. 93. Non-signatory Powers which have been *invited to* the *Second* Peace Conference may adhere to the present Convention.

The Power which desires to adhere notifies its intention in writing to the Netherland Government, forwarding to it the act of adhesion, which shall be deposited in the archives of the said Government.

This Government shall immediately forward to all the other Powers invited to the Second Peace Conference a duly certified copy of the notification as well as of the act of adhesion, mentioning the date on which it received the notification.

Art. 94. The conditions on which the Powers which have not been *invited* to the Second Peace Conference may adhere to the present Convention shall form the subject of a subsequent agreement between the contracting Powers.

Art. 95. *The present Convention shall take effect, in the case of the Powers which were not a party to the first deposit of ratifications, sixty days after the date of the procès-verbal of this deposit, and, in the case of the Powers which ratify subsequently or which adhere, sixty days after the notification of their ratification or of their adhesion has been received by the Netherland Government.*

Art. 96. In the event of one of the contracting *Powers wishing to* denounce the present Convention, *the* denunciation shall be notified in writing to the Netherland Government, *which shall* immediately communicate *a duly certified copy* of the notification to all the other Powers *informing them of the date on which it was received.*

The denunciation shall only have effect in regard to the notifying Power, *and one year after the notification has*

reached the Netherland Government.
Art. 97. *A register kept by the Netherland Minister for Foreign Affairs shall give the date of the deposit of ratifications effected in virtue of Article 92, paragraphs 3 and 4, as well as the date on which the notifications of adhesion (Article 93, paragraph 2) or of denunciation (Article 96, paragraph 1) have been received.*

Each contracting Power is entitled to have access to this register and to be *supplied with duly certified extracts from it.*

In faith whereof the plenipotentiaries have *appended their signatures to* the present Convention.

Done at The Hague, the *18th October, 1907,* in a single copy, which shall remain deposited in the archives of the Netherland Government, and duly certified copies of which shall be sent, through the diplomatic channel to the contracting Powers.

12. THE FINAL ACT OF THE SECOND HAGUE CONFERENCE, 18 OCTOBER 1907 [1]

In 1904 at the urging of the Inter-Parliamentary Union, then meeting in the United States, Theodore Roosevelt proposed a second conference to be held at the Hague for the purpose of continuing the work of the first. The Russo-Japanese war made postponement advisable. Later the Russian government intimated its desire to issue the invitations, a point Roosevelt cheerfully conceded. The agreements constituting the fruit of its labors are listed in this Final Act.

The Second International Peace Conference, proposed in the first instance by the President of the United States of America, having been convoked, on the invitation of His Majesty the Emperor of All the Russias, by Her Majesty the Queen of the Netherlands, assembled on the 15th June, 1907, at The Hague, in the Hall of the Knights, for the purpose of giving a fresh development to the humanitarian principles which served as a basis for the work of the First Conference of 1899.

The following Powers took part in the Conference, and appointed the delegates named below. . . .

At a series of meetings, held from the 15th June to the 18th October, 1907, in which the above delegates were throughout animated by the desire to realize, in the fullest possible measure, the generous views of the august initiator of the Conference and the intentions of their Governments, the Conference drew up, for submission for signature by the plenipotentiaries, the text of the Conventions and of the Declaration enumerated below and annexed to the present Act:

I. Convention for the pacific settlement of international disputes.

II. Convention respecting the limitation of the employment of force for the recovery of contract debts.

III. Convention relative to the opening of hostilities.

IV. Convention respecting the laws and customs of war on land.

V. Convention respecting the rights and duties of neutral powers and persons in case of war on land.

VI. Convention relative to the status of enemy merchant ships at the outbreak of hostilities.

VII. Convention relative to the conversion of merchant ships into warships.

VIII. Convention relative to the laying of automatic submarine contact mines.

IX. Convention respecting bombardment by naval forces in time of war.

X. Convention for the adaptation to naval war of the principles of the Geneva Convention.

XI. Convention relative to certain restrictions with regard to the exercise

[1] *Parliamentary Papers*, Misc. No. 4 (1908), pp. 66-69.

of the right of capture in naval war.

XII. Convention relative to the creation of an International Prize Court.

XIII. Convention concerning the rights and duties of neutral Powers in naval war.

XIV. Declaration prohibiting the discharge of projectiles and explosives from balloons.

These Conventions and Declaration shall form so many separate Acts. These Acts shall be dated this day, and may be signed up to the 30th June, 1908, at The Hague, by the plenipotentiaries of the Powers represented at the Second Peace Conference.

The Conference, actuated by the spirit of mutual agreement and concession characterizing its deliberations, has agreed upon the following Declaration, which, while reserving to each of the Powers represented full liberty of action as regards voting, enables them to affirm the principles which they regard as unanimously admitted:

It is unanimous—

1. In admitting the principle of compulsory arbitration.

2. In declaring that certain disputes, in particular those relating to the interpretation and application of the provisions of international agreements, may be submitted to compulsory arbitration without any restriction.

Finally, it is unanimous in proclaiming that, although it has not yet been found feasible to conclude a Convention in this sense, nevertheless the divergences of opinion which have come to light have not exceeded the bounds of judicial controversy, and that, by working together here during the past four months, the collected Powers not only have learnt to understand one another and to draw closer together, but have succeeded in the course of this long collaboration in evolving a very lofty conception of the common welfare of humanity.

The Conference has further unanimously adopted the following Resolution:

The Second Peace Conference confirms the Resolution adopted by the Conference of 1899 in regard to the limitation of military expenditure; and inasmuch as military expenditure has considerably increased in almost every country since that time, the Conference declares that it is eminently desirable that the Government should resume the serious examination of this question.

It has besides expressed the following *Vœux:*

1. The Conference recommends to the signatory Powers the adoption of the annexed draft Convention for the creation of a Judicial Arbitration Court, and the bringing it into force as soon as an agreement has been reached respecting the selection of the judges and the constitution of the Court.

2. The Conference expresses the opinion that, in case of war, the responsible authorities, civil as well as military, should make it their special duty to ensure and safeguard the maintenance of pacific relations, more especially of the commercial and industrial relations between the inhabitants of the belligerent States and neutral countries.

3. The Conference expresses the opinion that the Powers should regulate, by special treaties, the position, as regards military charges, of foreigners residing within their territories.

4. The Conference expresses the opinion that the preparation of regulations relative to the laws and customs of naval war should figure in the program of the next Conference, and that in any case the Powers may apply, as far as possible, to war by sea the principles of the Convention relative to the laws and customs of war on land.

Finally, the Conference recommends to the Powers the assembly of a Third Peace Conference, which might be held within a period corresponding to that which has elapsed since the preceding Conference, at a date to be fixed by common agreement between the Powers, and it calls their attention to the necessity of preparing the program of this Third Conference a sufficient time in advance to ensure its deliberations being conducted with the necessary authority and expedition.

In order to attain this object the Conference considers that it would be very desirable that, some two years before the probable date of the meeting, a preparatory committee should be charged by the Governments with the task of collecting the various proposals to be submitted to the Conference, of ascertaining what subjects are ripe for embodiment in an international regulation, and of preparing a program which the Governments should decide upon in sufficient time to enable it to be carefully examined by the countries interested. This committee should further be intrusted with the task of proposing a system of organization and procedure for the Conference itself.

In faith whereof the Plenipotentiaries have signed the present Act and have affixed their seals thereto.

Done at The Hague, the 18th October, 1907, in a single copy, which shall remain deposited in the archives of the Netherland Government, and duly certified copies of which shall be sent to all the Powers represented at the Conference.

13. THE DRAFT CONVENTION RELATIVE TO THE CREATION OF A JUDICIAL ARBITRATION COURT, 1908 [1]

The outstanding failure of the second Hague Conference concerned this "Draft Convention Relative to the Creation of a Judicial Arbitration Court." As they had done in 1899, the American delegates proposed a plan for a true court of law. The American plan became the basis for the draft convention annexed to the Final Act. But in the draft nothing is said about the number of judges or the method of their selection. Disagreement on these points prevented the adoption of the convention, thanks to the opposition of the smaller powers, determined that all states should be represented on the bench. The Final Act included a *voeu* that the signatories adopt the draft convention as soon as the question of the judges could be settled.[2]

PART I.—CONSTITUTION OF THE JUDICIAL ARBITRATION COURT

ART. I. With a view to promoting the cause of arbitration, the contracting Powers agree to constitute, without altering the status of the Permanent Court of Arbitration, a Judicial Arbitration Court, of free and easy access, composed of judges representing the various juridical systems of the world, and capable of insuring continuity in arbitral jurisprudence.

ART. 2. The Judicial Arbitration Court is composed of judges and deputy judges chosen from persons of the highest moral reputation, and all fulfilling conditions qualifying them, in their respective countries, to occupy high legal posts, or be jurists of recognized competence in matters of international law.

The judges and deputy judges of the Court are appointed, as far as possible, from the members of the Permanent Court of Arbitration. The appointment shall be made within the six months following the ratification of the present Convention.

ART. 3. The judges and deputy judges are appointed for a period of twelve years, counting from the date on which the appointment is notified to the Administrative Council created by the Convention for the pacific settlement of international disputes. Their appointments can be renewed.

Should a judge or deputy judge die or retire, the vacancy is filled in the manner in which his appointment was made. In this case, the appointment is

[1] *Parliamentary Papers*, Misc. No. 4 (1908), pp. 59-61, 257-301.
[2] The question was settled only with the Root-Phillimore proposal respecting the Permanent Court of International Justice in the League of Nations system (see Doc. 36).

made for a fresh period of twelve years.

ART. 4. The judges of the Judicial Arbitration Court are equal and rank according to the date on which their appointment was notified. The judge who is senior in point of age takes precedence when the date of notification is the same.

The deputy judges are assimilated, in the exercise of their functions, with the judges. They rank, however, below the latter.

ART. 5. The judges enjoy diplomatic privileges and immunities in the exercise of their functions, outside their own country.

Before taking their seat, the judges and deputy judges must, before the Administrative Council, swear or make a solemn affirmation to exercise their functions impartially and conscientiously.

ART. 6. The Court annually nominates three judges to form a special delegation and three more to replace them should the necessity arise. They may be reelected. They are balloted for. The persons who secure the largest number of votes are considered elected. The delegation itself elects its president, who, in default of a majority, is appointed by lot.

A member of the delegation can not exercise his duties when the Power which appointed him, or of which he is a national, is one of the parties.

The members of the delegation are to conclude all matters submitted to them, even if the period for which they have been appointed judges has expired.

ART. 7. A judge may not exercise his judicial functions in any case in which he has, in any way whatever, taken part in the decision of a national tribunal, of a tribunal of arbitration, or of a commission of inquiry, or has figured in the suit as counsel or advocate for one of the parties.

A judge can not act as agent or advocate before the Judicial Arbitration Court or the Permanent Court of Arbitration, before a special tribunal of arbitration or a commission of inquiry, nor act for one of the parties in any capacity whatsoever so long as his appointment lasts.

ART. 8. The Court elects its president and vice-president by an absolute majority of the votes cast. After two ballots, the election is made by a bare majority and, in case the votes are even, by lot.

ART. 9. The judges of the Judicial Arbitration Court receive an annual salary of 6,000 Netherland florins. This salary is paid at the end of each half-year, reckoned from the date on which the Court meets for the first time.

In the exercise of their duties during the sessions or in the special cases covered by the present Convention, they receive the sum of 100 florins *per diem*. They are further entitled to receive a traveling allowance fixed in accordance with regulations existing in their own country. The provisions of the present paragraph are applicable also to a deputy judge when acting for a judge.

These emoluments are included in the general expenses of the Court dealt with in Article 31, and are paid through the International Bureau created by the Convention for the pacific settlement of international disputes.

ART. 10. The judges may not accept from their own Government or from that of any other Power any remuneration for services connected with their duties in their capacity of members of the Court.

ART. 11. The seat of the Judicial Court of Arbitration is at The Hague, and can not be transferred, unless absolutely obliged by circumstances, elsewhere.

The delegation may choose, with the assent of the parties concerned, another site for its meetings, if special circumstances render such a step necessary.

ART. 12. The Administrative Council fulfils with regard to the Judicial Court of Arbitration the same functions as to the Permanent Court of Arbitration.

ART. 13. The International Bureau acts as registry to the Judicial Court of Arbitration, and must place its offices and staff at the disposal of the Court. It has charge of the archives and carries out the administrative work.

The secretary general of the Bureau discharges the functions of registrar.

The necessary secretaries to assist the registrar, translators and shorthand writers are appointed and sworn in by the Court.

ART. 14. The Court meets in session once a year. The session opens the third Wednesday in June and lasts until all the business on the agenda has been transacted.

The Court does not meet in session if the delegation considers that such meeting is unnecessary. However, when a Power is party in a case actually pending before the Court, the pleadings in which are closed, or about to be closed, it may insist that the session should be held.

When necessary, the delegation may summon the Court in extraordinary session.

ART. 15. A report of the doings of the Court shall be drawn up every year by the delegation. This report shall be forwarded to the contracting Powers through the International Bureau. It shall also be communicated to the judges and deputy judges of the Court.

ART. 16. The judges and deputy judges, members of the Judicial Arbitration Court, can also exercise the functions of judges and deputy judge in the International Prize Court.

PART II.—COMPETENCY AND
PROCEDURE

ART. 17. The Judicial Court of Arbitration is competent to deal with all cases submitted to it, in virtue either of a general undertaking to have recourse to arbitration or of a special agreement.

ART. 18. The delegation is competent—

1. To decide the arbitrations referred to in the preceding article, if the parties concerned are agreed that the summary procedure, laid down in Part IV, Chapter IV, of the Convention for the pacific settlement of international disputes is to be applied;

2. To hold an inquiry under and in accordance with Part III of the said Convention, in so far as the delegation is intrusted with such inquiry by the parties acting in common agreement. With the assent of the parties concerned, and as an exception to Article 7, paragraph 1, the members of the delegation who have taken part in the inquiry may sit as judges, if the case in dispute is submitted to the arbitration of the Court or of the delegation itself.

ART. 19. The delegation is also competent to settle the *compromis* referred to in Article 52 of the Convention for the pacific settlement of international disputes if the parties are agreed to leave it to the Court.

It is equally competent to do so, even when the request is only made by one of the parties concerned, if all attempts have failed to reach an understanding through the diplomatic channel, in the case of—

1. A dispute covered by a general treaty of arbitration concluded or renewed after the present Convention has come into force, providing for a *compromis* in all disputes, and not either explicitly or implicitly excluding the settlement of the *compromis* from the competence of the delegation. Recourse can not, however, be had to the Court if the other party declares that in its opinion the dispute does not belong to the category of questions to be submitted to compulsory arbitration, unless the treaty of arbitration confers upon the arbitration tribunal the power of deciding this preliminary question.

2. A dispute arising from contract

debts claimed from one Power by another Power as due to its nationals, and for the settlement of which the offer of arbitration has been accepted. This arrangement is not applicable if acceptance is subject to the condition that the *compromis* should be settled in some other way.

ART. 20. Each of the parties concerned may nominate a judge of the Court to take part, with power to vote, in the examination of the case submitted to the delegation.

If the delegation acts as a commission of inquiry, this task may be intrusted to persons other than the judges of the Court. The traveling expenses and remuneration to be given to the said persons are fixed and borne by the Powers appointing them.

ART. 21. The contracting Powers only may have access to the Judicial Arbitration Court set up by the present Convention.

ART. 22. The Judicial Court of Arbitration follows the rules of procedure laid down in the Convention for the pacific settlement of international disputes, except in so far as the procedure is laid down in the present Convention.

ART. 23. The Court determines what language it will itself use and what languages may be used before it.

ART. 24. The International Bureau serves as channel for all communications to be made to the judges during the interchange of pleadings provided for in Article 63, paragraph 2, of the Convention for the pacific settlement of international disputes.

ART. 25. For all notices to be served, in particular on the parties, witnesses, or experts, the Court may apply direct to the Government of the State on whose territory the service is to be carried out. The same rule applies in the case of steps being taken to procure evidence.

The requests addressed for this purpose can only be rejected when the Power applied to considers them likely to impair its sovereign rights or its safety. If the request is complied with, the fees charged must only comprise the expenses actually incurred.

The Court is equally entitled to act through the Power on whose territory it sits.

Notices to be given to parties in the place where the Court sits may be served through the International Bureau.

ART. 26. The discussions are under the control of the president or vice-president, or, in case they are absent or can not act, of the senior judge present.

The judge appointed by one of the parties can not preside.

ART. 27. The Court considers its decisions in private, and the proceedings are secret.

All decisions are arrived at by a majority of the judges present. If the number of judges is even and equally divided, the vote of the junior judge, in the order of precedence laid down in Article 4, paragraph 1, is not counted.

ART. 28. The judgment of the Court must give the reasons on which it is based. It contains the names of the judges taking part in it; it is signed by the president and registrar.

ART. 29. Each party pays its own costs and an equal share of the costs of the trial.

ART. 30. The provisions of Articles 21 to 29 are applicable by analogy to the procedure before the delegation.

When the right of attaching a member to the delegation has been exercised by one of the parties only, the vote of the member attached is not recorded if the votes are evenly divided.

ART. 31. The general expenses of the Court are borne by the contracting Powers.

The Administrative Council applies to the Powers to obtain the funds requisite for the working of the Court.

ART. 32. The Court itself draws up its own rules of procedure, which must be communicated to the contracting Powers.

After the ratification of the present Convention the Court shall meet as early as possible in order to elaborate these rules, elect the president and vice-president, and appoint the members of the delegation.

ART. 33. The Court may propose modifications in the provisions of the present Convention concerning procedure. These proposals are communicated through the Netherland Government to the contracting Powers, which will consider together as to the measures to be taken.

PART III.—FINAL PROVISIONS

ART. 34. The Present Convention shall be ratified as soon as possible.

The ratifications shall be deposited at The Hague.

A *procès-verbal* of the deposit of each ratification shall be drawn up, of which a duly certified copy shall be sent through the diplomatic channel to all the signatory Powers.

ART. 35. The Convention shall come into force six months after its ratification.

It shall remain in force for twelve years, and shall be tacitly renewed for periods of twelve years, unless denounced.

The denunciation must be notified, at least two years before the expiration of each period, to the Netherland Government, which will inform the other Powers.

The denunciation shall only have effect in regard to the notifying Power. The Convention shall continue in force as far as the other Powers are concerned.

Part Two

DOCUMENTS OF THE

FIRST EFFORT: THE

LEAGUE OF NATIONS

Chapter 6

Wartime Planning

14. HAMILTON HOLT, "THE WAY TO DISARM: A PRACTICAL PROPOSAL," 28 SEPTEMBER 1914 [1]

Planning which led to the League of Nations started on both sides of the Atlantic very early in the war years. Men and ideas both were contributed by the prewar movements for world peace, arbitration treaties, international law and the Hague conferences. Influential as a catalyst was this article, "The way to Disarm: a Practical Proposal," published in September 1914 in *The Independent*, New York City, by the editor, Hamilton Holt, a leading figure in the New York Peace Society. The article inspired the meetings out of which came the League to Enforce Peace. [2]

In his famous essay, *Perpetual Peace,* published in 1795, Emmanuel Kant, perhaps the greatest intellect the world has ever produced, declared that we never can have universal peace until the world is politically organized and it will never be possible to organize the world politically until the people, not the kings, rule.

If this be the true philosophy of peace, then when the Great War is over, and the stricken sobered peoples set about to rear a new civilization on the ashes of the old, they cannot hope to banish war from the earth unless they are prepared to extend democracy everywhere, and to organize the international realm on a basis of law rather than force.

The question of the extension of democracy is a domestic one. It can hardly be settled by joint action of the nations. World organization and disarmament, however, can be provided for in the terms of peace or by international agreement thereafter. As the United States seems destined to play an important part in the great reconstruction at the end of the war, this is perhaps the most important question now before American statesmanship.

LAW OR WAR

The only two powers that ever have governed or ever can govern human beings are reason and force—law and war. If we do not have the one we must have the other.

The peace movement is the process of substituting law for war. Peace follows justice, justice follows law, law follows political organization. The world has already achieved peace, thru justice, law and political organization in hamlets, towns, cities, states and even in the forty-six sovereign civilized nations of the world. But in that international realm over and above each nation, in which each nation is equally sovereign, the only way for a nation to secure its rights is by the use of force. Force, therefore—or war as it is called when exerted by a nation against another nation—is at present the only legal and final method of settling international differences. In other

---

[1] *The Independent*, LXXIX (28 September 1914), pp. 427-429.

[2] See Doc. 17.

words, the nations are in that state of civilization today where, without a qualm, they claim the right to settle their disputes in a manner which they would actually put their own subjects to death for imitating. The peace problem, then, is nothing but the problem of finding ways and means of doing *between* the nations what has already been done *within* the nations. International law follows private law. The "United Nations" follow the United States.

At present international law has reached the same state of development that private law reached in the tenth century. Professor T. J. Lawrence (in his essay the Evolution of Peace) distinguishes four stages in the evolution of private law:

1. Kinship is the sole bond; revenge and retaliation are unchecked, there being no authority whatever.

2. Organization is found an advantage and tribes under a chief subdue undisciplined hordes. The right of private vengeance within the tribe is regulated but not forbidden.

3. Courts of justice exist side by side with a limited right of vengeance.

4. Private war is abolished, all disputes being settled by the courts.

It is evident that in international relations we are entering into the third stage, because the nations have already created an international tribunal which exists side by side with the right of self-redress or war.

LIKE THE AMERICAN CONFEDERATION

Furthermore, a careful study of the formation of the thirteen American colonies from separate states into our present compact Union discloses the fact that the nations today are in the same stage of development that the American colonies were about the time of their first confederation. As the United States came into existence by the establishment of the Articles of Confederation and the Continental Congress, so the "United Nations" will come into existence thru the development of The Hague Court and the recurring Hague Conferences; The Hague Court being the promise of the Supreme Court of the world and The Hague Conferences being the prophecy of the parliament of man. We may look with confidence, therefore, to a future in which the world will have an established court with jurisdiction over all questions, self-governing conferences with power to legislate on all affairs of common concern, and an executive power of some form to carry out the decrees of both. To deny this is to ignore all the analogies of private law and the whole trend of the world's political history since the Declaration of Independence. As Secretary of State Knox said not long ago:

We have reached a point when it is evident that the future holds in store a time when war shall cease, when the nations of the world shall realize a federation as real and vital as that now subsisting between the component parts of a single state.

It would be difficult to recall a more far-visioned statement than this emanating from the chancellery of a great state. It means nothing less than that the age-long dreams of the poets, the prophets and the philosophers have at last entered the realms of practical statesmanship.

But now the Great War has come upon us. "When the storm is spent and the desolation is complete; when the flower of the manhood of Europe has passed into eternal tithe of childhood and age," will then the exhausted and beggared that live on be able to undertake the task of establishing that World Government which the historian Freeman has called "the most finished and the most artificial production of political ingenuity"?

THE HAGUE OR THE LEAGUE OF PEACE

If it can be done at all it can only be done in one of two ways.

First. By building on the foundations already laid at The Hague, the Federation of the World.

Second. By establishing a Great Confederation or League of Peace, composed of those few nations who thru political evolution or the suffering of war have at last seen the light and are ready here and now to disarm.

It is obvious that the time is scarcely ripe for voluntary and universal disarmament by joint agreement. There are too many medieval-minded nations still in existence. The Federation of the World must still be a dream for many years to come. It must be developed slowly, step by step.

The immediate establishment of a League of Peace, however, would in fact constitute a first step toward world federation and does not offer insuperable difficulties. The idea of a League of Peace is not novel. All federal governments and confederations of governments, both ancient and modern, are essentially leagues of peace, even tho they may have functions to perform which often lead directly to war.

The ancient Achaian League of Greece, the Confederation of Swiss Cantons, the United Provinces of The Netherlands, the United States of America, and the Commonwealth of Australia are the most nearly perfect systems of federated governments known to history. Less significant, but none the less interesting to students of government, are the Latin League of thirty cities, the Hanseatic League, the Holy Alliance, and in modern times, the German Confederation. Even the recent Concert of Europe was a more or less inchoate League of Peace. The ancient leagues as well as the modern confederations have generally been unions of offense and defense. They stood ready, if they did not actually propose, to use their common forces to compel outside states to obey their will. Thus they were as frequently leagues of oppression as leagues of peace.

THE PROBLEM OF FORCE

The problem of the League of Peace is therefore the problem of the use of force. Force internationally exprest is measured in armaments. The chief discussion which has been waged for the past decade between the pacifists and militarists has been over the question of armaments. The militarists claim that armaments insure national safety. The pacifists declare they inevitably lead to war. Both disputants insist that the present war furnishes irrefutable proof of their contentions.

As is usual in cases of this kind the shield has two sides. The confusion has arisen from a failure to recognize the threefold function of force:

1. Force used for the maintenance of order—police force.

2. Force used for attack—aggression.

3. Force used to neutralize aggression—defense.

Police force is almost wholly good.

Offense is almost wholly bad.

Defense is a necessary evil, and exists simply to neutralize force employed for aggression.

The problem of the peace movement is how to abolish the use of force for aggression, and yet to maintain it for police purposes. Force for defense will of course automatically cease when force for aggression is abolished.

The chief problem, then, of a League of Peace is this: Shall the members of the League "not only keep the peace themselves, but prevent by force if necessary its being broken by others," as ex-President Roosevelt suggested in his Nobel Peace Address delivered at Christiania, May 5, 1910? Or shall its force be exercised only within its membership and thus be on the side of law and order and ever on the side of arbitrary will or tyranny? Or shall it never be used at all? Whichever one of these conceptions finally prevails the Great War has conclusively demonstrated that as long as War Lords exist defensive force must be maintained. Hence the League must be prepared to use force against any nations which will not forswear force. Nevertheless a formula must be devised, for disarmament some how and some way must take place. How then can the maintenance of a force for defense and police power be reconciled with the theory of disarmament?

THE CONSTITUTION OF THE LEAGUE

In this way: Let the League of Peace be formed on the following five principles:

First. The nations of the League shall mutually agree to respect the territory and sovereignty of each other.

Second. All questions that cannot be settled by diplomacy shall be arbitrated.

Third. The nations of the League shall provide a periodical assembly to make all rules to become law unless vetoed by a nation within a stated period.

Fourth. The nations shall disarm to the point where the combined forces of the League shall be a certain per cent higher than those of the most heavily armed nation or alliance outside the League. Detailed rules for this pro rata disarmament shall be formulated by the Assembly.

Fifth. Any member of the League shall have the right to withdraw on due notice, or may be expelled by the unanimous vote of the others.

The advantages that a nation would gain in becoming a member of such a league are manifest. The risk of war would be eliminated within the League. Obviously the only things that are vital to a nation are its land and its independence. Since each nation in the League will have pledged itself to respect the territory and the sovereignty of every other, a refusal to do so will logically lead to expulsion from the League. Thus every vital question will be automatically reserved from both war and arbitration. All other questions are of secondary importance and can readily be arbitrated.

By the establishment of a periodical assembly a method would be devised whereby the members of the League could develop their common intercourse and interests as far and as fast as they could unanimously agree upon ways and means. As any law could be vetoed by a single nation, no nation could have any fear that it would be coerced against its will by a majority vote of the other nations. By such an assembly the League might in time agree to reduce tariffs and postal rates and in a thousand other ways promote commerce and comity among its members.

As a final safeguard against coercion by the other members of the League, each member will have the right of secession on due notice. This would prevent civil war within the League. The right of expulsion by the majority will prevent one nation by its veto power indefinitely blocking all progress of the League.

THE SCRAP OF PAPER

But it will be said that all these agreements will have no binding effect in a crisis. A covenant is a mere "scrap of paper" whose provisions will be violated by the first nation which fancies it is its interest to do so. In order to show that their faith is backed up by deeds, however, the nations on entering the League agree to disarm to a little above the danger point, and put all their defensive power under a federal authority. This is the real proof of their conversion to the peace idea.

Thus the nations which join the League will enjoy all the economic and political advantages which come from mutual cooperation and the extension of international friendship and at the same time will be protected by an adequate force against the aggressive force of the greatest nation or alliance outside the League. The League therefore reconciles the demand of the pacifists for the limitation of armaments and eventual disarmament and the demand of the militarists for the protection that armaments affords. Above all the establishment of such a league will give the liberal parties in the nations outside the League an issue on which they can attack their governments so as sooner or later to force them to apply to the League for membership. As each one enters there will be another pro rata reduction of the military forces of the League down to the armament of the next most powerful nation or alliance outside it; until finally the whole world is federated in a brotherhood of universal peace and armies and navies are reduced to an international police force.

This is the plan for a League of Peace. Is the hour about to strike when it can be realized? If only the United States, France, and England would lead in its formation, Belgium, Holland, Switzerland, Denmark, Norway, Sweden, Argentina, Brazil, Chile and others might perhaps join. Even if Russia and Germany and Japan and Italy stayed out, the League would still be powerful and large enough to begin with every auspicious hope of success.

THE DESTINY OF THE UNITED STATES

It would seem to be the manifest destiny of the United States to lead in the establishment of such a league. The United States is the world in miniature. The United States is the greatest league of peace known to history. The United States is a demonstration to the world that all the races and peoples of the earth can live in peace under one form of government, and its chief value to civilization is a demonstration of what this form of government is.

Prior to the formation "of a more perfect union" our original thirteen states were united in a confederacy strikingly similar to that now proposed on an international scale. They were obliged by the articles of this confederacy to respect each other's territory and sovereignty, to arbitrate all questions among themselves, to assist each other against any foreign foe, not to engage in war unless called upon by the confederation to do so or actually invaded by a foreign foe, and not to maintain armed forces in excess of the strength fixed for each state by all the states in congress assembled.

It is notable that security against aggression from states inside or outside the American Union accompanied the agreement to limit armaments. Thus danger of war and size of armaments were decreased contemporaneously.

It is also notable that from the birth of the Republic to this hour every President of the United States has advocated peace thru justice. From the first great Virginian to the last, all have abhorred what Thomas Jefferson called "the greatest scourge of mankind."

When the Great War is over and the United States is called upon to lead the nations in reconstructing a new order of civilization, why might not Woodrow Wilson do on a word scale something similar to what George Washington did on a continental scale?

Stranger things than this have happened in history. Let us add to the Declaration of Independence a Declaration of Interdependence.

15. THE CENTURY CLUB PROPOSALS AND PLATFORM, 9 APRIL 1915 [1]

Plans for the American League to Enforce Peace took shape at the Century Club in New York City in a series of meetings among a small number of private citizens long active in civic affairs. Ex-President Taft, who subsequently consented to assume the presidency of the projected "League of Peace," was present at the last meeting on 9 April. The Platform, as edited by Mr. Taft, was communicated to a much larger group of prominent citizens, who were invited to sponsor an inaugural meeting at Independence Hall, in June.[2]

LEAGUE OF PEACE

It is desirable for the United States to join a League of the great nations binding the signatories to the following:

First, all justiciable questions arising between the signatory powers not settled by negotiation, shall be submitted to a judicial tribunal for hearing and judgment both upon the merits and upon any issue as to its jurisdiction of the question.

Second, all non-justiciable questions arising between the signatories and not settled by negotiations, shall be submitted to a Council of Conciliation for hearing, consideration and recommendation.

Third, the signatory powers shall jointly use their military forces to prevent any one of their number from going to war or committing acts of hostility against another of the signatories before any question arising shall be submitted as provided in the foregoing.

Fourth, that conferences between signatory powers shall be held from time to time to formulate and codify rules of international law which, unless some signatory shall signify its dissent within a stated period, shall thereafter govern in the decisions of the Judicial Tribunal mentioned in article one.

16. THE "BRYCE GROUP" *PROPOSALS FOR THE AVOIDANCE OF WAR,* 24 FEBRUARY 1915 [1]*

In Britain shortly after the start of hostilities the "Council for the Study of International Relations," with Lord Bryce as president, was organized to explain means of preventing future wars. The mood of the British public, fearful of any weakening of the war effort, deterred the "Bryce Group," as the Council was known, from publishing its findings until after the United States entered the conflict. In the meantime, this preliminary draft entitled "Proposals for the Avoidance of War" was privately circulated.

JUSTICIABLE DISPUTES

1. The signatory Powers to agree to refer to the existing Permanent Court

of Arbitration at The Hague, or to the Court of Arbitral Justice proposed at the second Hague Conference, if and when such Court shall be established, or to some other arbitral tribunal, all disputes between them (including those affecting honour and vital interests), which are of a justiciable character and which the Powers concerned have failed to settle by diplomatic methods.

2. The signatory Powers so referring to arbitration to agree to accept, and give effect to the award of the tribunal.

[1] John H. Latané (ed.), *Development of the League of Nations Idea: Documents and Correspondence of Theodore Marburg,* (New York, 1932), II, p. 790.
[2] See Doc. 17.
[1]* Viscount James Bryce, *Proposals for the Avoidance of War (Private and Confidential,*

Not for Publication) (n.p., n.d.). The pamphlet is reprinted under the title, "Scheme Drafted by a British Group, 1915," in The Right Hon. Viscount Bryce, O.M., *Essays and Addresses in War Time* (New York, 1918), pp. 206-208.

3. "Disputes of a justiciable character" to be defined as "disputes as to the interpretation of a treaty, as to any question of international law, as to the existence of any fact which, if established, would constitute a breach of any international obligation, or as to the nature and extent of the reparation to be made for any such breach."

4. Any question which may arise as to whether a dispute is of a justiciable character, to be referred for decision to the Court of Arbitral Justice when constituted; or until it is constituted, to the existing Permanent Court of Arbitration at The Hague.

PERMANENT COUNCIL OF CONCILIATION

5. With a view to the prevention and settlement of disputes between the signatory Powers which are not of a justiciable character, a permanent Court of Conciliation to be constituted.

6. The members of the Council to be appointed by the several signatory Powers for a fixed term of years, and vacancies to be filled up by the appointing Powers, so that the Council shall always be complete and in being.

7. In order to provide for the case of disputes between a signatory Power and an outside Power which is willing to submit its case to the Council, provision to be made for the temporary representation of the latter.

8. The signatory Powers to agree that every party to a dispute, not of a justiciable character, the existence of which might ultimately endanger friendly relations with another signatory Power or Powers, and which has not been settled by diplomatic methods, will submit its case to the Council with a view to conciliation.

9. Where, in the opinion of the Council, any dispute exists between any of the signatory Powers which appears likely to endanger their good relations with each other, the Council to consider the dispute and to invite each Power concerned to submit its case with a view to conciliation.

10. Unless, through the good offices of the Council or otherwise, the dispute shall have previously been settled between the parties, the Council to make and publish, with regard to every dispute considered by it, a report or reports, containing recommendations for the amicable settlement of the dispute.

11. When it appears to the Council that, from any cause within its knowledge, the good relations between any of the signatory Powers are likely to be endangered, the Council to be at liberty to make suggestions to them with a view to conciliation, whether or not any dispute has actually arisen, and, if it considers it expedient to do so, to publish such suggestions.

12. The Council to be at liberty to make and submit for the consideration of the signatory Powers, suggestions as to the limitation or reduction of armaments, or any other suggestions which in its opinion would lead to the avoidance of war or the diminution of its evils.[2]

13. The signatory Powers to agree to furnish the Council with all the means and facilities required for the due discharge of its functions.

14. The Council to deliberate in public or in private, as it thinks fit.

15. The Council to have power to appoint committees, which may or may not be composed exclusively of its own members, to report to it on any matter within the scope of its functions.

MORATORIUM FOR HOSTILITIES

16. Every signatory Power to agree not to declare war or begin hostilities or hostile preparations against any other signatory Power (a) before the matter in dispute shall have been submitted to an arbitral tribunal or to the Council; or (b) within a period of twelve months after such submission; or (c) if the award of the arbitral tri-

---

[2] It will be observed that it is not proposed to confer any executive power on the Council.

bunal or the report of the Council, as the case may be, has been published within that time, then not to declare war or begin hostilities or hostile preparations within a period of six months after the publication of such award or report.[3]

LIMITATION OF EFFECT OF ALLIANCES

17. The signatory Powers to agree that no signatory Power commencing hostilities against another without first complying with the provisions of the precedure clauses, shall be entitled, by virtue of any now existing or future treaty of alliance or other engagement, to the military or other material support of any other signatory Power in such hostilities.

ENFORCEMENT OF THE PRECEDING PROVISIONS

18. Every signatory Power to undertake that in case any Power, whether or not a signatory Power, declares war or begins hostilities or hostile preparations against a signatory Power, (a) without first having submitted its case to an arbitral tribunal, or to the Council of Conciliation, or (b) before the expiration of the hereinbefore prescribed periods of delay, it will forthwith, in conjunction with the other signatory Powers, take such concerted measures, economic and forcible, against the Power so acting, as, in their judgment, are most effective and appropriate to the circumstances of the case.

19. The signatory Powers to undertake that if any Power shall fail to accept and give effect to the recommendations contained in any report of the Council, or in the award of the arbitral tribunal, they will, at a Conference to be forthwith summoned for the purpose, consider, in concert, the situation which has arisen by reason of such failure, and what collective action, if any, it is practicable to take in order to make such recommendations operative.[4]

17. THE INDEPENDENCE HALL PROGRAM OF THE LEAGUE TO ENFORCE PEACE, 17 JUNE 1915 [1]

The League to Enforce Peace was launched at an inaugural meeting in Independence Hall, Philadelphia, on 17 June 1915, with some 300 invited public figures in attendance. Ex-President Taft was elected president and this official platform adopted.

First: All justiciable questions arising between the signatory powers, not settled by negotiation, shall, subject to the limitations of treaties, be submitted to a judicial tribunal for hearing and judgment, both upon the merits and upon any issue as to its jurisdiction of the question.

Second: All other questions arising between the signatories and not settled by negotiation, shall be submitted to a council of conciliation for hearing, consideration and recommendation.

Third: The signatory powers shall jointly use forthwith both their economic and military forces against any one of their number that goes to war, or commits acts of hostility, against another of the signatories before any question arising shall be submitted as provided in the foregoing.

Fourth: Conferences between the

[3] If an agreement for limitation of armaments had been arrived at, any departure from the agreement would presumably be a "hostile preparation," until the contrary were shown.

[4] The measures contemplated in paragraphs 18, 19 would, of course, be taken by the gov-

ernments of the signatory Powers acting in concert, and not by the Council of Conciliation.

[1] John H. Latané (ed.), Development of the League of Nations Idea: Documents and Correspondence of Theodore Marburg, (New York, 1932), II, pp. 790 f.

signatory powers shall be held from time to time to formulate and codify rules of international law, which, unless some signatory shall signify its dissent within a stated period, shall thereafter govern in the decisions of the Judicial Tribunal mentioned in Article One.

18. WILSON'S ADDRESS TO THE CONGRESS, 8 JANUARY 1918; EXCERPT: THE FOURTEEN POINTS [1]

When President Wilson announced this "programme for the world's peace," which he did in an address to a joint session of the Congress 8 January 1918, it was formulated in the famous "Fourteen Points." In addition to eight provisions respecting particular peoples, there were six of general application including—in the fourteenth point—the establishment of a permanent arrangement for mutual security, the whole presupposing a new political morality among nations.[2]

The programme of the world's peace, therefore, is our programme; and that programme, the only possible, as we see it, is this:

I. Open covenants of peace, openly arrived at, after which there shall be no private international understandings of any kind, but diplomacy shall proceed always frankly and in the public view.

II. Absolute freedom of navigation upon the seas, outside territorial waters alike in peace and in war, except as the seas may be closed in whole or in part by international action for the enforcement of international covenants.

III. The removal, so far as possible, of all economic barriers and the establishment of an equality of trade conditions among all the nations consenting to the peace and associating themselves for its maintenance.

IV. Adequate guarantees given and taken that national armaments will be reduced to the lowest point consistent with domestic safety.

V. A free, open-minded, and absolutely impartial adjustment of all colonial claims, based upon a strict observance of the principle that, in determining all such questions of sovereignty, the interests of the populations concerned must have equal weight with the equitable claims of the Government whose title is to be determined.

VI. The evacuation of all Russian territory and such a settlement of all questions affecting Russia as will secure the best and freest cooperation of the other nations of the world in obtaining for her an unhampered and unembarrassed opportunity for the independent determination of her own political development and national policy and assure her of a sincere welcome into the society of free nations under institutions of her own choosing; and, more than a welcome, assistance also of every kind that she may need and may herself desire. The treatment accorded Russia by her sister nations in the months to come will be the acid test of their good-will, of their comprehension of her needs as distinguished from their own interests, and of their intelligent and unselfish sympathy.

VII. Belgium, the whole world will agree, must be evacuated and restored, without any attempt to limit the sovereignty which she enjoys in common with all other free nations. No other single act will serve as this will serve to restore confidence among the nations in the laws which they have themselves set and determined for the government of their relations with one another. Without this healing act, the

---

[1] *Congressional Record,* LVI, 65th Cong., 2nd sess., pp. 680 f.

[2] The Fourteen Points can profitably be compared with the Atlantic Charter (Doc. 41) which played a somewhat analogous role in World War II.

whole structure and validity of international law is for ever impaired.

VIII. All French territory should be freed and the invaded portions restored, and the wrong done to France by Prussia in 1871 in the matter of Alsace-Lorraine, which has unsettled the peace of the world for nearly fifty years, should be righted, in order that peace may once more be made secure in the interests of all.

IX. A readjustment of the frontiers of Italy should be effected along clearly recognisable lines of nationality.

X. The peoples of Austria-Hungary, whose place among the nations we wish to see safeguarded and assured, should be accorded the freest opportunity of autonomous development.

XI. Rumania, Serbia, and Montenegro should be evacuated; occupied territories restored; Serbia accorded free and secure access to the sea; and the relations of the several Balkan States to one another determined by friendly counsel along historically established lines of allegiance and nationality; and international guarantees of the political and economic independence and territorial integrity of the several Balkan States should be entered into.

XII. The Turkish portions of the present Ottoman Empire should be assured a secure sovereignty, but the other nationalities which are now under Turkish rule should be assured an undoubted security of life and an absolutely unmolested opportunity of autonomous development, and the Dardanelles should be permanently opened as a free passage to the ships and commerce of all nations under international guarantees.

XIII. An independent Polish State should be erected which should include the territories inhabited by indisputably Polish populations, which should be assured a free and secure access to the sea, and whose political and economic independence and territorial integrity should be guaranteed by international covenant.

XIV. A general association of nations must be formed under specific covenants for the purpose of affording mutual guarantees of political independence and territorial integrity to great and small States alike.

19. THE PHILLIMORE COMMITTEE DRAFT CONVENTION, 20 MARCH 1918 [1]

At the end of 1916, Lloyd George authorized the British Foreign Office to set up a "Committee on the League of Nations." The Committee, under the chairmanship of Sir Walter G. F. Phillimore, was to "enquire into the various schemes for establishing by means of a League of Nations or other device some alternative to war as a means of settling international disputes." [2] This Interim Report was submitted on 20 March 1918 and a final report followed on 3 July. Although the Committee's proposals amount to little more than a revival of the Concert of Europe with improved procedures and obligatory jurisdiction, many of the provisions of the reports were incorporated into the League of Nations Covenant. [3]

(There will be a Preamble reciting that the object of this Convention is to create a League of Nations which will, if possible, prevent all wars in the future.)

AVOIDANCE OF WAR

ART. 1. Each of the Allied States (being the parties to this Convention) agrees with the other Allied States collectively and separately that it will not go to war with another of the Allied States—

a. without previously submitting the matter in dispute to arbitration or to a Conference of the Allied States; and

b. until there has been an award or

---

[1] David Hunter Miller, *The Drafting of the Covenant* (New York, 1928), II, pp. 3-6.
[2] Foreign Office, Committee on the League of Nations, Interim Report, quoted in *ibid.*, I, p. 4.
[3] See Doc. 24.

a report by the Conference, provided that in the case mentioned in Article 12 the observance of this sub-clause is suspended;

and also that it will not go to war—

c. with another of the Allied States which complies with the award or with the recommendation (if any) made by the Conference in its report.

ART. 2. If, which may God avert, one of the Allied States should break the covenant contained in the preceding Article, this State will become *ipso facto* at war with all the other Allied States, and the latter agree to take and to support each other in taking jointly and severally all such measures—military, naval, financial, and economic—as will best avail for restraining the breach of covenant. Such financial and economic measures shall include severance of all relations of trade and finance with the subjects of the covenant-breaking State, prohibition against the subjects of the Allied States entering into any relations with the subjects of the covenant-breaking State, and the prevention, so far as possible, of the subjects of the covenant-breaking State from having any commercial or financial intercourse with the subjects of any other State, whether party to this Convention or not.

For the purpose of this Article, the Allied States shall detain any ship or goods belonging to any of the subjects of the covenant-breaking State or coming from or destined for any person residing in the territory of such state and shall take any other similar steps which shall be necessary for the same purpose.

Such of the Allied States (if any) as cannot make an effective contribution of military or naval force shall at the least take the other measures indicated in this Article.

PACIFIC SETTLEMENT OF INTERNATIONAL DISPUTES

ART. 3. If a dispute should hereafter arise between any of the Allied States as to the interpretation of a treaty, as to any question of international law, as to the existence of any fact which if established would constitute a breach of any international obligation, or as to the nature and extent of the reparation to be made for any such breach, if such dispute cannot be settled by negotiation, arbitration is recognized by the Allied States as the most effective and at the same time the most equitable means of settling the dispute.

ART. 4. But if the Allied States concerned do not agree that the dispute is suitable for reference to arbitration or do not agree as to the question to be referred or as to the composition of the tribunal of arbitration, or if for any other reason a reference to arbitration should prove impracticable, any one of the Allied States concerned may make application to the Conference of the Allied States to take the matter of the dispute into consideration.

ART. 5. The seat of the Conference shall be at X, the Convener shall be the Sovereign or President of the State of X, and his representative shall be the president of the Conference. The Allied States shall be represented at the Conference by their diplomatic representatives accredited to the State of X. In the event of X being one of the States parties to the dispute, either State may communicate with the Sovereign or President of Y, who thereupon shall become the Convener and shall fix the seat of the Conference and name its president.

The provisions of this Article shall not prejudice the right of any of the Allied States to send other representatives to the Conference, but the Conference shall be under no obligation to await their arrival.

ART. 6. It shall be the duty of the Convener of the Conference to give notice of the applications to the Conference to every State party to the dispute and to summon the Conference as speedily as possible.

ART. 7. The Conference shall regulate its own procedure, and may appoint Committees to enquire and report. In all matters covered by this Article the Conference may decide by the votes of a majority of the Allied States represented.

ART. 8. The function of the Conference shall be to ascertain the facts with regard to the dispute, and to make a recommendation based on the merits of the case, and calculated to ensure a just and lasting settlement. The recommendation shall not have the force of a decision.

ART. 9. The Allied States agree to place at the disposal of the Conference, or any Committee appointed by the Conference, to the fullest possible extent compatible with their interests, the information in their possession which bears upon the dispute.

ART. 10. The recommendation of the Conference shall be addressed to the parties to the dispute, and will not require their assent.

ART. 11. In the event of the Conference being unable to agree upon a recommendation to be addressed to the parties to the dispute, it shall be the duty of the representatives of such of the Allied States attending the Conference as shall be satisfied as to the nature of the recommendation which should be made—provided that they represent not less than a majority of the Allied States attending the Conference—to publish on behalf of the States which they represent a statement setting out what they believe to be the facts with regard to the dispute. They may also add thereto the text of the recommendation which they consider the Conference should have addressed to the parties to the dispute.

Alternative Article 11. If, in the event of the Conference being unable to agree upon a recommendation to be addressed to the parties to the dispute, any State or group of States having taken part in the Conference issues a public statement of the view which, as a result of the deliberations of the Conference, it takes of the dispute, such action shall not be regarded as an un-

friendly act by either of the parties to the dispute.

ART. 12. Any one of the Allied States having a dispute pending may apply to the Conference to be relieved from the moratorium imposed by Article 1 (b) on the ground that there is a continuing injury, or on the ground that unless some prompt provision for reparation or restitution is made the injury will be irreparable. The Conference shall, without deciding in any way upon the merits of the dispute, forthwith consider this application, and may relieve the applicant State from the provisions of the moratorium, or may suggest terms of temporary arrangement as a condition of not relieving the applicant State from the moratorium, and may from time to time consider the application and the terms which should be imposed. In the event of relief from the provisions of the moratorium being granted under this Article, any of the Allied States may, notwithstanding the provisions of Article 1, come to the assistance of the State so relieved.

RELATIONS BETWEEN THE ALLIED STATES AND STATES NOT PARTY TO THIS CONVENTION

ART. 13. As regards disputes between one of the Allied States and a State not party to this Convention, the Allied State shall endeavor to obtain submission of the dispute to arbitration, if it be of a suitable nature for arbitraton, and if the dispute be not of a nature suitable for arbitration, or if the other State will not agree to submit it to arbitration, the Allied State shall bring it before the Conference. In the latter event the Convener of the Conference shall, in the name of the League of Nations, invite the State not party to this Convention to become for this purpose a party to the Conference and to submit its case to the Conference, and in such case the provisions hereinbefore contained shall be applicable to the dispute both against and in favor of such State in all respects as if it were a party to this Convention.

Art. 14. If the State not party to this Convention will not accept the invitation to become *ad hoc* a party to the Conference, the Conference may enquire into the dispute *ex parte,* and may make a recommendation in the same way as if both parties were present.

Art. 15. If the Allied State shall be attacked by the other State before an award or a report of the Conference is made, or notwithstanding the compliance of the Allied State with the award or the recommendation (if any) made by the Conference in its report, any of the Allied States may come to its assistance.

Art. 16. In the case of a dispute between States none of whom are parties to this Convention, any of the Allied States may bring the matter before the Conference with a view to the Conference using its good offices to prevent war.

Art. 17. Any State not party to this Convention may apply to the Conference for leave to become a party. The Conference will forthwith examine the application favorably, and will determine whether it should be granted and whether it is necessary to impose any terms.

CONFLICT OF TREATIES

Art. 18. A. The Allied States severally agree that the present Convention abrogates all treaty obligations *inter se* inconsistent with the terms hereof, and that they will not enter into any engagements inconsistent with the terms hereof.

B. Where any of the Allied States, before becoming party to this Convention, shall have entered into any treaty imposing upon it obligations inconsistent with the terms of this Convention, it shall be the duty of such State to take immediate steps to procure its release from such obligations.

20. THE HOUSE DRAFT OF THE COVENANT, JULY 1918 [1]

Colonel Edward M. House, who was in touch with the League to Enforce Peace and who had received copies of the Phillimore Committee's Interim Report and the report (dated 8 June 1918) of the similar Bourgeois Committee in France,[2] prepared a draft plan for postwar organization which he forwarded to President Wilson 16 July. The House plan was used by Mr. Wilson later that month in preparing his first draft of the Covenant.[3]

SUGGESTION FOR A COVENANT OF A
LEAGUE OF NATIONS

Preamble

International civilization having proved a failure because there has not been constructed a fabric of law to which nations have yielded with the same obedience and deference as individuals submit to intra-national laws, and because public opinion has sanc-

tioned unmoral acts relating to international affairs, it is the purpose of the States signatory to this Convention to form a League of Nations having for its purpose the maintenance throughout the world of peace, security, progress and orderly government. Therefore it is agreed as follows:

Art. 1. The same standards of honor and ethics shall prevail internationally and in affairs of nations as in other matters. The agreement or promise of a Power shall be inviolate.

Art. 2. No official of a Power shall, either directly or by indirection on behalf of his Government, be expected or permitted to act or communicate other than consistently with the truth, the honor and the obligation of the power which he represents.

[1] David Hunter Miller, *The Drafting of the Covenant* (New York, 1928), II, pp. 7-11.
[2] Foreign Office, Committee on the League of Nations, *Interim Report,* quoted in Miller, *op. cit.,* I, p. 4.
[3] Doc. 24.

ART. 3. Any attempt by a Power, either openly or in secret, whether by propaganda or otherwise, to influence one Power or nation against another shall be deemed dishonorable.

ART. 4. Any open or direct inquiry regarding the acts or purposes of a Power may be made by another Power as of course, and shall be regarded as an act of friendship tending to promote frankness in international relations, but any secret inquiry to such end shall be deemed dishonorable.

ART. 5. Any war or threat of war is a matter of concern to the League of Nations, and to the Powers, members thereof.

ART. 6. The Ambassadors and Ministers of the Contracting Powers to X and the Minister for Foreign Affairs of X shall act as the respective delegates of the Powers in the League of Nations. The meetings of the delegates shall be held at the seat of government of X, and the Minister for Foreign Affairs of X shall be the presiding officer.

If the delegates deem it necessary or advisable, they may meet temporarily at the seat of government of Y or Z, in which case the Ambassador or Minister to X of the country in which the meeting is held, shall be the presiding officer *pro tempore*.

ART. 7. The Delegates shall meet in the interests of peace whenever war is rumored or threatened, and also whenever a Delegate of any power shall inform the Delegates that a meeting in the interests of peace is advisable.

ART. 8. The Delegates shall also meet at such other times as they shall from time to time determine.

ART. 9. The Delegates shall regulate their own procedure and may appoint committees to inquire and report. The Delegates shall constitute a Secretariat and fix the duties thereof and all expenses of the Secretariat shall be paid by the Contracting Powers as the Delegates may determine. In all matters covered by this article the Delegates may decide by the votes of a majority of the Contracting Powers represented.

ART. 10. An International Court composed of not more than fifteen members shall be constituted, which shall have jurisdiction to determine any difference between nations which has not been settled by diplomacy, arbitration, or otherwise, and which relates to the existence, interpretation, or effect of a treaty, or which may be submitted by consent, or which relates to matters of commerce, including in such matters, the validity or effect internationally of a statute, regulation or practice. The Delegates may at their discretion submit to the Court such other questions as may seem to them advisable.

The judges of the International Court, shall, both originally and from time to time as vacancies may occur, be chosen by the Delegates. A judge of the International Court shall retire from office when he shall have reached the age of seventy-two years, and may be so retired at any time by a vote of two thirds of the Delegates, but in case of retirement of a judge from office, the salary paid to him shall be continued to be so paid during his natural life.

A judge may be removed by a vote of two thirds of the Delegates. The International Court shall formulate its own rules of procedure.

ART. 11. Any difference between nations relating to matters of commerce and which involves the validity or effect internationally of a statute, regulation or practice, shall, if the Power having adopted such statute, regulation or practice so requests, be submitted to its highest national court for decision, before submission to the International Court.

ART. 12. The highest national court of each Contracting Power shall have jurisdiction to hear and finally determine any international dispute which may be submitted by consent for its decision.

ART. 13. The Contracting Powers agree that all disputes between or among them or any of them of any nature whatsoever which shall not be settled by diplomacy and which are not within the provisions of Article 10 shall be referred for arbitration before three arbitrators, one to be selected by each party to the dispute and one to be chosen by two arbitrators so selected, or in the event of their failure to agree to such choice, the third arbitrator shall be selected by the Delegates.

The decision of the arbitrators may be set aside on the appeal of a party to the dispute, by a vote of three fourths of the Delegates, if the decision of the arbitrators was unanimous, and by a vote of two thirds of the Delegates if the decision of the arbitrators was not unanimous, but shall otherwise be finally binding and conclusive.

When any decision of the arbitrators shall have been set aside by the Delegates, the dispute shall again be submitted to arbitration before three arbitrators, chosen as heretofore provided, but none of whom shall have previously acted as such and the decision of the arbitrators upon the second arbitration shall be finally binding and conclusive without right of appeal.

ART. 14. Any Power which the Delegates determine shall have failed to submit to the International Court any dispute of which that Court has jurisdiction as of course, or failed or neglected to carry out any decision of that Court, or of a national court to which a dispute has been submitted by consent for decision, or failed to submit to arbitration any dispute pursuant to Article 13 hereof, or failed to carry out any decision of the arbitrators, shall thereupon lose and be deprived of all rights of commerce and intercourse with the Contracting Powers.

ART. 15. If any Power shall declare war or begin hostilities before submitting a dispute with another Power as the case may be, either to the International Court or to Arbitrators, as herein provided, or shall declare war or begin hostilities in regard to any dispute which has been decided ad-

versely to it by said Court or by Arbitrators or pursuant to Article 12 hereof, as the case may be, the Contracting Powers shall not only cease all commerce and intercourse with that Power as in Article 14 provided, but shall also arrange to blockade and close the frontiers of that power to commerce and intercourse with the world.

ART. 16. As regards disputes between one of the Contracting Powers and a Power not a party to this Convention, the Contracting Power shall endeavor to obtain submission of the dispute to judicial decision or to arbitration. If the other state will not agree to submit the dispute to judicial decision or to arbitration the Contracting Powers shall bring it before the Delegates. In the latter event the Delegates shall in the name of the League of Nations invite the state not a party to this Convention to become *ad hoc* a party and to submit its case to judicial decision or to arbitration and in such case the provisions herein before contained shall be applicable to the dispute both against and in favor of such state in all respects as if it were a party to this Convention.

ART. 17. If the state not a party to this Convention will not accept the invitation to become *ad hoc* a party, the Delegates shall inquire into the dispute and shall make a recommendation in respect thereof.

ART. 18. If hostilities shall be commenced against the Contracting Power by the other state before a decision of the dispute, or before the recommendation made by the Delegates in respect thereof, or contrary to such recommendation, the Contracting Powers will thereupon cease all commerce and intercourse with the other state and will also arrange to blockade and close the frontiers of that state to commerce and intercourse with the world and any of the Contracting Powers may come to the assistance of the Contracting Power against which hostilities have been commenced.

ART. 19. In the case of a dispute between states not parties to this Convention, any Power may bring the matter before the Delegates, who shall tender the good offices of the League of Nations with a view to the peaceable settlement of the dispute.

If one of the Powers, party to the dispute, shall offer and agree to submit its interests and cause of action in regard thereto wholly to the control and decision of the League of Nations, that Power shall *ad hoc* be deemed a Contracting Power. If no one of the Powers, parties to such dispute, shall so offer and agree, the Delegates shall take such action and make such recommendations to their Governments as will preserve peace and prevent hostilities and result in the settlement of the dispute.

ART. 20. The Contracting Powers unite in several guarantees to each other of their territorial integrity and political independence, subject, however, to such territorial modifications, if any, as may become necessary in the future by reason of changes in present racial conditions and aspirations, pursuant to the principle of self-determination and as shall also be regarded by three fourths of the Delegates as necessary and proper for the welfare of the peoples concerned; recognizing also that all territorial changes involve equitable compensation and that the peace of the world is superior in importance and interest to questions of boundary.

ART. 21. The Contracting Powers recognize the principle that permanent peace will require that national armaments shall be reduced to the lowest point consistent with safety, and the Delegates are directed to formulate at once a plan by which such a reduction may be brought about. The plan so formulated shall not be binding until and unless unanimously approved by the Governments signatory to this Covenant.

The Contracting Powers agree that munitions and implements of war shall not be manufactured by private enterprise and that publicity as to all national armaments and programmes is essential.

ART. 22. Any Power not a party to this Convention may apply to the Delegates for leave to become a party. The Delegates may act favorably on the application if they shall regard the granting thereof as tending to promote the peace and security of the world.

ART. 23. A. The Contracting Powers severally agree that the present Convention abrogates all treaty obligations *inter se* inconsistent with the terms thereof, and that they will not enter into any engagements inconsistent with the terms hereof.

B. Where any of the Contracting Powers, before becoming party to this Convention, shall have entered into any treaty imposing upon it obligations inconsistent with the terms of this Convention, it shall be the duty of such Power to take immediate steps to procure its release from such obligations.

21. JAN CHRISTIAN SMUTS, *THE LEAGUE OF NATIONS: A PRACTICAL SUGGESTION,* 16 DECEMBER 1918; EXCERPTS [1]

Until near the end of 1918 the emphasis in discussions and plans dealing with postwar organization was almost exclusively upon

security and the maintenance of orderly relations among nations. With the publication in December of this essay by General Smuts,

[1] Lieut.-Gen. the Rt. Hon. J. C. Smuts, P.C., *The League of Nations: A Practical Suggestion* (London, Hodder and Stoughton, 1918). The Smuts "suggestion" took the form

of an extended essay in which 21 recommendations were set forth and supported. Only the recommendations are given here.

who had represented the Union of South Africa at the Imperial War Conference in 1917 and then become a member of the War Cabinet of Lloyd George, the discussion was lifted to a higher plane. Smuts saw the proposed League "not only as a possible means for preventing war, but much more as a great organ of the ordinary peaceful life of civilisation. . . ." [2]

(1) That in the vast multiplicity of territorial, economic, and other problems with which the conference will find itself confronted it should look upon the setting up of a league of nations as its primary and basic task, and as supplying the necessary organ by means of which most of those problems can find their only stable solution. Indeed, the conference should regard itself as the first or preliminary meeting of the league, intended to work out its organization, functions, and programme.

(2) That, so far at any rate as the peoples and territories formerly belonging to Russia, Austria-Hungary, and Turkey are concerned, the league of nations should be considered as the reversionary in the most general sense and as clothed with the right of ultimate disposal in accordance with certain fundamental principles. Reversion to the league of nations should be substituted for any policy of national annexation.

(3) That there shall be no annexation of any of these territories to any of the victorious Powers, and secondly, that in the future government of these territories and peoples the rule of self-determination, or the consent of the governed to their form of government, shall be fairly and reasonably applied.

(4) That any authority, control, or administration which may be necessary in respect of these territories and peoples, other than their own self-determined autonomy, shall be the exclusive function of and shall be vested in

the league of nations and exercised by or on behalf of it.

(5) That it shall be lawful for the league of nations to delegate its authority, control, or administration in respect of any people or territory to some other state whom it may appoint as its agent or mandatary, but that wherever possible the agent or mandatary so appointed shall be nominated or approved by the autonomous people or territory.

(6) That the degree of authority, control, or administration exercised by the mandatary state shall in each case be laid down by the league in a special act or charter, which shall reserve to it complete power to ultimate control and supervision, as well as the right of appeal to it from the territory or people affected against any gross breach of the mandate by the mandatary state.

(7) That the mandatary state shall in each case be bound to maintain the policy of the open door, or equal economic opportunity for all, and shall form no military forces beyond the standard laid down by the league for purposes of internal police.

(8) That no new state arising from the old empires be recognized or admitted into the league unless on condition that its military forces and armaments shall conform to a standard laid down by the league in respect of it from time to time.

(9) That, as the successor to the empires, the league of nations will directly and without power of delegation watch over the relations *inter se* of the new independent states arising from the break-up of those empires, and will regard as a very special task the duty of conciliating and composing differences between them with a view to the maintenance of good order and general peace.

(10) The constitution of the league

[2] *Ibid.*, p. 8. General Smuts, who was made a member of the League of Nations Commission to draft the Covenant at the Paris Conference (see Doc. 22), was also present for the drafting of the United Nations Charter at the San Francisco Conference in 1945 (see Doc. 47).

will be that of a permanent conference between the Governments of the constituent states for the purpose of joint international action in certain defined respects, and will not derogate from the independence of those states. It will consist of a general conference, a council and courts of arbitration and conciliation.

(11) The general conference, in which all constituent states will have equal voting power, will meet periodically to discuss matters submitted to it by the council. These matters will be general measures of international law or arrangements or general proposals for limitation of armaments for securing world peace, or any other general resolutions, the discussion of which by the conference is desired by the council before they are forwarded for the approval of the constituent Governments. Any resolutions passed by the conference will have the effect of recommendations to the national Governments and Parliaments.

(12) The council will be the executive committee of the league, and will consist of the Prime Ministers or Foreign Secretaries or other authoritative representatives of the Great Powers, together with the representatives drawn in rotation from two panels of the middle Powers and minor states respectively, in such a way that the Great Powers have a bare majority. A minority of three or more can veto any action or resolution of the council.

(13) The council will meet periodically, and will, in addition, hold an annual meeting of Prime Ministers or Foreign Secretaries for a general interchange of views, and for a review of the general policies of the league. It will appoint a permanent secretariat and staff, and will appoint joint committees for the study and coördination of the international questions with which the council deals, or questions likely to lead to international disputes. It will also take the necessary steps for keeping up proper liaison, not only with the Foreign Offices of the con-

stituent Governments, but also with the authorities acting on behalf of the league in various parts of the world.

(14) Its functions will be:

(a) To take executive action or control in regard to the matters set forth in Section A or under any international arrangements or conventions;

(b) To administer and control any property of an international character, such as international waterways, rivers, straits, railways, fortifications, air stations, etc.;

(c) To formulate for the approval of the Governments general measures of international law, or arrangements for limitation of armaments or promotion of world peace.

(Its remaining functions in regard to world peace are dealt with in the following Section C.)

(15) That all the states represented at the peace conference shall agree to the abolition of conscription or compulsory military service; and that their future defence forces shall consist of militia or volunteers, whose numbers and training shall, after expert inquiry, be fixed by the council of the league.

(16) That while the limitation of armaments in the general sense is impracticable, the council of the league shall determine what direct military equipment and armament is fair and reasonable in respect of the scale of forces laid down under paragraph 15, and that the limits fixed by the council shall not be exceeded without its permission.

(17) That all factories for the manufacture of direct weapons of war shall be nationalized and their production shall be subject to the inspection of the officers of the council; and that the council shall be furnished periodically with returns of imports and exports of munitions of war into or from the territories of its members and as far as possible into or from other countries.

(18) That the peace treaty shall provide that the members of the league bind themselves jointly and severally not to go to war with one another—

(a) without previously submitting the matter in dispute to arbitration, or to inquiry by the council of the league; and

(b) until there has been an award, or a report by the council; and

(c) not even then, as against a member which complies with the award, or with the recommendation (if any) made by the council in its report.

(19) That the peace treaty shall provide that if any member of the league breaks its covenant under paragraph 18, it shall ipso facto become at war with all the other members of the league which shall subject it to complete economic and financial boycott, including the Severance of all trade and financial relations and the prohibition of all intercourse between their subjects and the subjects of the covenant-breaking state and the prevention, as far as possible, of the subjects of the covenant-breaking state from having any commercial or financial intercourse with the subjects of any other state whether a member of the league or not.

While all members of the league are obliged to take the above measures, it is left to the council to recommend what effective naval or military force the members shall contribute and, if advisable, to absolve the smaller members of the league from making such contribution.

The covenant-breaking state shall after the restoration of peace be subject to perpetual disarmament and to the peaceful regime established for new states under paragraph 8.

(20) That the peace treaty shall further provide that if a dispute should arise between any members of the league as to the interpretation of a treaty, or as to any question of international law, or as to any fact which if established would constitute a breach of any international obligation, or as to any damage alleged and the nature and measure of the reparation to be made therefor, and if such dispute cannot be settled by negotiation, the members bind themselves to submit the dispute to arbitration and to carry out any award or decision which may be rendered.

(21) That if on any ground it proves impracticable to refer such dispute to arbitration, either party to the dispute may apply to the council to take the matter of the dispute into consideration. The council shall give notice of the application to the other party, and make the necessary arrangements for the hearing of the dispute. The council shall ascertain the facts with regard to the dispute and make recommendations based on the merits, and calculated to secure a just and lasting settlement. Other members of the league shall place at the disposal of the council all information in their possession which bears on the dispute. The council shall do its utmost by mediation and conciliation to induce the disputants to agree to a peaceful settlement. The recommendations shall be addressed to the disputants and shall not have the force of decisions. If either party threatens to go to war in spite of the recommendations, the council shall publish its recommendations. If the council fails to arrive at recommendations, both the majority and minority on the council may publish statements of the respective recommendations they favor, and such publication shall not be regarded as an unfriendly act by either of the disputants.

Chapter 7

The Paris Conference

22. THE PARIS CONFERENCE REGULATIONS, 1920 [1]

Whereas in 1815 the Congress of Vienna negotiated the reconstruction of Europe after peace had already been re-established by the first Treaty of Paris, in 1919 the Paris Conference negotiated both the peace and the reconstruction of the world community. At first intended only as a meeting to concert the policies of the victorious powers in preparation for a formal conference with the defeated enemy, the conference was in effect a continuation of the Allied war organization.[2]

I. The Conference, summoned with a view to lay down the conditions of peace, in the first place by peace preliminaries and later by a definite Treaty of Peace, shall include the representatives of the Allied or Associated belligerent Powers.

The belligerent Powers with general interests (the United States of America, the British Empire, France, Italy, Japan) shall attend all sessions and commissions.

The belligerent Powers with special interests (Belgium, Brazil, the British Dominions and India, China, Cuba, Greece, Guatemala, Hayti, the Hedjaz, Honduras, Liberia, Nicaragua, Panama, Poland, Portugal, Roumania, Serbia, Siam, the Czecho-Slovak Republic) shall attend the sessions at which questions concerning them are discussed.

Powers having broken off diplomatic relations with the enemy Powers (Bolivia, Ecuador, Peru, Uruguay) shall attend sessions at which questions interesting them will be discussed.

Neutral Powers and States in process of formation shall, on being summoned by the Powers with general interests, be heard, either orally or in writing, at sessions devoted especially to the examination of questions in which they are directly concerned, and only in so far as these questions are concerned.

II. The Powers shall be represented by Plenipotentiary Delegates to the number of:—

Five for the United States of America, the British Empire, France, Italy, Japan;

Three for Belgium, Brazil, Serbia;

Two for China, Greece, the Hedjax, Poland, Portugal, Roumania, Siam, the Czecho-Slovak Republic;

One for Cuba, Guatemala, Hayti, Honduras, Liberia, Nicaragua, Panama;

One for Bolivia, Ecuador, Peru, Uruguay.

[1] *U.S. Foreign Relations: The Paris Peace Conference 1919*, III, pp. 172-175.

[2] The organization of the Conference reflected both the new morality sought for international relations by the "League men" and the new power relations which were the result of the war. Thus, if in any general action of the world community the initiative and the required practical support remained with the Great Powers, it was also true that the concurrence of the great body of smaller powers now had become necessary (see Doc. 12).

The British Dominions and India shall be represented as follows:—

Two delegates each for Canada, Australia, South Africa, India (including the native States);

One Delegate for New Zealand.

Each Delegation shall be entitled to set up a panel, but the number of Plenipotentiaries shall not exceed the figures given above.

The representatives of the Dominions (including Newfoundland) and of India can, moreover, be included in the representation of the British Empire by means of the panel system.

Montenegro shall be represented by one Delegate, but the manner of his appointment shall not be decided until the present political situation of that country becomes clear.

The conditions governing the representation of Russia shall be settled by the Conference when Russian affairs come up for discussion.

III. Each Delegation of Plenipotentiaries may be accompanied by duly accredited Technical Delegates and by two shorthand writers.

The Technical Delegates may attend sessions in order to supply information when called upon. They may be asked to speak in order to give necessary explanations.

IV. The order of precedence shall follow the alphabetical order of the Powers in French.

V. The Conference shall be opened by the President of the French Republic. The President of the French Council of Ministers shall thereupon provisionally take the chair.

The credentials of members present shall at once be examined by a Committee composed of one Plenipotentiary for each of the Allied or Associated Powers.

VI. At the first meeting the permanent President and four Vice-Presidents shall be elected from among the Plenipotentiaries of the Great Powers in alphabetical order.

VII. A Secretariat chosen outside the ranks of the Plenipotentiaries, consisting of one representative each of the United States of America, the British Empire, France, Italy and Japan, shall be submitted for the approval of the Conference by the President, who shall be in control of and responsible for it.

The Secretariat shall draw up the protocols of the sessions, classify the archives, provide for the administrative organization of the Conferences and, generally, ensure the regular and punctual working of the services entrusted to it.

The head of the Secretariat shall be responsible for the safe custody of the protocols and archives.

The archives shall be accessible at all times to members of the Conference.

VIII. Publicity shall be given to the proceedings by means of official communiqués prepared by the Secretariat and made public. In case of disagreement as to the wording of such communiqués, the matter shall be referred to the chief Plenipotentiaries or their representatives.

IX. All documents to be incorporated in the protocols must be supplied in writing by the Plenipotentiaries originally responsible for them.

No document or proposal may be so supplied except by a Plenipotentiary or in his name.

X. With a view to facilitate discussion, any Plenipotentiary wishing to propose a resolution must give the President twenty-four hours notice thereof, except in the case of proposals connected with the order of the day and arising from the actual discussion.

Exceptions may, however, be made to this rule in the case of amendments or secondary questions which do not constitute actual proposals.

XI. All petitions, memoranda, observations and documents addressed to the Conference by any persons other than the Plenipotentiaries must be received and classified by the Secretariat.

Such of these communications as are of any political interest shall be briefly summarized in a list circulated to all the Plenipotentiaries. Supplementary editions of this list shall be issued as such communications are received.

All these documents shall be deposited in the archives.

XII. All questions to be decided shall be discussed at a first and second reading; the former shall afford occasion for a general discussion for the purpose of arriving at an agreement on points of principle; the second reading shall provide an opportunity of discussing details.

XIII. The Plenipotentiaries shall be entitled, subject to the approval of the Conference, to authorize their Technical Delegates to submit direct any technical explanations considered desirable regarding any particular question.

If the Conference shall think fit, the study of any particular question from the technical point of view may be entrusted to a Committee composed of Technical Delegates, who shall be instructed to present a report and suggest solutions.

XVI. The protocols drawn up by the Secretariat shall be printed and circulated in proof to the Delegates with the least possible delay.

To save time, this circulation of the protocols in advance shall take the place of reading them at the beginning of the sessions. Should no alterations be demanded by the Plenipotentiaries, the text shall be considered as approved and deposited in the archives.

Should any alteration be called for, it shall be read aloud by the President at the beginning of the following session.

The whole of the protocol shall, however, be read if one of the Plenipotentiary members shall so request.

XV. A committee shall be formed to draft the motions adopted.

This Committee shall deal only with questions which have been decided; its sole task shall be to draw up the text of the decisions adopted and to present them to the Conference for approval.

It shall consist of five members who shall not be Plenipotentiary Delegates and shall comprise one representative each of the United States of America, the British Empire, France, Italy and Japan.

23. THE HURST-MILLER DRAFT OF THE COVENANT, 3 FEBRUARY 1919 [1]

The legal advisers of the British and American delegation at the Paris Conference, respectively Cecil Hurst and David Hunter Miller, reconciled the divergent points in President Wilson's third draft of the Covenant and the British official draft. Their work, the so-called Hurst-Miller draft, became the basis of discussion in the deliberations of the League of Nations Commission [2] set up by the conference as a committee to draft the Covenant.[3]

[1] David Hunter Miller, *The Drafting of the Covenant* (New York, 1928), II, pp. 231-237.
[2] The Dumbarton Oaks Proposals, also primarily of Anglo-American authorship, played a similar part with respect to the United Nations Charter.
[3] The League of Nations Commission, accepted by the second plenary session of the conference on the proposal of its Supreme Council, had President Wilson as chairman and Sir Robert Cecil (Great Britain) as vice-

Preamble. In order to secure international peace and security by the acceptance of obligations not to resort to the use of armed force, by the prescription of open, just and honourable relations between nations, by the firm establishment of the understandings of international law as the actual rule of conduct among governments, and by

chairman, and included among its nineteen representatives such "League men" as Smuts (South Africa), Bourgeois (France), Scialoja (Italy) and Hymans (Belgium). The commission met in the evenings 3 February to 13 February. Without a preliminary discussion of general principles, it debated the Hurst-Miller draft article by article. The completed draft was presented by Mr. Wilson himself to the plenary session of the conference on 14 February.

the maintenance of justice and a scrupulous respect for all treaty obligations in the dealings of organized peoples with one another, and in order to promote international co-operation, the Powers signatory to this Covenant adopt this constitution of the League of Nations.

ART. 1. The action of the High Contracting Parties under the terms of this Covenant shall be effected through the instrumentality of meetings of Delegates representing the High Contracting Parties, of meetings at more frequent intervals of an Executive Council representing the States more immediately concerned in the matters under discussion, and of a permanent International Secretariat to be established at the capital of the League.

ART. 2. Meetings of the Body of Delegates shall be held from time to time as occasion may require for the purpose of dealing with matters within the sphere of action of the League.

Meetings of the Body of Delegates shall be held at the capital of the League, or at such other place as may be found convenient, and shall consist of not more than two representatives of each of the High Contracting Parties.

An Ambassador or Minister of one of the High Contracting Parties shall be competent to act as its representative.

All matters of procedure at meetings of the Body of Delegates, including the appointment of committees to investigate particular matters, shall be regulated by the Body of Delegates, and may be decided by a majority of those present at the meeting.

ART. 3. The representatives of the States, members of the League directly affected by matters within the sphere of action of the League, will meet as an Executive Council from time to time as occasion may require.

The United States of America, Great Britain, France, Italy, and Japan shall be deemed to be directly affected by all matters within the sphere of action of the League. Invitations will be sent to any Power whose interests are directly affected, and no decision taken at any meeting will be binding on a State which was not invited to be represented at the meeting.

Such meetings will be held at whatever place may be decided on, or, failing any such decision, at the capital of the League, and any matter affecting the interests of the League, or relating to matters within its sphere of action or likely to affect the peace of the world, may be dealt with.

ART. 4. The permanent Secretariat of the League shall be established at what shall constitute the capital of the League. The Secretariat shall comprise such secretaries and staff as may be required, under the general direction and control of a Chancellor of the League, by whom they shall be appointed.

The Chancellor shall act as Secretary at all meetings of the Body of Delegates or of the Executive Council.

The expenses of the Secretariat shall be borne by the States members of the League in accordance with the distribution among members of the Postal Union of the expenses of the International Postal Union.

ART. 5. Representatives of the High Contracting Parties and officials of the League when engaged on the business of the League shall enjoy diplomatic privileges and immunities, and the buildings occupied by the League or its officials or by representatives attending its meetings shall enjoy the benefits of extraterritoriality.

ART. 6. Admission to the League of States who are not signatories of this Covenant requires the assent of not less than two-thirds of the Body of Delegates.

No State shall be admitted to the League except on condition that its military and naval forces and armaments shall conform to standards prescribed by the League in respect of it from time to time.

ART. 7. The High Contracting Parties undertake to respect and preserve as against external aggression the territorial integrity and existing political independence of all States members of the League.

ART. 8. The High Contracting Parties recognize the principle that the maintenance of peace will require the reduction of national armaments to the lowest point consistent with domestic safety and the enforcement by common action of international obligations; and the Executive Council shall formulate plans for effecting such reduction. It shall also enquire into the feasibility of abolishing compulsory military service, and the substitution therefor of forces enrolled upon a voluntary basis, and into the military and naval equipment which it is reasonable to maintain.

The High Contracting Parties further agree that there shall be full and frank publicity as to all national armaments and military or naval programmes.

ART. 9. Any war or threat of war, whether immediately affecting any of the High Contracting Parties or not, is hereby declared a matter of concern to the League, and the High Contracting Parties reserve the right to take any action that may be deemed wise and effectual to safeguard the peace of nations.

It is hereby also declared and agreed to be the friendly right of each of the High Contracting Parties to draw the attention of the Body of Delegates, or of the Executive Council, to any circumstances anywhere which threaten to disturb international peace, or the good understanding between nations upon which peace depends.

ART. 10. The High Contracting Parties agree that should disputes arise between them which cannot be adjusted by the ordinary processes of diplomacy, they will in no case resort to armed force without previously submitting the questions and matters involved either to arbitration or to enquiry by the Executive Council, and

until three months after the award by the arbitrators, or a recommendation by the Executive Council; and that they will not even then resort to armed force as against a member of the League which complies with the award of the arbitrators, or the recommendation of the Executive Council.

ART. 11. The High Contracting Parties agree that whenever any dispute or difficulty shall arise between them which they recognize to be suitable for submission to arbitration, and which cannot be satisfactorily settled by diplomacy, they will submit the whole subject-matter to arbitration, and will carry out in full good faith any award or decision that may be rendered.

ART. 12. The Executive Council will formulate plans for the establishment of a Permanent Court of International Justice, and this Court will be competent to hear and determine any matter which the parties recognize as suitable for submission to it for arbitration under the foregoing Article.

ART. 13. If there should arise between States members of the League any dispute likely to lead to a rupture, which is not submitted to arbitration as above, the High Contracting Parties agree that they will refer the matter to the Executive Council; either party to the dispute may give notice to the Chancellor of the existence of the dispute, and the Chancellor will make all necessary arrangements for a full investigation and consideration thereof. For this purpose the parties agree to communicate to the Chancellor statements of their case with all the relevant facts and papers.

Where the efforts of the Council lead to the settlement of the dispute, a statement shall be prepared for publication indicating the nature of the dispute and the terms of settlement, together with such explanations as may be appropriate. If the dispute has not been settled, a report by the Council shall be published, setting forth with all necessary facts and explanations the recommendations which the Council think just and proper for the settlement of the dispute. If the report is unanimously agreed to by the members of the Council, other than the parties to the dispute, the High Contracting Parties agree that none of them will go to war with any party which complies with its recommendations. If no such unanimous report can be made, it shall be the duty of the majority to issue a statement indicating what they believe to be the facts and containing the recommendations which they consider to be just and proper.

The Executive Council may in any case under this article refer the dispute to the Body of Delegates. The dispute shall be so referred at the request of either party to the dispute. In any case referred to the Body of Delegates all the provisions of this Article relating to the action and powers of the Executive Council shall apply to the action and powers of the Body of Delegates.

ART. 14. Should any of the High Contracting Parties be found by the League to have broken or disregarded its covenants under Article 10, it shall thereby *ipso facto* be deemed to have committed an act of war against all the other members of the League, which shall immediately subject it to the severance of all trade or financial relations, the prohibition of all intercourse between their nationals and the nationals of the covenant-breaking State, and the prevention, so far as possible, of all financial, commercial, or personal intercourse between the nationals of the covenant-breaking State and the nationals of any other State, whether a member of the League or not.

It shall be the duty of the Executive Council in such a case to recommend what effective military or naval force the members of the League shall severally contribute to the armed forces to be used to protect the covenants of the League.

The High Contracting Parties agree, further, that they will mutually support one another in the financial and economic measures which are taken under this article in order to minimize the loss and inconvenience resulting from the above measures, and that they will mutually support one another in resisting any special measures aimed at one of their number by the covenant-breaking State, and that they will afford passage through their territory to the forces of any of the High Contracting Parties who are co-operating to protect the covenants of the League.

ART. 15. In the event of disputes between one State member of the League and another State which is not a member of the League, or between States not members of the League, the High Contracting Parties agree that the State or States not members of the League shall be invited to become *ad hoc* members of the League, and upon acceptance of any such invitation, the above provisions shall be applied with such modifications as may be deemed necessary by the League.

Upon such invitation being given the Executive Council shall immediately institute an enquiry into the circumstances and merits of the dispute and recommend such action as may seem best and most effectual in the circumstances.

In the event of a Power so invited refusing to become *ad hoc* a member of the League, and taking any action against a State member of the League, which in the case of a State member of the League would constitute a breach of Article 10, the provisions of Article 14 shall be applicable as against the State taking such action.

If both parties to the dispute when so invited refuse to become *ad hoc* members of the League, the Executive Council may take such action and make such recommendations as will prevent hostilities, and will result in the settlement of the dispute.

ART. 16. The High Contracting Parties entrust to the League the general supervision of the trade in arms and ammunition with the countries in

which the control of this traffic is necessary in the common interest.

ART. 17. The High Contracting Parties agree that in respect of territories
which formerly belonged to the German Empire or to Turkey, and which
are inhabited by peoples unable at present to secure for themselves the benefits of a stable administration, the well-
being of these peoples constitutes a
sacred trust for civilisation, and im-
poses upon the States members of the
League the obligation to render help
and guidance in the development of
the administration. They recognize
that all policies of administration or
economic development should be based
primarily upon the well-considered interests of the peoples themselves, upon
the maintenance of the policy of the
open door, and of equal opportunity
for all the High Contracting Parties in
respect of the use and development of
the economic resources of the territory.
No military or naval forces shall be
formed among the inhabitants of the
territories in excess of those required
for purposes of defence and of internal
police.

ART. 18. The High Contracting Parties will work to establish and maintain fair hours and humane conditions
of labour for all those within their
several jurisdictions, and they will
exert their influence in favour of the
adoption and maintenance of a similar
policy and like safeguards wherever
their industrial and commercial relations extend. Also they will appoint
commissions to study conditions of industry and labour in their international
aspects, and to make recommendations

thereon, including the extension and
improvement of existing conventions.

ART. 19. The High Contracting Parties agree that they will make no law
prohibiting or interfering with the
free exercise of religion, and that they
will in no way discriminate, either in
law or in fact, against those who practice any particular creed, religion, or
belief whose practices are not inconsistent with public order or public
morals.

ART. 20. The High Contracting Parties will agree upon provisions intended to secure and maintain freedom
of transit and just treatment for the
commerce of all States members of the
League.

ART. 21. The High Contracting Parties agree that any treaty or international engagement entered into between States members of the League
shall be forthwith registered with the
Chancellor, and as soon as possible
published by him.

ART. 22. The High Contracting Parties severally agree that the present
Covenant is accepted as abrogating all
obligations *inter se* which are inconsistent with the terms hereof, and solemnly engage that they will not hereafter enter into any engagements inconsistent with the terms hereof.

In case any of the Powers signatory
hereto, or subsequently admitted to
the League shall, before becoming a
party to this Covenant, have undertaken any obligations which are inconsistent with the terms of this Covenant,
it shall be the duty of such Power to
take immediate steps to procure its release from such obligations.

24. THE COVENANT OF THE LEAGUE OF NATIONS, 10 JANUARY 1920 AS AMENDED [1]

The Paris settlement was to have been embodied in a general act similar to the Act
of Vienna in 1815. The exigencies of peace-

[1] Originally Part I of the Treaties of Versailles, St. Germaine-en-Laye, Trianon and
Neuilly-sur-Seine, the Covenant was subsequently amended by the procedure prescribed

making in 1919 and the preliminary importance attached to the German treaty resulted
in a series of separate treaties worked out by

in Article 26. Paragraphs officially numbered
pursuant to Assembly resolution 21 September 1926. League of Nations, *Official Journal,*
spec. supp. No. 43, p. 10.

the Allies and imposed upon each of the defeated powers with little allowance for their views. In the first 26 articles comprising Part I of each of the treaties is to be found this Covenant of the League of Nations.[2]

COVENANT OF THE LEAGUE OF NATIONS

THE HIGH CONTRACTING PARTIES

In order to promote international co-operation and to achieve international peace and security

by the acceptance of obligations not to resort to war,

by the prescription of open, just and honorable relations between nations,

by the firm establishment of the understandings of international law as the actual rule of conduct among Governments, and

by the maintenance of justice and a scrupulous respect for all treaty obligations in the dealings of organized peoples with one another, Agree to this Covenant of the League of Nations.

ART. 1. 1. The original Members of the League of Nations shall be those of the Signatories which are named in the Annex to this Covenant, and also such of those other States named in the Annex as shall accede without reservation to this Covenant. Such accessions shall be effected by a declaration deposited with the Secretariat within two months of the coming into force of the Covenant. Notice thereof shall be sent to all other Members of the League.

2. Any fully self-governing State, Dominion or Colony not named in the Annex may become a Member of the League if its admission is agreed to by two-thirds of the Assembly, provided that it shall give effective guaranties of its sincere intention to observe its international obligations, and shall accept such regulations as may be prescribed by the League in regard to its military, naval and air forces and armaments.

3. Any Member of the League may, after two years' notice of its intention so to do, withdraw from the League, provided that all its international obligations and all its obligations under this Covenant shall have been fulfilled at the time of its withdrawal.

ART. 2. The action of the League under this Covenant shall be effected through the instrumentality of an Assembly and of a Council, with a permanent Secretariat.

ART. 3. 1. The Assembly shall consist of Representatives of the Members of the League.

2. The Assembly shall meet at stated intervals and from time to time as occasion may require at the Seat of the League or at such other place as may be decided upon.

3. The Assembly may deal at its meetings with any matter within the sphere of action of the League or affecting the peace of the world.

4. At meetings of the Assembly, each Member of the League shall have one vote, and may have not more than three Representatives.

ART. 4. 1. The Council shall consist of Representatives of the Principal Allied and Associated Powers, together with Representatives of four other Members of the League. These four Members of the League shall be selected by the Assembly from time to time in its discretion. Until the appointment of the Representatives of the four Members of the League first selected by the Assembly, Representatives of Belgium, Brazil, Spain and Greece shall be members of the Council.

2. With the approval of the majority of the Assembly, the Council may name additional Members of the League whose Representatives shall always be members of the Council; the Council with like approval may increase the number of Members of the

---

[2] Doc. 23. Accepted by the Conference with further changes proposed by Mr. Wilson, at the plenary session of 28 April. It came into force with the Versailles Treaty, 10 January 1920.

League to be selected by the Assembly for representation on the Council.

2 bis. The Assembly shall fix by a two-thirds majority the rules dealing with the election of the non-permanent members of the Council, and particularly such regulations as relate to their term of office and the conditions of re-eligibility.

3. The Council shall meet from time to time as occasion may require, and at least once a year, at the Seat of the League, or at such other place as may be decided upon.

4. The Council may deal at its meetings with any matter within the sphere of action of the League or affecting the peace of the world.

5. Any Member of the League not represented on the Council shall be invited to send a Representative to sit as a member at any meeting of the Council during the consideration of matters specially affecting the interests of that Member of the League.

6. At meetings of the Council, each Member of the League represented on the Council shall have one vote, and may have not more than one Representative.

ART. 5. 1. Except where otherwise expressly provided in this Covenant or by the terms of the present Treaty, decisions at any meeting of the Assembly or of the Council shall require the agreement of all the Members of the League represented at the meeting.

2. All matters of procedure at meetings of the Assembly or of the Council, including the appointment of Committees to investigate particular matters, shall be regulated by the Assembly or by the Council and may be decided by a majority of the Members of the League represented at the meeting.

3. The first meeting of the Assembly and the first meeting of the Council shall be summoned by the President of the United States of America.

ART. 6. 1. The permanent Secretariat shall be established at the Seat of the League. The Secretariat shall comprise a Secretary-General and such secretaries and staff as may be required.

2. The first Secretary-General shall be the person named in the Annex; thereafter the Secretary-General shall be appointed by the Council with the approval of the majority of the Assembly.

3. The secretaries and the staff of the Secretariat shall be appointed by the Secretary-General with the approval of the Council.

4. The Secretary-General shall act in that capacity at all meetings of the Assembly and of the Council.

5. *The expenses of the League shall be borne by the Members of the League in the proportion decided by the Assembly.*

ART. 7. 1. The Seat of the League is established at Geneva.

2. The Council may at any time decide that the Seat of the League shall be established elsewhere.

3. All positions under or in connection with the League, including the Secretariat, shall be open equally to men and women.

4. Representatives of the Members of the League and officials of the League when engaged on the business of the League shall enjoy diplomatic privileges and immunities.

5. The buildings and other property occupied by the League or its officials or by Representatives attending its meetings shall be inviolable.

ART. 8. 1. The Members of the League recognize that the maintenance of peace requires the reduction of national armaments to the lowest point consistent with national safety and the enforcement by common action of international obligations.

2. The Council, taking account of the geographical situation and circumstances of each State, shall formulate plans for such reduction for the consideration and action of the several Governments.

3. Such plans shall be subject to reconsideration and revision at least every 10 years.

4. After these plans shall have been adopted by the several Governments, the limits of armaments therein fixed shall not be exceeded without the concurrence of the Council.

5. The Members of the League agree that the manufacture by private enterprise of munitions and implements of war is open to grave objections. The Council shall advise how the evil effects attendant upon such manufacture can be prevented, due regard being had to the necessities of those Members of the League which are not able to manufacture the munitions and implements of war necessary for their safety.

6. The Members of the League undertake to interchange full and frank information as to the scale of their armaments, their military, naval and air programmes and the condition of such of their industries as are adaptable to war-like purposes.

ART. 9. A permanent Commission shall be constituted to advise the Council on the execution of the provisions of Articles 1 and 8 and on military, naval and air questions generally.

ART. 10. The Members of the League undertake to respect and preserve as against external aggression the territorial integrity and existing political independence of all Members of the League. In case of any such aggression or in case of any threat or danger of such aggression the Council shall advise upon the means by which this obligation shall be fulfilled.

ART. 11. 1. Any war or threat of war, whether immediately affecting any of the Members of the League or not, is hereby declared a matter of concern to the whole League, and the League shall take any action that may be deemed wise and effectual to safeguard the peace of nations. In case any such emergency should arise, the Secretary-General shall on the request of any Member of the League forthwith summon a meeting of the Council.

2. It is also declared to be the friendly right of each Member of the League to bring to the attention of the Assembly or of the Council any circumstance whatever affecting international relations which threatens to disturb international peace or the good understanding between nations upon which peace depends.

ART. 12.[3] 1. The Members of the League agree that if there should arise between them any dispute likely to lead to a rupture, they will submit the matter either to arbitration *or judicial settlement* or to inquiry by the Council, and they agree in no case to resort

[3] The Amendments printed in italics relating to these Articles came into force on September 26th, 1924, in accordance with Article 26 of the Covenant. The Articles, thus amended, replace the following texts:

"ART. 12. The Members of the League agree that if there should arise between them any dispute likely to lead to a rupture, they will submit the matter either to arbitration or to inquiry by the Council, and they agree in no case to resort to war until three months after the award by the arbitrators or the report by the Council.

"In any case under this Article the award of the arbitrators shall be made within a reasonable time, and the report of the Council shall be made within six months after the submission of the dispute."

"ART. 13. The Members of the League agree that whenever any dispute shall arise between them which they recognise to be suitable for submission to arbitration and which cannot be satisfactorily settled by diplomacy, they will submit the whole subject-matter to arbitration.

"Disputes as to the interpretation of a treaty, as to any question of International law, as to the existence of any fact which if established would constitute a breach of any international obligation, or as to the extent and nature of the reparation to be made for any such breach, are declared to be among those which are generally suitable for submission to arbitration.

"For the consideration of any such dispute the court of arbitration to which the case is referred shall be the Court agreed on by the parties to the dispute or stipulated in any convention existing between them.

"The Members of the League agree that they will carry out in full good faith any award that may be rendered, and that they will not resort to war against a Member of the League which complies therewith. In the event of any failure to carry out such an award, the Council shall propose what steps should be taken to give effect thereto."

to war until three months after the award by the arbitrators *or the judicial decision* or the report by the Council.

2. In any case under this Article the award of the arbitrators *or the judicial decision* shall be made within a reasonable time, and the report of the Council shall be made within six months after the submission of the dispute.

ART. 13. 1. The Members of the League agree that whenever any dispute shall arise between them which they recognise to be suitable for submission to arbitration *or judicial settlement,* and which cannot be satisfactorily settled by diplomacy, they will submit the whole subject-matter to arbitration *or judicial settlement.*

2. Disputes as to the interpretation of a treaty, as to any question of international law, as to the existence of any fact which if established would constitute a breach of any international obligation, or as to the extent and nature of the reparation to be made for any such breach, are declared to be among those which are generally suitable for submission to arbitration *or judicial settlement.*

3. *For the consideration of any such dispute, the court to which the case is referred shall be the Permanent Court of International Justice, established in accordance with Article 14, or any tribunal agreed on by the parties to the dispute or stipulated in any convention existing between them.*

4. The Members of the League agree that they will carry out in full good faith any award *or decision* that may be rendered, and that they will not resort to war against a Member of the League which complies therewith. In the event of any failure to carry out such an award *or decision,* the Council

shall propose what steps should be taken to give effect thereto.

ART. 14. The Council shall formulate and submit to the Members of the League for adoption plans for the establishment of a Permanent Court of International Justice. The Court shall be competent to hear and determine any dispute of an international character which the parties thereto submit to it. The Court may also give an advisory opinion upon any dispute or question referred to it by the Council or by the Assembly.

ART. 15. 1.[4] If there should arise between Members of the League any dispute likely to lead to a rupture, which is not submitted to arbitration *or judicial settlement* in accordance with Article 13, the Members of the League agree that they will submit the matter to the Council. Any party to the dispute may effect such submission by giving notice of the existence of the dispute to the Secretary-General, who will make all necessary arrangements for a full investigation and consideration thereof.

2. For this purpose the parties to the dispute will communicate to the Secretary-General, as promptly as possible, statements of their case with all the relevant facts and papers, and the Council may forthwith direct the publication thereof.

3. The Council shall endeavour to effect a settlement of the dispute, and if such efforts are successful, a statement shall be made public giving such facts and explanations regarding the dispute and the terms of settlement thereof as the Council may deem appropriate.

4. If the dispute is not thus settled, the Council either unanimously or by a majority vote shall make and publish

[4] The Amendment to the first paragraph of this Article came into force on September 26th, 1924, in accordance with Article 26 of the Covenant. This paragraph, thus amended, replaces the following text:
"ART. 15. If there should arise between Members of the League any dispute likely to lead to a rupture, which is not submitted to

arbitration in accordance with Article 13, the Members of the League agree that they will submit the matter to the Council. Any party to the dispute may effect such submission by giving notice of the existence of the dispute to the Secretary General, who will make all necessary arrangements for a full investigation and consideration thereof."

a report containing a statement of the facts of the dispute and the recommendations which are deemed just and proper in regard thereto.

5. Any Member of the League represented on the Council may make public a statement of the facts of the dispute and of its conclusions regarding the same.

6. If a report by the Council is unanimously agreed to by the members thereof other than the Representatives of one or more of the parties to the dispute, the Members of the League agree that they will not go to war with any party to the dispute which complies with the recommendations of the report.

7. If the Council fails to reach a report which is unanimously agreed to by the members thereof, other than the Representatives of one or more of the parties to the dispute, the Members of the League reserve to themselves the right to take such action as they shall consider necessary for the maintenance of right and justice.

8. If the dispute between the parties is claimed by one of them, and is found by the Council, to arise out of a matter which by international law is solely within the domestic jurisdiction of that party, the Council shall so report, and shall make no recommendation as to its settlement.

9. The Council may in any case under this Article refer the dispute to the Assembly. The dispute shall be so referred at the request of either party to the despute provided that such request be made within fourteen days after the submission of the dispute to the Council.

10. In any case referred to the Assembly, all the provisions of this Article and of Article 12 relating to the action and powers of the Council shall apply to the action and powers of the Assembly, provided that a report made by the Assembly, if concurred in by the Representatives of those Members of the League represented on the Council and of a majority of the other Members of the League, exclusive in each case of the Representatives of the parties to the dispute, shall have the same force as a report by the Council concurred in by all the members thereof other than the Representatives of one or more of the parties to the dispute.

ART. 16. 1. Should any Member of the League resort to war in disregard of its covenants under Articles 12, 13 or 15, it shall *ipso facto* be deemed to have committed an act of war against all other Members of the League, which hereby undertake immediately to subject it to the severance of all trade or financial relations, the prohibition of all intercourse between their nationals and the nationals of the covenant-breaking State, and the prevention of all financial, commercial or personal intercourse between the nationals of the covenant-breaking State and the nationals of any other State, whether a Member of the League or not.

2. It shall be the duty of the Council in such case to recommend to the several Governments concerned what effective military, naval or air force the Members of the League shall severally contribute to the armed forces to be used to protect the covenants of the League.

3. The Members of the League agree, further, that they will mutually support one another in the financial and economic measures which are taken under this Article, in order to minimize the loss and inconvenience resulting from the above measures, and that they will mutually support one another in resisting any special measures aimed at one of their number by the covenant-breaking State, and that they will take the necessary steps to afford passage through their territory to the forces of any of the Members of the League which are co-operating to protect the covenants of the League.

4. Any Member of the League which has violated any covenant of the League may be declared to be no

longer a Member of the League by a vote of the Council concurred in by the Representatives of all the other Members of the League represented thereon.

ART. 17. 1. In the event of a dispute between a Member of the League and a State which is not a member of the League, or between States not members of the League, the State or States not members of the League shall be invited to accept the obligations of membership in the League for the purposes of such dispute, upon such conditions as the Council may deem just. If such invitation is accepted, the provisions of Articles 12 to 16 inclusive shall be applied with such modifications as may be deemed necessary by the Council.

2. Upon such invitation being given the Council shall immediately institute an inquiry into the circumstances of the dispute and recommend such action as may seem best and most effectual in the circumstances.

3. If a State so invited shall refuse to accept the obligations of membership in the League for the purposes of such dispute, and shall resort to war against a Member of the League, the provisions of Article 16 shall be applicable as against the State taking such action.

4. If both parties to the dispute when so invited refuse to accept the obligations of membership in the League for the purposes of such dispute, the Council may take such measures and make such recommendations as will prevent hostilities and will result in the settlement of the dispute.

ART. 18. Every treaty or international engagement entered into hereafter by any Member of the League shall be forthwith registered with the Secretariat and shall as soon as possible be published by it. No such treaty or international engagement shall be binding until so registered.

ART. 19. The Assembly may from time to time advise the reconsideration by Members of the League of treaties which have become inapplicable and the consideration of international conditions whose continuance might endanger the peace of the world.

ART. 20. 1. The Members of the League severally agree that this Covenant is accepted as abrogating all obligations or understandings *inter se* which are inconsistent with the terms thereof, and solemnly undertake that they will not hereafter enter into any engagements inconsistent with the terms thereof.

2. In case any Member of the League shall, before becoming a Member of the League, have undertaken any obligations inconsistent with the terms of this Covenant, it shall be the duty of such Member to take immediate steps to procure its release from such obligations.

ART. 21. Nothing in this Covenant shall be deemed to affect the validity of international engagements, such as treaties of arbitration or regional understandings like the Monroe doctrine, for securing the maintenance of peace.

ART. 22. 1. To those colonies and territories which as a consequence of the late war have ceased to be under the sovereignty of the States which formerly governed them and which are inhabited by peoples not yet able to stand by themselves under the strenuous conditions of the modern world, there should be applied the principle that the well being and development of such peoples form a sacred trust of civilization and that securities for the performance of this trust should be embodied in this Covenant.

2. The best method of giving practical effect to this principle is that the tutelage of such peoples should be intrusted to advanced nations who, by reason of their resources, their experience or their geographical position, can best undertake this responsibility, and who are willing to accept it, and that this tutelage should be exercised by them as Mandatories on behalf of the League.

3. The character of the mandate

must differ according to the stage of the development of the people, the geographical situation of the territory, its economic conditions and other similar circumstances.

4. Certain communities formerly belonging to the Turkish Empire have reached a stage of development where their existence as independent nations can be provisionally recognized subject to the rendering of administrative advice and assistance by a Mandatory until such time as they are able to stand alone. The wishes of these communities must be a principal consideration in the selection of the Mandatory.

5. Other peoples, especially those of Central Africa, are at such a stage that the Mandatory must be responsible for the administration of the territory under conditions which will guarantee freedom of conscience and religion, subject only to the maintenance of public order and morals, the prohibition of abuses such as the slave trade, the arms traffic and the liquor traffic, and the prevention of the establishment of fortifications or military and naval bases and of military training of the natives for other than police purposes and the defense of territory, and will also secure equal opportunities for the trade and commerce of other Members of the League.

6. There are territories, such as Southwest Africa and certain of the South Pacific islands, which, owing to the sparseness of their population or their small size, or their remoteness from the centers of civilization, or their geographical contiguity to the territory of the Mandatory, and other circumstances, can be best administered under the laws of the Mandatory as integral portions of its territory, subject to the safeguards above mentioned in the interests of the indigenous population.

7. In every case of mandate, the Mandatory shall render to the Council an annual report in reference to the territory committed to its charge.

8. The degree of authority, control, or administration to be exercised by the Mandatory shall, if not previously agreed upon by the Members of the League, be explicitly defined in each case by the Council.

9. A permanent Commission shall be constituted to receive and examine the annual reports of the Mandatories and to advise the Council on all matters relating to the observance of the mandates.

ART. 23. Subject to and in accordance with the provisions of international conventions existing or hereafter to be agreed upon, the Members of the League:

(a) will endeavour to secure and maintain fair and humane conditions of labour for men, women, and children, both in their own countries and in all countries to which their commercial and industrial relations extend, and for that purpose will establish and maintain the necessary international organizations;

(b) undertake to secure just treatment of the native inhabitants of territories under their control;

(c) will entrust the League with the general supervision over the execution of agreements with regard to the traffic in women and children, and the traffic in opium and other dangerous drugs;

(d) will entrust the League with the general supervision of the trade in arms and ammunition with the countries in which the control of this traffic is necessary in the common interest;

(e) will make provision to secure and maintain freedom of communications and of transit and equitable treatment for the commerce of all Members of the League. In this connection, the special necessities of the regions devastated during the war of 1914-1918 shall be borne in mind;

(f) will endeavour to take steps in matters of international concern for the prevention and control of disease.

ART. 24. 1. There shall be placed under the direction of the League all international bureaux already established by general treaties if the parties to such treaties consent. All such international bureaux and all commissions for the regulation of matters of international interest hereafter constituted shall be placed under the direction of the League.

2. In all matters of international interest which are regulated by general conventions but which are not placed under the control of international bureaus or commissions, the Secretariat of the League shall, subject to the consent of the Council and if desired by the parties, collect and distribute all relevant information and shall render any other assistance which may be necessary or desirable.

3. The Council may include as part of the expenses of the Secretariat the expenses of any bureau or commission which is placed under the direction of the League.

ART. 25. The Members of the League agree to encourage and promote the establishment and co-operation of duly authorized voluntary national Red Cross organizations having as purposes the improvement of health, the prevention of disease and the mitigation of suffering throughout the world.

ART. 26. 1. Amendments to this Covenant will take effect when ratified by the Members of the League whose Representatives compose the Council and by a majority of the Members of the League whose Representatives compose the Assembly.

2. No such amendment shall bind any Member of the League which signifies its dissent therefrom, but in that case it shall cease to be a Member of the League.

ANNEX

I. Original Members of the League of Nations
Signatories of the Treaty of Peace

United States of America.	Cuba.	Nicaragua.
Belgium.	Ecuador.	Panama.
Bolivia.	France.	Peru.
Brazil.	Greece.	Poland.
British Empire.	Guatemala.	Portugal.
Canada.	Haiti.	Roumania.
Australia.	Hedjaz.	Serb-Kroat-Slovene State.
South Africa.	Honduras.	Siam.
New Zealand.	Italy.	Czecho-Slovakia.
India.	Japan.	Uruguay.
China.	Liberia.	

States invited to accede to the Covenant

Argentine Republic.	Norway.	Spain.
Chili.	Paraguay.	Sweden.
Colombia.	Persia.	Switzerland.
Denmark.	Salvador.	Venezuela.
Netherlands.		

II. First Secretary General of the League of Nations

The Honourable Sir James Eric DRUMMOND, K.C.M.G., C.B.

Chapter 8

Nature, Organization and Development of the League of Nations

25. REPORT ON THE RELATIONS BETWEEN AND THE RESPECTIVE COMPETENCE OF THE COUNCIL AND THE ASSEMBLY, ADOPTED BY THE ASSEMBLY, 7 DECEMBER 1920 [1]

The League of Nations, which was no league, still less a political entity like a state, was merely a political relationship among entities, the states members, and a political instrument for their cooperation.

The two bodies through which the formal decisions of the League were taken were the Assembly and the Council, both of which consisted of periodic conferences of governmental representatives. The Assembly was modeled upon the conferences of the Hague system and expected by the authors of the Covenant to inherit their "legislative" function. The Council, planned to be a standing conference of the Great Powers to which a few small powers, representative of the whole body of small powers, were admitted, was designed to be the guiding organ of the League carrying on in the tradition of the Concert of Europe and handling political matters much as they had been handled by the Concert.

The Covenant conferred upon each of these League organs general competence over the League's activities and left undefined the relationship between them and the limits of their respective jurisdictions. These were the subject of discussion and resolution at the first Assembly.[2]

1. We propose to seek in the Covenant the rights and duties attributed to the Council and the Assembly respectively. Before proceeding to this analysis, and in order to throw light upon it, we will attempt to take account, from the constitutional point of view, of the legal position of the League of Nations. We cannot attain a definite opinion until we have eliminated from the discussion certain hypotheses on which we must dwell for a moment.

(a) It is impossible to consider the Assembly as a Chamber of Deputies and the Council as an Upper Chamber. The objections to this view are that, while in certain matters the Council and the Assembly have identical rights, in others they have each their special rights; and that the two bodies are not called upon to discuss exactly the same points. If the Assembly was the Chamber of Deputies and the Council a sort of Upper Chamber, the same subjects would come first before the one and then before the other body.

(b) It is equally impossible to con-

[1] League of Nations Assembly, *Records*, sess. I, Plenary Meetings, pp. 318-320.
[2] In a very few years, custom made the Assembly the controlling and initiating body laying down the broad outlines of policy while the Council, increasingly relegated to a secondary role, found itself responsible for the efficient conduct of the League's work within the limits determined by the Assembly.

sider the Council as invested with the executive and the Assembly with the legislative power. The conclusive objection to this view is that the Assembly possesses executive prerogatives.

The truth is that the League of Nations has no analogy in ordinary constitutional law. Article 2 of the Covenant provides that the action of the League shall be effected through the instrumentality of an Assembly and a Council. It follows that the League is a single organism which has at its disposal two organs, whose distinct or similar attributes must now be considered.

II. *Competence of the Council.*—The Council has rights and duties which are peculiar to it; for example, those mentioned in Article 4 of the Covenant. The Council has the approval of the appointments made by the Secretary-General (Article 6), and may decide that the seat of the League shall be elsewhere than at Geneva (Article 7). The Council shall formulate plans for the reduction of armaments and must give its consent to armaments exceeding those limitations (Article 8). It shall advise as to the evil effects attendant upon manufacture of arms by private enterprise (Article 8). The Council shall advise in case of aggression (Article 10). It must formulate and submit proposals for the establishment of a Permanent Court of Justice (Article 14), and it may act as a Council of Mediation (Article 15). It must make recommendations to the Governments as to military contribution to the armed forces to be used to protect the covenants of the League (Article 16). It will define the conditions of the Mandates if they have not been previously agreed upon by the Members of the League (Article 22, paragraph 8). Its consent is required for the co-operation of the Secretariat with International Bureaux and Commissions (Article 24, paragraph 2).

The Council furthermore derives clearly-defined functions from the Peace Treaties (see Article 48, Article 50, Annex 17, Article 213 of the Treaty of Versailles; Article 159 of the Treaty with Austria: Article 104 of the Treaty with Bulgaria, etc.).

III. *Competence of the Assembly.*— The Assembly also has duties and rights which are peculiar to it; for example, admission of new members (Article 1); election of representatives on the Council (Article 4); approval of additional members on the Council (Article 4); approval of the Council's nomination for the office of Secretary-General (Article 6); hearing of disputes referred from the Council to the Assembly; etc. We find that on these very important matters the final decision rests with the Assembly and not with the Council.

IV. While, as we have seen, the Council and the Assembly have each their distinctive rights and duties, there are matters the decision of which is left to the League of Nations, without its being specified to which organ of the League the right of decision belongs (Articles 23 and 24 of the Covenant; Article 103, Article 336, Article 338, Article 376 of the Treaty of Versailles).

V. Finally our account of the provision of the Covenant in regard to the powers of the Council and the Assembly should be completed by setting out the relevant provisions of Articles 3 and 4. The former provides:

"The Assembly may deal at its meetings with any matter within the sphere of action of the League affecting the Peace of the world."

The latter Article provides:

"The Council may deal at its meetings with any matter within the sphere of action of the League or affecting the Peace of the world."

VI. In the opinion of the Committee it would not seem to be desirable or necessary to formulate in explicit language at the present time what are the precise functions which the Council and the Assembly are respectively expected to perform. In the report presented by Mr. Balfour and approved by the Council the following conclusion is reached:

"The moral I would draw from these broad considerations is that the less we attempt to formulate in explicit language the precise functions which the Council and the Assembly are respectively expected to perform, the better for the future of the League. . . .

"Let us substitute for any such formalism of our respective duties a resolve to deal with any difficulties between the Assembly and the Council, not according to pre-arranged rules, but according to the dictates of tact and commonsense, treating each case as it arises on its merits."

The Committee recommends the Assembly to accept and act upon this conclusion.

VII. In the report by Mr. Balfour already referred to, a proposal (No. *b* on p. 5) is made for the appointment of mixed committees to determine questions of doubtful competence between the Council and Assembly. While appreciating the purpose of this proposal, we think it is not necessary at the present time to decide this question.

VIII. It remains to solve a very important question: What is the nature of the executive effect of decisions of the Council and the Assembly? In our opinion, the Assembly and the Council should be considered to have complete authority in all matters which the Covenant or the Treaties have committed to them for decision. There are, however, matters referred to in the Covenant which are not within the competence of these organs, but require the concurrence and action of the Governments concerned in the form of international conventions, such as the serious questions contemplated by Article 23, paragraphs *a, b, e, f.* In these matters one must not forget that the responsibility of the Governments represented at the Assembly, which is external to the Assembly, cannot be engaged. The action of the Assembly should accordingly take the form of a recommendation or invitation leading up to agreement between the Governments.

IX. Two further questions were discussed in the Committee.

(*a*) The first question was whether a member of the Council, in rendering his decisions on the Council, represented the Member of the League which appointed him or acted in an independent capacity. Representatives on the Council and the Assembly are responsible to their own Governments and to those Governments alone. The Assembly has no right to interfere with the choice which a Member of the League may make of persons to represent it, nor to prevent a Representative from saying what he pleases; but it is essential that it should be thoroughly understood that, when a Representative votes, the vote is that of the Member which he represents, whether the vote be cast in the Council or the Assembly. (See Article 5.)

(*b*) The idea was suggested, not of permanent Committees continuing to function after the Assembly had risen, but of allowing Committees which had failed to complete their labours in the course of a session of the Assembly to retain their mandates until their discussions were completed. The Committee is unable to accept this proposal. Practical reasons render it unrealisable. As each Committee consists of one Representative from each State, it would be impossible to keep the Members of a Committee after the Assembly Session was over.

X. At the close of this purely juridical discussion, and as an assistance towards reaching a working basis for the time being, the Committee suggests the adoption of the following principles, which it has framed after close examination of the investigations upon the subject in question already made by the Secretary-General and Mr. Balfour:—

(*a*) The Council and the Assembly are each invested with particular powers and duties. Neither body has jurisdiction to render a decision in a matter which by the Treaties or the Covenant has been expressly committed to the other organ of the League. Either body may discuss and examine any matter which is within the competence of the League.

(*b*) Under the Covenant, Representatives sitting on the Council and the Assembly render their decisions as the Representatives of their respective States, and in rendering such decisions they have no standing except as such Representatives.

(*c*) The Council will present each year to the Assembly a report on the work performed by it.

26. THE BRUCE REPORT ON THE "DEVELOPMENT OF INTERNATIONAL COOPERATION IN ECONOMIC AND SOCIAL AFFAIRS," 22 AUGUST 1939; EXCERPTS [1]

A Special Committee on the Development of International Cooperation in Economic and Social Affairs, under the chairmanship of Stanley M. Bruce, of Australia, was appointed in May 1939. It studied the economic and social activities of the League of Nations in the light of past experience. In December 1939 the Assembly, approving the report, authorized the establishment of a Central Committee for Economic and Social Questions to replace the Council in coordinating the work of the auxiliary bodies in the economic and social field.[2]

We have thus reached the conclusion that the time has come when the Assembly should undertake a revision of the existing organisation of its economic and social work, in order to cope more effectively with the great developments which have taken place since 1920. For, though many improvements and reforms have been made since then, it is a fact that the essential character of the organisation remains to-day as then created.

In May 1938, the need for such a revision was foreshadowed by the Committee on the Structure and Functions of the Economic and Financial Organisation, which observed:

"Major structural changes with a view to widening the basis of international co-operation in the economic field might no doubt be suggested.

Should the situation develop in such a way as to enable suggestions of this kind to be made, the Committee considered that the opportunity should not be allowed to pass."

No doubt the Council had the same notion in mind when it adopted its decision of May 27th, 1939.

In making the proposal which follows, our first aim has been to increase the efficiency of the work as a whole, and in particular:

(*a*) To bring all this part of the work of the League under the supervision of an agency which should be both effective and representative;

(*b*) To meet the fact that the development in the nature of the work results in a growing inter-connection between the activities of the different organisations, and that therefore a coordinating direction is more and more required;

(*c*) To add fresh efficiency and vigour to the work itself, a result which may naturally be expected to follow if public knowledge in regard to it can be increased and if it becomes the primary interest of the directing organs; for under present conditions, at meetings whether of the Council or of the

[1] League of Nations, Doc. A. 33. 1939 (reprinted in League of Nations, *Monthly Summary*, Supp., August 1939).
[2] This development was not finally realized until the establishment of the Economic and Social Council under the Charter of the United Nations.

Assembly, the primary interest both of the delegates and of public opinion is concerned with such questions of international policy as appear on their agenda;

(*d*) To give States not members of the League the opportunity of the fullest possible co-operation in the work itself as well as in its direction and supervision.

We suggest, therefore, that the Assembly should set up a new organism, to be known as the Central Committee for Economic and Social Questions, to which should be entrusted the direction and supervision of the work of the League Committees dealing with economic and social questions. The proposed nature and functions of this organism are indicated in a formal text at the conclusion of the present report. Amongst the proposals made is the suggestion that the Secretary-General should make every year to the Assembly a separate report on the work done in the economic and social fields. This procedure should enable the discussion on this side of the League's work to be organised at the Assembly, without being overshadowed by the debates on foreign politics.

The Central Committee should appoint the members of the various standing technical committees—in so far as existing international conventions permit it to do so—and be entitled to appoint new committees, within the limits set by budgetary provisions, and to modify the existing structure of the economic and social organisations, should it find such a course desirable. But this fact should not be considered as depriving the Council or the Assembly of their normal channels of obtaining technical advice.

We have been impressed by the advantages of including non-official members in the body supervising the economic and social work of the League, and suggest that it should be authorised to secure the collaboration of persons experienced in economic and social affairs.

We further suggest that the whole budget relating to the economic and social work, covering indirect as well as direct charges, should be examined and approved by this widely representative body before being submitted to the Supervisory Commission and the Assembly.

It will be seen that the change which we propose is far-reaching, but it does not involve any fundamental constitutional question. We have suggested that the Central Committee should be entrusted with the direction and supervision of the work of the committees dealing with economic and social questions. This proposal cannot affect the powers and duties appertaining to the Council as a result of international treaties and conventions. Nor can any proposal we might make affect the rights and powers of Member States represented on the Assembly or the Council having their origin in the Covenant of the League.

We propose that the Central Committee should comprise in the first year the representatives of twenty-four States chosen by the Assembly, and not more than eight unofficial members co-opted on the ground of their special competence and authority. Further, we suggest that it should be authorised to take any steps it considers appropriate to facilitate the participation of other States desiring to share in this economic and social work.

Where reference is made in the text which follows to participating States which are not members of the League, it is to be understood that such States should participate in the economic and social work on the same footing as States Members of the League. Any such States should contribute to the cost of the economic and social work in the proportion in which they would contribute to such expenses if they were Members of the League. Their contribution would be applied exclusively to the expenses connected with that work.

While we hope that our general scheme will provide a permanent basis for the development of the economic and social work of the League, the Central Committee itself will no doubt judge in the light of experience whether any changes in detail are required. Thus, although we submit the proposed numbers of official and unofficial members only after most careful consideration, we feel that experience alone can determine the most appropriate proportions between these two elements. Moreover, our proposals, taken as a whole, must not be considered as more than a first step in the adaptation of the existing machinery to the changing conditions in the world.

With these brief explanations, we submit to the Assembly the following draft constitution for the new organism.

DRAFT CONSTITUTION FOR THE CENTRAL COMMITTEE FOR ECONOMIC AND SOCIAL QUESTIONS

1. A Central Committee shall be set up, to which shall be entrusted the direction and supervision of the work of the committees dealing with economic and social questions.

2. In the first instance, the Central Committee shall comprise representatives of twenty-four States chosen, for a period of one year, by the Assembly on the proposal of its Bureau. Thereafter, the Committee shall comprise such number for such period as may be determined in the light of experience.

3. Any Member of the League not represented on the Central Committee which considers itself specially interested in a particular matter shall be invited to send a representative to sit as a member at any meeting of the Committee during the consideration of such matter.

4. The Central Committee shall be authorised to co-opt not more than eight members appointed in a personal capacity on the grounds of their special competence and authority whose collaboration it considers would prove of special value.

5. The Central Committee shall be requested to study the conditions under which all States desiring to do so may participate in the work relating to economic and social questions, and shall be authorised to take such steps as appear to it appropriate in order to facilitate their participation. Any State so participating shall enjoy the rights conferred on Members of the League under paragraph 3.

6. The Secretary-General shall submit to the Central Committee the annual draft budget relating to economic and social work, which, after examination by the Central Committee, will be dealt with in accordance with the Financial Regulations of the League. This budget shall provide for all the expenditure, direct and indirect, incurred for the purpose of carrying out such work.

7. The Central Committee shall meet at least once a year. An annual report shall be submitted by the Secretary-General to the Assembly on its work and on the programme of future work for which budgetary credits are requested.

8. The Central Committee shall be authorised to draw up its own Rules of Procedure, to approve its agenda, elect its own President and its Bureau, appoint the members of the main standing committees, in so far as existing international conventions permit it to do so, and set up other committees when necessary. Its agenda shall include any questions which a State participating in its work refers to it for consideration. All matters shall be decided by a majority of the members present. The Central Committee shall be empowered to entrust its Bureau with the discharge, in the intervals between its own meetings, of any duties which it may determine.

27. THE BALFOUR REPORT ON THE SECRETARIAT, MAY 1920 [1]

A trail-blazing development in international relations was the establishment of the Secretariat of the League of Nations as an international civil service. No precedents existed for a secretariat international in composition, organization and responsibility. The policy of Sir Eric Drummond, the first Secretary-General, was confirmed by the Council in adopting this report on the "Staff of the Secretariat" by the British representative, Mr. A. J. Balfour, after whom the report is known.[2]

In dealing with the subject which has been entrusted to me, namely the course to be adopted by the Council as regards the Secretariat of the League, it will probably be convenient if I begin with a brief historical explanation:

The Secretary-General of the League was appointed by the Treaty of Versailles, and not only was the office then established, but its first occupant was mentioned by name; he is the present holder of the post. His duties are not only of immense importance, but he is the servant of two masters. He serves the Council of the League of Nations; he also serves the Assembly of the League of Nations—the two representative bodies who are entrusted with the general guidance of the policy of the League. When I remind you that on his shoulders has fallen the chief burden of organising the Secretariat in the first days of our still infant institution, you will be able to measure the importance of the responsibilities which he has to bear.

Soon after the appointment was thus made by Treaty, the Peace Conference, acting in plenary session, appointed a Committee to deal with the first stages of organisation. The Committee represented the nine Powers who send Representatives to the Council; Monsieur Pichon, then Foreign Minister of France, presided. They gave authority to the Secretary-General to make the necessary arrangements for the appointment of a staff, and they also fixed the amount of his remuneration. This remuneration, therefore, is the only one which so far has been made by the full authority of the Powers assembled in Paris.

As soon as these preliminary steps were accomplished, the Secretary-General set to work to collect the nucleus of his staff. At the moment, this appeared to be a matter of pressing necessity, for the general anticipation was that the Treaty of Versailles would be ratified soon after its signature, and as soon as the ratification took place the responsibilities of the League, and of its Secretariat, would immediately begin.

As you are all aware, these sanguine hopes were disappointed, and while the Treaty was signed on the 28th June, 1919, it was not ratified until the 10th January, 1920. For this reason, the foresight and energy of the Secretary-General led to the creation of a staff somewhat in anticipation of the duties which it had to perform. The blame, if blame there be, for this result falls evidently not upon him, but

---

[1] League of Nations, *Official Journal*, I (1920), pp. 136-139.
[2] To help preserve the international character of the Secretariat, Article 1 of the Staff regulations read:
"The officials of the Secretariat of the League of Nations are exclusively international officials, and their duties are not national but international. By accepting appointment, they pledge themselves to discharge their functions and to regulate their conduct with the interests of the League alone in view. . . . They may not seek or receive instructions from any government or other authority external to the Secretariat of the League of Nations" (*ibid.*, spec. supp. 88, Minutes of the Fourth Committee, p. 393). After 1930 Secretariat officials subscribed to a loyalty of substantially the same wording (*ibid.*, spec. supp. 103, p. 17). In the case of the United Nations, the international character of the Secretariat is provided for in similar terms by the Charter itself (see Doc. 49).

upon the complex conditions which produced a most regrettable delay.

By the terms of the Treaty, the duty of selecting the staff falls upon the Secretary-General, just as the duty of approving it falls upon the Council. In making his appointments, he had primarily to secure the best available men and women for the particular duties which had to be performed; but in doing so, it was necessary to have regard to the great importance of selecting the officials from various nations. Evidently, no one nation or group of nations ought to have a monopoly in providing the material for this international institution. I emphasise the word "International," because the members of the Secretariat once appointed are no longer the servants of the country of which they are citizens, but become for the time being the servants only of the League of Nations. Their duties are not national but international.

One further point of importance in this connection has to be noted. The International Labour Office is intimately connected by its constitution and origin with the League of Nations. Its Director and the Secretary-General are both alive to the immense importance of maintaining the closest co-operation between these two international organs and an agreement has been reached by which certain of the central services shall be common to both institutions.

I need hardly go into details as to the constitution of the Secretariat. So far, it has not been found necessary to create more than 10 separate sections, dealing with the various duties entrusted to the League by the Covenant, which forms part of the Treaty of Versailles; but there can be no doubt that, as our work increases, so the number of these sections will undergo corresponding augmentation.

The question of remuneration is one of considerable difficulty. This arises in part from the problems of exchange which are so deeply exercising the minds of all those who are concerned with International Finance, but it partly depends upon more permanent causes. The problem is to find a scale of pay appropriate to the members of an organisation who are drawn from different countries, between which there prevails a great difference in the ordinary scale of remuneration. It is clear on the one side that objection may be felt to paying any member of the staff a much higher salary than he would receive for work of equal difficulty and responsibility in his own country, and on the other hand, it would be most unfortunate if the scale of salaries were fixed at a rate which made it impossible to obtain first-class talent from those countries where the ordinary rate of remuneration is above the general average. While the final solution of this problem is not yet decided upon, and must receive further examination, I propose that the Council should approve the scale of salaries provisionally arranged by the Secretary-General until the confirmation of the budget by the Assembly.

One or two points of importance still remain to be mentioned.

I suggest that the Council should confirm the appointment of the members of the staff for five years. At the end of this period, a considerable number of them will probably be reappointed, and in many cases, no doubt, be promoted to higher posts. This seems to be necessary if only to secure smoothness and continuity of administration, but at the same time it is most desirable that at the end of the quinquennial period a certain infusion of new blood should be secured. This will obviate any danger of the staff of the League of Nations becoming as it were a separate bureaucratic caste, divided by their duties from the life of any particular community. It will also give room for the citizens of nations not at present represented on the staff, to obtain in their turn the intimate knowledge of the working of the

League which would be invaluable not only to the League as a whole but to the various nations which compose it.

I shall presently propose Resolutions covering, so far as is necessary, these various points, but I shall also propose two other Resolutions dealing with temporary or subsidiary matters which have a certain interest or importance. In the first of these Resolutions, I shall ask the Council to approve that the provisional seat of the Secretariat shall remain in London until the Assembly of the League comes to a decision as to the date of transfer. It seems quite clear that to remove the League from its provisional seat before the Assembly meets would be very detrimental to its efficiency. The amount of preliminary work which the meeting of the Assembly will throw upon it is very great, and it would be neither wise nor fair to add to these necessary labours the quite unnecessary exertions involved in a change of residence. This requires in itself a considerable organising effort, and if confusion is to be wholly avoided, it would certainly be wise to await the meeting of the Assembly and its decision as to the dates on which the movement of the Secretariat should take place.

My last Resolution touches what might at first sight seem to be only a personal issue, but I think it is of some importance. I shall propose that no member of the Secretariat, during his or her term of office, shall accept any honour or decoration except for services rendered prior to the appointment. The reasons for this proposal are fairly clear; they commend themselves, I know, to my colleagues, and I hope they will commend themselves to the public. The members of the staff carry out, as I have explained, not national but international duties. Nothing should be done to weaken the sense of their international allegiance; the acceptance of special marks of distinction or favour, either from their own or from any other country, militates in our view against the general spirit of the Covenant.

In accordance with these preliminary observations, I now beg to propose the four Resolutions whose general character and intentions I have endeavoured to explain.

RESOLUTIONS ADOPTED BY THE COUNCIL OF THE LEAGUE OF NATIONS

I. That in accordance with Article 6 of the Covenant, by which the secretaries and staff of the Secretariat shall be appointed by the Secretary-General with the approval of the Council, the Council approve the provisional appointments made by the Secretary-General acting under the authority of the Organisation Committee of the League of Nations. This approval is given for a period of five years, dating from the day of appointment if made after the coming into force of the Treaty, and for the other appointments from the date of the coming into force of the Treaty.

II. That the salaries provisionally allotted by the Secretary-General be approved by the Council until the budget has been confirmed by the Assembly.

III. That the continuance of the Secretariat in London, where the present provisional seat is established, be authorised, and that the date of transfer to the permanent seat be decided by the Council after the Assembly has had the opportunity of discussion.

IV. That no member of the International Secretariat during the term of his or her appointment accept any honour or decoration (except for services rendered prior to such appointment).

Chapter 9

Functions: Security

28. THE BRITISH AND AMERICAN TREATIES OF ASSISTANCE TO FRANCE, 28 JUNE 1919 [1]

At the Paris Peace Conference, President Wilson and Lloyd George agreed to enter into bilateral treaties with France providing that their countries could come to the aid of France if Germany, expected to be embittered by the terms of the peace treaty, should be guilty of aggression against France. The proposed treaties were part of the compromise over the Rhineland. Although the British treaty was ratified, neither came into force because the British ratification was conditional upon American ratification. The two treaties constitute the earliest application of the principle that regional security agreements were compatible with the general security provisions of the Covenant.

Whereas there is a danger that the stipulations relating to the left bank of the Rhine contained in the Treaty of Peace signed this day at Versailles may not at first provide adequate security and protection to the French Republic; and

Whereas His Britannic Majesty is willing, subject to the consent of His Parliament and provided that a similar obligation is entered into by the United States of America, to undertake to support the French Government in the case of an unprovoked movement of aggression being made against France by Germany; and

Whereas His Britannic Majesty and the President of the French Republic have determined to conclude a Treaty to that effect and have named as their

Plenipotentiaries for the purpose, that is to say:—

His Majesty the King of the United Kingdom of Great Britain and Ireland and of the British Dominions Beyond the Seas, Emperor of India:

The Right Honourable David Lloyd George, M.P., First Lord of His Treasury and Prime Minister;

The Right Honourable Arthur James Balfour, O.M., M.P., His Secretary of State for Foreign Affairs;

The President of the French Republic:

Mr. Georges Clemenceau, President of the Council, Minister of War;

Mr. Stephen Pichon, Minister of Foreign Affairs;

Who having communicated their full powers found in good and due form, have agreed as follows:—

ART. 1. In case the following stipulations relating to the left bank of the Rhine contained in the Treaty of Peace with Germany signed at Versailles the 28th day of June, 1919, by the British Empire, the French Republic and the United States of America among other Powers:

"Article 42. Germany is forbidden to maintain or construct any fortifications either on the left bank of the Rhine or

---

[1] *British and Foreign State Papers*, CXII, pp. 213-215, 216-218.

on the right bank to the west of a line drawn 50 kilom. to the East of the Rhine.

"Article 43. In the area defined above the maintenance and assembly of armed forces, either permanently or temporarily, and military manœuvres of any kind, as well as the upkeep of all permanent works for mobilisation, are in the same way forbidden.

"Article 44. In case Germany violates in any manner whatever the provisions of Articles 42 and 43, she shall be regarded as committing a hostile act against the Powers signatory of the present Treaty and as calculated to disturb the peace of world."

may not at first provide adequate security and protection to France, Great Britain agrees to come immediately to her assistance in the event of any unprovoked movement of aggression against her being made by Germany.

ART. 2. The present Treaty, in similar terms with the Treaty of even date for the same purpose concluded between the French Republic and the United States of America, a copy of which Treaty is annexed hereto, will only come into force when the latter is ratified.

ART. 3. The present Treaty must be submitted to the Council of the League of Nations and must be recognised by the Council, acting if need be by a majority, as an engagement which is consistent with the Covenant of the League; it will continue in force until on the application of one of the Parties to it the Council, acting if need be by a majority, agrees that the League itself affords sufficient protection.

ART. 4. The present Treaty shall before ratification by His Majesty be submitted to Parliament for approval.

It shall before ratification by the President of the French Republic be submitted to the French Chambers for approval.

ART. 5. The present Treaty shall impose no obligation upon any of the Dominions of the British Empire unless and until it is approved by the Parliament of the Dominion concerned.

The present Treaty shall be ratified, and shall, subject to Articles 2 and 4, come into force at the same time as the Treaty of Peace with Germany of even date comes into force for the British Empire and the French Republic.

In faith whereof the above-named Plenipotentiaries have signed the present Treaty, drawn up in the English and French languages.

Done in duplicate at Versailles, on the twenty-eighth day of June, 1919.

(L.S.) D. LLOYD GEORGE.
(L.S.) ARTHUR JAMES BALFOUR.
(L.S.) G. CLEMENCEAU.
(L.S.) S. PICHON.

Whereas the United States of America and the French Republic are equally animated by the desire to maintain the Peace of the world so happily restored by the Treaty of Peace signed at Versailles the 28th day of June, 1919, putting an end to the war begun by the aggression of the German Empire and ended by the defeat of that Power; and

Whereas the United States of America and the French Republic are fully persuaded that an unprovoked movement of aggression by Germany against France would not only violate both the letter and the spirit of the Treaty of Versailles to which the United States of America and the French Republic are parties, thus exposing France anew to the intolerable burdens of an unprovoked war, but that such aggression on the part of Germany would be and is so regarded by the Treaty of Versailles as a hostile act against all the Powers signatory to that Treaty and as calculated to disturb the Peace of the world by involving inevitably and directly the States of Europe and indirectly, as experience has amply and unfortunately demonstrated, the world at large; and

Whereas the United States of America and the French Republic fear that the stipulations relating to the left bank of the Rhine contained in the said Treaty of Versailles may not at first provide adequate security and protection to France, on the one hand, and the United States of America, as one of the signatories of the Treaty of Versailles, on the other;

Therefore, the United States of America and the French Republic having decided to conclude a treaty to effect these necessary purposes, Woodrow Wilson, President of the United States of America, and Robert Lansing, Secretary of State of the United States, specially authorised thereto by the President of the United States, and Georges Clemenceau, President of the Council, Minister of War, and Stephen Pichon, Minister of Foreign Affairs, specially authorised thereto by Raymond Poincaré, President of the French Republic, have agreed upon the following articles:

ART. 1. In case the following stipulations relating to the left bank of the Rhine, contained in the Treaty of Peace with Germany signed at Versailles on the 28th day of June, 1919, by the United States of America, the French Republic, and the British Empire among other Powers:

"*Article* 42. Germany is forbidden to maintain or construct any fortifications either on the left bank of the Rhine or on the right bank to the west of a line drawn 50 kilometres to the east of the Rhine.

"*Article* 43. In the area defined above, the maintenance and assembly of armed forces, either permanently or temporarily, and military manœuvres of any kind, as well as the upkeep of all permanent works for mobilisation, are in the same way forbidden.

"*Article* 44. In case Germany violates in any manner whatever the provisions of Articles 42 and 43, she shall be regarded as committing a hostile act against the Powers signatory of the present Treaty and as calculated to disturb the peace of the world."

may not at first provide adequate security and protection to France, the United States of America shall be bound to come immediately to her assistance in the event of any unprovoked movement of aggression against her being made by Germany.

ART. 2. The present Treaty, in similar terms with the Treaty of even date for the same purpose concluded between Great Britain and the French Republic, a copy of which Treaty is annexed hereto, will only come into force when the latter is ratified.

ART. 3. The present Treaty must be submitted to the Council of the League of nations and must be recognised by the Council, acting if need be by a majority, as an engagement which is consistent with the Covenant of the League; it will continue in force until on the application of one of the parties to it the Council, acting if need be by a majority, agrees that the League itself affords sufficient protection.

ART. 4. The present Treaty will be submitted to the Senate of the United States at the same time as the Treaty of Versailles is submitted to the Senate for its advice and consent to ratification. It will be submitted before ratification to the French Chamber of Deputies for approval. The ratifications thereof will be exchanged on the deposit of ratifications of the Treaty of Versailles at Paris or as soon thereafter as shall be possible.

In faith whereof the respective Plenipotentiaries, to wit; On the part of the United States of America, Woodrow Wilson, President, and Robert Lansing, Secretary of State, of the United States; and on the part of the French Republic, Georges Clemenceau, President of the Council of Ministers, Minister of War, and Stephen Pichon, Minister of Foreign Affairs, have signed the above articles both in English and French languages, and they have hereunto affixed their seals.

Done in duplicate at the City of Versailles, on the twenty-eighth day of June, in the year of our Lord one thousand nine hundred and nineteen, and the one hundred and forty-third of the

Independence of the United States of America.

(L.S.) WOODROW WILSON.
(L.S.) ROBERT LANSING.
(L.S.) CLEMENCEAU.
(L.S.) S. PICHON.

29. THE ASSEMBLY "RESOLUTION XIV" RELATIVE TO SECURITY AND DISARMAMENT, 27 SEPTEMBER 1922 [1]

Convinced that the armaments race of the prewar years had done most to bring on the war, the authors of the Covenant included a provision [2] for the systematic reduction of arms among the first duties of the new League. Despite the dramatic results of the Washington Naval Conference in the winter of 1921-1922, no progress was made in the matter of land armaments until the principle was accepted that national security was prerequisite to a reduction of arms. The principle was recognized in this "Resolution XIV," as it was subsequently known, which became the basis for the League's work thereafter in strengthening the security provisions of the Covenant, weakened by the absence of the United States, by additional security agreements expected to lead in turn to a reduction of arms.

XIV. (a) The Assembly, having considered the report of the Temporary Mixed Commission on the question of a general Treaty of Mutual Guarantee, being of opinion that this report can in no way affect the complete validity of all the Treaties of Peace or other agreements which are known to exist between States; and considering that this report contains valuable suggestions as to the methods by which a Treaty of Mutual Guarantee could be made effective, is of the opinion that:

1. No scheme for the reduction of armaments, within the meaning of Article 8 of the Covenant, can be fully successful unless it is general.

2. In the present state of the world many Governments would be unable to accept the responsibility for a serious reduction of armaments unless they re-

ceived in exchange a satisfactory guarantee of the safety of their country.

3. Such a guarantee can be found in a defensive agreement, which should be open to all countries, binding them to provide immediate and effective assistance in accordance with a pre-arranged plan in the event of one of them being attacked, provided that the obligation to render assistance to a country attacked shall be limited in principle to those countries situated in the same part of the globe. In cases, however, where, for historical, geographical, or other reasons, a country is in special danger of attack, detailed arrangements should be made for its defence in accordance with the above-mentioned plan.

4. As a general reduction of armaments is the object of the three preceding statements, and the Treaty of Mutual Guarantee the means of achieving that object, previous consent to this reduction is therefore the first condition for the Treaty.

This reduction could be carried out either by means of a general Treaty, which is the most desirable plan, or by means of partial treaties designed to be extended and open to all countries.

In the former case, the Treaty will carry with it a general reduction of armaments. In the latter case, the reduction should be porportionate to the guarantees afforded by the Treaty.

The Council of the League, after having taken the advice of the Tem-

[1] League of Nations, Assembly, sess. III, *Records of the Plenary Meetings*, p. 291.

[2] Articles VIII and IX.

porary Mixed Commission, which will examine how each of these two systems could be carried out, should further formulate and submit to the Governments for their consideration and sovereign decision the plan of the machinery, both political and military, necessary to bring them clearly into effect.

(b) The Assembly requests the Council to submit to the various Governments the above proposals for their observations, and requests the Temporary Mixed Commission to continue its investigations, and, in order to give precision to the above statements, to prepare a draft Treaty embodying the principles contained therein.

30. THE GENEVA PROTOCOL FOR THE PACIFIC SETTLEMENT OF INTERNATIONAL DISPUTES, 2 OCTOBER 1924 [1]

The fifth Assembly, led by the new prime ministers of Great Britain and France, Ramsay MacDonald and Edouard Herriot, witnessed the greatest advance to be made by the League as an organization for the maintenance of peace. There was then negotiated the Geneva Protocol, whose provisions elaborated the formula "arbitration, security, disarmament" for the maintenance of peace.

Animated by the firm desire to ensure the maintenance of the general peace and the security of nations whose existence, independence or territories may be threatened;

Recognising the solidarity of the members of the international community;

Asserting that a war of aggression constitutes a violation of this solidarity and an international crime;

Desirous of facilitating the complete application of the system provided in the Covenant of the League of Nations for the pacific settlement of disputes between States and of ensuring the repression of international crimes; and

For the purpose of realizing as contemplated by Article 8 of the Covenant, the reduction of national armaments to the lowest point consistent with national safety and the enforcement by common action of international obligations;

The undersigned, duly authorised to that effect, agree as follows:

ART. 1. The signatory States undertake to make every effort in their power to secure the introduction into the Covenant of amendments on the lines of the provisions contained in the following articles.

They agree that, as between themselves, these provisions shall be binding as from the coming into force of the present Protocol and that, so far as they are concerned, the Assembly and the Council of the League of Nations shall thenceforth have power to exercise all the rights and perform all the duties conferred upon them by the Protocol.

ART. 2. The signatory States agree in no case to resort to war either with one another or against a State which, if the occasion arises, accepts all the obligations hereinafter set out, except in case of resistance to acts of aggression or when acting in agreement with the Council or the Assembly of the League of Nations in accordance with the provisions of the Covenant and of the present Protocol.

ART. 3. The signatory States undertake to recognise as compulsory, ipso facto and without special agreement, the jurisdiction of the Permanent Court of International Justice in the cases covered by paragraph 2 of Article 36 of the Statute of the Court, but without prejudice to the right of any State, when acceding to the special protocol provided for in the said Article and opened for signature on December 16th, 1920, to make reservations compatible with the said clause.

[1] League of Nations, *Official Journal*, spec.   supp. No. 23, pp. 492-502.

Accession to this special protocol, opened for signature on December 16th, 1920, must be given within the month following the coming into force of the present Protocol.

States which accede to the present Protocol after its coming into force must carry out the above obligations within the month following their accession.

ART. 4. With a view to render more complete the provisions of paragraphs 4, 5, 6, and 7 of Article 15 of the Covenant, the signatory States agree to comply with following procedure:

1. If the dispute submitted to the Council is not settled as provided in paragraph 3 of the said Article 15, the Council shall endeavour to persuade the parties to submit the dispute to judicial settlement or arbitration.

2. (a) If the parties cannot agree to do so, there shall, at the request of at least one of the parties, be constituted a Committee of Arbitrators. The Committee shall so far as possible be constituted by agreement between the parties.

(b) If within the period fixed by the Council the parties have failed to agree, in whole or in part, upon the number, the names and the powers of the arbitrators and upon the procedure, the Council shall settle the points remaining in suspense. It shall with the utmost possible despatch select in consultation with the parties the arbitrators and their President from among persons who by their nationality, their personal character and their experience, appear to it to furnish the highest guarantees of competence and impartiality.

(c) After the claims of the parties have been formulated, the Committee of Arbitrators, on the request of any party, shall, through the medium of the Council request an advisory opinion upon any points of law in dispute from the Permanent Court of International Justice, which in such case shall

meet with the utmost possible despatch.

3. If none of the parties asks for arbitration, the Council shall again take the dispute under consideration. If the Council reaches a report which is unanimously agreed to by the members thereof other than the representatives of any of the parties to the dispute, the signatory States agree to comply with the recommendations therein.

4. If the Council fails to reach a report which is concurred in by all its members, other than the representatives of any of the parties to the dispute, it shall submit the dispute to arbitration. It shall itself determine the composition, the powers and the procedure of the Committee of Arbitrators and, in the choice of the arbitrators, shall bear in mind the guarantees of competence and impartiality referred to in Paragraph 2 (b) above.

5. In no case may a solution, upon which there has already been a unanimous recommendation of the Council accepted by one of the parties concerned, be again called in question.

6. The signatory States undertake that they will carry out in full good faith any judicial sentence or arbitral award that may be rendered and that they will comply, as provided in paragraph 3 above, with the solutions recommended by the Council. In the event of a State failing to carry out the above undertakings, the Council shall exert all its influence to secure compliance therewith. If it fails therein, it shall propose what steps should be taken to give effect thereto, in accordance with the provision contained at the end of Article 13 of the Covenant. Should a State in disregard of the above undertakings resort to war, the sanctions provided for by Article 16 of the Covenant, interpreted in the manner indicated in the present Protocol, shall immediately become applicable to it.

7. The provisions of the present article do not apply to the settlement of disputes which arise as the result of

measures of war taken by one or more signatory States in agreement with the Council or the Assembly.

ART. 5. The provisions of paragraph 8 of Article 15 of the Covenant shall continue to apply in proceedings before the Council.

If in the course of an arbitration, such as is contemplated in Article 4 above, one of the parties claims that the dispute, or part thereof, arises out of a matter which by international law is solely within the domestic jurisdiction of that party, the arbitrators shall on this point take the advice of the Permanent Court of International Justice through the medium of the Council. The opinion of the Court shall be binding upon the arbitrators, who, if the opinion is affirmative, shall confine themselves to so declaring in their award.

If the question is held by the Court or by the Council to be a matter solely within the domestic jurisdiction of the State, this decision shall not prevent consideration of the situation by the Council or by the Assembly under Article 11 of the Covenant.

ART. 6. If in accordance with paragraph 9 of Article 15 of the Covenant a dispute is referred to the Assembly, that body shall have for the settlement of the dispute all the powers conferred upon the Council as to endeavouring to reconcile the parties in the manner laid down in paragraphs 1, 2 and 3 of Article 15 of the Covenant and in paragraph 1 of Article 4 above.

Should the Assembly fail to achieve an amicable settlement:

If one of the parties asks for arbitration, the Council shall proceed to constitute the Committee of Arbitrators in the manner provided in sub-paragraphs (a), (b), and (c) of paragraph 2 of Article 4 above.

If no party asks for arbitration, the Assembly shall again take the dispute under consideration and shall have in this connection the same powers as the Council. Recommendations embodied in a report of the Assembly, provided

that it secures the measure of support stipulated at the end of paragraph 10 of Article 15 of the Covenant, shall have the same value and effect, as regards all matters dealt with in the present Protocol, as recommendations embodied in a report of the Council adopted as provided in paragraph 3 of Article 4 above.

If the necessary majority cannot be obtained, the dispute shall be submitted to arbitration and the Council shall determine the composition, the powers and the procedure of the Committee of Arbitrators as laid down in paragraph 4 of Article 4 above.

ART. 7. In the event of a dispute arising between two or more signatory States, these States agree that they will not, either before the dispute is submitted to proceedings for pacific settlement or during such proceedings, make any increase of their armaments or effectives which might modify the position established by the Conference for the Reduction of Armaments provided for by Article 17 of the present Protocol, nor will they take any measure of military, naval, air, industrial or economic mobilisation, nor, in general, any action of a nature likely to extend the dispute or render it more acute.

It shall by the duty of the Council, in accordance with the provisions of Article 11 of the Covenant, to take under consideration any complaint as to infraction of the above undertakings which is made to it by one or more of the States parties to the dispute. Should the Council be of opinion that the complaint requires investigation, it shall, if it deems it expedient, arrange for enquiries and investigations in one or more of the countries concerned. Such enquiries and investigations shall be carried out with the utmost possible despatch and the signatory States undertake to afford every facility for carrying them out.

The sole object of measures taken by the Council as above provided is to facilitate the pacific settlement of disputes and they shall in no way prejudge the actual settlement.

If the result of such enquiries and investigations is to establish an infraction of the provisions of the first paragraph of the present Article, it shall be the duty of the Council to summon the State or States guilty of the infraction to put an end thereto. Should the State or States in question fail to comply with such summons, the Council shall declare them to be guilty of a violation of the Covenant or of the present Protocol, and shall decide upon the measures to be taken with a view to end as soon as possible a situation of a nature to threaten the peace of the world.

For the purposes of the present Article decisions of the Council may be taken by a two-thirds majority.

ART. 8. The signatory States undertake to abstain from any act which might constitute a threat of aggression against another State.

If one of the signatory States is of opinion that another State is making preparations for war, it shall have the right to bring the matter to the notice of the Council.

The Council, if it ascertains that the facts are as alleged, shall proceed as provided in paragraphs 2, 4, and 5 of Article 7.

ART. 9. The existence of demilitarised zones being calculated to prevent aggression and to facilitate a definite finding of the nature provided for in Article 10 below, the establishment of such zones between States mutually consenting thereto is recommended as a means of avoiding violations of the present Protocol.

The demilitarised zones already existing under the terms of certain treaties or conventions, or which may be established in future between States mutually consenting thereto, may at the request and at the expense of one or more of the conterminous States, be placed under a temporary or permanent system of supervision to be organised by the Council.

ART. 10. Every State which resorts to war in violation of the undertakings contained in the Covenant or in the present Protocol is an aggressor. Violation of the rules laid down for a demilitarised zone shall be held equivalent of resort to war.

In the event of hostilities having broken out, any State shall be presumed to be an aggressor, unless a decision of the Council, which must be taken unanimously, shall otherwise declare:

1. If it has refused to submit the dispute to the procedure of pacific settlement provided by Articles 13 and 15 of the Covenant as amplified by the present Protocol, or to comply with a judicial sentence or arbitral award or with a unanimous recommendation of the Council, or has disregarded a unanimous report of the Council, a judicial sentence or an arbitral award recognising that the dispute between it and the other belligerent State arises out of a matter which by international law is solely within the domestic jurisdiction of the latter State; nevertheless, in the last case the State shall only be presumed to be an aggressor if it has not previously submitted the question to the Council or the Assembly, in accordance with Article 11 of the Covenant.

2. If it has violated provisional measures enjoined by the Council for the period while the proceedings are in progress as contemplated by Article 7 of the present Protocol.

Apart from the cases dealt with in paragraphs 1 and 2 of the present Article, if the Council does not at once succeed in determining the aggressor, it shall be bound to enjoin upon the belligerents an armistice, and shall fix the terms, acting, if need be, by a two-thirds majority and shall supervise its execution.

Any belligerent which has refused to accept the armistice or has violated its terms shall be deemed an aggressor.

The Council shall call upon the signatory States to apply forthwith against the aggressor the sanctions provided by Article 11 of the present Protocol, and any signatory State thus called upon shall thereupon be entitled to exercise the rights of a belligerent.

Art. 11. As soon as the Council has called upon the signatory States to apply sanctions, as provided in the last paragraph of Article 10 of the present Protocol, the obligations of the said States, in regard to the sanctions of all kinds mentioned in paragraphs 1 and 2 of Article 16 of the Covenant, will immediately become operative in order that such sanctions may forthwith be employed against the aggressor.

Those obligations shall be interpreted as obliging each of the signatory States to co-operate loyally and effectively in support of the Covenant of the League of Nations, and in resistance to any act of aggression, in the degree which its geographical position and its particular situation as regards armaments allow.

In accordance with paragraph 3 of Article 16 of the Covenant the signatory States give a joint and several undertaking to come to the assistance of the State attacked or threatened, and to give each other mutual support by means of facilities and reciprocal exchanges as regards the provision of raw materials and supplies of every kind, openings of credits, transport and transit, and for this purpose to take all measures in their power to preserve the safety of communications by land and by sea of the attacked on threatened State.

If both parties to the dispute are aggressors within the meaning of Article 10, the economic and financial sanctions shall be applied to both of them.

Art. 12. In view of the complexity of the conditions in which the Council may be called upon to exercise the functions mentioned in Article 11 of the present Protocol concerning economic and financial sanctions, and in order to determine more exactly the guarantees afforded by the present Protocol to the signatory States, the Council shall forthwith invite the economic and financial organisations of the League of Nations to consider and report as to the nature of the steps to be taken to give effect to the financial and economic sanctions and measures of co-operation contemplated in Article 16 of the Covenant and in Article 11 of this Protocol.

When in possession of this information, the Council shall draw up through its competent organs:

1. Plans of action for the application of the economic and financial sanctions against an aggressor State;

2. Plans of economic and financial co-operation between a State attacked and the different States assisting it;

and shall communicate these plans to the Members of the League and to the other signatory States.

Art. 13. In view of the contingent military, naval and air sanctions provided for by Article 16 of the Covenant and by Article 11 of the present Protocol, the Council shall be entitled to receive undertakings from States determining in advance the military, naval and air forces which they would be able to bring into action immediately to ensure the fulfilment of the obligations in regard to sanctions which result from the Covenant and the present Protocol.

Furthermore, as soon as the Council has called upon the signatory States to apply sanctions, as provided in the last paragraph of Article 10 above, the said States may, in accordance with any agreements which they may previously have concluded, bring to the assistance of a particular State, which is the victim of aggression, their military, naval and air forces.

The agreements mentioned in the preceding paragraphs shall be registered and published by the Secretariat of the League of Nations. They shall remain open to all States Members of the League which may desire to accede thereto.

Art. 14. The Council shall alone be

competent to declare that the application of sanctions shall cease and normal conditions be re-established.

ART. 15. In conformity with the spirit of the present Protocol, the signatory States agree that the whole cost of any military, naval or air operations undertaken for the repression of an aggression under the terms of the Protocol, and reparation for all losses suffered by individuals, whether civilians or combatants, and for all material damage caused by the operations of both sides, shall be borne by the aggressor State up to the extreme limit of its capacity.

Nevertheless, in view of Article 10 of the Covenant, neither the territorial integrity nor the political independence of the aggressor State shall in any case be affected as the result of the application of the sanctions mentioned in the present Protocol.

ART. 16. The signatory States agree that in the event of a dispute between one or more of them and one or more States which have not signed the present Protocol and are not Members of the League of Nations, such non-Member States shall be invited, on the conditions contemplated in Article 17 of the Covenant, to submit, for the purpose of a pacific settlement, to the obligations accepted by the States signatories of the present Protocol.

If the State so invited, having refused to accept the said conditions and obligations, resorts to war against a signatory State, the provisions of Article 16 of the Covenant, as defined by the present Protocol, shall be applicable against it.

ART. 17. The signatory States undertake to participate in an International Conference for the Reduction of Armaments which shall be convened by the Council and shall meet at Geneva on Monday, June 15th, 1925. All other States, whether Members of the League or not, shall be invited to this Conference.

In preparation for the convening of the Conference, the Council shall draw up with due regard to the undertakings contained in Articles 11 and 13 of the present Protocol, a general programme for the reduction and limitation of armaments, which shall be laid before the Conference and which shall be communicated to the Governments at the earliest possible date, and at the latest three months before the Conference meets.

If by May 1st, 1925, ratifications have not been deposited by at least a majority of the permanent Members of the Council and ten other Members of the League, the Secretary-General of the League shall immediately consult the Council as to whether he shall cancel the invitations or merely adjourn the Conference to a subsequent date so as to permit the necessary number of ratifications to be obtained.

ART. 18. Wherever mention is made in Article 10, or in any other provision of the present Protocol, of a decision of the Council, this shall be understood in the sense of Article 15 of the Covenant, namely, that the votes of the representatives of the parties to the dispute shall not be counted when reckoning unanimity or the necessary majority.

ART. 19. Except as expressly provided by its terms, the present Protocol shall not affect in any way the rights and obligations of Members of the League as determined by the Covenant.

ART. 20. Any dispute as to the interpretation of the present Protocol shall be submitted to the Permanent Court of International Justice.

ART. 21. The present Protocol, of which the French and English texts are both authentic, shall be ratified.

The deposit of ratifications shall be made at the Secretariat of the League of Nations as soon as possible.

States of which the seat of government is outside Europe will be entitled merely to inform the Secretariat of the League of Nations that their ratification has been given; in that case, they must transmit the instrument of ratification as soon as possible.

So soon as the majority of the permanent Members of the Council and ten other Members of the League have deposited or have effected their ratifications, a *procès-verbal* to that effect shall be drawn up by the Secretariat.

After the said *procès-verbal* has been drawn up, the Protocol shall come into force as soon as the plan for the reduction of armaments has been adopted by the Conference provided for in Article 17.

If within such period after the adoption of the plan for the reduction of armaments as shall be fixed by the said Conference, the plan has not been carried out, the Council shall make a declaration to that effect; this declaration shall render the present Protocol null and void.

The grounds on which the Council may declare that the plan drawn up by the International Conference for the Reduction of Armaments has not been carried out, and that in consequence the present Protocol has been rendered null and void, shall be laid down by the Conference itself.

A signatory State which, after the expiration of the period fixed by the Conference, fails to comply with the plan adopted by the Conference, shall not be admitted to benefit by the provisions of the present Protocol.

In faith whereof the undersigned, duly authorised for this purpose, have signed the present Protocol.

Done at Geneva, on the second day of October, nineteen hundred and twenty-four, in a single copy, which will be kept in the archives of the Secretariat of the League and registered by it on the date of its coming into force.

31. CHAMBERLAIN'S STATEMENT REJECTING THE GENEVA PROTOCOL, 12 MARCH 1925 [1]

The adoption of the Geneva Protocol by the Fifth Assembly reflected no change in the political realities. As the United States warned the British,[2] full recognition of its rights as a neutral would be expected; yet upon the British Navy in almost any conceivable case would fall the primary burden of enforcing economic sanctions. This was sufficient reason to lead the new government of Stanley Baldwin, which had succeeded that of Ramsay MacDonald in the fall of 1924, to reject the Protocol. The rejection, which had the support of the Dominions, was communicated to the Council at its meeting in March 1925 by Sir Austen Chamberlain, the new British foreign minister.

I. His Majesty's Government have given the most anxious consideration to the Protocol which was provisionally accepted last October by the Assembly of the League of Nations and submitted by the Council to the various States Members of the League. It is unnecessary to lay stress upon the sympathy felt throughout the British Empire with any effort to improve the international machinery for maintaining the peace of the world. Arbitration, disarmament and security are the main themes of the Protocol, and on all these great subjects the British Empire has shown, by deeds as well as words, that it is in the fullest accord with the ideals which have animated the fifth Assembly of the League. Successive administrations in Great Britain, with the full approval of the self-governing Dominions and India, have not only favoured arbitration in theory; they have largely availed themselves of it in practice. They have not contented themselves with preaching disarmament; they have disarmed to the limits of national safety. They have taken their full share in creating and supporting the League of Nations and the Court of International Justice; while the immense sacrifices they have been content to make in the cause of

[1] League of Nations, *Official Journal*, VI (1925), 446.

[2] *U.S. Foreign Relations, 1925*, I, pp. 17 f.

general security are matters of recent history.

If, therefore, His Majesty's present advisers, after discussing the subject with the self-governing Dominions and India, see insuperable objections to signing and ratifying the Protocol in its present shape, this is not because they feel themselves out of harmony with the purpose which it was intended to serve, or are opposed in principle to schemes for clarifying the meaning of the Covenant or strengthening its provisions. Amendment and interpretation may in themselves be desirable, but His Majesty's Government cannot believe that the Protocol as it stands provides the most suitable method of attempting that task.

II. The declared object of the Protocol is to facilitate disarmament, and it proposes to attain this most desirable end: (1) by closing certain gaps in the scheme originally laid down in the Covenant for peaceably settling international disputes, and (2) by sharpening the "sanctions," especially the economic sanctions, by which, under the existing system, aggression is to be discouraged and aggressors coerced. These two portions of the scheme are intimately connected, and it may be desirable on the present occasion to consider them together.

It was, of course, well known to the framers of the Covenant that international differences might conceivably take a form for which their peace preserving machinery provided no specific remedy; nor could they have doubted that this defect, if defect it was, could in theory be cured by insisting that every dispute should, at some stage or other, be submitted to arbitration. Therefore, they felt, as so many States Members of the League have felt since, that the objections to universal and compulsory arbitration might easily outweigh its theoretical advantages. So far as the Court of International Justice is concerned, this view was taken in 1920 by the British Delegation, while the British Delegation of

1924 made a reservation in the same connection which, so far as Great Britain is concerned, greatly limits the universal application of the compulsory principle.

Into this branch of the controversy, however, His Majesty's Government do not now propose to enter. It suffices to say that, so far from their objections to compulsory arbitration being diminished by the provisions of the Protocol, they have rather been increased, owing to the weakening of those reservations in clause 15 of the Covenant, which were designed to prevent any interference by the League in matters of domestic jurisdiction.

His Majesty's Government are now more immediately concerned to enquire how far the change in the Covenant effected by the Protocol is likely to increase the responsibilities already undertaken by the States Members of the League. On this there may conceivably be two opinions. Some have held that, although in the language of the First Committee . . . "there are numerous fissures in the wall of protection erected by the Covenant round the peace of the world," there is in fact but little danger that through these "fissures" any serious assaults will be attempted. The changes made by the Protocol are, in their judgment, formal rather than substantial; they aim at theoretical completeness rather than practical effect. On this view no material addition is made to responsibilities already incurred under the Covenant, nor (it must be added) is anything of importance accomplished in the cause of Peace and Disarmament.

But this (it need hardly be said) is not the view of the framers of the Protocol. They regard themselves as the authors of a "new system" . . . through which alone can be realised "the great ideal to which humanity aspires." . . . The last thing they contemplate is the possibility that their proposals will leave things very much as they stand under the Covenant. And in this His

Majesty's Government are entirely of their opinion. How, indeed, can it be otherwise? Fresh classes of disputes are to be decided by the League; fresh possibilities of defying its decisions are thereby created; fresh occasions for the application of coercive measures follow as a matter of course; and it is therefore not surprising that, quite apart from the problem of disarmament, the question of "sanctions" should by treated at length in the clauses of the Protocol.

III. It seems necessary to preface the comments called for by this part of the new scheme by recalling certain historic facts which, though very relevant to the subject, are never referred to in the documents by which the Protocol is justified and explained.

As all the world is aware, the League of Nations, in its present shape, is not the League designed by the framers of the Covenant. They no doubt contemplated, and, as far as they could, provided against, the difficulties that might arise from the non-inclusion of a certain number of States within the circle of League membership. But they never supposed that, among these States, would be found so many of the most powerful nations in the world; least of all did they foresee that one of them would be the United States of America.

It is no doubt true that there are many points of view from which these unfortunate facts have not proved to be of vital importance. The work of the League goes on, beneficent and full of promise. Though the United States remains in friendly aloofness, individual Americans have freely helped both by sympathy and service, while the generosity of the American public has greatly aided some causes in which the League is deeply interested. Could, therefore, attention be confined to the present and the past, it might be said with truth that the problems which even a weakened League has had to face have never overstrained its machinery.

The hope may be justified that this good fortune will continue. But surely it is most unwise to add to the liabilities already incurred without taking stock of the degree to which the machinery of the Covenant has been already weakened by the non-membership of certain great States. For in truth the change, especially as regards the "economic sanctions," amounts to a transformation. The "economic sanction," if simultaneously directed by all the world against a State which is not itself economically self-sufficing, would be a weapon of incalculable power. This, or something not very different from this, was the weapon originally devised by the authors of the Covenant. To them it appeared to be not only bloodless, but cheap, effective and easy to use, in the most improbable event of its use being necessary. But all this is changed by the mere existence of powerful economic communities outside the limits of the League. It might force trade into unaccustomed channels, but it could hardly stop it; and though the offending State would no doubt suffer, there is no presumption that it would be crushed or even that it would suffer most.

Were this the occasion for entering into a detailed discussion of the subsidiary provisions of the Protocol, it would be necessary to dwell at length on all those which, in the opinion of His Majesty's Government, are open to serious objection. But for the purposes of the present communication the following observations may suffice.

Articles 7 and 8 of the Protocol are designed for the purpose of preventing a State which has a difference with a neighbour from making any preparations for war between the moment when a dispute arises and the moment when proceedings for a pacific settlement have been concluded. The intentions of these provisions are most laudable. But the framers of the Protocol have not perhaps sufficiently considered that it may embarrass the victim of aggression even more than the aggressor. The aggressor is at liberty to select his own date for picking a quarrel. Until that date arrives he may distribute his armies as he pleases—provided only that he neither mobilizes them nor adds to them. When the distribution is as favourable to his designs as he can hope to make them, he starts the dispute. Immediately, the military position becomes temporarily unalterable. His troops, which are more or less in the right position for attack, may (indeed must) be kept there till he wants to use them. The troops, on the other hand, of his prospective victim are (by supposition) in the wrong position for defence. But there they must be kept, or the victim may find himself charged with a breach of the Protocol. Is this a tolerable situation? Is it one that could possibly survive the day of trial?

It may be replied that, if the aggressor attempts to concentrate troops for attack before the dispute arises, means may be found to stop him. Grant that such means exist, which is extremely doubtful, how does the Protocol deal with the case where the peace distribution of the troops belonging to the aggressor is normally more suitable for attack than the peace distribution of the troops belonging to its opponents is suitable for defence? If a dispute were to arise, would the defender be counted as an aggressor solely because he endeavoured to redress this accidental inequality?

These are some of the difficulties suggested by Articles 7 and 8 of the Protocol as these affect forces on land. But these articles raise even more embarrassing problems when applied to the case of forces at sea. The whole value of a fleet depends on its mobility. Its distribution is in all probability quite different in time of peace from what it would be under threat of war. To suggest that, directly a dispute arises which in any way concerns a maritime Power, its ships are to remain immovably fixed on the stations where the chance conveniences of peace

may happen to have placed them, is asking the threatened State to make a surrender of its inalienable right of self-defence, to which it is never likely to submit.

It may be desirable to add that, besides the obvious objections to those clauses already indicated, their great obscurity, and the inherent impossibility of distinguishing, in any paper definition, military movements genuinely intended for defence, and only for defence, from movements with some ulterior aggressive purpose, must always make them a danger to the unwary rather than a protection to the innocent. They could never be accepted as they stand.

There is one other article in the Protocol which cannot be passed over in complete silence, namely, Article 15.

This contains two provisions. By the first, the aggressor State is required to pay all the costs of the war for which it is responsible, and full reparation for all damages, public or private, which the war has caused. By the second, it is protected from any alteration of its frontiers and all interference with its internal affairs.

With the sentiments which have dictated these two provisions there will be general sympathy. His Majesty's Government, at all events, have no desire to relieve the aggressor of the duty of repairing to the utmost of his ability the damages for which he is responsible; they hold strongly to the view that frontiers are neither to be lightly made nor lightly violated; and they, of course, accept the broad principle that sovereign States should be left to manage their own affairs. But they cannot think it wise to embody these generalities in dogmas of inflexible rigidity, designed to control the actions of the League in all circumstances and for all time. In the sternest codes of law, mitigating circumstances are allowed to modify the judgments of the courts; and His Majesty's Government fail to see why the League of Nations should deliberately deprive itself of a discretion which all other tribunals are free to exercise.

Moreover, there is a certain want of harmony between the two provisions of the Article, which in rare and extreme cases (and it is for rare and extreme cases, among others, that we are asked to legislate) might well shock the conscience of the world. These cases cannot, indeed, be foreseen, but they may be imagined. Is it impossible (for example) that, in a war arising out of some very complicated situation involving perhaps a State not a member of the League, the guilt of the combatants might be fairly matched though only one of them was technically the aggressor? In such circumstances, would the League feel no misgivings when they found themselves compelled to throw all the cost of the war upon one party and none at all upon the other? Would not the universal verdict be that, under the first half of Article 15, the aggressor had in this case been hardly treated?

But now consider the second half of Article 15. This protects the aggressor, whatever his misdeeds, from losing anything under any circumstances but money or the equivalent of money. Is this quite satisfactory? The aggression may have been utterly unprovoked; it may have been barbarously conducted; it may be the work of a corrupt and tyrannical administration; and it may be the inevitable result of cruel misgovernment on the aggressor's side of an ill-drawn frontier. Are we to lay it down for all time that, in such a case, the League shall do nothing to prevent a repetition of the offence but ask for money? This may, indeed, be all that is possible; but would it not be wise to let the League itself resolve this problem, if unhappily the occasion should ever arise?

There is one general reflection which His Majesty's Government venture to add to the specific criticisms they have made in the preceding paragraphs. The Protocol purports to be little more than a completion of the work begun but not perfected by the authors of the Covenant. But surely this is a very inadequate description of its effects. The additions which it makes to the original document do something quite different from merely clarifying obscurities and filling in omissions. They destroy its balance and alter its spirit. The fresh emphasis laid upon sanctions, the new occasions discovered for their employment, the elaboration of military procedure, insensibly suggest the idea that the vital business of the League is not so much to promote friendly co-operation and reasoned harmony in the management of international affairs as to preserve peace by organising war, and (it may be) war on the largest scale. Now, it is unhappily true that circumstances may be easily imagined in which war, conducted by Members of the League, and with its collective assistance and approval, will become a tragic necessity. But such catastrophies belong to the pathology of international life, not to its normal condition. It is not wholesome for the ordinary man to be always brooding over the possibility of some severe surgical operation; nor is it wise for societies to pursue a similar course. It is more likely to hasten the dreaded consummation than to hinder it. And it certainly seems to His Majesty's Government that anything which fosters the idea that the main business of the League is with war rather than with peace is likely to weaken it in its fundamental task of diminishing the causes of war without making it in every respect a satisfactory instrument for organising great military operations should the necessity for them be forced upon the world.

IV. It may perhaps be urged that these objections to the Protocol, whatever be their value, are far outweighed by the blessings of the disarmament which would immediately follow its acceptance. But why should disarmament immediately follow its acceptance? Why should the new scheme succeed when the old scheme has so lamentably failed? It no doubt claims to have closed some "fissures in the wall of protection erected by the Covenant round the peace of the world." But it is not the possibility of an attack through these (alleged) weak places in the Covenant which haunts the imagination of those who hesitate to disarm. They do not doubt that the Covenant, if kept, would be sufficient to protect them, at least from attack by those who have signed it. What they doubt is whether when it comes to the point, the Covenant *will* be kept. Either some faithless Member of the League will break its pledge or some predatory nation outside the League will brush Covenant and Protocol ruthlessly aside, defying all the sanction by which they are protected. Brute force is what they fear, and only brute force enlisted in their defence can (as they believe) give them the security of which they feel the need.

His Majesty's Government fail altogether to see how this situation is bettered by the Protocol. Is it to be supposed that the "security" promised by the new system will be so complete that no armaments capable of being used or improvised for offensive purposes will remain in being? If not, is the balance of power between the States which desire peace and those which are plotting war to be adjusted in favour of the former? If so, on what principle? If not, then how are we advanced? How will the unscrupulous aggressors be relatively weakened? How will their potential victims be rendered more capable of defence?

And if the particular case of aggressors who are outside the League be considered, is not the weakness of the Protocol even more manifest? The aggressors within the League are traitors in the sight of all mankind. Their moral position in the face of any opposition within their own borders will be immensely weakened, while in neutral countries they will find none to plead their cause. However low the practical importance of moral consid-erations such as these may be rated, the eagerness of competing propaganda in times of international crisis may convince the most cynical that a good cause counts at least for something. If so, aggressors outside the League will have a smaller load of infamy to carry than aggressors within it, and will be by so much the more formidable. How does the Protocol deal with them? It requires them to treat the situation as if they were members of the League, to accept its methods and conform to its decisions. If they refuse they are counted as aggressors, they become the common enemy, and every signatory State is bound to go to war with them. They may be in the right and have nothing to fear from impartial judges. Yet national pride, in some cases perhaps the sense of power, dislike of compulsory arbitration, distrust of the League (to which presumably they have already refused to belong)—all these motives, or any of them, may harden their objections to outside interference. If so, the Protocol, designed to ensure universal peace may only extend the area of war—a possibility which, if realised, will not improve the chances of general disarmament.

V. It may perhaps be replied that, while every scheme of sanctions is open to criticism, some scheme of sanctions is certainly necessary. Without it a League of Nations would be as insecure as a civilised society without magistrates and police. International engagements which cannot be internationally enforced are little better than a sham. Those, therefore, who object to the plan proposed in the Protocol are bound to suggest a better.

To this challenge His Majesty's Government might be content to reply that, as between the Covenant unamended and the Covenant amended by the Protocol, they have already given reasons for preferring the former. But they are unwilling to conclude their argument on a purely critical note and, though they cannot believe that "security" can be reached by the route so carefully explored by the First and Third Committees of the League in 1924, they are willing to consider whether some approach to it may not be made from the side unsuccessfully attempted in 1923.

They do not agree, indeed, that without "sanctions" the League is powerless and treaties no better than waste paper. Doctrines like these seem to them not only mischievous but self-contradictory. Every "sanction" referred to either in the Covenant or the Protocol depends on treaties; and if no treaties are of value, all sanctions must be worthless. Do what we will, we have no choice but, in the last resort, to depend upon the plighted word.

But this, it must be admitted, does not settle the question whether the sanctions contemplated by the Covenant cannot in certain cases and for certain purposes be supplemented with advantage to the general scheme of the Covenant itself. That scheme may no doubt be trusted in ordinary cases to work smoothly and effectively. The mere threat to employ sanctions will commonly suffice. And if, unfortunately, it does not, their effect, when put into operation, will doubtless be speedy and conclusive. But it is easy to imagine extreme cases, about which we dare not speak with the same assurance; and it is precisely the possibility of these extreme cases, remote though that possibility may be, which fosters international suspicion, makes Governments hesitate to disarm and keeps the world on edge.

His Majesty's Government do not share these alarms, but they recognise their serious effect, and believe them to be the main obstacles to the complete recovery of our shaken civilisation from the disasters of war. How are they to be allayed?

The first expedient that naturally suggests itself is to strengthen the provisions of the Covenant. If the Covenant, as it stands, does not supply an adequate machinery for preserving peace in all conceivable cases, why not alter it till it does?

The futility of this plan is, in the opinion of His Majesty's Government, abundantly proved by the Protocol. For whatever else its proposals give us, they do not give us security. They multiply offences, but do nothing to strengthen remedies. They increase the responsibilities undertaken by individual Members of the League, but do nothing to readjust their burden.

What expedient remains? How is security and, above all, the feeling of security, to be attained? In answering this question it is necessary to keep in mind the characteristics of the "extreme cases," to which reference has already been made. The brooding fears that keep huge armaments in being have little relation to the ordinary misunderstandings inseparable from international (as from social) life—misunderstandings with which the League is so admirably fitted to deal. They spring from deep-lying causes of hostility which, for historic or other reasons, divide great and powerful States. These fears may be groundless; but if they exist they cannot be effectually laid by even the most perfect method of dealing with particular disputes by the machinery of enquiry and arbitration. For what is feared in such cases is not injustice but war—war deliberately undertaken for purposes of conquest or revenge. And, if so, can there be a better way of allaying fears like these than by adopting some scheme which should prove to all the world that such a war would fail?

Since the general provisions of the Covenant cannot be stiffened with advantage, and since the "extreme cases" with which the League may have to deal will probably affect certain nations or groups of nations more nearly than others, His Majesty's Government conclude that the best way of dealing with the situation is, with the co-operation of the League, to supplement the Covenant by making special arrangements in order to meet special needs. That these arrangements should be purely defensive in character, that they should be framed in the spirit of the Covenant, working in close harmony with the League and under its guidance, is manifest. And, in the opinion of His Majesty's Government, these objects can best be attained by knitting together the nations most immediately concerned, and whose differences might lead to a renewal of strife, by means of treaties framed with the sole object of maintaining, as between themselves, an unbroken peace. Within its limits no quicker remedy for our present ills can easily be found or any surer safeguard against future calamities.

That, gentlemen, is the declaration which His Majesty's Government have instructed me to make.

His Majesty's Government have found it impossible, in the time at their disposal, to confer personally with the representatives of the Dominions and of India, who are also Members of the League, but we have been in telegraphic communication with them, from which it appears that the Governments of the Dominion of Canada, of the Commonwealth of Australia, of New Zealand, of the Union of South Africa and of India are also unable to accept the Protocol. Their views will be made known in such a manner as they may think fit either by a communication to the Secretariat, or to the Assembly, or otherwise.

I am not yet in possession of the views of the Irish Free State.

32. THE LOCARNO PACTS: THE TREATY OF MUTUAL GUARANTEE, 16 OCTOBER 1925 [1]

With the failure of the Geneva Protocol and the setback given to the principle of general commitments in support of the Covenant, there was a new resort to regional and limited commitments. The group of agreements, initialed 16 October 1925 and known as the Locarno Pacts, consisted of this Treaty of Mutual Guarantee, four bilateral arbitration treaties between Germany and France, Belgium, Poland and Czechoslovakia and two bilateral treaties of guarantee between France and Poland and Czechoslovakia. The Locarno Pacts ushered in a era of good feeling in European relations animated by the "spirit of Locarno."

THE PRESIDENT OF THE GERMAN REICH, HIS MAJESTY THE KING OF THE BELGIANS, THE PRESIDENT OF THE FRENCH REPUBLIC, HIS MAJESTY THE KING OF THE UNITED KINGDOM OF GREAT BRITAIN AND IRELAND AND OF THE BRITISH DOMINIONS BEYOND THE SEAS, EMPEROR OF INDIA, HIS MAJESTY THE KING OF ITALY;

Anxious to satisfy the desire for security and protection which animates the peoples upon whom fell the scourge of the war of 1914-18;

Taking note of the abrogation of the treaties for the neutralisation of Belgium, and conscious of the necessity of ensuring peace in the area which has so frequently been the scene of European conflicts;

Animated also with the sincere desire of giving to all the signatory Powers concerned supplementary guarantees within the framework of the Covenant of the League of Nations and the treaties in force between them;

Have determined to conclude a treaty with these objects, and have appointed as their Plenipotentiaries:

PRESIDENT OF THE GERMAN EMPIRE:
   Dr. Hans LUTHER, Chancellor of the Empire;
   Dr. Gustav STRESEMANN, Minister for Foreign Affairs;
MAJESTY THE KING OF THE BELGIANS:
   M. Emile VANDERVELDE, Minister for Foreign Affairs;
PRESIDENT OF THE FRENCH REPUBLIC:
   M. Aristide BRIAND, Prime Minister

[1] *League of Nations Treaty Series,* LIV,   pp. 289 ff.

and Minister for Foreign Affairs;

MAJESTY THE KING OF THE UNITED KINGDOM OF GREAT BRITAIN AND IRELAND AND OF THE BRITISH DOMINIONS BEYOND THE SEAS, EMPEROR OF INDIA:

The Right Honourable Stanley BALDWIN, M.P., First Lord of the Treasury and Prime Minister;

The Right Honourable Joseph Austen CHAMBERLAIN, M.P., Principal Secretary of State for Foreign Affairs;

MAJESTY THE KING OF ITALY:

The Honourable Vittorio SCIALOJA, Senator of the Kingdom;

Who, having communicated their full powers, found in good and due form, have agreed as follows:

ART. 1. The High Contracting Parties collectively and severally guarantee, in the manner provided in the following Articles, the maintenance of the territorial *status quo* resulting from the frontiers between Germany and Belgium and between Germany and France, and the inviolability of the said frontiers as fixed by or in pursuance of the Treaty of Peace signed at Versailles on June 28, 1919, and also the observance of the stipulations of Articles 42 and 43 of the said Treaty concerning the demilitarised zone.

ART. 2. Germany and Belgium, and also Germany and France, mutually undertake that they will in no case attack or invade each other or resort to war against each other.

This stipulation shall not, however, apply in the case of:

(1) The exercise of the right of legitimate defence, that is to say, resistance to a violation of the undertaking contained in the previous paragraph or to a flagrant breach of Articles 42 or 43 of the said Treaty of Versailles, if such breach constitutes an unprovoked act of aggression and by reason of the assembly of armed forces in the demilitarised zone, immediate action is necessary;

(2) Action in pursuance of Article 16 of the Covenant of the League of Nations;

(3) Action as the result of a decision taken by the Assembly or by the Council of the League of Nations or in pursuance of Article 15, paragraph 7, of the Covenant of the League of Nations, provided that in this last event the action is directed against a State which was the first to attack.

ART. 3. In view of the undertakings entered into in Article 2 of the present Treaty, Germany and Belgium, and Germany and France, undertake to settle by peaceful means and in the manner laid down herein all questions of every kind which may arise between them and which it may not be possible to settle by the normal methods of diplomacy:

Any question with regard to which the Parties are in conflict as to their respective rights shall be submitted to judicial decision, and the Parties undertake to comply with such decision.

All other questions shall be submitted to a conciliation commission. If the proposals of this commission are not accepted by the two Parties, the question shall be brought before the Council of the League of Nations, which will deal with it in accordance with Article 15 of the Covenant of the League.

The detailed arrangements for effecting such peaceful settlement are the subject of special agreements signed this day.

ART. 4. (1) If one of the High Contracting Parties alleges that a violation of Article 2 of the present treaty or a breach of Articles 42 or 43 of the Treaty of Versailles has been or is being committed, it shall bring the question at once before the Council of the League of Nations.

(2) As soon as the Council of the League of Nations is satisfied that such violation or breach has been committed, it will notify its finding without delay to the Powers signatory of the present Treaty, who severally agree that in such case they will each of

LEAGUE OF NATIONS: SECURITY 109

them come immediately to the assistance of the Power against whom the act complained of is directed.

(3) In case of a flagrant violation of Article 2 of the present Treaty or of a flagrant breach of Articles 42 or 43 of the Treaty of Versailles by one of the High Contracting Parties, each of the other Contracting Parties hereby undertakes immediately to come to the help of the Party against whom such a violation or breach has been directed as soon as the said Power has been able to satisfy itself that this violation constitutes an unprovoked act of aggression and that by reason either of the crossing of the frontier or of the outbreak of hostilities or of the assembly of armed forces in the demilitarised zone immediate action is necessary. Nevertheless, the Council of the League of Nations, which will be seized of the question in accordance with the first paragraph of this Article, will issue its findings, and the High Contracting Parties undertake to act in accordance with the recommendations of the Council, provided that they are concurred in by all the Members other than the representatives of the Parties which have engaged in hostilities.

Art. 5. The provisions of Article 3 of the present Treaty are placed under the guarantee of the High Contracting Parties as provided by the following stipulations:

If one of the Powers referred to in Article 3 refuses to submit a dispute to peaceful settlement or to comply with an arbitral or judicial decision and commits a violation of Article 2 of the present Treaty or a breach of Articles 42 or 43 of the Treaty of Versailles, the provisions of Article 4 of the present Treaty shall apply.

Where one of the Powers referred to in Article 3, without committing a violation of Article 2 of the present Treaty or a breach of Articles 42 or 43 of the Treaty of Versailles, refuses to submit a dispute to peaceful settlement or to comply with an arbitral or judi-

cial decision, the other Party shall bring the matter before the Council of the League of Nations, and the Council shall propose what steps shall be taken; the High Contracting Parties shall comply with these proposals.

Art. 6. The provisions of the present Treaty do not affect the rights and obligations of the High Contracting Parties under the Treaty of Versailles or under arrangements supplementary thereto, including the Agreements signed in London on August 30, 1924.

Art. 7. The present Treaty, which is designed to ensure the maintenance of peace, and is in conformity with the Covenant of the League of Nations, shall not be interpreted as restricting the duty of the League to take whatever action may be deemed wise and effectual to safeguard the peace of the world.

Art. 8. The present Treaty shall be registered at the League of Nations in accordance with the Covenant of the League. It shall remain in force until the Council, acting on a request of one or other of the High Contracting Parties notified to the other signatory Powers three months in advance, and voting at least by a two-thirds' majority, decides that the League of Nations ensures sufficient protection to the High Contracting Parties; the Treaty shall cease to have effect on the expiration of a period of one year from such decision.

Art. 9. The present Treaty shall impose no obligation upon any of the British dominions, or upon India, unless the Government of such dominion, or of India, signifies its acceptance thereof.

Art. 10. The present Treaty shall be ratified and the ratifications shall be deposited at Geneva in the archives of the League of Nations as soon as possible.

It shall enter into force as soon as all the ratifications have been deposited and Germany has become a Member of the League of Nations.

The present Treaty, done in a single

copy, will be deposited in the archives of the League of Nations, and the Secretary-General will be requested to transmit certified copies to each of the High Contracting Parties.

In faith whereof the above-mentioned Plenipotentiaries have signed the present Treaty.

Done at Locarno, October 16, 1925.

(L.S.) (Signed) Hans LUTHER.
(L.S.) (Signed) Gustav STRESEMANN.
(L.S.) (Signed) Emile VANDERVELDE.
(L.S.) (Signed) Aristide BRIAND.
(L.S.) (Signed) Stanley BALDWIN.
(L.S.) (Signed) Austen CHAMBERLAIN.
(L.S.) (Signed) Vittorio SCIALOJA.

FINAL PROTOCOL OF THE LOCARNO
CONFERENCE

The representatives of the German, Belgian, British, French, Italian, Polish and Czechoslovak governments, who have met at Locarno from October 5 to 16, 1925, in order to seek by common agreement means for preserving their respective nations from the scourge of war and for providing for the peaceful settlement of disputes of every nature which might eventually arise between them,

Have given their approval to the draft Treaties and Conventions which respectively affect them and which, framed in the course of the present Conference, are mutually interdependent:

> Treaty between Germany, Belgium, France, Great Britain and Italy (Annex A).
> Arbitration Convention between Germany and Belgium (Annex B).
> Arbitration Convention between Germany and France (Annex C).
> Arbitration Treaty between Germany and Poland (Annex D).
> Arbitration Treaty between Germany and Czechoslovakia (Annex E).

These instruments, hereby initialled *ne varietur,* will bear to-day's date, the representatives of the interested Parties agreeing to meet in London on December 1 next, to proceed during the course of a single meeting to the formality of the signature of the instruments which affect them.

The Minister for Foreign Affairs of France states that as a result of the draft arbitration treaties mentioned above, France, Poland and Czechoslovakia have also concluded at Locarno draft agreements in order reciprocally to assure to themselves the benefit of the said treaties. These agreements will be duly deposited at the League of Nations, but M. Briand holds copies forthwith at the disposal of the Powers represented here.

The Secretary of State for Foreign Affairs of Great Britain proposes that, in reply to certain requests for explanations concerning Article 16 of the Covenant of the League of Nations presented by the Chancellor and the Minister for Foreign Affairs of Germany, a letter, of which the draft is similarly attached (Annex F) should be addressed to them at the same time as the formality of signature of the above-mentioned instruments takes place. This proposal is agreed to.

The representatives of the Governments represented here declare their firm conviction that the entry into force of these treaties and conventions will contribute greatly in bringing about a moral relaxation of the tension between nations, that it will help powerfully towards the solution of many political or economic problems in accordance with the interests and sentiments of peoples, and that, in strengthening peace and security in Europe, it will hasten on effectively the disarmament provided for in Article 8 of the Covenant of the League of Nations.

They undertake to give their sincere co-operation to the work relating to disarmament already undertaken by the League of Nations and to seek the realisation thereof in a general agreement.

Done at Locarno, October 16, 1925.

Dr. LUTHER.
STRESEMANN.

Emile VANDERVELDE.
Aristide BRIAND.
Austen CHAMBERLAIN.
Benito MUSSOLINI.
Al. SKRZYNSKI.
Eduard BENEŠ.

33. THE PACT OF PARIS, 27 AUGUST 1928 [1]

On 6 April 1927, the tenth anniversary of the entrance of the United States into World War I, Aristide Briand, perennial French Foreign Minister, proposed that France and the United States use the forthcoming renewal of the Franco-American Treaty of 1908 as the occasion for negotiating an agreement "outlawing war" between the two countries. Briand's suggestion led to this "General Pact for the Renunciation of War," signed by fifteen states at the Quai d'Orsay on 27 August 1928 and opened to adhesion by all nations. The Pact was generally welcomed as reflecting a new spirit of cooperation on the part of the United States, whose past negative attitude had been the principal block to a viable system of collective security. The existence of the Pact facilitated American cooperation with the League authorities during the next decade. The Pact was also destined to play an important role in connection with the war crimes trials following World War II.

The President of the German Reich, the President of the United States of America, His Majesty the King of the Belgians, the President of the French Republic, His Majesty the King of Great Britain, Ireland and the British Dominions beyond the Seas, Emperor of India, His Majesty the King of Italy, His Majesty the Emperor of Japan, the President of the Republic of Poland, the President of the Czechoslovak Republic,

Deeply sensible of their solemn duty to promote the welfare of mankind;

Persuaded that the time has come when a frank renunciation of war as an instrument of national policy should be made to the end that the peaceful and friendly relations now existing between their peoples may be perpetuated;

Convinced that all changes in their relations with one another should be sought only by pacific means and be the result of a peaceful and orderly process, and that any signatory Power which shall hereafter seek to promote its national interests by resort to war should be denied the benefits furnished by this Treaty;

Hopeful that, encouraged by their example, all the other nations of the world will join in this humane endeavor and by adhering to the present Treaty as soon as it comes into force bring their peoples within the scope of its beneficent provisions, thus uniting the civilized nations of the world in a common renunciation of war as an instrument of their national policy;

Have decided to conclude a Treaty and for that purpose have appointed as their respective Plenipotentiaries:

ART. I. The High Contracting Parties solemnly declare in the names of their respective peoples that they condemn recourse to war for the solution of international controversies, and renounce it as an instrument of national policy in their relations with one another.

ART. II. The High Contracting Parties agree that the settlement or solution of all disputes or conflicts of whatever nature or of whatever origin they may be, which may arise among them, shall never be sought except by pacific means.

ART. III. The present Treaty shall be ratified by the High Contracting Parties named in the Preamble in accordance with their respective constitutional requirements, and shall take effect as between them as soon as all

[1] United States Statutes at Large, XLVI   (1929-1931), pp. 2343-2347.

their several instruments of ratification shall have been deposited at Washington.

This Treaty shall, when it has come into effect as prescribed in the preceding paragraph, remain open as long as may be necessary for adherence by all the other Powers of the world. Every instrument evidencing the adherence of a Power shall be deposited at Washington and the Treaty shall immediately upon such deposit become effective as between the Power thus adhering and the other Powers parties hereto.

It shall be the duty of the Government of the United States to furnish each Government named in the Preamble and every Government subsequently adhering to this Treaty with a certified copy of the Treaty and of every instrument of ratification or adherence. It shall also be the duty of the Government of the United States telegraphically to notify such Governments immediately upon the deposit with it of each instrument of ratification or adherence.

In faith whereof the respective Plenipotentiaries have signed this Treaty in the French and English language, both texts having equal force, and hereunto affix their seals.

DONE at Paris, the twenty-seventh day of August in the year one thousand nine hundred and twenty-eight.

Chapter 10

Functions: Economic and Social

34. THE MANDATE FOR GERMAN EAST AFRICA (TANGANYIKA), 20 JULY 1922 [1]

The mandates system was established by Article XXII of the Covenant for certain territories surrendered by Germany and Turkey. It had for its object ensuring the well-being and development of the inhabitants, who were deemed unready for self-government and independence. Responsibility for the proper operation of the system was entrusted to the League of Nations. The territories themselves were handed over by the Principal Allied and Associated Powers to individual states to be administered in accordance with mandates approved by the Council, of which this one for German East Africa is a good example.

The Council of the League of Nations:

Whereas by Article 119 of the Treaty of Peace with Germany signed at Versailles on June 28th, 1919, Germany renounced in favour of the Principal Allied and Associated Powers all her rights over her oversea possessions, including therein German East Africa; and

Whereas, in accordance with the treaty of June 11th, 1891, between Her Britannic Majesty and His Majesty the King of Portugal, the River Rovuma is recognised as forming the northern boundary of the Portuguese possessions in East Africa from its mouth up to the confluence of the River M'Sinje; and

Whereas the Principal Allied and Associated Powers agreed that, in accordance with Article 22, Part I (Covenant of the League of Nations), of the said treaty, a mandate should be conferred upon His Britannic Majesty to administer part of the former colony of German East Africa, and have proposed that the mandate should be formulated in the following terms; and

Whereas His Britannic Majesty has agreed to accept the mandate in respect of the said territory, and has undertaken to exercise it on behalf of the League of Nations in accordance with the following provisions; and

Whereas by the afore-mentioned Article 22, paragraph 8, it is provided that the degree of authority, control or administration to be exercised by the Mandatory, not having been previously agreed upon by the Members of the League, shall be explicitly defined by the Council of the League of Nations;

Confirming the said mandate, defines its terms as follows:

ART. 1. The territory over which a mandate is conferred upon His Britannic Majesty (hereinafter called the Mandatory) comprises that part of the territory of the former colony of German East Africa situated to the east of the following line:

From the point where the frontier

[1] League of Nations, *Official Journal,* III (1922), pp. 865-868. The League of Nations mandate should be compared with the United Nations Trust Agreement for the same territory (Doc. 63).

between the Uganda Protectorate and German East Africa cuts the River Mavumba, a straight line in a south-easterly direction to point 1640, about 15 kilometres south-south-west of Mount Gabiro;

Thence a straight line in a southerly direction to the north shore of Lake Mohazi, where it terminates at the confluence of a river situated about 2½ kilometres west of the confluence of the River Msilala;

If the trace of the railway on the west of the River Kagera between Bugufi and Uganda approaches within 16 kilometres of the line defined above, the boundary will be carried to the west, following a minimum distance of 16 kilometres from the trace, without, however, passing to the west of the straight line joining the terminal point on Lake Mohazi and the top of Mount Kivisa, point 2100, situated on the Uganda-German East Africa frontier about 5 kilometres south-west of the point where the River Mavumba cuts this frontier;

Thence a line south-eastwards to meet the southern shore of Lake Mohazi;

Thence the watershed between the Taruka and the Mkarange and continuing southwards to the north-eastern end of Lake Mugesera;

Thence the median line of this lake and continuing southwards across Lake Ssake to meet the Kagera;

Thence the course of the Kagera downstream to meet the western boundary of Bugufi;

Thence this boundary to its junction with the eastern boundary of Urundi;

Thence the eastern and southern boundary of Urundi to Lake Tanganyika.

The line described above is shown on the attached British 1:1,000,000 map, G.S.G.S. 2932, sheet Ruanda and Urundi. The boundaries of Bugufi and Urundi are drawn as shown in the Deutscher Kolonialatlas (Dietrich-Reimer), scale 1:1,000,000, dated 1906.

ART. 2. Boundary Commissioners shall be appointed by His Britannic Majesty and His Majesty the King of the Belgians to trace on the spot the line described in Article 1 above.

In case any dispute should arise in connection with the work of these commissioners, the question shall be referred to the Council of the League of Nations, whose decision shall be final.

The final report by the Boundary Commission shall give the precise description of this boundary as actually demarcated on the ground; the necessary maps shall be annexed thereto and signed by the commissioners. The report, with its annexes, shall be made in triplicate; one copy shall be deposited in the archives of the League of Nations, one shall be kept by the Government of His Majesty the King of the Belgians and one by the Government of His Britannic Majesty.

ART. 3. The Mandatory shall be responsible for the peace, order and good government of the territory, and shall undertake to promote to the utmost the material and moral well-being and the social progress of its inhabitants. The Mandatory shall have full powers of legislation and administration.

ART. 4. The Mandatory shall not establish any military or naval bases, nor erect any fortifications, nor organise any native military force in the territory except for local police purposes and for the defence of the territory.

ART. 5. The Mandatory:

(1) shall provide for the eventual emancipation of all slaves and for as speedy an elimination of domestic and other slavery as social conditions will allow;

(2) shall suppress all forms of slave trade;

(3) shall prohibit all forms of forced or compulsory labour, except for essential public works and services, and then only in return for adequate remuneration;

(4) shall protect the natives from abuse and measures of fraud and force by the careful supervision of labour

contracts and the recruiting of labour;

(5) shall exercise a strict control over the traffic in arms and ammunition and the sale of spirituous liquors.

Art. 6. In the framing of laws relating to the holding or transfer of land, the Mandatory shall take into consideration native laws and customs, and shall respect the rights and safeguard the interests of the native population.

No native land may be transferred, except between natives, without the previous consent of the public authorities, and no real rights over native land in favour of non-natives may be created except with the same consent. The Mandatory will promulgate strict regulations against usury.

Art. 7. The Mandatory shall secure to all nationals of States Members of the League of Nations the same rights as are enjoyed in the territory by his own nationals in respect of entry into and residence in the territory, the protection afforded to their person and property, the acquisition of property, movable and immovable, and the exercise of their profession or trade, subject only to the requirements of public order, and on condition of compliance with the local law.

Further, the Mandatory shall ensure to all nationals of States Members of the League of Nations, on the same footing as to his own nationals, freedom of transit and navigation, and complete economic, commercial and industrial equality; provided that the Mandatory shall be free to organise essential public works and services on such terms and conditions as he thinks just.

Concessions for the development of the natural resources of the territory shall be granted by the Mandatory without distinction on grounds of nationality between the nationals of all States Members of the League of Nations, but on such conditions as will maintain intact the authority of the local Government.

Concessions having the character of a general monopoly shall not be granted. This provision does not affect the right of the Mandatory to create monopolies of a purely fiscal character in the interest of the territory under mandate, and in order to provide the territory with fiscal resources which seem best suited to the local requirements; or, in certain cases, to carry out the development of natural resources either directly by the State or by a controlled agency, provided that there shall result therefrom no monopoly of the natural resources for the benefit of the Mandatory or his nationals, directly or indirectly, nor any preferential advantage which shall be inconsistent with the economic, commercial and industrial equality hereinbefore guaranteed.

The rights conferred by this article extend equally to companies and associations organised in accordance with the law of any of the Members of the League of Nations, subject only to the requirements of public order, and on condition of compliance with the local law.

Art. 8. The Mandatory shall ensure in the territory complete freedom of conscience and the free exercise of all forms of worship which are consonant with public order and morality; missionaries who are nationals of States Members of the League of Nations shall be free to enter the territory and to travel and reside therein, to acquire and possess property, to erect religious buildings and to open schools throughout the territory; it being understood, however, that the Mandatory shall have the right to exercise such control as may be necessary for the maintenance of public order and good government, and to take all measures required for such control.

Art. 9. The Mandatory shall apply to the territory any general international conventions already existing, or which may be concluded hereafter, with the approval of the League of Nations, respecting the slave trade, the traffic in arms and ammunition, the liquor traffic, and the traffic in drugs, or relating to commercial equality, freedom of transit and navigation, aerial navigation, railways, postal, telegraphic and wireless communication, and industrial, literary and artistic property.

The Mandatory shall co-operate in the execution of any common policy adopted by the League of Nations for preventing and combating disease, including diseases of plants and animals.

ART. 10. The Mandatory shall be authorised to constitute the territory into a customs fiscal and administrative union or federation with the adjacent territories under his own sovereignty or control; provided always that the measures adopted to that end do not infringe the provisions of this mandate.

ART. 11. The Mandatory shall make to the Council of the League of Nations an annual report to the satisfaction of the Council, containing full information concerning the measures taken to apply the provisions of this mandate.

A copy of all laws and regulations made in the course of the year and affecting property, commerce, navigation or the moral and material well-being of the natives shall be annexed to this report.

ART. 12. The consent of the Council of the League of Nations is required for any modification of the terms of this mandate.

ART. 13. The Mandatory agrees that if any dispute whatever should arise between the Mandatory and another Member of the League of Nations relating to the interpretation or the application of the provisions of the mandate, such dispute, if it cannot be settled by negotiation, shall be submitted to the Permanent Court of International Justice provided for by Article 14 of the Covenant of the League of Nations.

States Members of the League of Nations may likewise bring any claims on behalf of their nationals for infractions of their rights under this mandate before the said Court for decision.

The present instrument shall be deposited in original in the archives of the League of Nations. Certified copies shall be forwarded by the Secretary-General of the League of Nations to all Members of the League.

Done at London, the twentieth day of July one thousand nine hundred and twenty-two.

Chapter 11

The United States and the League of Nations

35. THE PROPOSED SENATE RESOLUTION ADVISING AND CONSENTING TO THE TREATY OF VERSAILLES WITH THE "LODGE RESERVATIONS," 1919 [1]

President Wilson submitted the Treaty of Versailles, with the Covenant, to the Senate for its advice and consent on 10 July 1919. Because of the popular support which Wilson's peace program enjoyed throughout the country, the opponents of the President, led by Senator Henry Cabot Lodge, of Massachusetts, Chairman of the Senate Foreign Relations Committee, embarked upon a campaign to kill the treaty first by delaying tactics and then by attaching reservations which would be unacceptable to the President and his supporters. In the end, after having been defeated both with and without reservations on 19 November 1919 and then reconsidered, the treaty was finally killed on 19 March 1920 by a vote of 49 in favor of the treaty with reservations to 35 against, 7 votes less than the required two-thirds. Because of these "Lodge reservations" many Democratic senators voted against the treaty at the bidding of the President.

Resolved (two-thirds of the Senators present concurring therein), That the Senate advise and consent to the ratification of the treaty of peace with Germany concluded at Versailles on the 28th day of June, 1919, subject to the following reservations and understandings, which are hereby made a part and condition of this resolution of ratification, which ratification is not to take effect or bind the United States until the said reservations and understandings adopted by the Senate have

been accepted by an exchange of notes as a part and a condition of this resolution of ratification by at least three of the four principal allied and associated powers, to wit, Great Britain, France, Italy, and Japan:

1. The United States so understands and construes article 1 that in case of notice of withdrawal from the league of nations, as provided in said article, the United States shall be the sole judge as to whether all its international obligations and all its obligations under the said covenant have been fulfilled, and notice of withdrawal by the United States may be given by a concurrent resolution of the Congress of the United States.

2. The United States assumes no obligation to preserve the territorial integrity or political independence of any other country or to interfere in controversies between nations—whether members of the league or not—under the provisions of article 10, or to employ the military or naval forces of the United States under any article of the treaty for any purpose, unless in any particular case the Congress, which, under the Constitution, has the sole power to declare war or authorize the employment of the military or naval

[1] *Congressional Record,* 66th Cong. 1st sess. I . . . (November 1919), 8773; 2nd sess. LIX (19 March 1920), 4599.

forces of the United States, shall by act or joint resolution so provide.

3. No mandate shall be accepted by the United States under article 22, part 1, or any other provision of the treaty of peace with Germany, except by action of the Congress of the United States.

4. The United States reserves to itself exclusively the right to decide what questions are within its domestic jurisdiction and declares that all domestic and political questions relating wholly or in part to its internal affairs, including immigration, labor, coastwise traffic, the tariff, commerce, the suppression of traffic in women and children, and in opium and other dangerous drugs, and all other domestic questions, are solely within the jurisdiction of the United States and are not under this treaty to be submitted in any way either to arbitration or to the consideration of the council or of the assembly of the league of nations, or any agency thereof, or to the decision or recommendation of any other power.

5. The United States will not submit to arbitration or to inquiry by the assembly or by the council of the league of nations, provided for in said treaty of peace, any questions which in the judgment of the United States depend upon or relate to its long-established policy, commonly known as the Monroe doctrine; said doctrine is to be interpreted by the United States alone and is hereby declared to be wholly outside the jurisdiction of said league of nations and entirely unaffected by any provision contained in the said treaty of peace with Germany.

6. The United States withholds its assent to articles 156, 157, and 158, and reserves full liberty of action with respect to any controversy which may arise under said articles between the Republic of China and the Empire of Japan.

7. The Congress of the United States will provide by law for the appointment of the representatives of the United States in the assembly and the council of the league of nations, and may in its discretion provide for the participation of the United States in any commission, committee, tribunal, court, council, or conference, or in the selection of any members thereof and for the appointment of members of said commissions, committees, tribunals, courts, councils, or conferences, or any other representatives under the treaty of peace, or in carrying out its provisions, and until such participation and appointment have been so provided for and the powers and duties of such representatives have been defined by law, no person shall represent the United States under either said league of nations or the treaty of peace with Germany or be authorized to perform any act for or on behalf of the United States thereunder, and no citizen of the United States shall be selected or appointed as a member of said commissions, committees, tribunals, courts, councils, or conferences except with the approval of the Senate of the United States.

8. The United States understands that the reparation commission will regulate or interfere with exports from the United States to Germany, or from Germany to the United States, only when the United States by act or joint resolution of Congress approves such regulation or interference.

9. The United States shall not be obligated to contribute to any expenses of the league of nations, or of the secretariat, or of any commission, or committee, or conference, or other agency, organized under the league of nations or under the treaty or for the purpose of carrying out the treaty provisions, unless and until an appropriation of funds available for such expenses shall have been made by the Congress of the United States.

10. If the United States shall at any time adopt any plan for the limitation of armaments proposed by the council of the league of nations under the provisions of article 8, it reserves the right to increase such armaments without

the consent of the council whenever the United States is threatened with invasion or engaged in war.

11. The United States reserves the right to permit, in its discretion, the nationals of a covenant-breaking State, as defined in article 16 of the covenant of the league of nations, residing within the United States or in countries other than that violating said article 16, to continue their commercial, financial, and personal relations with the nationals of the United States.

12. Nothing in articles 296, 297, or in any of the annexes thereto or in any other article, section, or annex of the treaty of peace with Germany shall, as against citizens of the United States, be taken to mean any confirmation, ratification, or approval of any act otherwise illegal or in contravention of the rights of citizens of the United States.

13. The United States withholds its assent to Part XIII (articles 387 to 427, inclusive) unless Congress by act or joint resolution shall hereafter make provision for representation in the organization established by said Part XIII, and in such event the participation of the United States will be governed and conditioned by the provisions of such act or joint resolution.

14. The United States assumes no obligation to be bound by any election, decision, report, or finding of the council or assembly in which any member of the league and its self-governing dominions, colonies, or parts of empire, in the aggregate have cast more than one vote, and assumes no obligation to be bound by any decision, report, or finding of the council or assembly arising out of any dispute between the United States and any member of the league if such member, or any self-governing dominion, colony, empire, or part of empire united with it politically has voted.

Chapter 12

The Continuing Organs of the League System: The World Court

36. THE STATUTE OF THE INTERNATIONAL COURT OF JUSTICE,[1] 16 DECEMBER 1920, AS AMENDED[2]

In accordance with Article XIV of the Covenant, the League of Nations Council in February 1920 appointed a Commission of Jurists, including Elihu Root, to draft a plan for a Permanent Court of International Justice. The plan proposed by the Commission of Jurists was based in part on the 1907 draft "Convention Relative to the Creation of a Judicial Arbitration Court."[3] The Statute of the Court, adopted by the first Assembly with some amendments, came into force in September 1921 when its Protocol of Signature had been ratified by 28 states. The Statute was amended in 1929 and again in 1945, when the name of the Court was changed to International Court of Justice and the Statute was annexed to the United Nations Charter.[4]

ART. 1.[5] *The International Court of Justice established by the Charter of the United Nations as the principal judicial organ of the United Nations shall be constituted and shall function in accordance with the provisions of the present Statute.*

CHAPTER I. ORGANIZATION OF THE COURT

ART. 2. The Court shall be composed of a body of independent judges, elected regardless of their nationality from among persons of high moral character, who possess the qualifications required in their respective countries for appointment to the highest judicial offices, or are juris-consults of recognized competence in international law.

ART. 3.[6] 1. The Court shall consist of fifteen members, *no two of whom may be nationals of the same state.*

2. *A person who for the purposes of membership in the Court could be regarded as a national of more than one state shall be deemed to be a national of the one in which he ordinarily exercises civil and political rights.*

ART. 4. 1. The members of the Court

---

[1] Before 1945, it was known as the Permanent Court of International Justice.

[2] *Yearbook of the United Nations, 1946-1947,* pp. 833-850.

[3] Doc. 13. Mr. Root and Lord Phillimore suggested the procedure for selecting the judges which resolved the difficulties that beset the 1907 negotiations.

[4] Amendments to the 1929 Statute are indicated by italics, except for minor alterations such as "among" for "amongst," General Assembly" for "Assembly," etc. In cases other than mere additions, the original text is given

in footnotes. Asterisks before an article indicate changes from the 1920 text.

[5] A Permanent Court of International Justice is hereby established, in accordance with Article 14 of the Covenant of the League of Nations. This Court shall be in addition to the Court of Arbitration organized by the Conventions of The Hague of 1899 and 1907, and to the special Tribunals of Arbitration to which States are always at liberty to submit their disputes for settlement.

[6] The Court shall consist of fifteen members.

shall be elected by the General Assembly and by the Security Council from a list of persons nominated by the national groups in the Permanent Court of Arbitration, in accordance with the following provisions.

2. In the case of Members of the United Nations not represented in the Permanent Court of Arbitration, candidates shall be nominated by national groups appointed for this purpose by their governments under the same conditions as those prescribed for members of the Permanent Court of Arbitration by Article 44 of the Convention of The Hague of 1907 for the pacific settlement of international disputes.

3. The conditions under which a State which is a party to the present Statute but is not a Member of the United Nations may participate in electing the members of the Court shall, in the absence of a special agreement, be laid down by the General Assembly upon recommendation of the Security Council.

ART. 5. 1. At least three months before the date of the election, the Secretary-General of the United Nations shall address a written request to the members of the Permanent Court of Arbitration belonging to the states *which are parties to the present Statute,* and to the members of the national groups appointed under Article 4, paragraph 2, inviting them to undertake, within a given time, by national groups, the nomination of persons in a position to accept the duties of a member of the Court.

2. No group may nominate more than four persons, not more than two of whom shall be of their own nationality. In no case may the number of candidates nominated by a group be more than double the number of seats to be filled.

ART. 6. Before making these nominations, each national group is recommended to consult its highest court of justice, its legal faculties and schools of law, and its national academies and

national sections of international academies devoted to the study of law.

ART. 7. 1. The Secretary-General shall prepare a list in alphabetical order of all the persons thus nominated. Save as provided in Article 12, paragraph 2, these shall be the only persons eligible.

2. The Secretary-General shall submit this list to the General Assembly and to the Security Council.

ART. 8. The General Assembly and the Security Council shall proceed independently of one another to elect the members of the Court.

ART. 9. At every election, the electors shall bear in mind not only that the persons to be elected should individually possess the qualifications required, but also that in the body as a whole the representation of the main forms of civilization and of the principal legal systems of the world should be assured.

ART. 10. 1. Those candidates who obtain an absolute majority of votes in the General Assembly and in the Security Council shall be considered as elected.

2. *Any vote of the Security Council, whether for the election of judges or for the appointment of members of the conference envisaged in Article 12, shall be taken without any distinction between permanent and non-permanent members of the Security Council.*

3. In the event of more than one national of the same state obtaining an absolute majority of the votes both of the General Assembly and of the Security Council, the eldest of these only shall be considered as elected.

ART. 11. If, after the first meeting held for the purpose of the election, one or more seats remain to be filled, a second and, if necessary, a third meeting shall take place.

ART. 12. 1. If, after the third meeting, one or more seats still remain unfilled, a joint conference consisting of six members, three appointed by the General Assembly and three by the Security Council, may be formed at any time at the request of either the General Assembly or the Security Council, for the purpose of choosing *by the vote of an absolute majority* one name for each seat still vacant, to submit to the General Assembly and the Security Council for their respective acceptance.

2. If the joint conference is unanimously agreed upon any person who fulfils the required conditions, he may be included in its list, even though he was not included in the list of nominations referred to in Article 7.

3. If the joint conference is satisfied that it will not be successful in procuring an election, those members of the Court who have already been elected shall, within a period to be fixed by the Security Council, proceed to fill the vacant seats by selection from among those candidates who have obtained votes either in the General Assembly or in the Security Council.

4. In the event of an equality of votes among the judges, the eldest judge shall have a casting vote.

ART. 13. 1. The members of the Court shall be elected for nine years and may be re-elected; *provided, however, that of the judges elected at the first election, the terms of five judges shall expire at the end of three years and the terms of five more judges shall expire at the end of six years.*

2. *The judges whose terms are to expire at the end of the above-mentioned initial periods of three and six years shall be chosen by lot to be drawn by the Secretary-General immediately after the first election has been completed.*

3. The members of the Court shall continue to discharge their duties until their places have been filled. Though replaced, they shall finish any cases which they may have begun.

4. In the case of the resignation of a member of the Court, the resignation shall be addressed to the President of the Court for transmission to the Secretary-General. This last notification makes the place vacant.

ART. 14. Vacancies shall be filled by the same method as that laid down for the first election, subject to the following provision: the Secretary-General shall, within one month of the occurrence of the vacancy, proceed to issue the invitations provided for in Article 5, and the date of the election shall be fixed by the Security Council.

ART. 15. A member of the Court elected to replace a member whose term of office has not expired shall hold office for the remainder of his predecessor's term.

ART. 16. 1. No member of the Court may exercise any political or administrative function, or engage in any other occupation of a professional nature.

2. Any doubt on this point shall be settled by the decision of the Court.

ART. 17. 1. No member of the Court may act as agent, counsel, or advocate in any case.

2. No member may participate in the decision of any case in which he has previously taken part as agent, counsel, or advocate for one of the parties, or as a member of a national or international court, or of a commission of enquiry, or in any other capacity.

3. Any doubt on this point shall be settled by the decision of the Court.

ART. 18. 1. No member of the Court can be dismissed unless, in the unanimous opinion of the other members, he has ceased to fulfil the required conditions.

2. Formal notification thereof shall be made to the Secretary-General by the Registrar.

3. This notification makes the place vacant.

ART. 19. The members of the Court, when engaged on the business of the Court, shall enjoy diplomatic privileges and immunities.

ART. 20. Every member of the Court shall, before taking up his duties, make a solemn declaration in open court that he will exercise his powers impartially and conscientiously.

ART. 21. 1. The Court shall elect its President and Vice-President for three years; they may be re-elected.

2. The Court shall appoint its Registrar and may provide for the appointment of such other officers as may be necessary.

ART. 22. 1. The seat of the Court shall be established at The Hague. *This, however, shall not prevent the Court from sitting and exercising its functions elsewhere whenever the Court considers it desirable.*

2. The President and the Registrar shall reside at the seat of the Court.

ART. 23. 1. The Court shall remain permanently in session, except during the judicial vacations, the dates and duration of which shall be fixed by the Court.

2. Members of the Court are entitled to periodic leave, the dates and duration of which shall be fixed by the Court, having in mind the distance between The Hague and the home of each judge.

3. Members of the Court shall be bound, unless they are on leave or prevented from attending by illness or other serious reasons duly explained to the President, to hold themselves permanently at the disposal of the Court.

ART. 24. 1. If, for some special reason, a member of the Court considers that he should not take part in the decision of a particular case, he shall so inform the President.

2. If the President considers that for some special reason one of the members of the Court should not sit in a particular case, he shall give him notice accordingly.

3. If in any such case the member of the Court and the President disagree, the matter shall be settled by the decision of the Court.

ART. 25. 1. The full Court shall sit except when it is expressly provided otherwise in the present Statute.

2. Subject to the condition that the number of judges available to constitute the Court is not thereby reduced below eleven, the Rules of the Court may provide for allowing one or more judges, according to circumstances and in rotation, to be dispensed from sitting.

3. A quorum of nine judges shall suffice to constitute the Court.

ART. 26.[7] 1. *The Court may from*

---

[7] Article 26 of the 1945 Statute is a consolidation of Articles 26 and 27 of the 1929 Statute; certain substantive alterations are included. Articles 26 and 27 of the 1929 Statute follow:

Art. 26: Labor cases, particularly cases referred to in Part XIII (Labor) of the Treaty of Versailles and the corresponding portions of the other treaties of peace, shall be heard and determined by the Court under the following conditions:

The Court will appoint every three years a special Chamber of five judges, selected so far as possible with due regard to the provisions of Article 9. In addition, two judges shall be selected for the purpose of replacing a judge who finds it impossible to sit. If the parties so demand, cases will be heard and determined by this Chamber. In the absence of any such demand, the full Court will sit. In both cases, the judges will be assisted by four technical assessors sitting with them, but without the right to vote, and chosen with a view to ensuring a just representation of the competing interests.

The technical assessors shall be chosen for each particular case in accordance with rules of procedure under Article 30, from a list of "Assessors for Labor Cases" composed of two persons nominated by each Member of the League of Nations and an equivalent number nominated by the Governing Body of the Labor Office. The Governing Body will nominate, as to one-half, representatives of employers from the list referred to in Article 412 of the Treaty of Versailles and the corresponding articles of the other treaties of peace.

Recourse may always be had to the summary procedure provided for in Article 29, in the cases referred to in the first paragraph of the present Article, if the parties so request.

In Labor cases, the International Office shall be at liberty to furnish the Court with all relevant information, and for this purpose the Director of that Office shall receive copies of all the written proceedings.

Art. 27: Cases relating to transit and communications, particularly cases referred to in Part XII (Ports, Waterways and Railways) of the Treaty of Versailles and the corresponding portions of the other treaties of peace, shall be heard and determined by the Court under the following conditions:

The Court will appoint every three years a special Chamber of five judges, selected so far as possible with due regard to the pro-

time to time form one or more chambers, composed of three or more judges as the Court may determine, for dealing with particular categories of cases; for example, labor cases and cases relating to transit and communications.

2. The Court may at any time form a chamber for dealing with a particular case. The number of judges to constitute such a chamber shall be determined by the Court with the approval of the parties.

3. Cases shall be heard and determined by the chambers provided for in this Article if the parties so request.

ART. 27.[8] *A judgment given by any of the chambers provided for in Articles 26 and 29 shall be considered as rendered by the Court.*

ART. 28. The chambers provided for in Articles 26 and 29 may, with the consent of the parties, sit and exercise their functions elsewhere than at The Hague.

ART. 29. With a view to the speedy despatch of business, the Court shall form annually a chamber composed of five judges which, at the request of the parties, may hear and determine cases by summary procedure. In addition, two judges shall be selected for the purpose of replacing judges who find it impossible to sit.

ART. 30. 1. The Court shall frame rules for carrying out its functions. In particular, it shall lay down rules of procedure.

2. The Rules of the Court may provide for assessors to sit with the Court or with any of its chambers, without the right to vote.

ART. 31. 1. Judges of the nationality of each of the parties shall retain their right to sit in the case before the Court.

2. If the Court includes upon the Bench a judge of the nationality of one of the parties, any other party may choose a person to sit as judge. Such person shall be chosen preferably from among those persons who have been nominated as candidates as provided in Articles 4 and 5.

3. If the Court includes upon the Bench no judge of the nationality of the parties, each of these parties may proceed to choose a judge as provided in paragraph 2 of this Article.

4. The provisions of this Article shall apply to the case of Articles 26 and 29. In such cases, the President shall request one or, if necessary, two of the members of the Court forming the chamber to give place to the members of the Court of the nationality of the parties concerned, and, failing such, or if they are unable to be present, to the judges specially chosen by the parties.

5. Should there be several parties in the same interest, they shall, for the purpose of the preceding provisions, be reckoned as one party only. Any doubt upon this point shall be settled by the decision of the Court.

6. Judges chosen as laid down in paragraphs 2, 3, and 4 of this Article shall fulfil the conditions required by Articles 2, 17 (paragraph 2), 20, and 24 of the present Statute. They shall take part in the decision on terms of complete equality with their colleagues.

---

visions of Article 9. In addition, two judges shall be selected for the purpose of replacing a judge who finds it impossible to sit. If the parties so demand, cases will be heard and determined by this Chamber. In the absence of any such demand, the full Court will sit. When desired by the parties or decided by the Court, the judges will be assisted by four technical assessors sitting with them, but without the right to vote.

The technical assessors shall be chosen for each particular case in accordance with rules of procedure under Article 30, from a list of "Assessors for Transit and Communications

Cases" composed of two persons nominated by each Member of the League of Nations.

Recourse may always be had to the summary procedure provided for in Article 29, in the cases referred to in the first paragraph of the present Article, if the parties so request.

[8] Addition, 1945. In view of the consolidation of Articles 26 and 27 of the 1929 Statute, the addition of the new Article 27 in the 1945 Statute resulted in subsequent Articles numbers running parallel to the 1929 version.

Art. 32.[9] 1. Each member of the Court shall receive an annual salary.

2. The President shall receive a special annual allowance.

3. The Vice-President shall receive a special allowance for every day on which he acts as President.

4. The judges chosen under Article 31, other than members of the Court, shall receive compensation for each day on which they exercise their functions.

5. These salaries, allowances, and compensation shall be fixed by the General Assembly. They may not be decreased during the term of office.

6. The salary of the Registrar shall be fixed by the General Assembly on the proposal of the Court.

7. Regulations made by the General Assembly shall fix the conditions under which retirement pensions may be given to members of the Court and to the Registrar, and the conditions under which members of the Court and the Registrar shall have their traveling expenses refunded.

8. The above salaries, allowances, and compensation shall be free of all taxation.

Art. 33.[10] The expenses of the Court shall be borne by the United Nations in such a manner as shall be decided by the General Assembly.

CHAPTER II. COMPETENCE OF THE COURT

Art. 34. 1. Only states may be parties in cases before the Court.

2. *The Court, subject to and in conformity with its Rules, may request of public international organizations information relevant to cases before it, and shall receive such information presented by such organizations on their own initiative.*

3. *Whenever the construction of the constituent instrument of a public in-* *ternational organization or of an international convention adopted thereunder is in question in a case before the Court, the Registrar shall so notify the public international organization concerned and shall communicate to it copies of all the written proceedings.*

Art. 35.[11] 1. The Court shall be open to the *states parties to the present Statute.*

2. The conditions under which the Court shall be open to other states shall, subject to the special provisions contained in treaties in force, be laid down by the Security Council, but in no case shall such conditions place the parties in a position of inequality before the Court.

3. When a state which is not a Member of the United Nations is a party to a case, the Court shall fix the amount which that party is to contribute towards the expenses of the Court. This provision shall not apply if such state is bearing a share of the expenses of the Court.

Art. 36. 1. The jurisdiction of the Court comprises all cases which the parties refer to it and all matters specially provided for *in the Charter of the United Nations or* in treaties and conventions in force.

2. The states parties to the present Statute may at any time declare that they recognize as compulsory *ipso facto* and without special agreement, in relation to any other state accepting the same obligation, the jurisdiction of the Court in all legal disputes concerning:

a. the interpretation of a treaty;

b. any question of international law;

c. the existence of any fact which, if established, would constitute a breach of an international obligation;

d. the nature or extent of the reparation to be made for the breach of an international obligation.

---

[9] Paragraph 5. These salaries, allowances and indemnities shall be fixed by the Assembly on the proposal of the Council.

[10] The expenses of the Court shall be borne by the League of Nations in such a manner as shall be decided by the Assembly upon the proposal of the Council.

[11] Paragraph 1: The Court shall be open to the Members of the League and also to States mentioned in the Annex to the Covenant.

3. The declarations referred to above may be made unconditionally or on condition of reciprocity on the part of several or certain states, or for a certain time.

4. *Such declarations shall be deposited with the Secretary-General of the United Nations, who shall transmit copies thereof to the parties to the Statute and to the Registrar of the Court.*

5. *Declarations made under Article 36 of the Statute of the Permanent Court of International Justice and which are still in force shall be deemed, as between the parties to the present Statute, to be acceptances of the compulsory jurisdiction of the International Court of Justice for the period which they still have to run and in accordance with their terms.*

6. In the event of a dispute as to whether the Court has jurisdiction, the matter shall be settled by the decision of the Court.

ART. 37. Whenever a treaty or convention in force provides for reference of a matter to a tribunal to have been instituted by the League of Nations, or to the Permanent Court of International Justice, the matter shall, as between the parties to the present Statute, be referred to the International Court of Justice.

ART. 38. 1. The Court, whose function is to decide in accordance with international law such disputes as are submitted to it, shall apply:

a. international conventions, whether general or particular, establishing rules expressly recognized by the contesting states;

b. international custom, as evidence of a general practice accepted as law;

c. the general principles of law recognized by civilized nations;

d. subject to the provisions of Article 59, judicial decisions and the teachings of the most highly qualified publicists of the various nations, as subsidiary means for the determination of rules of law.

2. This provision shall not prejudice the power of the Court to decide a case *ex aequo et bono,* if the parties agree thereto.

CHAPTER III. PROCEDURE

ART. 39. 1. The official languages of the Court shall be French and English. If the parties agree that the case shall be conducted in French, the judgment shall be delivered in French. If the parties agree that the case shall be conducted in English, the judgment shall be delivered in English.

2. In the absence of an agreement as to which language shall be employed, each party may, in the pleadings, use the language which it prefers; the decision of the Court shall be given in French and English. In this case the Court shall at the same time determine which of the two texts shall be considered as authoritative.

3. The Court shall, at the request of any party, authorize a language other than French or English to be used by that party.

ART. 40. 1. Cases are brought before the Court, as the case may be, either by the notification of the special agreement or by a written application addressed to the Registrar. In either case the subject of the dispute and the parties shall be indicated.

2. The Registrar shall forthwith communicate the application to all concerned.

3. He shall also notify the Members of the United Nations through the Secretary-General, and also any other states entitled to appear before the Court.

ART. 41. 1. The Court shall have the power to indicate, if it considers that circumstances so require, any provisional measures which ought to be taken to preserve the respective rights of either party.

2. Pending the final decision, notice of the measures suggested shall forthwith be given to the parties and to the Security Council.

ART. 42. 1. The parties shall be represented by agents.

2. They may have the assistance of counsel or advocates before the Court.

3. *The agents, counsel, and advocates of parties before the Court shall enjoy the privileges and immunities necessary to the independent exercise of their duties.*

ART. 43. 1. The procedure shall consist of two parts: written and oral.

2. The written proceedings shall consist of the communication to the Court and to the parties of memorials, counter-memorials and, if necessary, replies; also all papers and documents in support.

3. These communications shall be made through the Registrar, in the order and within the time fixed by the Court.

4. A certified copy of every document produced by one party shall be communicated to the other party.

5. The oral proceedings shall consist of the hearing by the Court of witnesses, experts, agents, counsel, and advocates.

ART. 44. 1. For the service of all notices upon persons other than the agents, counsel, and advocates, the Court shall apply direct to the government of the state upon whose territory the notice has to be served.

2. The same provision shall apply whenever steps are to be taken to procure evidence on the spot.

ART. 45. The hearing shall be under the control of the President or, if he is unable to preside, of the Vice-President; if neither is able to preside, the senior judge present shall preside.

ART. 46. The hearing in Court shall be public, unless the Court shall decide otherwise, or unless the parties demand that the public be not admitted.

ART. 47. 1. Minutes shall be made at each hearing and signed by the Registrar and the President.

ART. 48. The Court shall make orders for the conduct of the case, shall decide the form and time in which each party must conclude its argu-ments, and make all arrangements connected with the taking of evidence.

ART. 49. The Court may, even before the hearing begins, call upon the agents to produce any document or to supply any explanations. Formal note shall be taken of any refusal.

ART. 50. The Court may, at any time, entrust any individual, body, bureau, commission, or other organization that it may select, with the task of carrying out an enquiry or giving an expert opinion.

ART. 51. During the hearing any relevant questions are to be put to the witnesses and experts under the conditions laid down by the Court in the rules of procedure referred to in Article 30.

ART. 52. After the Court has received the proofs and evidence within the time specified for the purpose, it may refuse to accept any further oral or written evidence that one party may desire to present unless the other side consents.

ART. 53. 1. Whenever one of the parties does not appear before the Court, or fails to defend its case, the other party may call upon the Court to decide in favor of its claim.

2. The Court must, before doing so, satisfy itself, not only that it has jurisdiction in accordance with Articles 36 and 37, but also that the claim is well founded in fact and law.

ART. 54. 1. When, subject to the control of the Court, the agents, counsel, and advocates have completed their presentation of the case, the President shall declare the hearing closed.

2. The Court shall withdraw to consider the judgment.

3. The deliberations of the Court shall take place in private and remain secret.

ART. 55. 1. All questions shall be decided by a majority of the judges present.

2. In the event of an equality of votes, the President or the judge who

acts in his place shall have a casting vote.

ART. 56. 1. The judgment shall state the reasons on which it is based.

2. It shall contain the names of the judges who have taken part in the decision.

ART. 57. If the judgment does not represent in whole or in part the unanimous opinion of the judges, any judge shall be entitled to deliver a separate opinion.

ART. 58. The judgment shall be signed by the President and by the Registrar. It shall be read in open court, due notice having been given to the agents.

ART. 59. The decision of the Court has no binding force except between the parties and in respect of that particular case.

ART. 60. The judgment is final and without appeal. In the event of dispute as to the meaning or scope of the judgment, the Court shall construe it upon the request of any party.

ART. 61. 1. An application for revision of a judgment may be made only when it is based upon the discovery of some fact of such a nature as to be a decisive factor, which fact was, when the judgment was given, unknown to the Court and also to the party claiming revision, always provided that such ignorance was not due to negligence.

2. The proceedings for revision shall be opened by a judgment of the Court expressly recording the existence of the new fact, recognizing that it has such a character as to lay the case open to revision, and declaring the application admissible on this ground.

3. The Court may require previous compliance with the terms of the judgment before it admits proceedings in revision.

4. The application for revision must be made at latest within six months of the discovery of the new fact.

5. No application for revision may be made after the lapse of ten years from the date of the judgment.

ART. 62. 1. Should a state consider that it has an interest of a legal nature which may be affected by the decision in the case, it may submit a request to the Court to be permitted to intervene.

2. It shall be for the Court to decide upon this request.

ART. 63. 1. Whenever the construction of a convention to which states other than those concerned in the case are parties is in question, the Registrar shall notify all such states forthwith.

2. Every state so notified has the right to intervene in the proceedings; but if it uses this right, the construction given by the judgment will be equally binding upon it.

ART. 64. Unless otherwise decided by the Court, each party shall bear its own costs.

CHAPTER IV. ADVISORY OPINIONS

ART. 65.[12] *1. The Court may give an advisory opinion on any legal question at the request of whatever body may be authorized by or in accordance with the Charter of the United Nations to make such a request.*

2. Questions upon which the advisory opinion of the Court is asked shall be laid before the Court by means of a written request containing an exact statement of the question upon which an opinion is required, and accompanied by all documents likely to throw light upon the question.

ART. 66. 1. The Registrar shall forthwith give notice of the request for an advisory opinion to all states entitled to appear before the Court.

2. The Registrar shall also, by means of a special and direct communication,

---

[12] Paragraph 1: Questions upon which the advisory opinion of the Court is asked shall be laid before the Court by means of a written request, signed either by the President of the Assembly or the President of the Council of the League of Nations, or by the Secretary-General of the League under instructions from the Assembly or the Council.

notify any state entitled to appear before the Court or international organization considered by the Court, or, should it not be sitting, by the President, as likely to be able to furnish information on the question, that the Court will be prepared to receive, within a time limit to be fixed by the President, written statements, or to hear, at a public sitting to be held for the purpose, oral statements relating to the question.

3. Should any such state entitled to appear before the Court have failed to receive the special communication referred to in paragraph 2 of this Article, such state may express a desire to submit a written statement or to be heard; and the Court will decide.

4. States and organizations having presented written or oral statements or both shall be permitted to comment on the statements made by other states or organizations in the form, to the extent, and within the time limits which the Court, or, should it not be sitting, the President, shall decide in each particular case. Accordingly, the Registrar shall in due time communicate any such written statements to states and organizations having submitted similar statements.

ART. 67. The Court shall deliver its advisory opinions in open court, notice having been given to the Secretary-General and to the representatives of Members of the United Nations, of other states and of international organizations immediately concerned.

ART. 68. In the exercise of its advisory functions the Court shall further be guided by the provisions of the present Statute which apply in contentious cases to the extent to which it recognizes them to be applicable.

CHAPTER V. AMENDMENT

ART. 69. *Amendments to the present Statute shall be effected by the same procedure as is provided by the Charter of the United Nations for amendments to that Charter, subject however to any provisions which the General Assembly upon recommendation of the Security Council may adopt concerning the participation of states which are parties to the present Statute but are not Members of the United Nations.*

ART. 70. *The Court shall have power to propose such amendments to the present Statute as it may deem necessary, through written communications to the Secretary-General, for consideration in conformity with the provisions of Article 69.*

37. THE SENATE RESERVATIONS TO THE PROTOCOL OF SIGNATURE, 27 JANUARY 1926 [1]

In February 1923, two years after receiving from the Secretary General of the League of Nations the Protocol of Signature for the World Court, Secretary of State Hughes recommended, and President Harding asked, that the Senate advise and consent to United States adhesion. Hughes' recommendation incorporated four reservations designed to placate Senate opposition. A fifth reservation was added before the Senate, three years later, voted its approval 76 to 17.[2]

Whereas the President, under date of February 24, 1923, transmitted a message to the Senate, accompanied by a letter from the Secretary of State, dated February 17th, 1923, asking the

---

[1] *Congressional Record,* 69th Cong., 1st sess., LXVII, pp. 2824 f.

[2] Only the second part of the fifth reservation proved unacceptable to the other signatories. At first unwilling to reconsider, the United States four years later negotiated an interpretive agreement, which President Hoover transmitted to the Senate on 10 December 1930. Four more years of controversy and parliamentary maneuvering ended on 29 January 1935 when, by a vote of 52 in favor to 36 opposed, the Senate failed to give its approval, being short of the necessary two thirds by 7 votes. Thus the matter was closed, only to be opened by World War II.

favorable advice and consent of the Senate to the adherence on the part of the United States to the protocol of December 16, 1920, of signature of the statute for the Permanent Court of International Justice, set out in the said message of the President (without accepting or agreeing to the optional clause for compulsory jurisdiction contained therein), upon the conditions and understandings hereafter stated, to be made a part of the instrument of adherence:

Therefore be it

Resolved (two-thirds of the Senators present concurring), That the Senate advise and consent to the adherence on the part of the United States to the said protocol of December 16, 1920, and the adjoined statute for the Permanent Court of International Justice (without accepting or agreeing to the optional clause for compulsory jurisdiction contained in said statute), and that the signature of the United States be affixed to the said protocol, subject to the following reservations and understandings, which are hereby made a part and condition of this resolution, namely:

1. That such adherence shall not be taken to involve any legal relation on the part of the United States to the League of Nations or the assumption of any obligations by the United States under the Treaty of Versailles.

2. That the United States shall be permitted to participate, through representatives designated for the purpose and upon an equality with the other states, members, respectively, of the Council and Assembly of the League of Nations, in any and all proceedings of either the council or the Assembly for the election of judges or deputy judges of the Permanent Court of International Justice or for the filling of vacancies.

3. That the United States will pay a fair share of the expenses of the court as determined and appropriated from time to time by the Congress of the United States.

4. That the United States may at any time withdraw its adherence to the said protocol and that the statute for the Permanent Court of International Justice adjoined to the protocol shall not be amended without the consent of the United States.

5. That the court shall not render any advisory opinion except publicly after due notice to all states adhering to the court and to all interested states and after public hearing or opportunity for hearing given to any state concerned; nor shall it, without the consent of the United States, entertain any request for an advisory opinion touching any dispute or question in which the United States has or claims an interest.

The signature of the United States to the said protocol shall not be affixed until the powers signatory to such protocol shall have indicated, through an exchange of notes, their acceptance of the foregoing reservations and understandings as a part and a condition of adherence by the United States to the said protocol.

Resolved further, as a part of this act of ratification, that the United States approve the protocol and statute hereinabove mentioned, with the understanding that recourse to the Permanent Court of International Justice for the settlement of differences between the United States and any other state or states can be had only by agreement thereto through general or special treaties concluded between the parties in dispute; and

Resolved further, That adherence to the said protocol and statute hereby approved shall not be so construed as to require the United States to depart from its traditional policy of not intruding upon, interfering with, or entangling itself in the political questions of policy or internal administration of any foreign State; nor shall adherence to the said protocol and statute be construed to imply a relinquishment by the United States of its traditional attitude toward purely American questions.

Agreed to, January 16th (Calendar day, January 27th), 1926.

38. UNITED STATES DECLARATION ACCEPTING COMPULSORY JURISDICTION OF THE INTERNATIONAL COURT OF JUSTICE, 14 AUGUST 1946 [1]

Following World War II, the United States not only accepted the Statute of the World Court, whose name was now changed from the older and less apt Permanent Court of International Justice to International Court of Justice, but also went on to accept, although not without qualifications, the compulsory jurisdiction of the Court under Article XXXVI, the "optional clause," of the Statute.

DECLARATION ON THE PART OF THE
UNITED STATES OF AMERICA

I, Harry S. Truman, President of the United States of America, declare on behalf of the United States of America, under Article 36, paragraph 2, of the Statute of the International Court of Justice, and in accordance with the Resolution of August 2, 1946, of the Senate of the United States of America (two-thirds of the Senators present concurring therein), that the United States of America recognizes as compulsory *ipso facto* and without special agreement, in relation to any other state accepting the same obligation, the jurisdiction of the International Court of Justice in all legal disputes hereafter arising concerning
  a. the interpretation of a treaty;
  b. any question of international law;
  c. the existence of any fact which, if established, would constitute a

breach of an international obligation;
  d. the nature of extent of the reparation to be made for the breach of an international obligation;
Provided, that this declaration shall not apply to
  a. disputes the solution of which the parties shall entrust to other tribunals by virtue of agreements already in existence or which may be concluded in the future; or
  b. disputes with regard to matters which are essentially within the domestic jurisdiction of the United States of America as determined by the United States of America; or
  c. disputes arising under a multilateral treaty, unless (1) all parties to the treaty affected by the decision are also parties to the case before the Court, or (2) the United States of America specially agrees to jurisdiction; and
Provided further, that this declaration shall remain in force for a period of five years and thereafter until the expiration of six months after notice may be given to terminate this declaration.

Done at Washington this fourteenth day of August 1946.

HARRY S. TRUMAN

[1] *United States Statutes at Large,* LXI (1947), p. 1218.

Chapter 13

The Continuing Organs of the League System:
The International Labor Organization

39. THE CONSTITUTION OF THE INTERNATIONAL
LABOR ORGANIZATION,[1] 28 JUNE 1919, AS AMENDED [2]

At the outbreak of World War I the movement to ameliorate the condition of workers through joint action among governments had been slowly gathering force since England's Robert Owen first memorialized the Congress Powers at Aix-la-Chapelle in 1818. But organized labor had taken little part, suspicious of the intentions of its would-be benefactors and preferring to work through the trade unions, which avoided government action, or through the socialist international, which sought to socialize the state. World War I, with its manpower demands, brought the two movements together. At the Paris Peace Conference in 1919 a Commission on Labor Legislation under the chairmanship of

Samuel Gompers, President of the American Federation of Labor, drafted a labor chapter for the peace treaties. The Commission worked on the basis of a draft convention, debated article by article after only a perfunctory discussion of general principles, which the British delegation brought to the Conference. Thus, the "Constitution" of the International Labor Organization, like the Covenant of the League of Nations, was largely Anglo-Saxon in its authorship. After World War II, such extensive revisions were made in the Constitution (as it was now called) that the two versions are given here in parallel columns.

PART XIII (LABOR) OF THE TREATY OF VERSAILLES

(June 28, 1919)

SECTION I
ORGANIZATION OF LABOR

[PREAMBLE]

Whereas the League of Nations has for its object the establishment of universal peace, and such a peace can be established only if it is based upon social justice;

And whereas conditions of labor ex-

THE CONSTITUTION OF THE INTERNATIONAL ORGANIZATION AS AMENDED BY THE CONSTITUTION OF THE INTERNATIONAL LABOR ORGANIZATION INSTRUMENT OF AMENDMENT, 1946

PREAMBLE

Whereas universal and lasting peace can be established only if it is based upon social justice;

And whereas conditions of labor exist involving such injustice, hardship and privation to large numbers of peo-

---

[1] Originally Part XIII of the Treaties of Versailles, St-Germain-en-Laye and Trianon and Part XII of the Treaty of Neuilly-sur-Seine, the constitution of the International Labor Organization was subsequently amended by the procedure prescribed in Article 422

and by the Constitution of the International Labor Organization Instrument of Amendment of 1945.

[2] *Yearbook of the United Nations, 1946-1947*, pp. 670-679.

ist involving such injustice, hardship and privation to large numbers of people as to produce unrest so great that the peace and harmony of the world are imperilled; and an improvement of those conditions is urgently required: as, for example, by the regulation of the hours of work, including the establishment of a maximum working day and week, the regulation of the labor supply, the prevention of unemployment, the provision of an adequate living wage, the protection of the worker against sickness, disease and injury arising out of his employment, the protection of children, young persons and women, provision for old age and injury, protection of the interests of workers when employed in countries other than their own, recognition of the principle of freedom of association, the organization of vocational and technical education and other measures;

Whereas also the failure of any nation to adopt humane conditions of labor is an obstacle in the way of other nations which desire to improve the conditions in their own countries;

The High Contracting Parties, moved by sentiments of justice and humanity as well as by the desire to secure the permanent peace of the world, agree to the following:

ple as to produce unrest so great that the peace and harmony of the world are imperilled; and an improvement of those conditions is urgently required: as, for example, by the regulation of the hours of work, including the establishment of a maximum working day and week, the regulation of the labor supply, the prevention of unemployment, the provision of an adequate living wage, the protection of the worker against sickness, disease and injury arising out of his employment, the protection of children, young persons and women, provision for old age and injury, protection of the interests of workers when employed in countries other than their own, recognition of the principle of equal remuneration for work of equal value, recognition of the principle of freedom of association, the organization of vocational and technical education and other measures;

Whereas also the failure of any nation to adopt humane conditions of labor is an obstacle in the way of other nations which desire to improve the conditions in their own countries;

The High Contracting Parties, moved by sentiments of justice and humanity as well as by the desire to secure the permanent peace of the world, and with a view to attaining the objectives set forth in this Preamble, agree to the following Constitution of the International Labor Organization:

Chapter I—ORGANIZATION

Art. 387 [MEMBERSHIP]. 1. A permanent organization is hereby established for the promotion of the objects set forth in the Preamble.

CHAPTER I—ORGANIZATION

Art. 1. 1. A permanent organization is hereby established for the promotion of the objects set forth in the Preamble to this Constitution and in the Declaration concerning the aims and purposes of the International Labor Organization adopted at Philadelphia on 10 May 1944 the text of which is annexed to this Constitution.

2. The Members of the International Labor Organization shall be the States which were Members of the Organization on 1 November 1945, and such other States as may become Members

2. The original Members of the League of Nations shall be the original Members of this organization, and hereafter membership of the League of Nations shall carry with it membership of the said organization.

in pursuance of the provisions of paragraphs 3 and 4 of this Article.

3. Any original Member of the United Nations and any State admitted to membership of the United Nations by a decision of the General Assembly in accordance with the provisions of the Charter may become a Member of the International Labor Organization by communicating to the Director-General of the International Labor Office its formal acceptance of the obligations of the Constitution of the International Labor Organization.

4. The General Conference of the International Labor Organization may also admit Members to the Organization by a vote concurred in by two-thirds of the delegates attending the session, including two-thirds of the Government delegates present and voting. Such admission shall take effect on the communication to the Director-General of the International Labor Office by the Government of the new Member of its formal acceptance of the obligations of the Constitution of the Organization.

5. No Member of the International Labor Organization may withdraw from the Organization without giving notice of its intention so to do to the Director-General of the International Labor Office. Such notice shall take effect two years after the date of its reception by the Director-General, subject to the Member having at that time fulfilled all financial obligations arising out of its membership. When a Member has ratified any International Labor Convention, such withdrawal shall not affect the continued validity for the period provided for in the Convention of all obligations arising thereunder or relating thereto.

6. In the event of any State having ceased to be a Member of the Organization, its re-admission to membership shall be governed by the provisions of paragraph 3 or paragraph 4 of this Article as the case may be.

ART. 388 [MACHINERY]. The permanent organization shall consist of:
1. A General Conference of Representatives of the Members and
2. An International Labor Office controlled by the Governing Body described in Article 393.

ART. 389 [CONFERENCE, PERIODICITY, DELEGATIONS]. 1. The meetings of the General Conference of Representatives of the Members shall be held from time to time as occasion may require, and at least once in every year. It shall be composed of four Representatives of each of the Members, of whom two shall be Government Delegates and the two others shall be Delegates representing respectively the employers and the workpeople of each of the Members.
2. Each Delegate may be accompanied by advisers, who shall not exceed two in number for each item on the agenda of the meeting. When questions specially affecting women are to be considered by the Conference, one at least of the advisers should be a woman.

3. The Members undertake to nominate non-Government Delegates and advisers chosen in agreement with the industrial organizations, if such organizations exist, which are most representative of employers or work-people,

ART. 2. The permanent organization shall consist of:
(a) a General Conference of representatives of the Members;
(b) a Governing Body composed as described in Article 7; and
(c) an International Labor Office controlled by the Governing Body.

ART. 3. 1. The meetings of the General Conference of representatives of the Members shall be held from time to time as occasion may require, and at least once in every year. It shall be composed of four representatives of each of the Members, of whom two shall be Government delegates and the two others shall be delegates representing respectively the employers and the workpeople of each of the Members.

2. Each delegate may be accompanied by advisers, who shall not exceed two in number for each item on the agenda of the meeting. When questions specially affecting women are to be considered by the Conference, one at least of the advisers should be a woman.
3. Each Member which is responsible for the international relations of non-metropolitan territories may appoint as additional advisers to each of its delegates:
(a) persons nominated by it as representatives of any such territory in regard to matters within the self-governing powers of that territory; and
(b) persons nominated by it to advise its delegates in regard to matters concerning non-self-governing territories.
4. In the case of a territory under the joint authority of two or more Members, persons may be nominated to advise the delegates of such Members.
5. The Members undertake to nominate non-Government delegates and advisers chosen in agreement with the industrial organizations, if such organizations exist, which are most representative of employers or workpeople,

as the case may be, in their respective countries.

4. Advisers shall not speak except on a request made by the Delegate whom they accompany and by the special authorization of the President of the Conference, and may not vote.

5. A Delegate may by notice in writing addressed to the President appoint one of his advisers to act as his deputy, and the adviser, while so acting, shall be allowed to speak and vote.

6. The names of the Delegates and their advisers will be communicated to the International Labor Office by the Government of each of the Members.

7. The credentials of Delegates and their advisers shall be subject to scrutiny by the Conference, which may, by two-thirds of the votes cast by the Delegates present, refuse to admit any Delegate or adviser whom it deems not to have been nominated in accordance with this Article.

ART. 390 [VOTING]. 1. Every Delegate shall be entitled to vote individually on all matters which are taken into consideration by the Conference.

2. If one of the Members fails to nominate one of the non-Government Delegates whom it is entitled to nominate, the other non-Government Delegate shall be allowed to sit and speak at the Conference, but not to vote.

3. If in accordance with Article 389 the Conference refuses admission to a Delegate of one of the Members, the provisions of the present Article shall apply as if that Delegate had not been nominated.

ART. 391 [PLACE OF MEETING]. The meetings of the Conference shall be held at the seat of the League of Nations, or at such other place as may be decided by the Conference at a previous meeting by two-thirds of the votes cast by the Delegates present.

ART. 392 [SEAT OF OFFICE]. The International Labor Office shall be established as the seat of the League of Nations as part of the organization of the League.

as the case may be, in their respective countries.

6. Advisers shall not speak except on a request made by the delegate whom they accompany and by the special authorisation of the President of the Conference, and may not vote.

7. A delegate may by notice in writing addressed to the President appoint one of his advisers to act as his deputy, and the adviser, while so acting, shall be allowed to speak and vote.

8. The names of the delegates and their advisers will be communicated to the International Labor Office by the Government of each of the Members.

9. The credentials of delegates and their advisers shall be subject to scrutiny by the Conference, which may, by two-thirds of the votes cast by the delegates present, refuse to admit any delegate or adviser whom it deems not to have been nominated in accordance with this Article.

ART. 4. 1. Every delegate shall be entitled to vote individually on all matters which are taken into consideration by the Conference.

2. If one of the Members fails to nominate one of the non-Government delegates whom it is entitled to nominate, the other non-Government delegate shall be allowed to sit and speak at the Conference, but not to vote.

3. If in accordance with Article 3 the Conference refuses admission to a delegate of one of the Members, the provisions of the present Article shall apply as if that delegate had not been nominated.

ART. 5. The meetings of the Conference shall, subject to any decisions which may have been taken by the Conference itself at a previous meeting, be held at such place as may be decided by the Governing Body.

ART. 6. Any change in the seat of the International Labor Office shall be decided by the Conference by a two-thirds majority of the votes cast by the delegates present.

Art. 393 [3] [GOVERNING BODY]. 1. The International Labor Office shall be under the control of a Governing Body consisting of thirty-two persons:

Sixteen representing Governments,
Eight representing the Employers, and
Eight representing the Workers.

2. Of the sixteen persons representing Governments, eight shall be appointed by the Members of chief industrial importance, and eight shall be appointed by the Members selected for that purpose by the Government Delegates to the Conference excluding the Delegates of the eight Members mentioned above. Of the sixteen Members represented six shall be non-European States.

3. Any question as to which are the Members of chief industrial importance shall be decided by the Council of the League of Nations.

4. The persons representing the Employers and the persons representing the Workers shall be elected respectively by the Employers' Delegates and the Workers' Delegates to the Conference. Two Employers' representatives and two Workers' representatives shall belong to non-European States.

5. The period of office of the Governing Body shall be three years.

Art. 7.[4] 1. The Governing Body shall consist of thirty-two persons:

Sixteen representing Governments,
Eight representing the employers, and
Eight representing the workers.

2. Of the sixteen persons representing Governments, eight shall be appointed by the Members of chief industrial importance, and eight shall be appointed by the Members selected for that purpose by the Government delegates to the Conference, excluding the delegates of the eight Members mentioned above. Of the sixteen Members represented, six shall be non-European States.

3. The Governing Body shall as occasion requires determine which are the Members of the Organization of chief industrial importance and shall make rules to ensure that all questions relating to the selection of the Members of chief industrial importance are considered by an impartial committee before being decided by the Governing Body. Any appeal made by a Member from the declaration of the Governing Body as to which are the Members of chief industrial importance shall be decided by the Conference, but an appeal to the Conference shall not suspend the application of the declaration until such time as the Conference decides the appeal.

4. The persons representing the employers and the persons representing the workers shall be elected respectively by the employers' delegates and the workers' delegates to the Conference. Two employers' representatives and two workers' representatives shall belong to non-European States.

5. The period of office of the Governing Body shall be three years. If for any reason the Governing Body elec-

---

[3] Under the original Constitution (as contained in the various postwar treaties) the Governing Body consisted of 24 persons: 12 representing governments, 6 representing employers, and 6 representing workers.

[4] This 1946 Instrument of Amendment does not include a subsequent amendment which changed the composition of the Governing Body to 40 persons: 20 government, 10 employer, and 10 worker members.

tions do not take place on the expiry of this period, the Governing Body shall remain in office until such elections are held.

6. The method of filling vacancies and of appointing substitutes and other similar questions may be decided by the Governing Body subject to the approval of the Conference.

6. The method of filling vacancies and of appointing substitutes and other similar questions may be decided by the Governing Body subject to the approval of the Conference.

7. The Governing Body shall, from time to time, elect one of its number to act as its Chairman, shall regulate its own procedure, and shall fix its own times of meeting. A special meeting shall be held if a written request to that effect is made by at least twelve of the representatives on the Governing Body.

7. The Governing Body shall, from time to time, elect from its number a Chairman and two Vice-Chairmen, of whom one shall be a person representing a Government, one a person representing the employers, and one a person representing the workers.

8. The Governing Body shall regulate its own procedure and shall fix its own times of meeting. A special meeting shall be held if a written request to that effect is made by at least twelve of the representatives on the Governing Body.

ART. 394 [DIRECTOR]. 1. There shall be a Director of the International Labor Office, who shall be appointed by the Governing Body, and, subject to the instructions of the Governing Body, shall be responsible for the efficient conduct of the International Labor Office and for such other duties as may be assigned to him.

ART. 8. 1. There shall be a Director-General of the International Labor Office, who shall be appointed by the Governing Body, and, subject to the instructions of the Governing Body, shall be responsible for the efficient conduct of the International Labor Office and, for such other duties as may be assigned to him.

2. The Director or his deputy shall attend all meetings of the Governing Body.

2. The Director-General or his deputy shall attend all meetings of the Governing Body.

ART. 395 [STAFF]. The staff of the International Labor Office shall be appointed by the Director, who shall, so far as is possible with due regard to the efficiency of the work of the Office, select persons of different nationalities. A certain number of these persons shall be women.

ART. 9. 1. The staff of the International Labor Office shall be appointed by the Director-General under regulations approved by the Governing Body.

2. So far as is possible with due regard to the efficiency of the work of the Office, the Director-General shall select persons of different nationalities.

3. A certain number of these persons shall be women.

4. The responsibilities of the Director-General and the staff shall be exclusively international in character. In the performance of their duties, the Director-General and the staff shall not seek or receive instructions from any Government or from any other au-

thority external to the Organization. They shall refrain from any action which might reflect on their position as international officials responsible only to the Organization.

5. Each Member of the Organization undertakes to respect the exclusively international character of the responsibilities of the Director-General and the staff and not to seek to influence them in the discharge of their responsibilities.

ART. 396 [FUNCTIONS OF OFFICE]. 1. The functions of the International Labor Office shall include the collection and distribution of information on all subjects relating to the international adjustment of conditions of industrial life and labor, and particularly the examination of subjects which it is proposed to bring before the Conference with a view to the conclusion of international conventions, and the conduct of such special investigations as may be ordered by the Conference.

2. It will prepare the agenda for the meetings of the Conference.

3. It will carry out the duties required of it by the provisions of this Part of the present Treaty in connection with international disputes.

4. It will edit and publish in French and English, and in such other languages as the Governing Body may think desirable, a periodical paper dealing with problems of industry and employment of international interest.

ART. 10. 1. The functions of the International Labor Office shall include the collection and distribution of information on all subjects relating to the international adjustment of conditions of industrial life and labour, and particularly the examination of subjects which it is proposed to bring before the Conference with a view to the conclusion of international Conventions, and the conduct of such special investigations as may be ordered by the Conference or by the Governing Body.

2. Subject to such directions as the Governing Body may give, the Office will—

(*a*) prepare the documents on the various items of the agenda for the meetings of the Conference;

(*b*) accord to Governments at their request all appropriate assistance within its power in connection with the framing of laws and regulations on the basis of the decisions of the Conference and the improvement of administrative practices and systems of inspection;

(*c*) carry out the duties required of it by the provisions of this Constitution in connection with the effective observance of Conventions;

(*d*) edit and issue, in such languages as the Governing Body may think desirable, publications dealing with problems of industry and employment of international interest.

5. Generally, in addition to the functions set out in this Article, it shall have such other powers and duties as may be assigned to it by the Conference.

ART. 397 [COMMUNICATION WITH GOVERNMENTS]. The Government De-

3. Generally, it shall have such other powers and duties as may be assigned to it by the Conference or by the Governing Body.

ART. 11. The Government departments of any of the Members which

partments of any of the Members which deal with questions of industry and employment may communicate directly with the Director through the Representative of their Government on the Governing Body of the International Labor Office, or failing any such Representative, through such other qualified official as the Government may nominate for the purpose.

ART. 398 [ASSISTANCE OF LEAGUE SECRETARY-GENERAL]. The International Labor Office shall be entitled to the assistance of the Secretary-General of the League of Nations in any matter in which it can be given.

ART. 399 [FINANCE]. 1. Each of the Members will pay the travelling and subsistence expenses of its Delegates and their advisers and of its Representatives attending the meetings of the Conference or Governing Body, as the case may be.

2. All the other expenses of the International Labor Office and of the meetings of the Conference or Governing Body shall be paid to the Director

deal with questions of industry and employment may communicate directly with the Director-General through the representative of their Government on the Governing Body of the International Labor Office or, failing any such representative, through such other qualified official as the Government may nominate for the purpose.

ART. 12. 1. The International Labor Organization shall co-operate within the terms of this Constitution with any general international organization entrusted with the co-ordination of the activities of public international organizations having specialized responsibilities and with public international organizations having specialized responsibilities in related fields.

2. The International Labor Organization may make appropriate arrangements for the representatives of public international organizations to participate without vote in its deliberations.

3. The International Labor Organization may make suitable arrangements for such consultation as it may think desirable with recognized non-governmental international organizations, including international organizations of employers, workers, agriculturists and co-operators.

ART. 13. 1. The International Labor Organization may make such financial and budgetary arrangements with the United Nations as may appear appropriate.

2. Pending the conclusion of such arrangements or if at any time no such arrangements are in force—

(a) each of the Members will pay the travelling and subsistence expenses of its delegates and their advisers and of its representatives attending the meetings of the Conference or the Governing Body, as the case may be;

(b) all other expenses of the International Labor Office and of the meetings of the Conference or Governing Body shall be paid by the Director-General of by the Secretary-General of the League of Nations out of the general funds of the League.

the International Labor Office out of the general funds of the International Labor Organization;

(c) the arrangements for the approval, allocation and collection of the budget of the International Labor Organization shall be determined by the Conference by a two-thirds majority of the votes cast by the delegates present, and shall provide for the approval of the budget and of the arrangements for the allocation of expenses among the Members of the Organization by a committee of Government representatives.

3. The expenses of the International Labor Organization shall be borne by the Members in accordance with the arrangements in force in virtue of paragraph 1 or paragraph 2 (c) of this Article.

4. A Member of the Organization which is in arrears in the payment of its financial contribution to the Organization shall have no vote in the Conference, in the Governing Body, in any committee, or in the elections of members of the Governing Body, if the amount of its arrears equals or exceeds the amount of the contributions due from it for the preceding two full years: Provided that the Conference may by a two-thirds majority of the votes cast by the delegates present permit such a Member to vote if it is satisfied that the failure to pay is due to conditions beyond the control of the Member.

3. The Director shall be responsible to the Secretary-General of the League for the proper expenditure of all moneys paid to him in pursuance of this Article.

5. The Director-General of the International Labor Office shall be responsible to the Governing Body for the proper expenditure of the funds of the International Labor Organization.

CHAPTER II—PROCEDURE

ART. 400 [AGENDA FOR CONFERENCE]. The agenda for all meetings of the Conference will be settled by the Governing Body, who shall consider any suggestion as to the agenda that may be made by the Government of any of the Members or by any representative

CHAPTER II—PROCEDURE

ART. 14. 1. The agenda for all meetings of the Conference will be settled by the Governing Body, which shall consider any suggestion as to the agenda that may be made by the Government of any of the Members or by any representative organization recog-

organization recognized for the purpose of Article 389.

ART. 401 [SECRETARY. NOTICE OF AGENDA]. The Director shall act as the Secretary of the Conference, and shall transmit the agenda so as to reach the Members four months before the meeting of the Conference, and, through them, the non-Government Delegates when appointed.

ART. 402 [OBJECTIONS TO AGENDA]. 1. Any of the Governments of the Members may formally object to the inclusion of any item or items in the agenda. The grounds for such objection shall be set forth in a reasoned statement addressed to the Director, who shall circulate it to all the Members of the Permanent Organization.

2. Items to which such objection has been made shall not, however, be excluded from the agenda, if at the Conference a majority of two-thirds of the votes cast by the Delegates present is in favor of considering them.

3. If the Conference decides (otherwise than under the preceding paragraph) by two-thirds of the votes cast by the Delegates present that any subject shall be considered by the Conference, that subject shall be included in the agenda for the following meeting.

ART. 403 [PRESIDENT. VOTING]. 1. The Conference shall regulate its own procedure, shall elect its own President,

nized for the purpose of Article 3, or by any public international organization.

2. The Governing Body shall make rules to ensure thorough technical preparation and adequate consultation of the Members primarily concerned, by means of a preparatory Conference or otherwise, prior to the adoption of a Convention or Recommendation by the Conference.

ART. 15. 1. The Director-General shall act as the Secretary-General of the Conference, and shall transmit the agenda so as to reach the Members four months before the meeting of the Conference, and, through them, the non-Government delegates when appointed.

2. The reports on each item of the agenda shall be despatched so as to reach the Members in time to permit adequate consideration before the meeting of the Conference. The Governing Body shall make rules for the application of this provision.

ART. 16. 1. Any of the Governments of the Members may formally object to the inclusion of any item or items in the agenda. The grounds for such objection shall be set forth in a statement addressed to the Director-General who shall circulate it to all the Members of the Organization.

2. Items to which such objection has been made shall not, however, be excluded from the agenda, if at the Conference a majority of two-thirds of the votes cast by the delegates present is in favour of considering them.

3. If the Conference decides (otherwise than under the preceding paragraph) by two-thirds of the votes cast by the delegates present that any subject shall be considered by the Conference, that subject shall be included in the agenda for the following meeting.

ART. 17. 1. The Conference shall elect a President and three Vice-Presidents. One of the Vice-Presidents shall

and may appoint committees to consider and report on any matter.

2. Except as otherwise expressly provided in this Part of the present Treaty, all matters shall be decided by a simple majority of the votes cast by the Delegates present.

3. The voting is void unless the total number of votes cast is equal to half the number of the Delegates attending the Conference.

ART. 404 [COMMITTEES. ASSESSORS]. The Conference may add to any committees which it appoints technical experts, who shall be assessors without power to vote.

ART. 405 [CONVENTIONS AND RECOMMENDATIONS. VOTING. OBLIGATION OF GOVERNMENTS]. 1. When the Conference has decided on the adoption of proposals with regard to an item in the agenda, it will rest with the Conference to determine whether these proposals should take the form: (a) of a recommendation to be submitted to the Members for consideration with a view to effect being given to it by national legislation or otherwise, or (b) of a draft international convention for ratification by the Members.

2. In either case a majority of two-thirds of the votes cast by the Delegates present shall be necessary on the final vote for the adoption of the recommendation or draft convention, as the case may be, by the Conference.

3. In framing any recommendation or draft convention of general application the Conference shall have due regard to those countries in which climatic conditions, the imperfect development of industrial organization, or other special circumstances make the industrial conditions substantially different, and shall suggest the modi-

be a Government delegate, one an employers' delegate and one a workers' delegate. The Conference shall regulate its own procedure and may appoint committees to consider and report on any matter.

2. Except as otherwise expressly provided in this Constitution or by the terms of any Convention or other instrument conferring powers on the Conference or of the financial and budgetary arrangements adopted in virtue of Article 13, all matters shall be decided by a simple majority of the votes cast by the delegates present.

3. The voting is void unless the total number of votes cast is equal to half the number of the delegates attending the Conference.

ART. 18. The Conference may add to any committees which it appoints technical experts without power to vote.

ART. 19. 1. When the Conference has decided on the adoption of proposals with regard to an item in the agenda, it will rest with the Conference to determine whether these proposals should take the form: (a) of an international Convention, or (b) of a Recommendation to meet circumstances where the subject, or aspect of it, dealt with is not considered suitable or appropriate at that time for a Convention.

2. In either case a majority of two-thirds of the votes cast by the delegates present shall be necessary on the final vote for the adoption of the Convention or Recommendation, as the case may be, by the Conference.

3. In framing any Convention or Recommendation of general application the Conference shall have due regard to those countries in which climatic conditions, the imperfect development of industrial organization, or other special circumstances make the industrial conditions substantially different and shall suggest the modifications, if any,

fications, if any, which it considers may be required to meet the case of such countries.

4. A copy of the recommendation or draft convention shall be authenticated by the signature of the President of the Conference and of the Director and shall be deposited with the Secretary-General of the League of Nations. The Secretary-General will communicate a certified copy of the recommendation or draft convention to each of the Members.

5. Each of the Members undertakes that it will, within the period of one year at most from the closing of the session of the Conference, or if it is impossible owing to exceptional circumstances to do so within the period of one year, then at the earliest practicable moment and in no case later than eighteen months from the closing of the session of the Conference, bring the recommendation or draft convention before the authority or authorities within whose competence the matter lies, for the enactment of legislation or other action.

6. In the case of a draft convention, the Member will, if it obtains the consent of the authority or authorities within whose competence the matter lies, communicate the formal ratification of the convention to the Secretary-General and will take such action as may be necessary to make effective the provisions of such convention.

which it considers may be required to meet the case of such countries.

4. Two copies of the Convention or Recommendation shall be authenticated by the signatures of the President of the Conference and of the Director-General. Of these copies one shall be deposited in the archives of the International Labor Office and the other with the Secretary-General of the United Nations. The Director-General will communicate a certified copy of the Convention or Recommendation to each of the Members.

5. In the case of a Convention—

(a) the Convention will be communicated to all Members for ratification;

(b) each of the Members undertakes that it will, within the period of one year at most from the closing of the session of the Conference, or if it is impossible owing to exceptional circumstances to do so within the period of one year, then at the earliest practicable moment and in no case later than eighteen months from the closing of the session of the Conference, bring the Convention before the authority or authorities within whose competence the matter lies, for the enactment of legislation or other action;

(c) Members shall inform the Director-General of the International Labor Office of the measures taken in accordance with this Article to bring the Convention before the said competent authority or authorities, with particulars of the authority or authorities regarded as competent, and of the action taken by them;

(d) if the Member obtains the consent of the authority or authorities within whose competence the matter lies, it will communicate the formal ratification of the Convention to the Director-General and will take such action as may be necessary to make effective the provisions of such Convention;

(e) if the Member does not obtain the consent of the authority or authorities within whose competence the matter lies, no further obligation shall rest upon the Member except that it shall report to the Director-General of the International Labor Office, at appropriate intervals as requested by the Governing Body, the position of its law and practice in regard to the matters dealt with in the Convention, showing the extent to which effect has been given, or is proposed to be given, to any of the provisions of the Convention by legislation, administrative action, collective agreement or otherwise and stating the difficulties which prevent or delay the ratification of such Convention.

6. In the case of a Recommendation—

(*a*) the Recommendation will be communicated to all Members for their consideration with a view to effect being given to it by national legislation or otherwise;

(*b*) each of the Members undertakes that it will, within a period of one year at most from the closing of the session of the Conference, or if it is impossible owing to exceptional circumstances to do so within the period of one year, then at the earliest practicable moment and in no case later than eighteen months after the closing of the Conference, bring the Recommendation before the authority or authorities within whose competence the matter lies for the enactment of legislation or other action;

7. In the case of a recommendation, the Members will inform the Secretary-General of the action taken.

(*c*) the Members shall inform the Director-General of the International Labor Office of the measures taken in accordance with this Article to bring the Recommendation before the said competent authority or authorities with particulars of the authority or authorities regarded as competent, and of the action taken by them;

(*d*) apart from bringing the Recommendation before the said competent authority or authorities, no further obligation shall rest upon the Members, except that they shall report to the Director-General of the International La-

8. If on a recommendation no legislative or other action is taken to make a recommendation effective, or if the draft convention fails to obtain the consent of the authority or authorities within whose competence the matter

lies, no further obligation shall rest upon the Members.

9. In the case of a federal State, the power of which to enter into conventions on labor matters is subject to limitations, it shall be in the discretion of that Government to treat a draft convention to which such limitations apply as a recommendation only, and the provisions of this Article with respect to recommendations shall apply in such case.

bor Office, at appropriate intervals as requested by the Governing Body, the position of the law and practice in their country in regard to the matters dealt with in the Recommendation, showing the extent to which effect has been given, or is proposed to be given, to the provisions of the Recommendation and such modifications of these provisions as it has been found or may be found necessary to make in adopting or applying them.

7. In the case of a federal State, the following provisions shall apply:

(a) in respect of Conventions and Recommendations which the federal Government regards as appropriate under its constitutional system for federal action, the obligations of the federal State shall be the same as those of Members which are not federal States;

(b) in respect of Conventions and Recommendations which the federal Government regards as appropriate under its constitutional system, in whole or in part, for action by the constituent States, provinces, or cantons rather than for federal action, the federal Government shall—

(i) make, in accordance with its Constitution and the Constitutions of the States, provinces or cantons concerned, effective arrangements for the reference of such Conventions and Recomendations not later than eighteen months from the closing of the session of the Conference to the appropriate federal, State, provincial or cantonal authorities for the enactment of legislation or other action;

(ii) arrange, subject to the concurrence of the State, provincial or cantonal Governments concerned, for periodical consultations between the federal and the State, provincial or cantonal authorities with a view to promoting within the federal State co-ordinated action to give effect to the provisions of such Conventions and Recommendations;

(iii) inform the Director-General of the International Labor Office of the measures taken in accordance with this Article to bring such Conventions and Recommendations before the appropriate federal, State, provincial or cantonal authorities with particulars of the authorities regarded as appropriate and of the action taken by them;

(iv) in respect of each such Convention which it has not ratified, report to the Director-General of the International Labor Office, at appropriate intervals as requested by the Governing Body, the position of the law and practice of the federation and its constituent States, provinces or cantons in regard to the Convention, showing the extent to which effect has been given, or is proposed to be given, to any of the provisions of the Convention by legislation, administrative action, collective agreement, or otherwise;

(v) in respect of each such Recommendation, report to the Director-General of the International Labor Office, at appropriate intervals as requested by the Governing Body, the position of the law and practice of the federation and its constituent States, provinces or cantons in regard to the Recommendation, showing the extent to which effect has been given, or is proposed to be given, to the provisions of the Recommendation and such modifications of these provisions as have been found or may be found necessary in adopting or applying them.

8. In no case shall the adoption of any Convention or Recommendation by the Conference, or the ratification of any Convention by any Member, be deemed to affect any law, award, custom or agreement which ensures more favourable conditions to the workers concerned than those provided for in the Convention or Recommendation.

10. The above Article shall be interpreted in accordance with the following principle:

11. In no case shall any Member be asked or required, as a result of the adoption of any recommendation or draft convention by the Conference, to lessen the protection afforded by its existing legislation to the workers concerned.

ART. 406 [RATIFICATION]. Any convention so ratified shall be registered by the Secretary-General of the League of Nations, but shall only be binding upon the Members which ratify it.

ART. 20. Any Convention so ratified shall be communicated by the Director-General of the International Labor Office to the Secretary-General of the United Nations for registration in accordance with the provisions of Article

ART. 407 [AGREEMENT ON UNADOPTED CONVENTIONS]. 1. If any convention coming before the Conference for final consideration fails to secure the support of two-thirds of the votes cast by the Delegates present, it shall nevertheless be within the right of any of the Members of the Permanent Organization to agree to such convention among themselves.

2. Any convention so agreed to shall be communicated by the Governments concerned to the Secretary-General of the League of Nations, who shall register it.

ART. 408 [ANNUAL REPORTS]. Each of the Members agrees to make an annual report to the International Labor Office on the measures which it has taken to give effect to the provisions of conventions to which it is a party. These reports shall be made in such form and shall contain such particulars as the Governing Body may request. The Director shall lay a summary of these reports before the next meeting of the Conference.

ART. 409 [COMPLAINT OF DEFAULT FROM AN INDUSTRIAL ORGANIZATION]. In the event of any representation being made to the International Labor Office by an industrial association of employers or of workers that any of the Members has failed to secure in any respect the effective observance within its jur-

102 of the Charter of the United Nations but shall only be binding upon the Members which ratify it.

ART. 21. 1. If any Convention coming before the Conference for final consideration fails to secure the support of two-thirds of the votes cast by the delegates present, it shall nevertheless be within the right of any of the Members of the Organization to agree to such Convention among themselves.

2. Any Convention so agreed to shall be communicated by the Governments concerned to the Director-General of the International Labor Office and to the Secretary-General of the United Nations for registration in accordance with the provisions of Article 102 of the Charter of the United Nations.

ART. 22. Each of the Members agrees to make an annual report to the International Labor Office on the measures which it has taken to give effect to the provisions of Conventions to which it is a party. These reports shall be made in such form and shall contain such particulars as the Governing Body may request.

ART 23.[5] 1. The Director-General shall lay before the next meeting of the Conference a summary of the information and reports communicated to him by Members in pursuance of Articles 19 and 22.

2. Each Member shall communicate to the representative organizations recognized for the purpose of Article 3 copies of the information and reports communicated to the Director-General in pursuance of Articles 19 and 22.

ART. 24. In the event of any representation being made to the International Labor Office by an industrial association of employers or of workers that any of the Members has failed to secure in any respect the effective ob-

[5] Article 23 has no parallel article in the 1919 original.

isdiction of any convention to which it is a party, the Governing Body may communicate this representation to the Government against which it is made, and may invite that Government to make such statement on the subject as it may think fit.

ART. 410 [PROCEDURE]. If no statement is received within a reasonable time from the Government in question, or if the statement when received is not deemed to be satisfactory by the Governing Body, the latter shall have the right to publish the representation and the statement, if any, made in reply to it.

ART. 411 [COMPLAINT OF DEFAULT FROM A GOVERNMENT]. 1. Any of the Members shall have the right to file a complaint with the International Labor Office if it is not satisfied that any other Member is securing the effective observance of any convention which both have ratified in accordance with the foregoing Articles.

2. The Governing Body may, if it thinks fit, before referring such a complaint to a Commission of Inquiry, as hereinafter provided for, communicate with the Government in question in the manner described in Article 409.

3. If the Governing Body does not think it necessary to communicate the complaint to the Government in question, or if, when they have made such communication, no statement in reply has been received within a reasonable time which the Governing Body considers to be satisfactory, the Governing Body may apply for the appointment of a Commission of Inquiry to consider the complaint and to report thereon.

4. The Governing Body may adopt the same procedure either on its own motion or on receipt of a complaint from a Delegate to the Conference.

5. When any matter arising out of Articles 410 or 411 is being considered by the Governing Body, the Government in question shall, if not already represented thereon, be entitled to send a representative to take part in the pro-

servance within its jurisdiction of any Convention to which it is a party, the Governing Body may communicate this representation to the Government against which it is made, and may invite that Government to make such statement on the subject as it may think fit.

ART. 25. If no statement is received within a reasonable time from the Government in question, or if the statement when received is not deemed to be satisfactory by the Governing Body, the latter shall have the right to publish the representation and the statement, if any, made in reply to it.

ART. 26. 1. Any of the Members shall have the right to file a complaint with the International Labor Office if it is not satisfied that any other Member is securing the effective observance of any Convention which both have ratified in accordance with the foregoing Articles.

2. The Governing Body may, if it thinks fit, before referring such a complaint to a Commission of Enquiry, as hereinafter provided for, communicate with the Government in question in the manner described in Article 24.

3. If the Governing Body does not think it necessary to communicate the complaint to the Government in question, or if, when it has made such communication, no statement in reply has been received within a reasonable time which the Governing Body considers to be satisfactory, the Governing Body may appoint a Commission of Enquiry to consider the complaint and to report thereon.

4. The Governing Body may adopt the same procedure either of its own motion or on receipt of a complaint from a delegate to the Conference.

5. When any matter arising out of Articles 25 or 26 is being considered by the Governing Body, the Government in question shall, if not already represented thereon, be entitled to send a representative to take part in the pro-

ceedings of the Governing Body while the matter is under consideration. Adequate notice of the date on which the matter will be considered shall be given to the Government in question.

ART. 412 [6] [COMMISSION OF INQUIRY. CONSTITUTION]. 1. The Commission of Inquiry shall be constituted in accordance with the following provisions:

2. Each of the Members agrees to nominate within six months of the date on which the present Treaty comes into force three persons of industrial experience, of whom one shall be a representative of employers, one a representative of workers, and one a person of independent standing, who shall together form a panel from which the members of the Commission of Inquiry shall be drawn.

3. The qualifications of the persons so nominated shall be subject to scrutiny by the Governing Body, which may by two-thirds of the votes cast by the representatives present refuse to accept the nomination of any person whose qualifications do not in its opinion comply with the requirements of the present Article.

4. Upon the application of the Governing Body, the Secretary-General of the League of Nations shall nominate three persons, one from each section of this panel, to constitute the Commission of Inquiry, and shall designate one of them as the President of the Commission. None of these three persons shall be a person nominated to the panel by any Member directly concerned in the complaint.

ART. 413 [COMMUNICATION OF INFORMATION]. The Members agree that, in the event of the reference of a complaint to a Commission of Inquiry under Article 411, they will each, whether directly concerned in the complaint or not, place at the disposal of the Commission all the information in their possession which bears upon the subject matter of the complaint.

ART. 414 [REPORT OF COMMISSION].

[6] Article 412 has no parallel article in the present constitution.

ceedings of the Governing Body while the matter is under consideration. Adequate notice of the date on which the matter will be considered shall be given to the Government in question.

ART. 27. The Members agree that, in the event of the reference of a complaint to a Commission of Inquiry under Article 26, they will each, whether directly concerned in the complaint or not, place at the disposal of the Commission all the information in their possession which bears upon the subject matter of the complaint.

ART. 28. When the Commission of Inquiry has fully considered the complaint, it shall prepare a report embody-

1. When the Commission of Inquiry has fully considered the complaint, it shall prepare a report embodying its findings on all questions of fact relevant to determining the issue between the parties and containing such recommendations as it may think proper as to the steps which should be taken to meet the complaint and the time within which they should be taken.

2. It shall also indicate in this report the measures, if any, of an economic character against a defaulting Government which it considers to be appropriate, and which it considers other Governments would be justified in adopting.

ART. 415 [COMMUNICATION OF REPORT]. 1. The Secretary-General of the League of Nations shall communicate the report of the Commission of Inquiry to each of the Governments concerned in the complaint, and shall cause it to be published.

2. Each of these Governments shall within one month inform the Secretary-General of the League of Nations whether or not it accepts the recommendations contained in the report of the Commission; and if not, whether it proposes to refer the complaint to the Permanent Court of International Justice of the League of Nations.

ART. 416 [COMPLAINT OF BREACH OF ARTICLE 405]. In the event of any Member failing to take the action required by Article 405, with regard to a recommendation or draft convention, any other Member shall be entitled to refer the matter to the Permanent Court of International Justice.

ART. 417 [NO APPEAL FROM PERMANENT COURT]. The decision of the Permanent Court of International Justice in regard to a complaint or matter which has been referred to it in pursuance of Article 415 or Article 416 shall be final.

ART. 418 [POWERS OF PERMANENT COURT]. The Permanent Court of In-

ing its findings on all questions of fact relevant to determining the issue between the parties and containing such recommendations as it may think proper as to the steps which should be taken to meet the complaint and the time within which they should be taken.

ART. 29. 1. The Director-General of the International Labor Office shall communicate the report of the Commission of Inquiry to the Governing Body and to each of the Governments concerned in the complaint, and shall cause it to be published.

2. Each of these Governments shall within three months inform the Director-General of the International Labor Office whether or not it accepts the recommendations contained in the report of the Commission; and if not, whether it proposes to refer the complaint to the International Court of Justice.

ART. 30. In the event of any Member failing to take the action required by paragraphs 5 (*b*), 6 (*b*) or 7 (*b*) (i) of Article 19 with regard to a Convention or Recommendation, any other Member shall be entitled to refer the matter to the Governing Body. In the event of the Governing Body finding that there has been such a failure, it shall report the matter to the Conference.

ART. 31. The decision of the International Court of Justice in regard to a complaint or matter which has been referred to it in pursuance of Article 29 shall be final.

ART. 32. The International Court of Justice may affirm, vary or reverse any

ternational Justice may affirm, vary or reverse any of the findings or recommendations of the Commission of Inquiry, if any, and shall in its decision indicate the measures, if any, of an economic character which it considers to be appropriate, and which other Governments would be justified in adopting against a defaulting Government.

ART. 419 [PENALTIES]. In the event of any Member failing to carry out within the time specified the recommendations, if any, contained in the report of the Commission of Inquiry, or in the decision of the Permanent Court of International Justice, as the case may be, any other Member may take against that Member the measures of an economic character indicated in the report of the Commission or in the decision of the Court as appropriate to the case.

ART. 420 [CESSATION OF DEFAULT]. The defaulting Government may at any time inform the Governing Body that it has taken the steps necessary to comply with the recommendations of the Commission of Inquiry or with those in the decision of the Permanent Court of International Justice, as the case may be, and may request it to apply to the Secretary-General of the League to constitute a Commission of Inquiry to verify its contention. In this case the provisions of Articles 412, 413, 414, 415, 417 and 418 shall apply and if the report of the Commission of Inquiry or the decision of the Permanent Court of International Justice is in favor of the defaulting Government, the other Governments shall forthwith discontinue the measures of an economic character that they have taken against the defaulting Government.

of the findings or recommendations of the Commission of Inquiry, if any.

ART. 33. In the event of any Member failing to carry out within the time specified the recommendations, if any, contained in the report of the Commission of Inquiry, or in the decision of the International Court of Justice, as the case may be, the Governing Body may recommend to the Conference such action as it may deem wise and expedient to secure compliance therewith.

ART. 34. The defaulting Government may at any time inform the Governing Body that it has taken the steps necessary to comply with the recommendations of the Commission of Inquiry or with those in the decision of the International Court of Justice, as the case may be, and may request it to constitute a Commission of Inquiry to verify its contention. In this case the provisions of Articles 27, 28, 29, 31 and 32 shall apply, and if the report of the Commission of Inquiry or the decision of the International Court of Justice is in favour of the defaulting Government, the Governing Body shall forthwith recommend the discontinuance of any action taken in pursuance of Article 33.

CHAPTER III—GENERAL

ART. 421 [APPLICATION TO COLONIES]. 1. The Members engage to apply conventions which they have ratified in accordance with the provisions of this Part of the present Treaty to their

CHAPTER III—GENERAL

ART. 35. 1. The Members undertake that Conventions which they have ratified in accordance with the provisions of this Constitution shall be applied to the non-metropolitan territories for colonies, protectorates and possessions which are not fully self-governing:

(1) Except where owing to the local conditions the convention is inapplicable, or

(2) Subject to such modifications as may be necessary to adapt the convention to local conditions.

2. And each of the Members shall notify to the International Labor Office the action taken in respect of each of its colonies, protectorates and possessions which are not fully self-governing.

whose international relations they are responsible, including any trust territories for which they are the administering authority, except where the subject matter of the Convention is within the self-governing powers of the territory or the Convention is inapplicable owing to the local conditions or subject to such modifications as may be necessary to adapt the Convention to local conditions.

2. Each Member which ratifies a Convention shall as soon as possible after ratification communicate to the Director-General of the International Labour Office a declaration stating in respect of the territories other than those referred to in paragraphs 4 and 5 below the extent to which it undertakes that the provisions of the Convention shall be applied and giving such particulars as may be prescribed by the Convention.

3. Each Member which has communicated a declaration in virtue of the preceding paragraph may from time to time, in accordance with the terms of the Convention, communicate a further declaration modifying the terms of any former declaration and stating the present position in respect of such territories.

4. Where the subject matter of the Convention is within the self-governing powers of any non-metropolitan territory the Member responsible for the international relations of that territory shall bring the Convention to the notice of the Government of the territory as soon as possible with a view to the enactment of legislation or other action by such Government. Thereafter the Member, in agreement with the Government of the territory, may communicate to the Director-General of the International Labor Office a declaration accepting the obligations of the Convention on behalf of such territory.

5. A declaration accepting the obligations of any Convention may be communicated to the Director-General of the International Labor Office—

(a) by two or more Members of the

Organization in respect of any territory which is under their joint authority; or

(b) by any international authority responsible for the administration of any territory, in virtue of the Charter of the United Nations or otherwise, in respect of any such territory.

6. Acceptance of the obligations of a Convention in virtue of paragraph 4 or paragraph 5 shall involve the acceptance on behalf of the territory concerned of the obligations stipulated by the terms of the Convention and the obligations under the Constitution of the Organization which apply to ratified Conventions. A declaration of acceptance may specify such modification of the provisions of the Conventions as may be necessary to adapt the Convention to local conditions.

7. Each Member or international authority which has communicated a declaration in virtue of paragraph 4 or paragraph 5 of this Article may from time to time, in accordance with the terms of the Convention, communicate a further declaration modifying the terms of any former declaration or terminating the acceptance of the obligations of the Convention on behalf of the territory concerned.

8. If the obligations of a Convention are not accepted on behalf of a territory to which paragraph 4 or paragraph 5 of this Article relates, the Member or Members or international authority concerned shall report to the Director-General of the International Labor Office the position of the law and practice of that territory in regard to the matters dealt with in the Convention and the report shall show the extent to which effect has been given, or is proposed to be given, to any of the provisions of the Convention by legislation, administrative action, collective agreement or otherwise and shall state the difficulties which prevent or delay the acceptance of such Convention.

ART. 422 [AMENDMENT OF TREATY]. Amendments to this part of the present Treaty which are adopted by the Con-

ART. 36. Amendments to this Constitution which are adopted by the Conference by a majority of two-thirds of

ference by a majority of two-thirds of the votes cast by the Delegates present shall take effect when ratified by the States whose representatives compose the Council of the League of Nations and by three-fourths of the Members.

ART. 423 [QUESTIONS OF INTERPRETATION]. Any question or dispute relating to the interpretation of this Part of the present Treaty or of any subsequent convention concluded by the Members in pursuance of the provisions of this Part of the present Treaty shall be referred for decision to the Permanent Court of International Justice.

CHAPTER IV—TRANSITORY PROVISIONS

ART. 424 [7] [FIRST CONFERENCE. ORGANIZATION AND FINANCE]. 1. The first meeting of the Conference shall take place in October, 1919. The place and agenda for this meeting shall be as specified in the Annex hereto.

2. Arrangements for the convening and the organization of the first meeting of the Conference will be made by the Government designated for the

[7] Article 424 has no parallel article in the present constitution.

the votes cast by the delegates present shall take effect when ratified or accepted by two-thirds of the Members of the Organization including five of the eight Members which are represented on the Governing Body as Members of chief industrial importance in accordance with the provisions of paragraph 3 of Article 7 of this Constitution.

ART. 37. 1. Any question or dispute relating to the interpretation of this Constitution or of any subsequent Convention concluded by the Members in pursuance of the provisions of this Constitution shall be referred for decision to the International Court of Justice.

2. Notwithstanding the provisions of paragraph 1 of this Article the Governing Body may make and submit to the Conference for approval rules providing for the appointment of a tribunal for the expeditious determination of any dispute or question relating to the interpretation of a Convention which may be referred thereto by the Governing Body or in accordance with the terms of the Convention. Any applicable judgment or advisory opinion of the International Court of Justice shall be binding upon any tribunal established in virtue of this paragraph. Any award made by such a tribunal shall be circulated to the Members of the Organization and any observations which they may make thereon shall be brought before the Conference.

ART. 38 [8] 1. The International Labor Organization may convene such regional conferences and establish such regional agencies as may be desirable to promote the aims and purposes of the Organization.

2. The powers, functions and procedure of regional conferences shall be governed by rules drawn up by the Governing Body and submitted to the General Conference for confirmation.

[8] Article 38 has no parallel article in the 1919 original.

purpose in the said Annex. That Government shall be assisted in the preparation of the documents for submission to the Conference by an International Committee constituted as provided in the said Annex.

3. The expenses of the first meeting and of all subsequent meetings held before the League of Nations has been able to establish a general fund, other than the expenses of Delegates and their advisers, will be borne by the Members in accordance with the apportionment of the expenses of the International Bureau of the Universal Postal Union.

ART. 425 [9] [RECEIPT OF COMMUNICATIONS]. Until the League of Nations has been constituted all communications which under the provisions of the foregoing Articles should be addressed to the Secretary-General of the League will be preserved by the Director of the International Labor Office, who will transmit them to the Secretary-General of the League.

ART. 426 [10] [TEMPORARY TRIBUNAL]. Pending the creation of a Permanent Court of International Justice, disputes which in accordance with this Part of the present Treaty would be submitted to it for decision will be referred to a tribunal of three persons appointed by the Council of the League of Nations.

CHAPTER IV—MISCELLANEOUS PROVISIONS

ART. 39.[11] The International Labor Organization shall possess full juridical personality and in particular the capacity—

(a) to contract;

(b) to acquire and dispose of immovable and movable property;

(c) to institute legal proceedings.

ART. 40.[12] 1. The International Labor Organization shall enjoy in the territory of each of its Members such privileges and immunities as are necessary for the fulfilment of its purposes.

2. Delegates to the Conference, members of the Governing Body and the Director-General and officials of the Office shall likewise enjoy such privileges and immunities as are necessary for the independent exercise of their functions in connection with the Organization.

3. Such privileges and immunities shall be defined in a separate agreement to be prepared by the Organization with a view to its acceptance by the Members.

ANNEX [13]—FIRST MEETING OF ANNUAL
LABOR CONFERENCE, 1919

1. The place of meeting will be Washington.

2. The Government of the United States of America is requested to convene the Conference.

3. The International Organizing Committee will consist of seven members appointed by the United States of

ANNEX [14]

DECLARATION CONCERNING THE AIMS AND
PURPOSES OF THE INTERNATIONAL
LABOR ORGANIZATION

The General Conference of the International Labor Organization, meeting in its Twenty-sixth Session in Philadelphia, hereby adopts, this tenth day of May in the year nineteen hundred

---

[9] Article 425 has no parallel article in the present constitution.

[10] Article 426 has no parallel article in the present constitution.

[13] Inasmuch as the Annex of the present (1946) Constitution is quite different from the 1919 original, they cannot be successfully paralleled.

[11] Article 39 has no parallel article in the 1919 original.

[12] Article 40 has no parallel article in the 1919 original.

[14] This Annex is the so-called "Declaration of Philadelphia," adopted at Philadelphia on May 10, 1944.

America, Great Britain, France, Italy, Japan, Belgium and Switzerland. The Committee may, if it thinks necessary, invite other Members to appoint representatives.

4. *Agenda:*
   (1) Application of principle of the 8-hours day or of the 48-hours week.
   (2) Question of preventing or providing against unemployment.
   (3) Women's employment:
       (*a*) Before and after childbirth, including the question of maternity benefit;
       (*b*) During the night;
       (*c*) In unhealthy processes.
   (4) Employment of children:
       (*a*) Minimum age of employment;
       (*b*) During the night;
       (*c*) In unhealthy processes.
   (5) Extension and application of the International Conventions adopted at Berne in 1906 on the prohibition of night work for women employed in industry and the prohibition of the use of white phosphorus in the manufacture of matches.

SECTION II.—GENERAL PRINCIPLES

ART. 427 [NINE GUIDING POINTS]. The High Contracting Parties, recognizing that the well-being, physical, moral and intellectual, of industrial wage-earners is of supreme international importance, have framed, in order to further this great end, the permanent machinery provided for in Section I, and associated with that of the League of Nations.

They recognize that differences of climate, habits and customs, of economic opportunity and industrial tradition, make strict uniformity in the conditions of labor difficult of immediate attainment. But, holding as they do that labor should not be regarded and forty-four, the present Declaration of the aims and purposes of the International Labor Organization and of the principles which should inspire the policy of its Members.

I. The Conference reaffirms the fundamental principles on which the Organization is based and, in particular, that:

(*a*) labor is not a commodity;

(*b*) freedom of expression and of association are essential to sustained progress;

(*c*) poverty anywhere constitutes a danger to prosperity everywhere;

(*d*) the war against want requires to be carried on with unrelenting vigour within each nation, and by continuous and concerted international effort in which the representatives of workers and employers, enjoying equal status with those of Governments, join with them in free discussion and democratic decision with a view to the promotion of the common welfare.

II. Believing that experience has fully demonstrated the truth of the statement in the Constitution of the International Labor Organization that lasting peace can be established only if it is based on social justice, the Conference affirms that:

(*a*) all human beings, irrespective of race, creed or sex, have the right to pursue both their material well-being and their spiritual development in conditions of freedom and dignity, of economic security and equal opportunity;

(*b*) the attainment of the conditions in which this shall be possible must constitute the central aim of national and international policy;

(*c*) all national and international policies and measures, in particular those of an economic and financial character, should be judged in this light and accepted only in so far as they may be held to promote and not to hinder the achievement of this fundamental objective;

(*d*) it is a responsibility of the International Labor Organization to examine and consider all international

merely as an article of commerce, they think that there are methods and principles for regulating labor conditions which all industrial communities should endeavor to apply, so far as their special circumstances will permit.

Among these methods and principles, the following seem to the High Contracting Parties to be of special and urgent importance:

First.—The guiding principle above enunciated that labor should not be regarded merely as a commodity or article of commerce.

Second.—The right of association for all lawful purposes by the employed as well as by the employers.

Third.—The payment to the employed of a wage adequate to maintain a reasonable standard of life as this is understood in their time and country.

Fourth.—The adoption of an eight-hour day or a forty-eight hour week as the standard to be aimed at where it has not already been attained.

Fifth.—The adoption of a weekly rest of at least twenty-four hours, which should include Sunday wherever practicable.

Sixth.—The abolition of child labor and the imposition of such limitations on the labor of young persons as shall permit the continuation of their education and assure their proper physical development.

Seventh.—The principle that men and women should receive equal remuneration for work of equal value.

Eighth.—The standard set by law in each country with respect to the conditions of labor should have due regard to the equitable economic treatment of all workers lawfully resident therein.

Ninth.—Each State should make provision for a system of inspection in which women should take part, in order to insure the enforcement of the laws and regulations for the protection of the employed.

Without claiming that these methods and principles are either complete

economic and financial policies and measures in the light of this fundamental objective;

(e) in discharging the tasks entrusted to it the International Labor Organization, having considered all relevant economic and financial factors, may include in its decisions and recommendations any provisions which it considers appropriate.

III. The Conference recognizes the solemn obligation of the International Labor Organization to further among the nations of the world programmes which will achieve:

(a) full employment and the raising of standards of living;

(b) the employment of workers in the occupations in which they can have the satisfaction of giving the fullest measure of their skill and attainments and make their greatest contribution to the common well-being;

(c) the provision, as a means to the attainment of this end and under adequate guarantees for all concerned, of facilities for training and the transfer of labour, including migration for employment and settlement;

(d) policies in regard to wages and earnings, hours and other conditions of work calculated to ensure a just share of the fruits of progress to all, and a minimum living wage to all employed and in need of such protection;

(e) the effective recognition of the right of collective bargaining, the co-operation of management and labor in the continuous improvement of productive efficiency, and the collaboration of workers and employers in the preparation and application of social and economic measures;

(f) the extension of social security measures to provide a basic income to all in need of such protection and comprehensive medical care;

(g) adequate protection for the life and health of workers in all occupations;

(h) provision for child welfare and maternity protection;

(i) the provision of adequate nutri-

or final, the High Contracting Parties are of opinion that they are well fitted to guide the policy of the League of Nations; and that, if adopted by the industrial communities who are Members of the League, and safeguarded in practice by an adequate system of such inspection, they will confer lasting benefits upon the wage-earners of the world.

tion, housing and facilities for recreation and culture;

(j) the assurance of equality of educational and vocational opportunity.

IV. Confident that the fuller and broader utilisation of the world's productive resources necessary for the achievement of the objectives set forth in this Declaration can be secured by effective international and national action, including measures to expand production and consumption, to avoid severe economic fluctuations, to promote the economic and social advancement of the less developed regions of the world, to assure greater stability in world prices of primary products, and to promote a high and steady volume of international trade, the Conference pledges the full co-operation of the International Labor Organization with such international bodies as may be entrusted with a share of the responsibility for this great task and for the promotion of the health, education and well-being of all peoples.

The Conference affirms that the principles set forth in this Declaration are fully applicable to all peoples everywhere and that, while the manner of their application must be determined with due regard to the stage of social and economic development reached by each people, their progressive application to peoples who are still dependent, as well as to those who have already achieved self-government, is a matter of concern to the whole civilized world.

40. THE SENATE JOINT RESOLUTION 131 (HOUSE JOINT RESOLUTION 368) PROVIDING FOR MEMBERSHIP IN THE INTERNATIONAL LABOR ORGANIZATION, APPROVED 18 JUNE 1934 [1]

Despite the American share in drafting the Constitution of the International Labor Organization and the first meeting of the Conference at Washington in 1919, the defeat of the Treaty of Versailles resulted in the failure of the United States to participate in

the Organization until 1934. In that year the new administration of Franklin D. Roosevelt, as part of its program for raising labor standards, secured the adoption by the Congress of this joint resolution authorizing the President to accept membership in the In-

[1] *Congressional Record,* 73rd Cong., 2nd sess., Part 10, p. 11343; *United States Stat-* *utes at Large,* XLVIII (1934), 1182.

ternational Labor Organization. The vote was unanimous in the Senate and by more than two-thirds in the House.

Whereas progress toward the solution of the problems of international competition in industry can be made through international action concerning the welfare of wage earners, and

Whereas the failure of a nation to establish humane conditions of labor is an obstacle in the way of other nations which desire to maintain and improve the conditions in their own countries, and

Whereas the United States early recognized the desirability of international cooperation in matters pertaining to labor and took part in 1900 in establishing and for many years thereafter supported the International Association for Labor Legislation, and

Whereas the International Labor Organization has advanced the welfare of labor throughout the world through studies, recommendations, conferences and conventions concerning conditions of labor, and

Whereas other nations have joined the International Labor Organization without being members of the League of Nations, and

Whereas special provision has been made in the constitution of the International Labor Organization by which membership of the United States would not impose or be deemed to impose an obligation or agreement upon the United States to accept the proposals of that body as involving anything more than recommendations for its consideration:

Therefore be it

Resolved by the Senate and House of Representatives of the United States of America in Congress assembled that the President is hereby authorized to accept membership for the Government of the United States of America in the International Labor Organization which through its general conference of representatives of its members and through its International Labor Office collects information concerning labor throughout the world and prepares international conventions for the consideration of member governments with a view to improving conditions of labor.

Sec. 2. That in accepting such membership, the President shall assume on behalf of the United States no obligation under the Covenant of the League of Nations.

Part Three

DOCUMENTS OF THE

SECOND EFFORT:

THE UNITED NATIONS

Chapter 14

Wartime Developments

41. THE ATLANTIC CHARTER, 14 AUGUST 1941 [1]

The earliest commitment foreshadowing the establishment of a new general security system at the end of World War II appears in the eighth article of this joint declaration of principles by President Roosevelt and Prime Minister Churchill. Subsequently called the "Atlantic Charter," it was released to the press in the course of a conference on board the cruiser U.S.S. *Atlanta* off Newfoundland in August 1941, at which other decisions affecting the struggle then in progress were made.[2]

Joint declaration of the President of the United States of America and the Prime Minister, Mr. Churchill, representing His Majesty's Government in the United Kingdom, being met together, deem it right to make known certain common principles in the national policies of their respective countries on which they base their hopes for a better future for the world.

First, their countries seek no aggrandizement, territorial or other;

Second, they desire to see no territorial changes that do not accord with the freely expressed wishes of the peoples concerned;

Third, they respect the right of all peoples to choose the form of government under which they will live; and they wish to see sovereign rights and self-government restored to those who have been forcibly deprived of them;

Fourth, they will endeavor, with due respect for their existing obligations, to further the enjoyment by all States, great or small, victor or vanquished, of access, on equal terms, to the trade and to the raw materials of the world which are needed for their economic prosperity;

Fifth, they desire to bring about the fullest collaboration between all nations in the economic field with the object of securing, for all, improved labor standards, economic advancement and social security;

Sixth, after the final destruction of the Nazi tyranny, they hope to see established a peace which will afford to all nations the means of dwelling in safety within their own boundaries, and which will afford assurance that all the men in all the lands may live out their lives in freedom from fear and want;

Seventh, such a peace should enable all men to traverse the high seas and oceans without hindrance;

Eighth, they believe that all of the nations of the world, for realistic as well as spiritual reasons must come to the abandonment of the use of force. Since no future peace can be maintained if land, sea or air armaments continue to be employed by nations

---

[1] *Executive Agreement Series,* No. 236 (1942), p. 4. The declaration should bear the date of August 12th, when it was signed. But custom has given it the 14th, when it was published.

[2] The Atlantic Charter should be compared with President Wilson's "Fourteen Points" (see Doc. 18). For references to the Atlantic Charter in the Declaration by United Nations, see Doc. 42.

which threaten, or may threaten, aggression outside of their frontiers, they believe, pending the establishment of a wider and permanent system of general security, that the disarmament of such nations is essential. They will likewise aid and encourage all other practicable measures which will lighten for peace-loving peoples the crushing burden of armaments.

42. DECLARATION BY UNITED NATIONS, 1 JANUARY 1942 [1]

Following the Japanese strike at Pearl Harbor and the entrance of the United States into the war, this pledge to carry on the common struggle against the Axis powers was signed by 26 states, with another 21 subsequently adhering. By subscribing to the program of the Altantic Charter, they thereby, if indirectly, approved the principle of a general security system.

The Governments signatory hereto,

Having subscribed to a common program of purposes and principles embodied in the Joint Declaration of the President of the United States of America and the Prime Minister of the United Kingdom of Great Britain and Northern Ireland dated August 14, 1941, known as the Atlantic Charter.

Being convinced that complete victory over their enemies is essential to defend life, liberty, independence and religious freedom, and to preserve human rights and justice in their own lands as well as in other lands, and that they are now engaged in a common struggle against savage and brutal forces seeking to subjugate the world,

Declare:

(1) Each Government pledges itself to employ its full resources, military or economic, against those members of the Tripartite Pact and its adherents with which such government is at war.

(2) Each Government pledges itself to cooperate with the Governments signatory hereto and not to make a separate armistice or peace with the enemies.

The foregoing declaration may be adhered to by other nations which are, or which may be, rendering material assistance and contributions in the struggle for victory over Hitlerism.

Done at Washington

January First, 1942.

43. THE STATE DEPARTMENT STAFF DRAFT "CHARTER OF THE UNITED NATIONS," 14 AUGUST 1943 [1]*

Within three weeks of Pearl Harbor an Advisory Committee on Post War Foreign Policy was set up by the State Department to study, among other things, postwar international organization. A special subcommittee on international organization, with Sumner Welles, Under-Secretary of State, as chairman, studied past experience with international organization, not excluding the Covenant of the League of Nations. A year's work of the Welles committee culminated in a "Draft Constitution" [2] based, however, upon principles which proved to be unacceptable to the Department.

Following the rejection of the Welles "Draft Constitution," a group of ten staff members in the State Department's Division of Political Studies, all of them with wide knowledge of the League of Nations and its work, drafted this "Charter of the United Nations," which follows closely the lines of the League of Nations Covenant.[3]

[1] *Executive Agreement Series,* No. 236 (1942), p. 4. U.S. *Department of State Bulletin,* (3 January 1942), pp. 3-4. The name United Nations, later employed to designate the general international organization established at San Francisco in 1945 (Doc. 49) has here its first official use.

[1]* (Harley A. Notter), *Postwar Foreign*

Policy Preparation, 1939-1945 (Department of State Publication 3840, Washington, 1950), pp. 526-534.

[2] *Ibid.,* pp. 472-483.

[3] The work was done in the few days between 4-14 August, the latter date being the second anniversary of the publication of the Atlantic Charter. Here for the first time in

PREAMBLE

The United Nations, determined to banish the scourge of war, to establish the rule of law among states, and to promote the freedom, dignity and welfare of all peoples, do ordain and establish this Charter.

ART. 1. THE UNITED NATIONS

1. The community of nations organized within the framework of this Charter shall be known as The United Nations.
2. The seat of The United Nations shall be at ——————————.

ART. 2. MEMBERSHIP

1. Membership in The United Nations shall be open to states signing and ratifying this Charter.
2. By a vote of three-fourths of the Members represented in the General Conference, any other independent state may be admitted to membership by adherence to this Charter.
3. Admission to membership in The United Nations shall constitute acknowledgment by all Members of the international rights and privileges of the state so admitted.

ART. 3. THE GENERAL CONFERENCE

1. The General Conference shall consist of representatives of the Members of The United Nations.
2. In matters of international concern affecting the community of nations, the General Conference shall determine the general policies of The United Nations and may initiate action where the initiative is not specifically reserved to the Council.
3. The General Conference shall review the work of the organs of The United Nations, shall vote the appropriations for their activities, and shall exercise such other specific powers as

are conferred upon it by this Charter.
4. Each Member of The United Nations shall have one vote in the General Conference and shall have not more than six representatives, including representation from the national legislative body.
5. Except as otherwise provided in this instrument, decisions by the General Conference shall be by a three-fourths vote of the Members present and voting. Procedural questions, including the appointment of committees, shall be decided by a majority of the Members present and voting.
6. The General Conference shall meet annually at the seat of The United Nations. Special sessions may be convened upon the request of any five Members. The Conference shall elect a President and Vice-President, for annual terms, and otherwise perfect its organization. It shall adopt its own rules of procedure.

ART. 4. THE COUNCIL

1. The Council shall consist of representatives of certain Members with indeterminate tenure whose special position devolves upon them exceptional responsibilities for the maintenance of international security, together with the representatives of an equal number less one of Members elected by the General Conference for annual terms and not immediately eligible for reelection. Upon nomination of the Council, the General Conference may name additional Members to the Council.
2. Initially, the United States of America, the United Kingdom of Great Britain and Northern Ireland, the Republic of China, and the Union of Soviet Socialist Republics shall be the Members of the Council with indeterminate tenure, and three other Members shall be elected by the General Conference for annual terms.

official planning the name "United Nations" was attached to the future organization and

the word "Charter" to its proposed constitution.

3. The Council shall have primary responsibility for the maintenance of international security, and general responsibility for giving executive effect to policies determined by the General Conference. Between sessions of the General Conference the Council may initiate any necessary action within the competence of The United Nations, subject to review by the General Conference. It shall exercise such specific powers as are conferred upon it by this Charter.

4. Any Member of The United Nations not represented on the Council shall be entitled, subject to approval by a majority of the Council, to attend and be heard during the consideration of matters specially affecting that Member.

5. If the Council, in giving executive effect to a decision of the General Conference, deems that certain modifications are desirable, it may request the General Conference to reconsider the matter.

6. The [Director General] of The United Nations shall preside over the Council. He may participate in its deliberations without the right to vote.

7. Each Member of the Council shall have one representative and one vote. Except as otherwise provided in this Charter, decisions by the Council shall be by a two-thirds majority of the Members present and voting, provided all the Members with indeterminate tenure present and voting concur. Procedural questions, including the appointment of committees, shall be decided by a majority of the Members present and voting. The Council shall adopt its own rules of procedure.

ART. 5. THE ADMINISTRATIVE OFFICES

1. The General Administrative Office shall be established at the seat of The United Nations. Other administrative offices, wherever established, shall be subject to the staff regulations governing the General Administrative Office.

2. All administrative offices shall be under the direction of a [Director General] who shall be assisted by such directors and other officers as may be required. All general officers shall be appointed by the Council and confirmed by the General Conference. In making appointments the widest distribution, compatible with technical efficiency, shall be made among nationalities.

3. There shall be established such administrative offices as may be required for the various technical organisations and commissions, including offices in the fields of economics and finance, labor, food and agriculture, communications, health, social welfare, education and culture, and international territorial administration. Each office shall be in charge of a Director appointed by the Council upon the nomination of the highest executive authority of the technical organization concerned.

4. The Directors of the several offices, together with the [Director General], shall constitute an Administrative Committee to supervise and coordinate the administrative work of the various offices. This Administrative Committee shall sit with and advise the Council in coordinating the policies of the technical organizations. The Director of each technical office shall report and make recommendations directly to the Council on the work of the technical organization concerned.

5. The permanent officials of the administrative staffs shall agree to discharge their duties and regulate their conduct with the interests of The United Nations alone in view. The Members shall impose no obligations upon their nationals, officials of The United Nations, which are inconsistent with the performance of their duties.

6. Officials of The United Nations when engaged on the business of The United Nations, or when traveling to and from the seat of The United Nations, shall enjoy diplomatic privileges and immunities.

ART. 6. THE JUDICIARY

1. The International Court of Justice is constituted in accordance with the terms of the Statute annexed to this Charter.

2. The General Conference is authorized to formulate and submit to the Members of The United Nations for adoption plans for the establishment of such other tribunals as may be required.

3. Any state, or any agency of The United Nations which is so authorized by the terms of the instrument by which it was created, may be a party to cases before the Court.

4. The Court shall be competent to hear and determine all cases involving disputes as to the respective rights of the parties, or as to the interpretation of this Charter, which are referred to it: (a) by agreement of the parties; (b) in accordance with the provisions of agreements, treaties or conventions in force; and (c) by the Council, in the event that a menace to the peace of nations exists. The Court may also give its opinion upon the legal aspects of any question within the competence of The United Nations, when so requested by a majority of the Members of the Council present and voting.

ART. 7. PEACEFUL ADJUSTMENT

1. The Members of The United Nations agree to settle by peaceful means any of their disputes which may threaten the peace and security of nations.

2. Any dispute, the continuance of which may disturb the peace or the good understanding between nations, which is not settled by diplomacy, shall be submitted to conciliation, arbitration, judicial settlement or to the procedures of this Article.

3. In the event that any dispute has not been settled by other peaceful means, the Council, upon its own initiative or that of any party or any other state, shall endeavor to effect a settle-ment between the parties. The Council, by a majority of the Members present and voting, may undertake an investigation and make proposals for a settlement.

4. Should such a settlement not be effected the Council shall make recommendations which it deems just and equitable.

5. The Council may refer the dispute to the General Conference, which shall make such recommendations for settlement as it deems just and equitable.

6. In the event that any party to a dispute shall fail to observe or execute a recommendation by the Council or by the General Conference, the Council shall take steps to ensure compliance therewith.

7. In any decision taken by the Council or the General Conference under paragraphs 4, 5, or 6 of this Article, the votes of the parties shall be excluded.

ART. 8. SECURITY AND ARMAMENTS

1. Any threat to international peace and security is declared to be a matter of concern to all Members of The United Nations, which hereby undertake effectively to support measures adopted by the Council and the General Conference for safeguarding or restoring peace.

2. In the event of a threat to, or a breach of, the peace between nations, the Chairman of the Council, after consultation with the Members of the Council, shall request the parties involved to desist from any action which might prejudice a peaceful settlement. States failing to comply with this request shall be regarded as intending a breach of the peace, and the Council shall forthwith institute such measures, including measures of force, as it deems appropriate for the maintenance or restoration of the peace. The Council shall apprise the General Conference of its action, and request the Members to take appropriate supporting action.

3. Members of The United Nations agree to prohibit all assistance to a state

which is declared by the Council to have committed, or to be threatening, a breach of the peace.

4. In the event of Council action under paragraph 2, the Members of The United Nations agree to make available such of their national armaments, facilities and installations, strategic areas, and contingents of armed forces as the Council, in consultation with the Member concerned, shall determine to be necessary. For this purpose, the Council shall be advised by a General Security and Armaments Commission whose composition and functions are set forth in a Protocol annexed to this Charter. In considering the contributions of a Member to a joint effort for the maintenance or restoration of peace, the Council shall take account of its geographical position, regional or special obligations, and relative resources. Freedom of passage shall be afforded by Members to all forces operating in behalf of The United Nations.

5. Members of The United Nations agree to cooperate in executing such economic, commercial or financial measures against a state threatening, or committing a breach of, the peace as the Council or the General Conference shall determine to be necessary. They further agree to support one another in resisting measures resulting from such action, and in equalizing excessive losses incurred thereby.

6. Members of The United Nations undertake to maintain their armaments at the lowest point consistent with their internal order and with the effective discharge of their respective obligations for maintaining international security. An appropriate system of armaments regulation shall be established by the Council, with the advice of the General Security and Armaments Commission, and in consultation with the Members of The United Nations. Account shall be taken of the special responsibilities for security assumed by Members of the Council with indeterminate tenure, and the collective responsibility assumed by all.

7. Limitations and regulations established under paragraph 6 shall be enforced by a system of inspection carried out by an Armaments Inspection Commission under the direction of the General Security and Armaments Commission. Members shall accord this Commission every facility for the effective discharge of its responsibility.

8. Any action by the Council under this Article shall require a two-thirds majority vote of the Members present and voting, including three-fourths of the Members with indeterminate tenure.

ART. 9. HUMAN RIGHTS

The Members of The United Nations agree to give legislative effect to the Declaration of Human Rights annexed to this Charter. Measures of enforcement shall be applied by the administrative and judicial authorities of each Member without discrimination as to nationality, language, race, political opinion, or religious belief.

ART. 10. ECONOMIC AND SOCIAL COOPERATION

1. The United Nations shall assist its Members in developing collaboration in economic and social matters. For this purpose the General Conference is authorized to establish or to bring within the framework of the United Nations appropriate technical organizations, including organizations in the fields of economics and finance, labor, food and agriculture, communications, health, social welfare, and education and culture.

2. The General Conference, taking into account the recommendations of each organization, shall determine the general policies of technical organizations of The United Nations.

3. The Council, with the advice and assistance of the Administrative Committee provided for in Article 5, shall coordinate the activities of the technical organizations.

4. Each technical organization shall

have a statute which shall be consistent with this Charter.

ART. 11. TERRITORIAL ADMINISTRATION

1. The Council shall establish a system of administration for territories which may be placed under the authority of The United Nations by treaty or other agreement.

2. The Council shall establish by separate instruments for each such territory the terms and conditions under which it shall be administered. All instruments shall include provisions to assure:

(*a*) the education and cultural advancement of the inhabitants;

(*b*) freedom of conscience and speech;

(*c*) protection of the inhabitants from exploitation;

(*d*) promotion of economic and social welfare;

(*e*) establishment and maintenance of non-discriminatory commercial treatment;

(*f*) promotion of equality of economic opportunity consistent with the safeguarding of the interests of the local inhabitants.

3. The Council, on behalf of The United Nations, shall administer these territories either directly or through such authorities as it may recognize or establish.

4. To assist the Council in exercising its powers of administration and supervision, commissions shall be established whose number, composition and powers shall be defined by the Council. Each commission shall have the right to conduct inspections in territories under its supervision to ensure that the policies of the Council are being carried out, and it shall make periodic reports and recommendations to the Council.

5. The Council shall be the final authority in all matters relating to modification or termination of the provisions of this Article. It shall also decide to what degree any of the provisions shall be modified for special reasons of international security.

6. Each Member of The United Nations undertakes to observe in the other non-self-governing territories under its control the same standards of administration as are required by the terms of this Article.

ART. 12. REGIONAL ARRANGEMENTS

Nothing in this Charter shall affect regional arrangements, agreements, or associations, now existing or which may be entered into between Members, which are consistent with the obligations assumed under this Charter.

ART. 13. FINANCIAL PROVISIONS

1. The expenses of The United Nations shall be borne by the Members on a basis of apportionment determined by the General Conference with the approval of the Council.

2. Regulations for the financial administration of The United Nations, including provision for the payment of the travel expenses of official representatives to meetings of the General Conference and the Council, shall be approved by the General Conference.

3. A Treasurer, appointed by the Council and confirmed by the General Conference, shall receive and administer all funds of The United Nations.

ART. 14. REGISTRATION OF TREATIES

Every treaty and agreement entered into by the Members of The United Nations shall be registered with the General Administrative Office for publication. The texts of the instruments so registered shall be regarded by The United Nations as authentic.

ART. 15. RATIFICATION AND BINDING FORCE

1. This Charter shall be ratified, and shall come into force when ratifications have been deposited with the President

of the United States of America by 25 states, including those Members of the Council with indeterminate tenure. It shall remain in force indefinitely.

2. The authorities of each Member shall take such measures as may be necessary to give full force and effect to the provisions of this Charter.

3. The Members agree to take such steps as may be required to obtain their release from any obligations inconsistent with the undertakings of this Charter; and they further agree that they will not hereafter enter into any treaty or agreement inconsistent with these undertakings.

ART. 16. WITHDRAWAL FROM MEMBERSHIP

1. Membership in The United Nations shall be for a period of ten years, and shall continue for successive periods of ten years unless a Member shall, not less than two years before the expiration of a ten-year period, give notice to the President of the General Conference of its intention to withdraw.

2. Withdrawal from membership shall not release a state from any obligations whatsoever which it has in-

curred while a Member of The United Nations, nor shall it affect the binding force of this Charter for the remaining Members.

ART. 17. AMENDMENTS

Amendments to this Charter shall be adopted by the General Conference and be submitted forthwith by the [Director General] to the Members of The United Nations. They shall come into force if ratified within five years by four-fifths of the number of Members of The United Nations at the time of the adoption of the amendment, including all Members of the Council with indeterminate tenure.

TRANSITORY ARTICLES

1. The first meetings of the General Conference and of the Council of The United Nations shall be called by the President of the United States of America, within six months after this Charter enters into force, at such time and place as he may designate.

2. The Council shall determine the time and manner in which provisional agencies shall be superseded by permanent organs of The United Nations.

44. THE FULBRIGHT RESOLUTION, 21 SEPTEMBER 1943 [1]

As planning for postwar organization went forward in the executive branch and in private circles, fears of adverse action in the Congress began to be allayed after the adoption by the House of this resolution whose first draft was introduced by Congressman J. William Fulbright, of Arkansas. Without committing the Congress to any final action, the resolution was intended to reflect the support of the American people for United States participation in a general system of collective security.

[1] *Congressional Record,* (House of Representatives) 78th Cong. 1st sess., LXXXIX (21 September 1943), p. 7225.
[2] The Fulbright resolution as House Con-

Resolved by the House of Representatives (the Senate concurring) [2] That the Congress hereby expresses itself as favoring the creation of appropriate international machinery with power adequate to establish and to maintain a just and lasting peace, among the nations of the world, and as favoring participation by the United States therein through its constitutional processes.

current Resolution 25 was referred to the Senate, which preferred to draw up a resolution of its own (see Doc. 45).

45. THE MOSCOW DECLARATION ON GENERAL SECURITY, 1 NOVEMBER 1943 [1]

Although by the end of 1942 responsible government figures in all the other leading powers among the wartime United Nations had publicly espoused a policy of establishing a new international organization after the war, nearly a year was to pass before the Kremlin was brought into line. The first explicit Soviet agreement came with the October 1943 conference of foreign ministers from the United States, Russia and Great Britain and the Chinese ambassador to Russia. In the Moscow Declaration are set forth the principles upon which the postwar organization was to be based. It would be a general international organization, composed of sovereign states, with both great and small powers included.[2]

(c) DECLARATION OF FOUR NATIONS ON GENERAL SECURITY, NOVEMBER 1, 1943

The Governments of the United States of America, the United Kingdom, the Soviet Union and China:

united in their determination, in accordance with the Declaration by the United Nations of January 1, 1942, and subsequent declarations, to continue hostilities against those Axis powers with which they respectively are at war until such powers have laid down their arms on the basis of unconditional surrender;

conscious of their responsibility to secure the liberation of themselves and the peoples allied with them from the menace of aggression;

recognizing the necessity of ensuring a rapid and orderly transition from war to peace and of establishing and maintaining international peace and security with the least diversion of the world's human and economic resources for armaments;

jointly declare:

1. That their united action, pledged for the prosecution of the war against their respective enemies, will be continued for the organization and maintenance of peace and security.

2. That those of them at war with a common enemy will act together in all matters relating to the surrender and disarmament of that enemy.

3. That they will take all measures deemed by them to be necessary to provide against any violation of the terms imposed upon the enemy.

4. That they recognise the necessity of establishing at the earliest practicable date a general international organization, based on the principle of the sovereign equality of all peace-loving states, and open to membership by all such states, large and small, for the maintenance of international peace and security.

5. That for the purpose of maintaining international peace and security pending the re-establishment of law and order and the inauguration of a system of general security, they will consult with one another and as occasion requires with other members of the United Nations with a view to joint action on behalf of the community of nations.

6. That after the termination of hostilities they will not employ their military forces within the territories of other states except for the purposes envisaged in this declaration and after joint consultation.

7. That they will confer and co-operate with one another and with other members of the United Nations to bring about a practicable general agreement with respect to the regulation of armaments in the post-war period.

V. MOLOTOV
ANTHONY EDEN
CORDELL HULL
FOO PING-SHEUNG

MOSCOW, *30th October, 1943.*

[1] *Department of State Bulletin,* IX (6 November 1943), pp. 308 f.

[2] Regionalism, federalism and a revived Concert of Great Powers were thus rejected.

46. THE CONNALLY RESOLUTION, 5 NOVEMBER 1943 [1]

Early in 1943 the United States Senate began consideration of a number of resolutions supporting the principle of international organization and calling for United States participation therein. Its efforts culminated in the adoption of this Connally Resolution, 85 to 5, in November, by which time the House had adopted the Fulbright Resolution [2] and the Moscow Conference of Foreign Ministers had taken place. To the original text of the resolution was added the fourth point of the Moscow Declaration.[3]

Resolved, That the war against all our enemies be waged until complete victory is achieved.

That the United States cooperate with its comrades-in-arms in securing a just and honorable peace.

That the United States, acting through its constitutional processes, join with free and sovereign nations in the establishment and maintenance of international authority with power to prevent aggression and to preserve the peace of the world.

That the Senate recognizes the necessity of their being established at the earliest practicable date a general international organization, based on the principle of the sovereign equality of all peace-loving states, and open to membership by all such states, large and small, for the maintenance of international peace and security.

That, pursuant to the Constitution of the United States, any treaty made to effect the purposes of this resolution, on behalf of the Government of the United States with any other nation or any association of nations, shall be made only by and with the advice and consent of the Senate of the United States, provided two-thirds of the Senators present concur.

[1] *Congressional Record* (Senate), 78th Cong., 1st sess., LXXXIX (5 November 1943), p. 9222.

[2] See Doc. 44.
[3] See Doc. 45.

Chapter 15

Establishment of the United Nations

47. THE UNITED NATIONS CONFERENCE ON INTERNATIONAL ORGANIZATION, RULES OF PROCEDURE,[1] 1945

The United Nations Conference on International Organization opened on 25 April 1945 with forty-six nations in attendance; later four others were admitted. The organization of the Conference included four Commissions served by a total of twelve technical committees. A Steering Committee and an Executive Committee guided the work of the Conference. A Coordination Committee and a Committee of Jurists put the Charter into final form. In addition there was a Credentials Committee. Plenary sessions of the conference heard reports and took formal action.

The work of the Conference was based upon the "Proposals for the Establishment of a General International Organization" adopted by the Big Four on 7 October 1944 at the end of their "conversations" at Dumbarton Oaks, the Yalta agreement respecting voting in the Security Council, and other suggestions forwarded by the members of the wartime United Nations in preparation for the conference.

Although they governed the work of the Conference, by an apparent oversight the Executive Committee failed to submit these Rules of Procedure for adoption by the Conference in plenary session.[2]

RULES OF PROCEDURE [3]

Doc. 177, May 9
I. Establishment of Commissions, Technical Committees and Sub-Committees

1. Upon adoption by the Conference in plenary session of the Report of the

Meeting of the Heads of Delegations To Organize the Conference, the President of the Conference will request the presidents of the commissions, in consultation with the Secretary-General of the Conference, to call the first meetings of their respective commissions as soon as possible. The secretary-general of each delegation as soon as possible will inform the Secretary-General of the Conference as to the commissions and technical committees on which his delegation desires to be represented and the name of the member or members designated in each case.

2. At the appropriate time the presidents of the respective commissions will request the chairmen of the technical committees to call the first meetings of their respective committees.

3. Subcommittees will begin meetings when requested to do so by the respective technical committees.

II. Submission and Allocation of Formal Proposals

Formal proposals which a delegation desires to submit to the Conference shall be deposited with, or forwarded to, the Secretary-General and shall be circulated to all delegations. All such

---

[1] *The United Nations Conference on International Organization, San Francisco, California, April 24-June 26, 1945: Selected Documents* (Department of State Publication 2490), pp. 74-76.
[2] *Ibid.*, pp. 87 ff.

[3] This document is still to be submitted to the Conference in plenary session. [Footnote in the original; the document was never submitted to a plenary session and consequently was never approved.]

proposals should be submitted before midnight, Friday, May 4, it being understood that drafting changes may be put forward at any time. Formal proposals received after Friday, May 4, can be accepted only upon authorization of the Executive Committee, before which body the Secretary-General will lay them. The Secretary-General will provisionally allocate all proposals submitted by the various delegations to the appropriate commissions and their committees.

III. Communications from Non-Participants in the Conference

Communications from governments, organizations, and individuals not participating in the Conference which are sent to the Secretariat will be distributed to the delegations only if, in the discretion of the Secretary-General, they are relevant to the subject-matter of the Conference and if the facilities of the Secretariat are available to handle them without delay to official work.

IV. Right to Address the Conference

Speakers shall be recognized by the presiding officer in the order in which they have signified their desire to speak. The president, chairman, or rapporteur of a commission or committee may be accorded precedence for the purpose of explaining or clarifying the conclusions arrived at by the commission or committee.

V. Voting

1. Each delegation shall have one vote in each body of the Conference on which it is represented.

2. Any question of procedure put to the vote shall be decided by a majority of the votes of the delegations present and voting. All other questions put to the vote shall be decided by two thirds of the votes of the delegations present and voting.

3. If there is a substantial degree of uncertainty prior to a vote on any given question as to whether that question is or is not one of procedure, the presiding officer of the body concerned shall submit the question to the Executive Committee, which shall decide.

4. The Conference shall normally vote by a show of hands, except that any delegation in any body of the Conference may request a roll call, which shall then be taken by countries in English alphabetical order.

VI. Languages

1. English, Russian, Chinese, French, and Spanish shall be the official languages of the Conference.

2. English and French shall be the working languages of the Conference.

3. At plenary sessions of the Conference addresses in English or French shall not be interpreted into the other language unless the speaker so requests, but a translation will appear subsequently in the verbatim minutes.

Delegates shall be free to use any other language besides English or French, but in this case they shall provide interpretations thereof into either English or French at their choice. Interpretations will be provided by the Secretariat into the other of these two languages if the speaker so requests. As regards meetings of commissions, technical committees, and subcommittees, interpretations from English into French and from French into English will be provided. Delegates shall be free in these bodies also to speak in any other language, but shall provide their own interpretations into either English or French at their choice; the Secretariat will provide interpretations into the other of these two languages if the speaker so requests.

4. The Dumbarton Oaks Proposals, as supplemented at the Crimea Conference and by the Chinese proposals agreed to by all of the sponsoring governments, will be issued in each of the five official languages as the first document of the Conference.

5. The final text of the Charter will be prepared and opened for signature in each of the five official languages. If

time does not permit the completion of the texts in each of these languages before the closing of the Conference, the texts which have not been completed by that time shall be opened for signature at a later date.

6. All Conference documents, records, and the official *Journal* will be issued in the two working languages of the Conference.

7. The following categories of documents will be published (i.e. issued in printed, mimeographed, hectographed, or other appropriate form) upon request in any or all of the five official languages in addition to English and French.

a. All proposals presented to the Conference or its subordinate bodies;

b. All decisions of plenary sessions, commissions, or committees;

c. Summaries or records of meetings of the committees or sub-committees.

VII. Records

1. No stenographic transcript of proceedings will be kept except at plenary sessions of the Conference and at public meetings of the commissions.

2. The Secretariat will prepare a brief summary of the proceedings in other meetings.

3. Both stenographic transcripts and summaries of proceedings will be prepared first in provisional form and be subject to correction. After corrections have been made the transcript or summary will be issued in final form.

VIII. Document Classification

There will be two classifications of documents:

1. *Unrestricted,* for distribution to all delegations, to accredited press, radio, and newsreel representatives, and to the public so far as the supply permits;

2. *Restricted,* for distribution only to delegations.

IX. Public-Information Policy

Plenary sessions of the Conference and meetings of the commissions will be held in public, subject to the reservation that the commissions in their discretion may hold closed meetings. In addition, principal officers of the Conference will hold regular meetings with the accredited press, radio, and newsreel representatives. The meetings of the technical committees and subcommittees will be closed.

X. Hours of Assembly

1. Plenary sessions of the Conference will normally convene at 10:30 a.m. or 3:30 p.m. Meetings of the commissions will normally take place at 10:30 a.m. and 2:45 p.m. For the technical committees there will be four sittings each day, at 10:30 a.m., 2:45 p.m., 5:00 p.m., and 8:30 p.m. At each of these hours three committees will normally convene. If the work of technical committees, or their subcommittees, makes it essential for them to hold special meetings at hours differing from the established schedule, they should consult with the Office of the Executive Secretary.

48. THE FOUR POWER STATEMENT ON SECURITY COUNCIL VOTING PROCEDURE, 7 JUNE 1945 [1]

Toward the close of the San Francisco Conference, in answer to the objections and questions of the smaller powers, this Four Power Statement on voting in the Security Council was drafted and issued. It explains the proposed Article 27 and attempts to defend the so-called "veto," which the smaller nations regarded as placing the permanent members of the Council, if not above the law, at least beyond any effective application of the law.[2]

[1] *The United Nations Conference on International Organization, San Francisco, California, April 24-June 26, 1945: Selected Documents* (Department of State Publication 2490), pp. 751-754.

[2] The "veto" provision is the requirement that among the seven (out of eleven) votes needed for approving a substantive question, those of all five permanent members must be included. In the course of the constitu-

I

Specific questions covering the voting procedure in the Security Council have been submitted by a Sub-Committee of the Conference Committee on Structure and Procedures of the Security Council to the Delegations of the four Governments sponsoring the Conference—the United States of America, the United Kingdom of Great Britain and Northern Ireland, the Union of Soviet Socialist Republics, and the Republic of China. In dealing with these questions, the four Delegations desire to make the following statement of their general attitude towards the whole question of unanimity of permanent members in the decisions of the Security Council.

1. The Yalta voting formula recognizes that the Security Council, in discharging its responsibilities for the maintenance of international peace and security, will have two broad groups of functions. Under Chapter VIII, the Council will have to make decisions which involve its taking direct measures in connection with settlement of disputes, adjustment of situations likely to lead to disputes, determination of threats to the peace, removal of threats to the peace, and suppression of breaches of the peace. It will also have to make decisions which do not involve the taking of such measures. The Yalta formula provides that the second of these two groups of decisions will be governed by a procedural vote—that is, the vote of any seven members. The first group of decisions will be governed by a qualified vote—that is, the vote of seven members, including the concurring votes of the five permanent members, subject to the proviso that in decisions under section A and a part of

section C of chapter VIII parties to a dispute shall abstain from voting.

2. For example, under the Yalta formula a procedural vote will govern the decisions made under the entire section D of chapter VI. This means that the Council will, by a vote of any seven of its members, adopt or alter its rules of procedure; determine the method of selecting its president; organize itself in such a way as to be able to function continuously; select the times and places of its regular and special meetings; establish such bodies or agencies as it may deem necessary for the performance of its functions; invite a member of the Organization not represented on the Council to participate in its discussions when that Member's interests are specially affected; and invite any state when it is a party to a dispute being considered by the Council to participate in the discussion relating to that dispute.

3. Further, no individual member of the Council can alone prevent consideration and discussion by the Council of a dispute or situation brought to its attention under paragraph 2, section A, chapter VIII. Nor can parties to such dispute be prevented by these means from being heard by the Council. Likewise, the requirement for unanimity of the permanent members cannot prevent any member of the Council from reminding the members of the Organization of their general obligations assumed under the Charter as regards peaceful settlement of international disputes.

4. Beyond this point, decisions and actions by the Security Council may well have major political consequences and may even initiate a chain of events which might, in the end, require the Council under its responsibilities to in-

---

tional development of the United Nations since 1945, the practice has developed that abstention from voting or absence is not a failure to vote affirmatively, within the meaning of Article 27, so far as substantive questions before the Security Council are concerned. This in effect means that to exercise the "veto" power a permanent member must actually cast a negative vote. Precedents with respect to abstentions (although, because of the wording of Article 5, paragraph 1, of the Covenant, not with respect to absences) are to be found in the practice of the League of Nations.

voke measures of enforcement under section B, chapter VIII. This chain of events begins when [the] Council decides to make an investigation, or determines that the time has come to call upon states to settle their differences, or makes recommendations to the parties. It is to such decisions and actions that unanimity of the permanent members applies, with the important proviso, referred to above, for abstention from voting by parties to a dispute.

5. To illustrate: In ordering an investigation, the Council has to consider whether the investigation—which may involve calling for reports, hearing witnesses, dispatching a commission of inquiry, or other means—might not further aggravate the situation. After investigation, the Council must determine whether the continuance of the situation or dispute would be likely to endanger international peace and security. If it so determines, the Council would be under obligation to take further steps. Similarly, the decision to make recommendations, even when all parties request it to do so, or to call upon parties to a dispute to fulfill their obligations under the Charter, might be the first step on a course of action from which the Security Council could withdraw only at the risk of failing to discharge its responsibilities.

6. In appraising the significance of the vote required to take such decisions or actions, it is useful to make comparison with the requirements of the League Covenant with reference to decisions of the League Council. Substantive decisions of the League of Nations Council could be taken only by the unanimous vote of all its members, whether permanent or not, with the exception of parties to a dispute under article XV of the League Covenant. Under article XI, under which most of the disputes brought before the League were dealt with and decisions to make investigations taken, the unanimity rule was invariably interpreted to include even the votes of the parties to a dispute.

7. The Yalta voting formula substitutes for the rule of complete unanimity of the League Council a system of qualified majority voting in the Security Council. Under this system nonpermanent members of the Security Council individually would have no veto. As regards the permanent members, there is no question under the Yalta formula of investing them with a new right; namely, the right to veto, a right which the permanent members of the League Council always had. The formula proposed for the taking of action in the Security Council by a majority of seven would make the operation of the Council less subject to obstruction than was the case under the League of Nations rule of complete unanimity.

8. It should also be remembered that under the Yalta formula the five major powers could not act by themselves, since even under the unanimity requirement any decisions of the Council would have to include the concurring votes of at least two of the nonpermanent members. In other words, it would be possible for five nonpermanent members as a group to exercise a veto. It is not to be assumed, however, that the permanent members, any more than the nonpermanent members, would use their veto power willfully to obstruct the operation of the Council.

9. In view of the primary responsibilities of the permanent members they could not be expected, in the present condition of the world, to assume the obligation to act in so serious a matter as the maintenance of international peace and security in consequence of a decision in which they had not concurred. Therefore, if majority voting in the Security Council is to be made possible, the only practicable method is to provide, in respect of nonprocedural decisions, for unanimity of the permanent members plus the concurring votes of at least two of the nonpermanent members.

10. For all these reasons, the four sponsoring governments agreed on the

Yalta formula and have presented it to this Conference as essential if an international organization is to be created through which all peace-loving nations can effectively discharge their common responsibilities for the maintenance of international peace and security.

II

In the light of the considerations set forth in part 1 of this statement, it is clear what the answers to the questions submitted by the subcommittee should be, with the exception of question 19. The answer to that question is as follows:

1. In the opinion of the delegations

of the sponsoring governments, the Draft Charter itself contains an indication of the application of the voting procedures to the various functions of the Council.

2. In this case, it will be unlikely that there will arise in the future any matters of great importance on which a decision will have to be made as to whether a procedural vote would apply. Should, however, such a matter arise the decision regarding the preliminary question as to whether or not such a matter is procedural must be taken by a vote of seven members of the Security Council, including the concurring votes of the permanent members.

49. THE CHARTER OF THE UNITED NATIONS, 26 JUNE 1945 [1]

After nine weeks of arduous negotiation involving compromises on many issues, some of which were serious enough to threaten the success of the Conference, the United Nations Charter was signed by all the nations represented at San Francisco.[2]

We the peoples of the United Nations determined

to save succeeding generations from the scourge of war, which twice in our lifetime has brought untold sorrow to mankind, and

to reaffirm faith in fundamental human rights, in the dignity and worth of the human person, in the equal rights of men and women and of nations large and small, and

to establish conditions under which justice and respect for the obligations arising from treaties and other sources of international law can be maintained, and

to promote social progress and better standards of life in larger freedom,

and for these ends

to practice tolerance and live together in peace with one another as good neighbors, and

to unite our strength to maintain international peace and security, and

to ensure, by the acceptance of principles and the institution of methods, that armed force shall not be used, save in the common interest, and

to employ international machinery for the promotion of economic and social advancement of all peoples,

have resolved to combine our efforts to accomplish these aims.

Accordingly, our respective Governments, through representatives assembled in the city of San Francisco, who have exhibited their full powers found to be in good and due form, have agreed to the present Charter of the United Nations and do hereby estab-

[1] United States Statutes at Large, LIX (1945), pp. 1033 ff. For the annexed Statute of the International Court of Justice, see Doc. 36.

[2] In addition to the nations originally attending or later admitted to the Conference, Poland also signed and became a Charter member.

lish an international organization to be known as the United Nations.

CHAPTER I. PURPOSES AND PRINCIPLES

ART. 1. The Purposes of the United Nations are:

1. To maintain international peace and security, and to that end: to take effective collective measures for the prevention and removal of threats to the peace, and for the suppression of acts of aggression or other breaches of the peace, and to bring about by peaceful means, and in conformity with the principles of justice and international law, adjustment or settlement of international disputes or situations which might lead to a breach of the peace;

2. To develop friendly relations among nations based on respect for the principle of equal rights and self-determination of peoples, and to take other appropriate measures to strengthen universal peace;

3. To achieve international cooperation in solving international problems of an economic, social, cultural, or humanitarian character, and in promoting and encouraging respect for human rights and for fundamental freedoms for all without distinction as to race, sex, language, or religion; and

4. To be a center for harmonizing the actions of nations in the attainment of these common ends.

ART. 2. The Organization and its Members, in pursuit of the Purposes stated in Article 1, shall act in accordance with the following Principles.

1. The Organization is based on the principle of the sovereign equality of all its Members.

2. All Members, in order to ensure to all of them the rights and benefits resulting from membership, shall fulfil in good faith the obligations assumed by them in accordance with the present Charter.

3. All Members shall settle their international disputes by peaceful means in such a manner that international peace and security, and justice, are not endangered.

4. All Members shall refrain in their international relations from the threat or use of force against the territorial integrity or political independence of any state, or in any other manner inconsistent with the Purposes of the United Nations.

5. All Members shall give the United Nations every assistance in any action it takes in accordance with the present Charter, and shall refrain from giving assistance to any state against which the United Nations is taking preventive or enforcement action.

6. The Organization shall ensure that states which are not Members of the United Nations act in accordance with these Principles so far as may be necessary for the maintenance of international peace and security.

7. Nothing contained in the present Charter shall authorize the United Nations to intervene in matters which are essentially within the domestic jurisdiction of any state or shall require the Members to submit such matters to settlement under the present Charter; but this principle shall not prejudice the application of enforcement measures under Chapter VII.

CHAPTER II. MEMBERSHIP

ART. 3. The original Members of the United Nations shall be the states which, having participated in the United Nations Conference on International Organization at San Francisco, or having previously signed the Declaration by United Nations of January 1, 1942, sign the present Charter and ratify it in accordance with Article 110.

ART. 4. 1. Membership in the United Nations is open to all other peace-loving states which accept the obligations contained in the present Charter and, in the judgment of the Organization, are able and willing to carry out these obligations.

2. The admission of any such state to membership in the United Nations

will be effected by a decision of the General Assembly upon the recommendation of the Security Council.

ART. 5. A Member of the United Nations against which preventive or enforcement action has been taken by the Security Council may be suspended from the exercise of the rights and privileges of membership by the General Assembly upon the recommendation of the Security Council. The exercise of these rights and privileges may be restored by the Security Council.

ART. 6. A Member of the United Nations which has persistently violated the Principles contained in the present Charter may be expelled from the Organization by the General Assembly upon the recommendation of the Security Council.

CHAPTER III. ORGANS

ART. 7. There are established as the principal organs of the United Nations: a General Assembly, a Security Council, an Economic and Social Council, a Trusteeship Council, an International Court of Justice, and a Secretariat.

2. Such subsidiary organs as may be found necessary may be established in accordance with the present Charter.

ART. 8. The United Nations shall place no restrictions on the eligibility of men and women to participate in any capacity and under conditions of equality in its principal and subsidiary organs.

CHAPTER IV. THE GENERAL ASSEMBLY

Composition

ART. 9. 1. The General Assembly shall consist of all the Members of the United Nations.

2. Each Member shall have not more than five representatives in the General Assembly.

Functions and Powers

ART. 10. The General Assembly may discuss any questions or any matters within the scope of the present Charter or relating to the powers and functions of any organs provided for in the Present Charter, and, except as provided in Article 12, may make recommendations to the Members of the United Nations or to the Security Council or to both on any such questions or matters.

ART. 11. 1. The General Assembly may consider the general principles of cooperation in the maintenance of international peace and security, including the principles governing disarmament and the regulation of armaments, and may make recommendations with regard to such principles to the Members or to the Security Council or to both.

2. The General Assembly may discuss any questions relating to the maintenance of international peace and security brought before it by any Member of the United Nations, or by the Security Council, or by a state which is not a Member of the United Nations in accordance with Article 35, paragraph 2, and, except as provided in Article 12, may make recommendations with regard to any such questions to the state or states concerned or to the Security Council or to both. Any such question on which action is necessary shall be referred to the Security Council by the General Assembly either before or after discussion.

3. The General Assembly may call the attention of the Security Council to situations which are likely to endanger international peace and security.

4. The powers of the General Assembly set forth in this Article shall not limit the general scope of Article 10.

ART. 12. 1. While the Security Council is exercising in respect of any dispute or situation the functions assigned to it in the present Charter, the General Assembly shall not make any recommendation with regard to that dispute or situation unless the Security Council so requests.

2. The Secretary-General, with the consent of the Security Council, shall notify the General Assembly at each

session of any matters relative to the maintenance of international peace and security which are being dealt with by the Security Council and shall similarly notify the General Assembly, or the Members of the United Nations if the General Assembly is not in session, immediately the Security Council ceases to deal with such matters.

ART. 13. 1. The General Assembly shall initiate studies and make recommendations for the purpose of:

a. promoting international cooperation in the political field and encouraging the progressive development of international law and its codification;

b. promoting international cooperation in the economic, social, cultural, educational, and health fields, and assisting in the realization of human rights and fundamental freedoms for all without distinction as to race, sex, language, or religion.

2. The further responsibilities, functions, and powers of the General Assembly with respect to matters mentioned in paragraph 1 (b) above are set forth in Chapters IX and X.

ART. 14. Subject to the provisions of Article 12, the General Assembly may recommend measures for the peaceful adjustment of any situation, regardless of origin, which it deems likely to impair the general welfare or friendly relations among nations, including situations resulting from a violation of the provisions of the present Charter setting forth the Purposes and Principles of the United Nations.

ART. 15. 1. The General Assembly shall receive and consider annual and special reports from the Security Council; these reports shall include an account of the measures that the Security Council has decided upon or taken to maintain international peace and security.

2. The General Assembly shall receive and consider reports from the other organs of the United Nations.

ART. 16. The General Assembly shall perform such functions with respect to the international trusteeship system as are assigned to it under Chapters XII and XIII, including the approval of the trusteeship agreements for areas not designated as strategic.

ART. 17. 1. The General Assembly shall consider and approve the budget of the Organization.

2. The expenses of the Organization shall be borne by the Members as apportioned by the General Assembly.

3. The General Assembly shall consider and approve any financial and budgetary arrangements with specialized agencies referred to in Article 57 and shall examine the administrative budgets of such specialized agencies with a view to making recommendations to the agencies concerned.

Voting

ART. 18. 1. Each member of the General Assembly shall have one vote.

2. Decisions of the General Assembly on important questions shall be made by a two-thirds majority of the members present and voting. These questions shall include: recommendations with respect to the maintenance of international peace and security, the election of the non-permanent members of the Security Council, the election of the members of the Economic and Social Council, the election of members of the Trusteeship Council in accordance with paragraph 1 (c) of Article 86, the admission of new Members to the United Nations, the suspension of the rights and privileges of membership, the expulsion of Members, questions relating to the operation of the trusteeship system, and budgetary questions.

3. Decisions on other questions, including the determination of additional categories of questions to be decided by a two-thirds majority, shall be made by a majority of the members present and voting.

ART. 19. A Member of the United Nations which is in arrears in the payment of its financial contributions to the Organization shall have no vote in the General Assembly if the amount of its arrears equals or exceeds the amount of the contributions due from it for the preceding two full years. The General Assembly may, nevertheless, permit such a Member to vote if it is satisfied that the failure to pay is due to conditions beyond the control of the Member.

Procedure

ART. 20. The General Assembly shall meet in regular annual sessions and in such special sessions as occasion may require. Special sessions shall be convoked by the Secretary-General at the request of the Security Council or of a majority of the Members of the United Nations.

ART. 21. The General Assembly shall adopt its own rules of procedure. It shall elect its President for each session.

ART. 22. The General Assembly may establish such subsidiary organs as it deems necessary for the performance of its functions.

CHAPTER V. THE SECURITY COUNCIL

Composition

ART. 23. 1. The Security Council shall consist of eleven Members of the United Nations. The Republic of China, France, the Union of Soviet Socialist Republics, the United Kingdom of Great Britain and Northern Ireland, and the United States of America shall be permanent members of the Security Council. The General Assembly shall elect six other Members of the United Nations to be non-permanent members of the Security Council, due regard being specially paid, in the first instance to the contribution of Members of the United Nations to the maintenance of international peace and security and to the other purposes of the Organization, and also to equitable geographical distribution.

2. The non-permanent members of the Security Council shall be elected for a term of two years. In the first election of the non-permanent members, however, three shall be chosen for a term of one year. A retiring member shall not be eligible for immediate re-election.

3. Each member of the Security Council shall have one representative.

Functions and Powers

ART. 24. 1. In order to ensure prompt and effective action by the United Nations, its Members confer on the Security Council primary responsibility for the maintenance of international peace and security, and agree that in carrying out its duties under this responsibility the Security Council acts on their behalf.

2. In discharging these duties the Security Council shall act in accordance with the Purposes and Principles of the United Nations. The specific powers granted to the Security Council for the discharge of these duties are laid down in Chapters VI, VII, VIII, and XII.

3. The Security Council shall submit annual and, when necessary, special reports to the General Assembly for its consideration.

ART. 25. The Members of the United Nations agree to accept and carry out the decisions of the Security Council in accordance with the present Charter.

ART. 26. In order to promote the establishment and maintenance of international peace and security with the least diversion for armaments of the world's human and economic resources, the Security Council shall be responsible for formulating, with the assistance of the Military Staff Committee referred to in Article 47, plans to be submitted to the Members of the United Nations for the establishment of a system for the regulation of armaments.

Voting

ART. 27. 1. Each member of the Security Council shall have one vote.

2. Decisions of the Security Council

on procedural matters shall be made by an affirmative vote of seven members.

3. Decisions of the Security Council on all other matters shall be made by an affirmative vote of seven members including the concurring votes of the permanent members; provided that, in decisions under Chapter VI, and under paragraph 3 of Article 52, a party to a dispute shall abstain from voting.

Procedure

ART. 28. 1. The Security Council shall be so organized as to be able to function continuously. Each member of the Security Council shall for this purpose be represented at all times at the seat of the Organization.

2. The Security Council shall hold periodic meetings at which each of its members may, if it so desires, be represented by a member of the government or by some other specially designated representative.

3. The Security Council may hold meetings at such places other than the seat of the Organization as in its judgment will best facilitate its work.

ART. 29. The Security Council may establish such subsidiary organs as it deems necessary for the performance of its functions.

ART. 30. The Security Council shall adopt its own rules of procedure, including the method of selecting its President.

ART. 31. Any Member of the United Nations which is not a member of the Security Council may participate, without vote, in the discussion of any question brought before the Security Council whenever the latter considers that the interests of that Member are specially affected.

ART. 32. Any Member of the United Nations which is not a member of the Security Council or any state which is not a Member of the United Nations, if it is a party to a dispute under consideration by the Security Council, shall be invited to participate, without vote, in the discussion relating to the dis-

pute. The Security Council shall lay down such conditions as it deems just for the participation of a state which is not a Member of the United Nations.

CHAPTER VI. PACIFIC SETTLEMENT OF DISPUTES

ART. 33. 1. The parties to any dispute, the continuance of which is likely to endanger the maintenance of international peace and security, shall, first of all, seek a solution by negotiation, enquiry, mediation, conciliation, arbitration, judicial settlement, resort to regional agencies or arrangements, or other peaceful means of their own choice.

2. The Security Council shall, when it deems necessary, call upon the parties to settle their dispute by such means.

ART. 34. The Security Council may investigate any dispute, or any situation which might lead to international friction or give rise to a dispute, in order to determine whether the continuance of the dispute or situation is likely to endanger the maintenance of international peace and security.

ART. 35. 1. Any member of the United Nations may bring any dispute, or any situation of the nature referred to in Article 34, to the attention of the Security Council or of the General Assembly.

2. A state which is not a Member of the United Nations may bring to the attention of the Security Council or of the General Assembly any dispute to which it is a party if it accepts in advance, for the purposes of the dispute, the obligations of pacific settlement provided in the present Charter.

3. The proceedings of the General Assembly in respect of matters brought to its attention under this Article will be subject to the provisions of Articles 11 and 12.

ART. 36. 1. The Security Council may, at any stage of a dispute of the nature referred to in Article 33 or of a situation of like nature, recommend appropriate procedures or methods of adjustment.

2. The Security Council should take into consideration any procedures for the settlement of the dispute which have already been adopted by the parties.

3. In making recommendations under this Article the Security Council should also take into consideration that legal disputes should as a general rule be deferred by the parties to the International Court of Justice in accordance with the provisions of the Statute of the Court.

ART. 37. 1. Should the parties to a dispute of the nature referred to in Article 33 fail to settle it by the means indicated in that Article, they shall refer it to the Security Council.

2. If the Security Council deems that the continuance of the dispute is in fact likely to endanger the maintenance of international peace and security, it shall decide whether to take action under Article 36 or to recommend such terms of settlement as it may consider appropriate.

ART. 38. Without prejudice to the provisions of Articles 33 to 37, the Security Council may, if all the parties to any dispute so request, make recommendations to the parties with a view to a pacific settlement of the dispute.

CHAPTER VII. ACTION WITH RESPECT TO THREATS TO THE PEACE, BREACHES OF THE PEACE, AND ACTS OF AGGRESSION

ART. 39. The Security Council shall determine the existence of any threat to the peace, breach of the peace, or act of aggression and shall make recommendations, or decide what measures shall be taken in accordance with Articles 41 and 42, to maintain or restore international peace and security.

ART. 40. In order to prevent an aggravation of the situation, the Security Council may, before making the recommendations or deciding upon the measures provided for in Article 39,

call upon the parties concerned to comply with such provisional measures as it deems necessary or desirable. Such provisional measures shall be without prejudice to the rights, claims, or position of the parties concerned. The Security Council shall duly take account of failure to comply with such provisional measures.

ART. 41. The Security Council may decide what measures not involving the use of armed force are to be employed to give effect to its decisions, and it may call upon the Members of the United Nations to apply such measures. These may include complete or partial interruption of economic relations and of rail, sea, air, postal, telegraphic, radio, and other means of communication, and the severance of diplomatic relations.

ART. 42. Should the Security Council consider that measures provided for in Article 41 would be inadequate or have proved to be inadequate, it may take such action by air, sea, or land forces as may be necessary to maintain or restore international peace and security. Such action may include demonstrations, blockade, and other operations by air, sea, or land forces of Members of the United Nations.

ART. 43. 1. All Members of the United Nations, in order to contribute to the maintenance of international peace and security, undertake to make available to the Security Council, on its call and in accordance with a special agreement or agreements, armed forces, assistance, and facilities, including rights of passage, necessary for the purpose of maintaining international peace and security.

2. Such agreement or agreemnts shall govern the numbers and types of forces, their degree of readiness and general location, and the nature of the facilities and assistance to be provided.

3. The agreement or agreements shall be negotiated as soon as possible on the initiative of the Security Council. They shall be concluded between the Security Council and Members or between the

Security Council and groups of Members and shall be subject to ratification by the signatory states in accordance with their respective constitutional processes.

ART. 44. When the Security Council has decided to use force it shall, before calling upon a Member not represented on it to provide armed forces in fulfilment of the obligations assumed under Article 43, invite that Member, if the Member so desires, to participate in the decisions of the Security Council concerning the employment of contingents of that Member's armed forces.

ART. 45. In order to enable the United Nations to take urgent military measures, Members shall hold immediately available national airforce contingents for combined international enforcement action. The strength and degree of readiness of these contingents and plans for their combined action shall be determined, within the limits laid down in the special agreement or agreements referred to in Article 43, by the Security Council with the assistance of the Military Staff Committee.

ART. 46. Plans for the application of armed force shall be made by the Security Council with the assistance of the Military Staff Committee.

ART. 47. 1. There shall be established a Military Staff Committee to advise and assist the Security Council on all questions relating to the Security Council's military requirements for the maintenance of international peace and security, the employment and command of forces placed at its disposal, the regulation of armaments, and possible disarmament.

2. The Military Staff Committee shall consist of the Chiefs of Staff of the permanent Members of the Security Council or their representatives. Any Member of the United Nations not permanently represented on the Committee shall be invited by the Committee to be associated with it when the efficient discharge of the Committee's responsibilities requires the participation of that Member in its work.

3. The Military Staff Committee shall be responsible under the Security Council for the strategic direction of any armed forces placed at the disposal of the Security Council. Questions relating to the command of such forces shall be worked out subsequently.

4. The Military Staff Committee, with the authorization of the Security Council and after consultation with appropriate regional agencies, may establish regional subcommittees.

ART. 48. 1. The action required to carry out the decisions of the Security Council for the maintenance of international peace and security shall be taken by all the Members of the United Nations or by some of them, as the Security Council may determine.

2. Such decisions shall be carried out by the Members of the United Nations directly and through their action in the appropriate international agencies of which they are members.

ART. 49. The Members of the United Nations shall join in affording mutual assistance in carrying out the measures decided upon by the Security Council.

ART. 50. If preventive or enforcement measures against any state are taken by the Security Council, any other state, whether a Member of the United Nations or not, which finds itself confronted with special economic problems arising from the carrying out of those measures shall have the right to consult the Security Council with regard to a solution of those problems.

ART. 51. Nothing in the present Charter shall impair the inherent right of individual or collective self-defense if an armed attack occurs against a Member of the United Nations, until the Security Council has taken the measures necessary to maintain international peace and security. Measures taken by Members in the exercise of this right of self-defense shall be immediately reported to the Security Council and shall not in any way affect the authority and responsibility of the Security Council under the present Charter to take at any time such action as it deems necessary in order to maintain or restore international peace and security.

CHAPTER VIII. REGIONAL ARRANGEMENTS

ART. 52. 1. Nothing in the present Charter precludes the existence of regional arrangements or agencies for dealing with such matters relating to the maintenance of international peace and security as are appropriate for regional action, provided that such arrangements or agencies and their activities are consistent with the Purposes and Principles of the United Nations.

2. The Members of the United Nations entering into such arrangements or constituting such agencies shall make every effort to achieve pacific settlement of local disputes through such regional arrangements or by such regional agencies before referring them to the Security Council.

3. The Security Council shall encourage the development of pacific settlement of local disputes through such regional arrangements or by such regional agencies either on the initiative of the states concerned or by reference from the Security Council.

4. This Article in no way impairs the application of Articles 34 and 35.

ART. 53. 1. The Security Council shall, where appropriate, utilize such regional arrangements or agencies for enforcement action under its authority. But no enforcement action shall be taken under regional arrangements or by regional agencies without the authorization of the Security Council, with the exception of measures against any enemy state, as defined in paragraph 2 of this Article, provided for pursuant to Article 107 or in regional arrangements directed against renewal of aggressive policy on the part of any such state, until such time as the Organization may, on request of the Governments concerned, be charged with the responsibility for preventing further aggression by such a state.

2. The term enemy state as used in paragraph 1 of this Article applies to any state which during the Second World War has been an enemy of any signatory of the present Charter.

ART. 54. The Security Council shall at all times be kept fully informed of activities undertaken or in contemplation under regional arrangements or by regional agencies for the maintenance of international peace and security.

CHAPTER IX. INTERNATIONAL ECONOMIC AND SOCIAL COOPERATION

ART. 55. With a view to the creation of conditions of stability and well-being which are necessary for peaceful and friendly relations among nations based on respect for the principle of equal rights and self-determination of peoples, the United Nations shall promote:

a. higher standards of living, full employment, and conditions of economic and social progress and development;

b. solutions of international economic, social, health, and related problems; and international cultural and educational cooperation; and

c. universal respect for, and observance of, human rights and fundamental freedoms for all without distinction as to race, sex, language, or religion.

ART. 56. All Members pledge themselves to take joint and separate action in cooperation with the Organization for the achievement of the purposes set forth in Article 55.

ART. 57. 1. The various specialized agencies, established by intergovernmental agreement and having wide international responsibilities, as defined in their basic instruments, in economic, social, cultural, educational, health, and related fields, shall be brought into relationship with the United Nations in accordance with the provisions of Article 63.

2. Such agencies thus brought into relationship with the United Nations are hereinafter referred to as specialized agencies.

ART. 58. The Organization shall make recommendations for the coordination of the policies and activities of the specialized agencies.

ART. 59. The Organization shall, where appropriate, initiate negotiations among the states concerned for the creation of any new specialized agencies required for the accomplishment of the purposes set forth in Article 55.

ART. 60. Responsibility for the discharge of the functions of the Organization set forth in this Chapter shall be vested in the General Assembly and, under the authority of the General Assembly, in the Economic and Social Council, which shall have for this purpose the powers set forth in Chapter X.

CHAPTER X. THE ECONOMIC AND SOCIAL COUNCIL

Composition

ART. 61. 1. The Economic and Social Council shall consist of eighteen Members of the United Nations elected by the General Assembly.

2. Subject to the provisions of paragraph 3, six members of the Economic and Social Council shall be elected each year for a term of three years. A retiring member shall be eligible for immediate re-election.

3. At the first election, eighteen members of the Economic and Social Council shall be chosen. The term of office of six members so chosen shall expire at the end of one year, and of six other members at the end of two years, in accordance with arrangements made by the General Assembly.

4. Each member of the Economic and Social Council shall have one representative.

Functions and Powers

ART. 62. 1. The Economic and Social Council may make or initiate studies and reports with respect to international economic, social, cultural, educational, health, and related matters and may make recommendations with respect to any such matters to the General Assembly, to the Members of the United Nations, and to the specialized agencies concerned.

2. It may make recommendations for the purpose of promoting respect for, and observance of, human rights and fundamental freedoms for all.

3. It may prepare draft conventions for submission to the General Assembly, with respect to matters falling within its competence.

4. It may call, in accordance with the rules prescribed by the United Nations, international conferences on matters falling within its competence.

ART. 63. 1. The Economic and Social Council may enter into agreements with any of the agencies referred to in Article 57, defining the terms on which the agency concerned shall be brought into relationship with the United Nations. Such agreements shall be subject to approval by the General Assembly.

2. It may coordinate the activities of the specialized agencies through consultation with and recommendations to such agencies and through recommendations to the General Assembly and to the Members of the United Nations.

ART. 64. 1. The Economic and Social Council may take appropriate steps to obtain regular reports from the specialized agencies. It may make arrangements with the Members of the United Nations and with the specialized agencies to obtain reports on the steps taken to give effect to its own recommendations and to recommendations on matters falling within its competence made by the General Assembly.

2. It may communicate its observations on these reports to the General Assembly.

ART. 65. The Economic and Social Council may furnish information to the Security Council and shall assist the Security Council upon its request.

ART. 66. 1. The Economic and Social Council shall perform such functions as fall within its competence in connection with the carrying out of the recommendations of the General Assembly.

2. It may, with the approval of the General Assembly, perform services at the request of Members of the United Nations and at the request of specialized agencies.

3. It shall perform such other functions as are specified elsewhere in the present Charter or as may be assigned to it by the General Assembly.

Voting

ART. 67. 1. Each member of the Economic and Social Council shall have one vote.

2. Decisions of the Economic and Social Council shall be made by a majority of the members present and voting.

Procedure

ART. 68. The Economic and Social Council shall set up commissions in economic and social fields and for the promotion of human rights, and such other commissions as may be required for the performance of its functions.

ART. 69. The Economic and Social Council shall invite any Member of the United Nations to participate, without vote, in its deliberations on any matter of particular concern to that Member.

ART. 70. The Economic and Social Council may make arrangements for representatives of the specialized agencies to participate, without vote, in its deliberations and in those of the commissions established by it, and for its representatives to participate in the deliberations of the specialized agencies.

ART. 71. The Economic and Social Council may make suitable arrangements for consultation with non-governmental organizations which are concerned with matters within its competence. Such arrangements may be made with international organizations and, where appropriate, with national organizations after consultation with the Member of the United Nations concerned.

ART. 72. 1. The Economic and Social Council shall adopt its own rules of procedure, including the method of selecting its President.

2. The Economic and Social Council shall meet as required in accordance with its rules, which shall include provision for the convening of meetings on the request of a majority of its members.

CHAPTER XI. DECLARATION REGARDING NON-SELF-GOVERNING TERRITORIES

ART. 73. Members of the United Nations which have or assume responsibilities for the administration of territories whose peoples have not yet attained a full measure of self-government recognize the principle that the interests of the inhabitants of these territories are paramount, and accept as a sacred trust the obligation to promote to the utmost, within the system of international peace and security established by the present Charter, the well-being of the inhabitants of these territories, and, to this end:

a. to ensure, with due respect for the culture of the peoples concerned, their political, economic, social, and educational advancement, their just treatment, and their protection against abuses;

b. to develop self-government, to take due account of the political aspirations of the peoples, and to assist them in the progressive development of their free political institutions, according to the particular circumstances of each territory and its peoples and their varying stages of advancement;

c. to further international peace and security;

d. to promote constructive measures of development, to encourage research, and to cooperate with one another and, when and where appropriate, with specialized international bodies with a view to the practical achievement of the social, economic, and scientific purposes set forth in this Article; and

e. to transmit regularly to the Secretary-General for information purposes, subject to such limitation as security and constitutional considerations may require, statistical and other information of a technical nature relating to economic, social, and educational conditions in the territories for which they are respectively responsible other than those territories to which Chapters XII and XIII apply.

ART. 74. Members of the United Nations also agree that their policy in respect of the territories to which this Chapter applies, no less than in respect of their metropolitan areas, must be based on the general principal of good-neighborliness, due account being taken of the interests and well-being of the rest of the world, in social, economic, and commercial matters.

CHAPTER XII. INTERNATIONAL TRUSTEE-SHIP SYSTEM

ART. 75. The United Nations shall establish under its authority an international trusteeship system for the administration and supervision of such territories as may be placed thereunder by subsequent individual agreements. These territories are hereinafter referred to as trust territories.

ART. 76. The basic objectives of the trusteeship system, in accordance with the Purposes of the United Nations laid down in Article 1 of the present Charter, shall be:

a. to further international peace and security;

b. to promote the political, economic, social, and educational advancement of the inhabitants of the trust territories, and their progressive development towards self-government or independence as may be appropriate to the particular circumstances of each territory and its peoples and the freely expressed wishes of the peoples concerned, and as may be provided by the terms of each trusteeship agreement;

c. to encourage respect for human rights and for fundamental freedoms for all without distinction as to race, sex, language, or religion, and to encourage recognition of the interdepend-

ence of the peoples of the world; and

d. to ensure equal treatment in social, economic, and commercial matters for all Members of the United Nations and their nationals, and also equal treatment for the latter in the administration of justice, without prejudice to the attainment of the foregoing objectives and subject to the provisions of Article 80.

ART. 77. 1. The trusteeship system shall apply to such territories in the following categories as may be placed thereunder by means of trusteeship agreements:

a. territories now held under mandate;

b. territories which may be detached from enemy states as a result of the Second World War; and

c. territories voluntarily placed under the system by states responsible for their administration.

2. It will be a matter for subsequent agreement as to which territories in the foregoing categories will be brought under the trusteeship system and upon what terms.

ART. 78. The trusteeship system shall not apply to territories which have become Members of the United Nations, relationship among which shall be based on respect for the principle of sovereign equality.

ART. 79. The terms of trusteeship for each territory to be placed under the trusteeship system, including any alteration or amendment, shall be agreed upon by the states directly concerned, including the mandatory power in the case of territories held under mandate by a Member of the United Nations, and shall be approved as provided for in Articles 83 and 85.

ART. 80. 1. Except as may be agreed upon in individual trusteeship agreements, made under Articles 77, 79, and 81, placing each territory under the trusteeship system, and until such agreements have been concluded, nothing in this Chapter shall be construed in or of itself to alter in any manner the rights whatsoever of any states or any peoples or the terms of existing international instruments to which Members of the United Nations may respectively be parties.

2. Paragraph 1 of this Article shall not be interpreted as giving grounds for delay or postponement of the negotiation and conclusion of agreements for placing mandated and other territories under the trusteeship system as provided for in Article 77.

ART. 81. The trusteeship agreement shall in each case include the terms under which the trust territory will be administered and designate the authority which will exercise the administration of the trust territory. Such authority, hereinafter called the administering authority, may be one or more states or the Organization itself.

ART. 82. There may be designated, in any trusteeship agreement, a strategic area or areas which may include part or all of the trust territory to which the agreement applies, without prejudice to any special agreement or agreements made under Article 43.

ART. 83. 1. All functions of the United Nations relating to strategic areas, including the approval of the terms of the trusteeship agreements and of their alteration or amendment, shall be exercised by the Security Council.

2. The basic objectives set forth in Article 76 shall be applicable to the people of each strategic area.

3. The Security Council shall, subject to the provisions of the trusteeship agreements and without prejudice to security considerations, avail itself of the assistance of the Trusteeship Council to perform those functions of the United Nations under the trusteeship system relating to political, economic, social, and educational matters in the strategic areas.

ART. 84. It shall be the duty of the administering authority to ensure that the trust territory shall play its part in the maintenance of international peace and security. To this end the administering authority may make use of volunteer forces, facilities, and assistance

from the trust territory in carrying out the obligations towards the Security Council undertaken in this regard by the administering authority, as well as for local defense and the maintenance of law and order within the trust territory.

ART. 85. 1. The functions of the United Nations with regard to trusteeship agreements for all areas not designated as strategic, including the approval of the terms of the trusteeship agreements and of their alteration or amendment, shall be exercised by the General Assembly.

2. The Trusteeship Council, operating under the authority of the General Assembly shall assist the General Assembly in carrying out these functions.

CHAPTER XIII. THE TRUSTEESHIP COUNCIL

Composition

ART. 86. 1. The Trusteeship Council shall consist of the following Members of the United Nations:

a. those Members administering trust territories;

b. such of those Members mentioned by name in Article 23 as are not administering trust territories; and

c. as many other Members elected for three-year terms by the General Assembly as may be necessary to ensure that the total number of members of the trusteeship Council is equally divided between those Members of the United Nations which administer trust territories and those which do not.

2. Each member of the Trusteeship Council shall designate one specially qualified person to represent it therein.

Functions and Powers

ART. 87. The General Assembly and, under its authority, the Trusteeship Council, in carrying out their functions, may:

a. consider reports submitted by the administering authority;

b. accept petitions and examine them

in consultation with the administering authority;

c. provide for periodic visits to the respective trust territories at times agreed upon with the administering authority; and

d. take these and other actions in conformity with the terms of the trusteeship agreements.

ART. 88. The Trusteeship Council shall formulate a questionnaire on the political, economic, social, and educational advancement of the inhabitants of each trust territory, and the administering authority for each trust territory within the competence of the General Assembly shall make an annual report to the General Assembly upon the basis of such questionnaire.

Voting

ART. 89. 1. Each member of the Trusteeship Council shall have one vote.

2. Decisions of the Trusteeship Council shall be made by a majority of the members present and voting.

Procedure

ART. 90. 1. The Trusteeship Council shall adopt its own rules of procedure, including the method of selecting its President.

2. The Trusteeship Council shall meet as required in accordance with its rules, which shall include provision for the convening of meetings on the request of a majority of its members.

ART. 91. The Trusteeship Council shall, when appropriate, avail itself of the assistance of the Economic and Social Council and of the specialized agencies in regard to matters with which they are respectively concerned.

CHAPTER XIV. THE INTERNATIONAL COURT OF JUSTICE

ART. 92. The International Court of Justice shall be the principal judicial organ of the United Nations. It shall function in accordance with the an-

nexed Statute, which is based upon the Statute of the Permanent Court of International Justice and forms an integral part of the present Charter.

ART. 93. 1. All Members of the United Nations are *ipso facto* parties to the Statute of the International Court of Justice.

2. A state which is not a Member of the United Nations may become a party to the Statute of the International Court of Justice on conditions to be determined in each case by the General Assembly upon the recommendation of the Security Council.

ART. 94. 1. Each Member of the United Nations undertakes to comply with the decision of the International Court of Justice in any case to which it is a party.

2. If any party to a case fails to perform the obligations incumbent upon it under a judgment rendered by the Court, the other party may have recourse to the Security Council, which may, if it deems necessary, make recommendations or decide upon measures to be taken to give effect to the judgment.

ART. 95. Nothing in the present Charter shall prevent Members of the United Nations from entrusting the solution of their differences to other tribunals by virtue of agreements already in existence or which may be concluded in the future.

ART. 96. 1. The General Assembly or the Security Council may request the International Court of Justice to give an advisory opinion on any legal question.

2. Other organs of the United Nations and specialized agencies, which may at any time be so authorized by the General Assembly, may also request advisory opinions of the Court on legal questions arising within the scope of their activities.

CHAPTER XV. THE SECRETARIAT

ART. 97. The Secretariat shall comprise a Secretary-General and such staff as the Organization may require. The Secretary-General shall be appointed by the General Assembly upon the recommendation of the Security Council. He shall be the chief administrative officer of the Organization.

ART. 98. The Secretary-General shall act in that capacity in all meetings of the General Assembly, of the Security Council, of the Economic and Social Council, and of the Trusteeship Council, and shall perform such other functions as are entrusted to him by these organs. The Secretary-General shall make an annual report to the General Assembly on the work of the Organization.

ART. 99. The Secretary-General may bring to the attention of the Security Council any matter which in his opinion may threaten the maintenance of international peace and security.

ART. 100. 1. In the performance of their duties the Secretary-General and the staff shall not seek or receive instructions from any government or from any other authority external to the Organization. They shall refrain from any action which might reflect on their position as international officials responsible only to the Organization.

2. Each Member of the United Nations undertakes to respect the exclusively international character of the responsibilities of the Secretary-General and the staff and not to seek to influence them in the discharge of their responsibilities.

ART. 101. 1. The staff shall be appointed by the Secretary-General under regulations established by the General Assembly.

2. Appropriate staffs shall be permanently assigned to the Economic and Social Council, the Trusteeship Council, and, as required, to other organs of the United Nations. These staffs shall form a part of the Secretariat.

3. The paramount consideration in the employment of the staff and in the determination of the conditions of service shall be the necessity of securing the highest standards of efficiency, competence, and integrity. Due regard shall be paid to the importance of recruiting the staff on as wide a geographical basis as possible.

CHAPTER XVI. MISCELLANEOUS PROVISIONS

ART. 102. 1. Every treaty and every international agreement entered into by any Member of the United Nations after the present Charter comes into force shall as soon as possible be registered with the Secretariat and published by it.

2. No party to any such treaty or international agreement which has not been registered in accordance with the provisions of paragraph 1 of this Article may invoke that treaty or agreement before any organ of the United Nations.

ART. 103. In the event of a conflict between the obligations of the Members of the United Nations under the present Charter and their obligations under any other international agreement, their obligations under the present Charter shall prevail.

ART. 104. The Organization shall enjoy in the territory of each of its Members such legal capacity as may be necessary for the exercise of its functions and the fulfillment of its purposes.

ART. 105. 1. The Organization shall enjoy in the territory of each of its Members such privileges and immunities as are necessary for the fulfillment of its purposes.

2. Representatives of the Members of the United Nations and officials of the Organization shall similarly enjoy such privileges and immunities as are necessary for the independent exercise of their functions in connection with the Organization.

3. The General Assembly may make recommendations with a view to determining the details of the application of paragraphs 1 and 2 of this Article or may propose conventions to the

Members of the United Nations for this purpose.

CHAPTER XVII. TRANSITIONAL SECURITY ARRANGEMENTS

ART. 106. Pending the coming into force of such special agreements referred to in Article 43 as in the opinion of the Security Council enable it to begin the exercise of its responsibilities under Article 42, the parties to the Four-Nation Declaration, signed at Moscow, October 30, 1943, and France, shall, in accordance with the provisions of paragraph 5 of that Declaration, consult with one another and as occasion requires with other Members of the United Nations with a view to such joint action on behalf of the Organization as may be necessary for the purpose of maintaining international peace and security.

ART. 107. Nothing in the present Charter shall invalidate or preclude action, in relation to any state which during the Second World War has been an enemy of any signatory to the present Charter, taken or authorized as a result of that war by the Governments having responsibility for such action.

CHAPTER XVIII. AMENDMENTS

ART. 108. Amendments to the present Charter shall come into force for all Members of the United Nations when they have been adopted by a vote of two thirds of the members of the General Assembly and ratified in accordance with their respective constitutional processes by two thirds of the Members of the United Nations, including all the permanent members of the Security Council.

ART. 109. 1. A General Conference of the Members of the United Nations for the purpose of reviewing the present Charter may be held at a date and place to be fixed by a two-thirds vote of the members of the General Assembly and by a vote of any seven members of the Security Council. Each Member of

the United Nations shall have one vote in the conference.

2. Any alteration of the present Charter recommended by a two-thirds vote of the conference shall take effect when ratified in accordance with their respective constitutional processes by two thirds of the Members of the United Nations including all the permanent members of the Security Council.

3. If such a conference has not been held before the tenth annual session of the General Assembly following the coming into force of the present Charter, the proposal to call such a conference shall be placed on the agenda of that session of the General Assembly, and the conference shall be held if so decided by a majority vote of the members of the General Assembly and by a vote of any seven members of the Security Council.

CHAPTER XIX. RATIFICATION AND SIGNATURE

ART. 110. 1. The present Charter shall be ratified by the signatory states in accordance with their respective constitutional processes.

2. The ratifications shall be deposited with the Government of the United States of America, which shall notify all the signatory states of each deposit as well as the Secretary-General of the Organization when he has been appointed.

3. The present Charter shall come into force upon the deposit of ratifications by the Republic of China, France, the Union of Soviet Socialist Republics, the United Kingdom of Great Britain and Northern Ireland, and the United States of America, and by a majority of the other signatory states. A protocol of the ratifications deposited shall thereupon be drawn up by the Government of the United States of America which shall communicate copies thereof to all the signatory states.

4. The states signatory to the present Charter which ratify it after it has come into force will become original

Members of the United Nations on the date of the deposit of their respective ratifications.

Art. 111. The present Charter, of which the Chinese, French, Russian, English, and Spanish texts are equally authentic, shall remain deposited in the archives of the Government of the United States of America. Duly certified copies thereof shall be transmitted by that Government to the Governments of the other signatory states.

In faith whereof the representatives of the Governments of the United Nations have signed the present Charter.

Done at the city of San Francisco the twenty-sixth day of June, one thousand nine hundred and forty-five.

Chapter 16

Functions: Security

50. THE TRUMAN DOCTRINE: MESSAGE OF THE PRESIDENT TO A JOINT SESSION OF THE CONGRESS, 12 MARCH 1947 [1]

By the spring of 1947, the United States government and the American public by and large had come to the conclusion that, in the expansion of Soviet communism, the free world faced a new threat in place of that from the Axis powers. It seemed clear that, if the United Nations, designed as it was to rest upon the cornerstone of Great Power unity, were to see the peaceful conditions it was established to maintain but not to achieve, prompt and vigorous measures were necessary to prevent a collapse in the face of Soviet aggression. A halt must be put on Soviet expansion, specifically in the eastern Mediterranean, where both Greece and Turkey were under pressures from the Soviets and their satellites. By mutual efforts, the economic health and military strength of the free world must be restored. Within the framework of the Charter greater effectiveness must be achieved through the invention of novel means. The enunciation of the Truman Doctrine was the first step.

MR. PRESIDENT, MR. SPEAKER, MEMBERS OF THE CONGRESS OF THE UNITED STATES:

The gravity of the situation which confronts the world today necessitates my appearance before a joint session of the Congress.

The foreign policy and the national security of this country are involved.

One aspect of the present situation, which I wish to present to you at this time for your consideration and decision, concerns Greece and Turkey.

The United States has received from the Greek Government an urgent appeal for financial and economic assistance. Preliminary reports from the American Ambassador in Greece corroborate the statement of the Greek Government that assistance is imperative if Greece is to survive as a free nation.

I do not believe that the American people and the Congress wish to turn a deaf ear to the appeal of the Greek Government.

Greece is not a rich country. Lack of sufficient natural resources has always forced the Greek people to work hard to make both ends meet. Since 1940 this industrious and peace-loving country has suffered invasion, four years of cruel enemy occupation, and bitter internal strife.

When forces of liberation entered Greece they found that the retreating Germans had destroyed virtually all the railways, roads, port facilities, communications, and merchant marine. More than a thousand villages had been burned. Eighty-five percent of the children were tubercular. Livestock, poultry, and draft animals had almost disappeared. Inflation had wiped out practically all savings.

As a result of these tragic conditions, a militant minority, exploiting human want and misery, was able to create

[1] U.S., *Department of State Bulletin*, XVI (23 March 1947), pp. 534-537.

political chaos which, until now, has made economic recovery impossible.

Greece is today without funds to finance the importation of those goods which are essential to bare subsistence. Under these circumstances the people of Greece cannot make progress in solving their problems of reconstruction. Greece is in desperate need of financial and economic assistance to enable it to resume purchases of food, clothing, fuel, and seeds. These are indispensable for the subsistence of its people and are obtainable only from abroad. Greece must have help to import the goods necessary to restore internal order and security so essential for economic and political recovery.

The Greek Government has also asked for the assistance of experienced American administrators, economists, and technicians to insure that the financial and other aid given to Greece shall be used effectively in creating a stable and self-sustaining economy and in improving its public administration.

The very existence of the Greek state is today threatened by the terrorist activities of several thousand armed men, led by Communists, who defy the Government's authority at a number of points, particularly along the northern boundaries. A commission appointed by the United Nations Security Council is at present investigating disturbed conditions in northern Greece and alleged border violations along the frontier between Greece on the one hand and Albania, Bulgaria, and Yugoslavia on the other.

Meanwhile, the Greek Government is unable to cope with the situation. The Greek Army is small and poorly equipped. It needs supplies and equipment if it is to restore authority to the Government throughout Greek territory.

Greece must have assistance if it is to become a self-supporting and self-respecting democracy.

The United States must supply that assistance. We have already extended to Greece certain types of relief and economic aid, but these are inadequate.

There is no other country to which democratic Greece can turn.

No other nation is willing and able to provide the necessary support for a democratic Greek Government.

The British Government, which has been helping Greece, can give no further financial or economic aid after March 31. Great Britain finds itself under the necessity of reducing or liquidating its commitments in several parts of the world, including Greece.

We have considered how the United Nations might assist in this crisis. But the situation is an urgent one requiring immediate action, and the United Nations and its related organizations are not in a position to extend help of the kind that is required.

It is important to note that the Greek Government has asked for our aid in utilizing effectively the financial and other assistance we may give to Greece, and in improving its public administration. It is of the utmost importance that we supervise the use of any funds made available to Greece, in such a manner that each dollar spent will count toward making Greece self-supporting, and will help to build an economy in which a healthy democracy can flourish.

No government is perfect. One of the chief virtues of a democracy, however, is that its defects are always visible and under democratic processes can be pointed out and corrected. The Government of Greece is not perfect. Nevertheless it represents 85 percent of the members of the Greek Parliament who were chosen in an election last year. Foreign observers, including 692 Americans, considered this election to be a fair expression of the views of the Greek people.

The Greek Government has been operating in an atmosphere of chaos and extremism. It has made mistakes. The extension of aid by this country does not mean that the United States condones everything that the Greek Government has done or will do. We have condemned in the past, and we condemn now, extremist measures of the right or the left. We have in the past advised tolerance, and we advise tolerance now.

Greece's neighbor, Turkey, also deserves our attention.

The future of Turkey as an independent and economically sound state is clearly no less important to the freedom-loving peoples of the world than the future of Greece. The circumstances in which Turkey finds itself today are considerably different from those of Greece. Turkey has been spared the disasters that have beset Greece. And during the war the United States and Great Britain furnished Turkey with material aid.

Nevertheless, Turkey now needs our support.

Since the war Turkey has sought additional financial assistance from Great Britain and the United States for the purpose of effecting that modernization necessary for the maintenance of its national integrity.

That integrity is essential to the preservation of order in the Middle East.

The British Government has informed us that, owing to its own difficulties, it can no longer extend financial or economic aid to Turkey.

As in the case of Greece, if Turkey is to have the assistance it needs, the United States must supply it. We are the only country able to provide that help.

I am fully aware of the broad implications involved if the United States extends assistance to Greece and Turkey, and I shall discuss these implications with you at this time.

One of the primary objectives of the foreign policy of the United States is the creation of conditions in which we and other nations will be able to work out a way of life free from coercion. This was a fundamental issue in the war with Germany and Japan. Our victory was won over countries which

sought to impose their will, and their way of life, upon other nations.

To insure the peaceful development of nations, free from coercion, the United States has taken a leading part in establishing the United Nations. The United Nations is designed to make possible lasting freedom and independence for all its members. We shall not realize our objectives, however, unless we are willing to help free peoples to maintain their free institutions and their national integrity against aggressive movements that seek to impose upon them totalitarian regimes. This is no more than a frank recognition that totalitarian regimes imposed upon free peoples, by direct or indirect aggression, undermine the foundations of international peace and hence the security of the United States.

The peoples of a number of countries of the world have recently had totalitarian regimes forced upon them against their will. The Government of the United States has made frequent protests against coercion and intimidation, in violation of the Yalta agreement, in Poland, Rumania, and Bulgaria. I must also state that in a number of other countries there have been similar developments.

At the present moment in world history nearly every nation must choose between alternative ways of life. The choice is too often not a free one.

One way of life is based upon the will of the majority, and is distinguished by free institutions, representative government, free elections, guaranties, of individual liberty, freedom of speech and religion, and freedom from political oppression.

The second way of life is based upon the will of a minority forcibly imposed upon the majority. It relies upon terror and oppression, a controlled press and radio, fixed elections, and the suppression of personal freedoms.

I believe that it must be the policy of the United States to support free peoples who are resisting attempted subjugation by armed minorities or by outside pressures.

I believe that we must assist free peoples to work out their own destinies in their own way.

I believe that our help should be primarily through economic and financial aid which is essential to economic stability and orderly political processes.

The world is not static, and the *status quo* is not sacred. But we cannot allow changes in the *status quo* in violation of the Charter of the United Nations by such methods as coercion, or by such subterfuges as political infiltration. In helping free and independent nations to maintain their freedom, the United States will be giving effect to the principles of the Charter of the United Nations.

It is necessary only to glance at a map to realize that the survival and integrity of the Greek nation are of grave importance in a much wider situation. If Greece should fall under the control of an armed minority, the effect upon its neighbor, Turkey, would be immediate and serious. Confusion and disorder might well spread throughout the entire Middle East.

Moreover, the disappearance of Greece as an independent state would have a profound effect upon those countries in Europe whose peoples are struggling against great difficulties to maintain their freedoms and their independence while they repair the damages of war.

It would be an unspeakable tragedy if these countries, which have struggled so long against overwhelming odds, should lose that victory for which they sacrificed so much. Collapse of free institutions and loss of independence would be disastrous not only for them but for the world. Discouragement and possibly failure would quickly be the lot of neighboring peoples striving to maintain their freedom and independence.

Should we fail to aid Greece and Turkey in this fateful hour, the effect will be far reaching to the West as well as to the East.

We must take immediate and resolute action.

I therefore ask the Congress to provide authority for assistance to Greece and Turkey in the amount of $400,-000,000 for the period ending June 30, 1948. In requesting these funds, I have taken into consideration the maximum amount of relief assistance which would be furnished to Greece out of the $350,000,000 which I recently requested that the Congress authorize for the prevention of starvation and suffering in countries devastated by the war.

In addition to funds, I ask the Congress to authorize the detail of American civilian and military personnel to Greece and Turkey, at the request of those countries, to assist in the tasks of reconstruction, and for the purpose of supervising the use of such financial and material assistance as may be furnished. I recommend that authority also be provided for the instruction and training of selected Greek and Turkish personnel.

Finally, I ask that the Congress provide authority which will permit the speediest and most effective use, in terms of needed commodities, supplies, and equipment, of such funds as may be authorized.

If further funds, or further authority, should be needed for purposes indicated in this message, I shall not hesitate to bring the situation before the Congress. On this subject the Executive and Legislative branches of the Government must work together.

This is a serious course upon which we embark.

I would not recommend it except that the alternative is much more serious.

The United States contributed $341,-000,000,000 toward winning World War II. This is an investment in world freedom and world peace.

The assistance that I am recommending for Greece and Turkey amounts to little more than one-tenth of one percent of this investment. It is only common sense that we should safeguard this investment and make sure that it was not in vain.

The seeds of totalitarian regimes are nurtured by misery and want. They spread and grow in the evil soul of poverty and strife. They reach their full growth when the hope of a people for a better life has died.

We must keep that hope alive.

The free peoples of the world look to us for support in maintaining their freedoms.

If we falter in our leadership, we may endanger the peace of the world—and we shall surely endanger the welfare of our own Nation.

Great responsibilities have been placed upon us by the swift movement of events.

I am confident that the Congress will face these responsibilities squarely.

51. SECRETARY MARSHALL'S HARVARD UNIVERSITY ADDRESS, 5 JUNE 1947 [1]

Two years after the end of World War II, the states of Western Europe, unable by their own efforts to recover from the destruction wrought by the war on their industry, agriculture, and distribution systems, were reeling on the brink of economic chaos. The growing despair of the population was also fed in 1946-47 by the worst winter in a generation, followed in the spring by conditions of acute drought. Within each country subversive forces, sustained by Soviet support from abroad, threatened the established order. A further deterioration by inviting Soviet intervention would have undermined the United Nations and also have impaired the security and economy of the United States. At the beginning of the summer, Secretary of State Marshall asked the states of Europe to unite in a program of recovery. The appeal was the more dramatic because of its understatement. Out of this "Marshall Plan" came the European Recovery Program and its related institutions on both sides of the Atlantic. These gave effect to the economic implications of the Truman Doctrine in the case of Europe.

I need not tell you gentlemen that the world situation is very serious. That must be apparent to all intelligent people. I think one difficulty is that the problem is one of such enormous complexity that the very mass of facts presented to the public by press and radio make it exceedingly difficult for the man in the street to reach a clear appraisement of the situation. Furthermore, the people of this country are distant from the troubled areas of the

earth and it is hard for them to comprehend the plight and consequent reactions of the long-suffering peoples, and the effect of those reactions on their governments in connection with our efforts to promote peace in the world.

In considering the requirements for the rehabilitation of Europe, the physical loss of life, the visible destruction of cities, factories, mines, and railroads was correctly estimated, but it has become obvious during recent months that this visible destruction was probably less serious than the dislocation of the entire fabric of European economy. For the past ten years conditions have been highly abnormal. The feverish preparation for war and the more feverish maintenance of the war effort engulfed all aspects of national economies. Machinery has fallen into disrepair or is entirely obsolete. Under the arbitrary and destructive Nazi rule, virtually every possible enterprise was geared into the German war machine. Long-standing commercial ties, private institutions, banks, insurance companies, and shipping companies disappeared, through loss of capital, absorption through nationalization, or by simple destruction. In many countries, confidence in the local currency has been severely shaken. The breakdown of the

[1] U.S., *Department of State Bulletin*, XVI (15 June 1947), pp. 159 f.

business structure of Europe during the war was complete. Recovery has been seriously retarded by the fact that two years after the close of hostilities a peace settlement with Germany and Austria has not been agreed upon. But even given a more prompt solution of these difficult problems, the rehabilitation of the economic structure of Europe quite evidently will require a much longer time and greater effort than had been foreseen.

There is a phase of this matter which is both interesting and serious. The farmer has always produced the foodstuffs to exchange with the city dweller for the other necessities of life. This division of labour is the basis of modern civilization. At the present time it is threatened with breakdown. The town and city industries are not producing adequate goods to exchange with the food-producing farmer. Raw materials and fuel are in short supply. Machinery is lacking or worn out. The farmer or the peasant cannot find the goods for sale which he desires to purchase. So the sale of his farm produce for money which he cannot use seems to him an unprofitable transaction. He, therefore, has withdrawn many fields from crop cultivation and is using them for grazing. He feeds more grain to stock and finds for himself and his family an ample supply of food, however short he may be on clothing and the other ordinary gadgets of civilization. Meanwhile people in the cities are short of food and fuel. So the governments are forced to use their foreign money and credits to procure these necessities abroad. This process exhausts funds which are urgently needed for reconstruction. Thus a very serious situation is rapidly developing which bodes no good for the world. The modern system of the division of labour upon which the exchange of products is based is in danger of breaking down.

The truth of the matter is that Europe's requirements for the next three or four years of foreign food and other essential products—principally from America—are so much greater than her present ability to pay that she must have substantial additional help or face economic, social, and political deterioration of a very grave character.

The remedy lies in breaking the vicious circle and restoring the confidence of the European people in the economic future of their own countries and of Europe as a whole. The manufacturer and the farmer throughout wide areas must be able and willing to exchange their products for currencies the continuing value of which is not open to question.

Aside from the demoralizing effect on the world at large and the possibilities of disturbances arising as a result of the desperation of the people concerned, the consequences to the economy of the United States should be apparent to all. It is logical that the United States should do whatever it is able to do to assist in the return of normal economic health in the world, without which there can be no political stability and no assured peace. Our policy is directed not against any country or doctrine but against hunger, poverty, desperation, and chaos. Its purpose should be the revival of a working economy in the world so as to permit the emergence of political and social conditions in which free institutions can exist. Such assistance, I am convinced, must not be on a piecemeal basis as crises develop. Any assistance that this Government may render in the future should provide a cure rather than a mere palliative. Any government that is willing to assist in the task of recovery will find full co-operation, I am sure, on the part of the United States Government. Any government which manoeuvres to block the recovery of other countries cannot expect help from us. Furthermore, governments, political parties, or groups which seek to perpetuate human misery in order to profit therefrom politically or otherwise will encounter the opposition of the United States.

It is already evident that, before the the United States Government can proceed much further in its efforts to alleviate the situation and help start the European world on its way to recovery, there must be some agreement among the countries of Europe as to the requirements of the situation and the part of those countries themselves will take in order to give proper effect to whatever action might be undertaken by this Government. It would be neither fitting or efficacious for this Government to undertake to draw up unilaterally a programme designed to place Europe on its feet economically. This is the business of the Europeans. The initiative, I think, must come from Europe. The role of this country should

consist of friendly aid in the drafting of a European programme and of later support of such a programme so far as it may be practical for us to do so. The programme should be a joint one, agreed to by a number of, if not all, European nations.

An essential part of any successful action on the part of the United States is an understanding on the part of the people of America of the character of the problem and the remedies to be applied. Political passion and prejudice should have no part. With foresight, and a willingness on the part of our people to face up to the vast responsibility which history has clearly placed upon our country, the difficulties I have outlined can and will be overcome.

52. SECRETARY MARSHALL'S ADDRESS IN THE GENERAL DEBATE OF THE UNITED NATIONS ASSEMBLY, 17 SEPTEMBER 1947[1]

The obstructionist tactics adopted by Soviet Russia from the inception of the United Nations, including especially the abuse of the "veto" power in the Security Council, rendered inoperative or ineffective many of the provisions of the Charter both for the settlement of international disputes and for the prevention of aggression. By the opening of the second session of the Assembly it was clear that, if the United Nations organization was not to degenerate into a forum for mere debate and propaganda, other means consistent with the Charter must be devised. With this address, in which he set forth a "Program for a More Effective United Nations," Secretary of State Marshall launched the United Nations on a course in which the peace-keeping functions, originally intended for the Security Council, have been increasingly assumed by the Assembly, due to the paralysis of the former. The consequent shift in the prestige and authority of the two bodies has been as salutary as it was inevitable.

MR. PRESIDENT; FELLOW DELEGATES:

I have been asked by the President of the United States to extend to you the cordial greetings of the Government and people of the United States, as well as his own warm personal welcome. We are happy to have you with us in

this country. We trust that your stay will be productive of the far-reaching results which the peoples of all countries expect from this gathering.

Our point of departure for the deliberations of this Assembly might well be the annual report of the Secretary-General on the work of the organization. It is a noteworthy document. It records realistically the progress and development of the United Nations, and its failures. It reflects the diligent efforts of the Secretary-General and his staff to expedite the rapidly growing volume of United Nations business.

The situation we face today may be summarized by the statement that more than two years after the end of the war the fruits of peace and victory are still beyond our grasp. Men look anxiously toward the future, wondering whether a new and more terrible conflict will engulf them. We have not yet succeeded in establishing a basis for peace with Germany and Japan, nor have we restored Austria as an independent state.

[1] United Nations, General Assembly, *Official Records*, 2nd Sess., I, pp. 19-35.

Reconstruction lags everywhere; the basic requirements of life are scarce; there is desperate need throughout great areas. The complex economic machinery which was thrown out of joint by the war has not yet been put back into running order. In place of peace, liberty, and economic security, we find menace, repression, and dire want.

A supreme effort is required from us all if we are to succeed in breaking through the vicious circles of deepening political and economic crisis. That is why the United States has placed on the agenda of this Assembly the question of threats to the political independence and territorial integrity of Greece.

The history of the Greek case in the United Nations is well known in this Assembly. You are aware that the Security Council last December adopted a resolution establishing an investigating commission to inquire into the situation along the northern frontier of Greece and report the facts to the Security Council. You know that that commission and its subsidiary group, by large majorities, have attributed the disturbances principally to the illegal assistance and support furnished by Yugoslavia, Albania, and Bulgaria to guerrilla forces fighting against the Greek Government. The extent or effectiveness of such assistance to the Greek guerrillas is not the point at issue here. It is a universally accepted principle of international law that for one nation to arm or otherwise assist rebellious forces against another government is a hostile and aggressive act. Not only has this principle been upheld in a number of famous cases in international law, but it has also found expression in international agreements. The majority of the members of the Security Council have recorded their support of this principle by their action in this case. One permanent member of the Security Council, however, has three times vetoed the efforts of the Council to deal with the situation.

This Assembly cannot stand by as a mere spectator while a member of the United Nations is endangered by attacks from abroad. If the United Nations should fail to protect the integrity of one small state, the security of all small states would be placed in jeopardy. The inability of the Security Council to take effective action in this case passes a grave responsibility to the General Assembly. I am confident that the General Assembly will not fail to meet this responsibility. It must do so if the organization is to carry out its fundamental purposes.

The United States Delegation will therefore submit to the Assembly a resolution which will contain a finding of responsibility, call upon Albania, Bulgaria, and Yugoslavia to cease and desist from rendering further assistance or support to the guerrillas in Greece, establish a commission to assist in the implementation of these recommendations and to investigate the facts with regard to compliance therewith, and make other appropriate recommendations to the states concerned.

The General Assembly is also faced with the problem of Palestine. The Government of the United States intends to do everything within its power at this session of the General Assembly to assist in finding a solution for this difficult problem which has stirred up such violent passions and which is now resulting in the shedding of blood and in great mental and moral anguish. The solution will require of each of us courage and resolution. It will also require restraint.

The Special Committee on Palestine is to be highly commended for its contribution to the solution of this problem. Although the members of this Committee were not able to agree unanimously upon a number of important issues, including that of partition, they have been able to find the basis for agreement on 11 recommendations to this Assembly. Their achievement in reaching unanimity on so many points represents definite progress.

We realize that, whatever the solution recommended by the General Assembly, it cannot be ideally satisfactory to either of the two great peoples primarily concerned. While the final decision of this Assembly must properly await the detailed consideration of the report, the Government of the United States gives great weight not only to the recommendations which have met with the unanimous approval of the Special Committee but also to those which have been approved by the majority of that Committee.

I turn now to the question of the independence of Korea. At Cairo in December 1943, the United States, the United Kingdom, and China joined in declaring that, in due course, Korea should become free and independent. This multilateral pledge was reaffirmed in the Potsdam declaration of July 1945 and subscribed to by the Union of Soviet Socialist Republics when it entered the war against Japan. In Moscow in December of 1945, the Foreign Ministers of the U.S.S.R., the United Kingdom, and the United States concluded an agreement designed to bring about the independence of Korea. This agreement was later adhered to by the Government of China. It provided for the establishment of a Joint U.S.-U.S.S.R. Commission to meet in Korea and, through consultations with Korean democratic parties and social organizations, to decide on methods for establishing a provisional Korean government. The Joint Commission was then to consult with that provisional government on methods of giving aid and assistance to Korea; any agreement reached being submitted for approval to the four powers adhering to the Moscow agreement.

For about two years the United States Government has been trying to reach agreement with the Soviet Government, through the Joint Commission and otherwise, on methods of implementing the Moscow agreement and thus bringing about the independence of Korea. The United States representatives have insisted that any settlement of the Korean problem must in no way infringe the fundamental democratic right of freedom of opinion. That is still the position of my Government. Today the independence of Korea is no further advanced than it was two years ago. Korea remains divided at the 38th parallel with Soviet forces in the industrial north and United States forces in the agricultural south. There is little or no exchange of goods or services between the two zones. Korea's economy is thus crippled.

The Korean people, not former enemies, but a people liberated from 40 years of Japanese oppression, are still not free. This situation must not be allowed to continue indefinitely. In an effort to make progress the United States Government recently made certain proposals designed to achieve the purposes of the Moscow agreement and requested the powers adhering to that agreement to join in discussion of these proposals. China and the United Kingdom agreed to this procedure. The Soviet Government did not. Furthermore, the United States and Soviet Delegations to the Joint Commission have not even been able to agree on a joint report on the status of their deliberations. It appears evident that further attempts to solve the Korean problem by means of bilateral negotiations will only serve to delay the establishment of an independent, united Korea.

It is therefore the intention of the United States Government to present the problem of Korean independence to this session of the General Assembly. Although we shall be prepared to submit suggestions as to how the early attainment of Korean independence might be effected, we believe that this is a matter which now requires the impartial judgment of the other members. We do not wish to have the inability of two powers to reach agreement delay any further the urgent and rightful claims of the Korean people to independence.

For the achievement of international security and the well-being of the peoples of the world, it is necessary that the United Nations press forward on many fronts. Among these the control of atomic and other weapons of mass destruction has perhaps the highest priority if we are to remove the specter of a war of annihilation.

The preponderant majority of the Atomic Energy Commission has made real progress in spelling out in detail the functions and powers of an international control agency which would provide a framework for effective atomic energy control. Two nations, however, have been unwilling to join the majority in the conclusions reached. This is a disturbing and ominous fact. In dealing with the facts presented by the advent of atomic energy, the majority has devised a system of control which, while it is bold and daring, is, in our view, essential for security against atomic warfare. The minority has evidently been unwilling to face these same facts realistically. The mandate of the General Assembly remains unfulfilled. Failure to agree on a system of control which can provide security against atomic warfare will inevitably retard the development of the peaceful uses of atomic energy for the benefits of the peoples of the world and will accelerate an atomic armaments race.

The initial offer made by the United States on June 14, 1946, by which this country would give up its present advantage in exchange for an effective system of control, has found most gratifying acceptance by the majority of the nations represented on the Commission. They have worked earnestly together to hammer out specific proposals whereby such a system could be put into effect. All have made important contributions to the end product. The majority is convinced that its proposals provide the only adequate basis for effective control.

Since the United States realizes fully the consequences of failure to attain effective international control, we shall continue our efforts in the Atomic Energy Commission to carry forward

our work along the lines of the majority views. We must state frankly, however, that in the absence of unanimous agreement on the essential functions and powers which the majority has concluded must be given to the international agency, there will necessarily be limitations on the extent to which the remaining aspects of the problem can be worked out in detail. If the minority persists in refusing to join with the majority, the Atomic Energy Commission may soon be faced with the conclusion that it is unable to complete the task assigned it under its terms of reference laid down in the General Assembly resolution of January 24, 1946.

The United States also recognizes the importance of regulating conventional armaments. We regret that much more progress has not been made in this field. From this rostrum it is very easy to pay lip service to the sincere aspirations of all peoples for the limitation and reduction of armed forces. This is a serious matter which should not be the subject of demagogic appeals and irresponsible propaganda. I say frankly to the General Assembly that it is the conviction of my Government that a workable system for the regulation of armaments cannot be put into operation until conditions of international confidence prevail. We have consistently and repeatedly made it clear that the regulation of armaments presupposes enough international understanding to make possible the settlement of peace terms with Germany and Japan, the implementation of agreements putting military forces and facilities at the disposal of the Security Council, and an international arrangement for the control of atomic energy.

Nevertheless, we believe it is important not to delay the formulation of a system of arms regulation for implementation when conditions permit. The Security Council has accepted a logical plan of work for the Commission for Conventional Armaments. We believe that the Commission should proceed vigorously to develop a system for the regulation of armaments in the businesslike manner outlined in its plan of work.

The effective operation of the United Nations Security Council is one of the crucial conditions for the maintenance of international security. The exercise of the veto power in the Security Council has the closest bearing on the success and the vitality of the United Nations.

In the past the United States has been reluctant to encourage proposals for changes in the system of voting in the Security Council. Having accepted the Charter provisions on this subject and having joined with other permanent members at San Francisco in a statement of general attitude toward the question of permanent member unanimity, we wished to permit full opportunity for practical testing. We were always fully aware that the successful operation of the rule of unanimity would require the exercise of restraint by the permanent members, and we so expressed ourselves at San Francisco.

It is our hope that, despite our experience to date, such restraint will be practiced in the future by the permanent members. The abuse of the right of unanimity has prevented the Security Council from fulfilling its true functions. That has been especially true in cases arising under chapter VI and in the admission of new members.

The Government of the United States has come to the conclusion that the only practicable method for improving this situation is a liberalization of the voting procedure in the Council.

The United States would be willing to accept, by whatever means may be appropriate, the elimination of the unanimity requirement with respect to matters arising under chapter VI of the Charter and such matters as applications for membership.

We recognize that this is a matter of significance and complexity for the United Nations. We consider that the problem of how to achieve the objective of liberalization of the Security Council voting procedure deserves careful study. Consequently, we shall propose that this matter be referred to a special committee for study and report to the next session of the Assembly. Measures should be pressed concurrently in the Security Council to bring about improvements within the existing provisions of the Charter, through amendments to the rules of procedure or other feasible means.

The scope and complexity of the problems on the agenda of this Assembly have given rise to the question whether the General Assembly can adequately discharge its responsibilities in its regular annual sessions. There is a limit to the number of items which can receive thorough consideration during the few weeks in which this body meets. There would seem to be a definite need for constant attention to the work of the Assembly in order to deal with continuing problems. Occasional special sessions are not enough. The General Assembly has a definite and continuing responsibility, under articles 11 and 14 of the Charter, in the broad field of political security and the preservation of friendly relations among nations. In our fast-moving world an annual review of developments in this field is not sufficient.

The facilities of the General Assembly must be developed to meet this need. I am therefore proposing, today, that this Assembly proceed at this session to create a standing committee of the General Assembly, which might be known as the Interim Committee on Peace and Security, to serve until the beginning of its third regular session next September. The Committtee would not, of course, impinge on matters which are the primary responsibility of the Security Council or of special commissions, but, subject to that, it might consider situations and disputes impairing friendly relations brought to its attention by member states or by the

Security Council pursuant to articles 11 and 14 of the Charter and report to the Assembly or to the Security Council thereon; recommend to the members the calling of special sessions of the General Assembly when necessary; and might report at the next regular session on the desirability of establishing such a committee on a permanent basis.

In our opinion, every Member of the United Nations should be seated on this body.

The creation of the Interim Committee will make the facilities of the General Assembly continually available during this next year to all its members. It will strengthen the machinery for peaceful settlement and place the responsibility for such settlement broadly upon all the Members of the United Nations. Without infringing on the jurisdiction of the Security Council, it will provide an unsurpassed opportunity for continuing study, after the adjournment of this Assembly, of the problems with which the United Nations must contend if it is to succeed.

The attitude of the United States toward the whole range of problems before the United Nations is founded on a very genuine desire to perfect the Organization so as to safeguard the security of states and the well-being of their peoples.

These aims can be accomplished only if the untapped resources of the United Nations are brought to bear with full effect through the General Assembly and in other organs. The Assembly cannot dodge its responsibilities; it must organize itself effectively, not as an agency of intermittent action but on a continuous basis. It is for us, the members of the Assembly, to construct a record of achievement in dealing with crucial problems which will buttress the authority of the Organization and enable it to fulfil its promise to all peoples.

The large powers bear special responsibilities because of their strength and resources. While these responsibilities bring with them special advantages, the Great Powers must recognize that restraint is an essential companion of power and privilege. The United Nations will never endure if there is insistence on privilege to the point of frustration of the collective will. In this spirit we have indicated our own willingness to accept a modification of our special voting rights in the Security Council. In the same spirit we appeal to the other permanent members of the Security Council, in this and in all matters, to use their privileged position to promote the attainment of the purposes of the Organization.

The Government of the United States believes that the surest foundation for permanent peace lies in the extension of the benefits and the restraints of the rule of law to all peoples and to all governments. This is the heart of the Charter and of the structure of the United Nations. It is the best hope of mankind.

53. THE CHARTER OF THE ORGANIZATION OF AMERICAN STATES, 30 APRIL 1948[1]

The Inter-American Conference on Questions of War and Peace held at Mexico City in February and March 1945 to reconcile the Inter-American system with the proposed world system did more than concert the policies of the Western Hemisphere states with respect to general international organization. It also committed them to negotiating a treaty of mutual assistance and a treaty providing for the pacific settlement of international disputes. From the first commitment came the Inter-American Treaty of Reciprocal Assistance (the Rio Pact) drafted at Petropolis in August 1947; and from the second the American Treaty of Pacific Settlement drafted at the Ninth Inter-American Con-

[1] *United States Statutes at Large,* LXII (1948), p. 1681.

ference at Bogota in April 1948. A third commitment of the Mexico City Conference led to negotiating a treaty basis for the Inter-American system, which had theretofore existed principally by virtue of a series of conference resolutions. Accordingly, there was drafted also at the Bogota meeting this Charter of the Organization of American States.

In the name of their peoples, the States represented at the Ninth International Conference of American States,

Convinced that the historic mission of America is to offer to man a land of liberty, and a favorable environment for the development of his personality and the realization of his just aspirations;

Conscious that that mission has already inspired numerous agreements, whose essential value lies in the desire of the American peoples to live together in peace, and, through their mutual understanding and respect for the sovereignty of each one, to provide for the betterment of all, in independence, in equality and under law;

Confident that true significance of American solidarity and good neighborliness can only mean the consolidation on this continent, within the framework of democratic institutions, of a system of individual liberty and social justice based on respect for the essential rights of man;

Persuaded that their welfare and their contribution to the progress and the civilization of the world will increasingly require intensive continental cooperation;

Resolved to persevere in the noble undertaking that humanity has conferred upon the United Nations, whose principles and purposes they solemnly reaffirm;

Convinced that juridical organization is a necessary condition for security and peace founded on moral order and on justice; and

In accordance with Resolution IX of the Inter-American Conference on

Problems of War and Peace, held at Mexico City,

Have agreed upon the following

CHARTER OF THE ORGANIZATION OF AMERICAN STATES

PART ONE

CHAPTER I: NATURE AND PURPOSES

Art. 1. The American States establish by this Charter the international organization that they have developed to achieve an order of peace and justice, to promote their solidarity, to strengthen their collaboration, and to defend their sovereignty, their territorial integrity and their independence. Within the United Nations, the Organization of American States is a regional agency.

Art. 2. All American States that ratify the present Charter are Members of the Organization.

Art. 3. Any new political entity that arises from the union of several Member States and that, as such, ratifies the present Charter, shall become a Member of the Organization. The entry of the new political entity into the Organization shall result in the loss of membership of each one of the States which constitute it.

Art. 4. The Organization of American States, in order to put into practice the principles on which it is founded and to fulfill its regional obligations under the Charter of the United Nations, proclaims the following essential purposes:

a) To strengthen the peace and security of the continent;

b) To prevent possible causes of difficulties and to ensure the pacific settlement of disputes that may arise among the Member States;

c) To provide for common action on the part of those States in the event of aggression;

d) To seek the solution of political, juridical and economic problems that may arise among them; and

e) To promote, by cooperative action,

their economic, social and cultural development.

CHAPTER II: PRINCIPLES

ART. 5. The American States reaffirm the following principles:

a) International law is the standard of conduct of States in their reciprocal relations;

b) International order consists essentially of respect for the personality, sovereignty and independence of States, and the faithful fulfillment of obligations derived from treaties and other sources of international law;

c) Good faith shall govern the relations between States;

d) The solidarity of the American States and the high aims which are sought through it require the political organization of those States on the basis of the effective exercise of representative democracy;

e) The American States condemn war of aggression: victory does not give rights;

f) An act of aggression against one American State is an act of aggression against all the other American States;

g) Controversies of an international character arising between two or more American States shall be settled by peaceful procedures;

h) Social justice and social security are bases of lasting peace;

i) Economic cooperation is essential to the common welfare and prosperity of the peoples of the continent;

j) The American States proclaim the fundamental rights of the individual without distinction as to race, nationality, creed or sex;

k) The spiritual unity of the continent is based on respect for the cultural values of the American countries and requires their close cooperation for the high purposes of civilization;

l) The education of peoples should be directed toward justice, freedom and peace.

CHAPTER III: FUNDAMENTAL RIGHTS AND DUTIES OF STATES

ART. 6. States are juridically equal, enjoy equal rights and equal capacity to exercise these rights, and have equal duties. The rights of each State depend not upon its power to ensure the exercise thereof, but upon the mere fact of its existence as a person under international law.

ART. 7. Every American State has the duty to respect the rights enjoyed by every other State in accordance with international law.

ART. 8. The fundamental rights of States may not be impaired in any manner whatsoever.

ART. 9. The political existence of the State is independent of recognition by other States. Even before being recognized, the State has the right to defend its integrity and independence, to provide for its preservation and prosperity, and consequently to organize itself as it sees fit, to legislate concerning its interests, to administer its services, and to determine the jurisdiction and competence of its courts. The exercise of these rights is limited only by the exercise of the rights of other States in accordance with international law.

ART. 10. Recognition implies that the State granting it accepts the personality of the new State, with all the rights and duties that international law prescribes for the two States.

ART. 11. The right of each State to protect itself and live its own life does not authorize it to commit unjust acts against another State.

ART. 12. The jurisdiction of States within the limits of their national territory is exercised equally over all the inhabitants, whether nationals or aliens.

ART. 13. Each State has the right to develop its cultural, political and economic life freely and naturally. In this free development, the State shall respect the rights of the individual and the principles of universal morality.

ART. 14. Respect for and the faithful observance of treaties constitute standards for the development of peaceful relations among States. International treaties and agreements should be public.

ART. 15. No State or group of States has the right to intervene, directly or indirectly, for any reason whatever, in the internal or external affairs of any other State. The foregoing principle prohibits not only armed force but also any other form of interference or attempted threat against the personality of the State or against its political, economic and cultural elements.

ART. 16. No State may use or encourage the use of coercive measures of an economic or political character in order to force the sovereign will of another State and obtain from it advantages of any kind.

ART. 17. The territory of a State is inviolable; it may not be the object, even temporarily, of military occupation or of other measures of force taken by another State, directly or indirectly, on any grounds whatever. No territorial acquisitions or special advantages obtained either by force or by other means of coercion shall be recognized.

ART. 18. The American States bind themselves in their international relations not to have recourse to the use of force, except in the case of self-defense in accordance with existing treaties or in fulfillment thereof.

ART. 19. Measures adopted for the maintenance of peace and security in accordance with existing treaties do not constitute a violation of the principles set forth in Articles 15 and 17.

CHAPTER IV: PACIFIC SETTLEMENT
OF DISPUTES

ART. 20. All international disputes that may arise between American States shall be submitted to the peaceful procedures set forth in this Charter, before being referred to the Security Council of the United Nations.

ART. 21. The following are peaceful procedures: direct negotiation, good offices, mediation, investigation and conciliation, judicial settlement, arbitration, and those which the parties to the dispute may especially agree upon at any time.

ART. 22. In the event that a dispute arises between two or more American States which, in the opinion of one of them, cannot be settled through the usual diplomatic channels, the Parties shall agree on some other peaceful procedure that will enable them to reach a solution.

ART. 23. A special treaty will establish adequate procedures for the pacific settlement of disputes and will determine the appropriate means for their application, so that no dispute between American States will fail of definitive settlement within a reasonable period.

CHAPTER V: COLLECTIVE SECURITY

ART. 24. Every act of aggression by a State against the territorial integrity or the inviolability of the territory or against the sovereignty or political independence of an American State shall be considered an act of aggression against the other American States.

ART. 25. If the inviolability or the integrity of the territory or the sovereignty or political independence of any American State should be affected by an armed attack or by an act of aggression that is not an armed attack, or by an extra-continental conflict, or by a conflict between two or more American States, or by any other fact or situation that might endanger the peace of America, the American States, in furtherance of the principles of continental solidarity or collective self-defense, shall apply the measures and procedures established in the special treaties on the subject.

CHAPTER VI: ECONOMIC STANDARDS

ART. 26. The Member States agree to cooperate with one another, as far as their resources may permit and their laws may provide, in the broadest spirit of good neighborliness, in order to strengthen their economic structure, develop their agriculture and mining, promote their industry and increase their trade.

ART. 27. If the economy of an American State is affected by serious conditions that cannot be satisfactorily remedied by its own unaided effort, such State may place its economic problems before the Inter-American Economic and Social Council to seek through consultation the most appropriate solution for such problems.

CHAPTER VII: SOCIAL STANDARDS

ART. 28. The Member States agree to cooperate with one another to achieve just and decent living conditions for their entire populations.

ART. 29. The Member States agree upon the desirability of developing their social legislation on the following bases:

a) All human beings, without distinction as to race, nationality, sex, creed or social condition, have the right to attain material well-being and spiritual growth under circumstances of liberty, dignity, equality of opportunity, and economic security;

b) Work is a right and a social duty; it shall not be considered as an article of commerce; it demands respect for freedom of association and for the dignity of the worker; and it is to be performed under conditions that ensure life, health and a decent standard of living, both during the working years and during old age, or when any circumstance deprives the individual of the possibility of working.

CHAPTER VIII: CULTURAL STANDARDS

ART. 30. The Member States agree to promote, in accordance with their constitutional provisions and their material resources, the exercise of the right to education, on the following bases:

a) Elementary education shall be compulsory and, when provided by the State, shall be without cost;

b) Higher education shall be available to all, without distinction as to race, nationality, sex, language, creed or social condition.

ART. 31. With due consideration for the national character of each State, the Member States undertake to facilitate free cultural interchange by every medium of expression.

PART TWO

CHAPTER IX: THE ORGANS

ART. 32. The Organization of American States accomplishes its purposes by means of:

a) The Inter-American Conference;

b) The Meeting of Consultation of Ministers of Foreign Affairs;

c) The Council;

d) The Pan American Union;

e) The Specialized Conferences; and

f) The Specialized Organizations.

CHAPTER X: THE INTER-AMERICAN CONFERENCE

ART. 33. The Inter-American Conference is the supreme organ of the Organization of American States. It decides the general action and policy of the Organization and determines the structure and functions of its Organs, and has the authority to consider any matter relating to friendly relations among the American States. These functions shall be carried out in accordance with the provisions of this Charter and of other inter-American treaties.

ART. 34. All Member States have the right to be represented at the Inter-American Conference. Each State has the right to one vote.

ART. 35. The Conference shall convene every five years at the time fixed by the Council of the Organization, after consultation with the government of the country where the Conference is to be held.

ART. 36. In special circumstances and with the approval of two-thirds of the

American Governments, a special Inter-American Conference may be held, or the date of the next regular Conference may be changed.

Art. 37. Each Inter-American Conference shall designate the place of meeting of the next Conference. If for any unforeseen reason the Conference cannot be held at the place designated, the Council of the Organization shall designate a new place.

Art. 38. The program and regulations of the Inter-American Conference shall be prepared by the Council of the Organization and submitted to the Member States for consideration.

CHAPTER XI: THE MEETING OF CONSULTATION OF MINISTERS OF FOREIGN AFFAIRS

Art. 39. The Meeting of Consultation of Ministers of Foreign Affairs shall be held in order to consider problems of an urgent nature and of common interest to the American States, and to serve as the Organ of Consultation.

Art. 40. Any Member State may request that a Meeting of Consultation be called. The request shall be addressed to the Council of the Organization, which shall decide by an absolute majority whether a meeting should be held.

Art. 41. The program and regulations of the Meeting of Consultation shall be prepared by the Council of the Organization and submitted to the Member States for consideration.

Art. 42. If, for exceptional reasons, a Minister of Foreign Affairs is unable to attend the meeting, he shall be represented by a special delegate.

Art. 43. In case of an armed attack within the territory of an American State or within the region of security delimited by treaties in force, a Meeting of Consultation shall be held without delay. Such Meeting shall be called immediately by the Chairman of the Council of the Organization, who shall at the same time call a meeting of the Council itself.

Art. 44. An Advisory Defense Committee shall be established to advise the Organ of Consultation on problems of military cooperation that may arise in connection with the application of existing special treaties on collective security.

Art. 45. The Advisory Defense Committee shall be composed of the highest military authorities of the American States participating in the Meeting of Consultation. Under exceptional circumstances the Governments may appoint substitutes. Each State shall be entitled to one vote.

Art. 46. The Advisory Defense Committee shall be convoked under the same conditions as the Organ of Consultation, when the latter deals with matters relating to defense against aggression.

Art. 47. The Committee shall also meet when the Conference or the Meeting of Consultation or the Governments, by a two-thirds majority of the Member States, assign to it technical studies or reports on specific subjects.

CHAPTER XII: THE COUNCIL

Art. 48. The Council of the Organization of American States is composed of one Representative of each Member State of the Organization, especially appointed by the respective Government, with the rank of Ambassador. The appointment may be given to the diplomatic representative accredited to the Government of the country in which the Council has its seat. During the absence of the titular Representative, the Government may appoint an interim Representative.

Art. 49. The Council shall elect a Chairman and a Vice Chairman, who shall serve for one year and shall not be eligible for election to either of those positions for the term immediately following.

Art. 50. The Council takes cognizance, within the limits of the present Charter and of inter-American treaties and agreements, of any matter referred to it by the Inter-American Conference or the Meeting of Consultation of Ministers of Foreign Affairs.

Art. 51. The Council shall be responsible for the proper discharge by the Pan American Union of the duties assigned to it.

Art. 52. The Council shall serve provisionally as the Organ of Consultation when the circumstances contemplated in Article 43 of this Charter arise.

Article 53. It is also the duty of the Council:

a) To draft and submit to the Governments and to the Inter-American Conference proposals for the creation of new Specialized Organizations or for the combination, adaptation or elimination of existing ones, including matters relating to the financing and support thereof;

b) To draft recommendations to the Governments, the Inter-American Conference, the Specialized Conferences or the Specialized Organizations, for the coordination of the activities and programs of such organizations, after consultation with them;

c) To conclude agreements with the Inter-American Specialized Organizations to determine the relations that shall exist between the respective agency and the Organization;

d) To conclude agreements or special arrangements for cooperation with other American organizations of recognized international standing;

e) To promote and facilitate collaboration between the Organization of American States and the United Nations, as well as between Inter-American Specialized Organizations and similar international agencies;

f) To adopt resolutions that will enable the Secretary General to perform the duties envisaged in Article 84;

g) To perform the other duties assigned to it by the present Charter.

Art. 54. The Council shall establish the bases for fixing the quota that each Government is to contribute to the maintenance of the Pan American Un-

ion, taking into account the ability to pay of the respective countries and their determination to contribute in an equitable manner. The budget, after approval by the Council, shall be transmitted to the Governments at least six months before the first day of the fiscal year, with a statement of the annual quota of each country. Decisions on budgetary matters require the approval of two-thirds of the members of the Council.

Art. 55. The Council shall formulate its own regulations.

Art. 56. The Council shall function at the seat of the Pan American Union.

Art. 57. The following are organs of the Council of the Organization of American States:

a) The Inter-American Economic and Social Council;

b) The Inter-American Council of Jurists; and

c) The Inter-American Cultural Council.

Art. 58. The organs referred to in the preceding article shall have technical autonomy within the limits of this Charter; but their decisions shall not encroach upon the sphere of action of the Council of the Organization.

Art. 59. The organs of the Council of the Organization are composed of representatives of all the Member States of the Organization.

Art. 60. The organs of the Council of the Organization shall, as far as possible, render to the Governments such technical services as the latter may request; and they shall advise the Council of the Organization on matters within their jurisdiction.

Art. 61. The organs of the Council of the Organization shall, in agreement with the Council, establish cooperative relations with the corresponding organs of the United Nations and with the national or international agencies that function within their respective spheres of action.

Art. 62. The Council of the Organization, with the advice of the appropriate bodies and after consultation with the Governments, shall formulate the statutes of its organs in accordance with and in the execution of the provisions of this Charter. The organs shall formulate their own regulations.

A) THE INTER-AMERICAN ECONOMIC AND SOCIAL COUNCIL

ART. 63. The Inter-American Economic and Social Council has for its principal purpose the promotion of the economic and social welfare of the American nations through effective cooperation for the better utilization of their natural resources, the development of their agriculture and industry and the raising of the standards of living of their peoples.

ART. 64. To accomplish this purpose the Council shall:

a) Propose the means by which the American nations may give each other technical assistance in making studies and formulating and executing plans to carry out the purposes referred to in Article 26 and to develop and improve their social services;

b) Act as coordinating agency for all official inter-American activities of an economic and social nature;

c) Undertake studies on its own initiative or at the request of any Member State;

d) Assemble and prepare reports on economic and social matters for the use of the Member States;

e) Suggest to the Council of the Organization the advisibility of holding specialized conferences on economic and social matters;

f) Carry on such other activities as may be assigned to it by the Inter-American Conference, the Meeting of Consultation of Ministers of Foreign Affairs, or the Council of the Organization.

ART. 65. The Inter-American Economic and Social Council, composed of technical delegates appointed by each Member State, shall meet on its own initiative or on that of the Council of the Organization.

ART. 66. The Inter-American Economic and Social Council shall function at the seat of the Pan American Union, but it may hold meetings in any American city by a majority decision of the Member States.

B) THE INTER-AMERICAN COUNCIL OF JURISTS

ART. 67. The purpose of the Inter-American Council of Jurists is to serve as an advisory body on juridical matters; to promote the development and codification of public and private international law; and to study the possibility of attaining uniformity in the legislation of the various American countries, insofar as it may appear desirable.

ART. 68. The Inter-American Juridical Committee of Rio de Janeiro shall be the permanent committee of the Inter-American Council of Jurists.

ART. 69. The Juridical Committee shall be composed of jurists of the nine countries selected by the Inter-American Conference. The selection of the jurists shall be made by the Inter-American Council of Jurists from a panel submitted by each country chosen by the Conference. The Members of the Juridical Committee represent all Member States of the Organization. The Council of the Organization is empowered to fill any vacancies that occur during the intervals between Intervals between Inter-American Conferences and between meetings of the Inter-American Council of Jurists.

ART. 70. The Juridical Committee shall undertake such studies and preparatory work as are assigned to it by the Inter-American Council of Jurists, the Inter-American Conference, the Meeting of Consultation of Ministers of Foreign Affairs, or the Council of the Organization. It may also undertake those studies and projects which, on its own initiative, it considers advisable.

ART. 71. The Inter-American Council of Jurists and the Juridical Committee should seek the cooperation of national committees for the codification of international law, of institutes of international and comparative law, and of other specialized agencies.

ART. 72. The Inter-American Council of Jurists shall meet when convened by the Council of the Organization, at the place determined by the Council of Jurists at its previous meeting.

C) THE INTER-AMERICAN CULTURAL COUNCIL

ART. 73. The purpose of the Inter-American Cultural Council is to promote friendly relations and mutual understanding among the American peoples, in order to strengthen the peaceful sentiments that have characterized the evolution of America, through the promotion of educational, scientific and cultural exchange.

ART. 74. To this end the principal functions of the Council shall be:

a) To sponsor inter-American cultural activities;

b) To collect and supply information on cultural activities carried on in and among the American States by private and official agencies both national and international in character;

c) To promote the adoption of basic educational programs adapted to the needs of all population groups in the American countries;

d) To promote, in addition, the adoption of special programs of training, education and culture for the indigenous groups of the American countries;

e) To cooperate in the protection, preservation and increase of the cultural heritage of the continent;

f) To promote cooperation among the American nations in the fields of education, science and culture, by means of the exchange of materials for research and study, as well as the exchange of teachers, students, specialists and, in general such other persons and materials as are useful for the realization of these ends;

g) To encourage the education of the peoples for harmonious international relations;

h) To carry on such other activities as may be assigned to it by the Inter-American Conference, the Meeting of Consultation of Ministers of Foreign Affairs, or the Council of the Organization.

ART. 75. The Inter-American Cultural Council shall determine the place of its next meeting and shall be convened by the Council of the Organization on the date chosen by the latter in agreement with the Government of the country selected as the seat of the meeting.

ART. 76. There shall be a Committee for Cultural Action of which five States, chosen at each Inter-American Conference, shall be members. The individuals composing the Committee for Cultural Action shall be selected by the Inter-American Cultural Council from a panel submitted by each country chosen by the Conference, and they shall be specialists in education or cultural matters. When the Inter-American Cultural Council and the Inter-American Conference are not in session, the Council of the Organization may fill vacancies that arise and replace those countries that find it necessary to discontinue their cooperation.

ART. 77. The Committee for Cultural Action shall function as the permanent committee of the Inter-American Cultural Council, for the purpose of preparing any studies that the latter may assign to it. With respect to these studies the Council shall have the final decision.

CHAPTER XIII. THE PAN AMERICAN UNION

ART. 78. The Pan American Union is the central and permanent organ of the Organization of American States and the General Secretariat of the Organization. It shall perform the duties assigned to it in this Charter and such other duties as may be assigned to it in other inter-American treaties and agreements.

ART. 79. There shall be a Secretary General of the Organization, who shall be elected by the Council for a ten-year term and who may not be reelected or be succeeded by a person of the same nationality. In the event of a vacancy in the office of Secretary General, the Council shall, within the next ninety days, elect a successor to fill the office for the remainder of the term, who may be reelected if the vacancy occurs during the second half of the term.

ART. 80. The Secretary General shall direct the Pan American Union and be the legal representative thereof.

ART. 81. The Secretary General shall participate with voice, but without vote, in the deliberations of the Inter-American Conference, the Meeting of Consultation of Ministers of Foreign Affairs, the Specialized Conferences, and the Council and its organs.

ART. 82. The Pan American Union, through its technical and information offices, shall, under the direction of the Council, promote economic, social, juridical and cultural relations among all the Member States of the Organization.

ART. 83. The Pan American Union shall also perform the following functions:

a) Transmit *ex officio* to Member States the convocation to the Inter-American Conference, the Meeting of Consultation of Ministers of Foreign Affairs, and the Specialized Conferences;

b) Advise the Council and its organs in the preparation of programs and regulations of the Inter-American Conference, the Meeting of Consultation of Ministers of Foreign Affairs, and the Specialized Conferences;

c) Place, to the extent of its ability, at the disposal of the Government of the country where a conference is to be held, the technical aid and personnel which such Government may request;

d) Serve as custodian of the documents and archives of the Inter-American Conference, of the Meeting of Consultation of Ministers of Foreign Affairs, and, insofar as possible, of the Specialized Conferences;

e) Serve as depository of the instruments of ratification of inter-American agreements;

f) Perform the functions entrusted to it by the Inter-American Conference, and the Meeting of Consultation of Ministers of Foreign Affairs;

g) Submit to the Council an annual report on the activities of the Organization;

h) Submit to the Inter-American Conference a report on the work accomplished by the Organs of the Organization since the previous Conference.

ART. 84. It is the duty of the Secretary General:

a) To establish, with the approval of the Council, such technical and administrative offices of the Pan American Union as are necessary to accomplish its purposes;

b) To determine the number of department heads, officers and employees of the Pan American Union; to appoint them, regulate their powers and duties, and fix their compensation, in accordance with general standards established by the Council.

ART. 85. There shall be an Assistant Secretary General, elected by the Council for a term of ten years and eligible for reelection. In the event of a vacancy in the office of Assistant Secretary General, the Council shall, within the next ninety days, elect a successor to fill such office for the remainder of the term.

ART. 86. The Assistant Secretary General shall be the Secretary of the Council. He shall perform the duties of the Secretary General during the temporary absence or disability of the latter, or during the ninety-day vacancy referred to in Article 79. He shall also serve as advisory officer to the Secretary General, with the power to act as his delegate in all matters that the Secretary General may entrust to him.

ART. 87. The Council, by a two-thirds vote of its members, may remove the Secretary General or the Assistant Secretary General whenever the proper functioning of the Organization so demands.

ART. 88. The heads of the respective departments of the Pan American Union, appointed by the Secretary General, shall be the Executive Secretaries of the Inter-American Economic and Social Council, the Council of Jurists and the Cultural Council.

ART. 89. In the performance of their duties the personnel shall not seek or receive instructions from any government or from any other authority outside the Pan American Union. They shall refrain from any action that might reflect upon their position as international officials responsible only to the Union.

ART. 90. Every Member of the Organization of American States pledges itself to respect the exclusively international character of the responsibilities of the Secretary General and the personnel, and not to seek to influence them in the discharge of their duties.

ART. 91. In selecting its personnel the Pan American Union shall give first consideration to efficiency, competence and integrity; but at the same time importance shall be given to the necessity of recruiting personnel on as broad a geographical basis as possible.

ART. 92. The seat of the Pan American Union is the city of Washington.

CHAPTER XIV: THE SPECIALIZED CONFERENCES

ART. 93. The Specialized Conferences shall meet to deal with special technical matters or to develop specific aspects of inter-American cooperation, when it is so decided by the Inter-American Conference or the Meeting of Consultation of Ministers of Foreign Affairs; when inter-American agreements so provide; or when the Council of the Organization considers it necessary, either on its own initiative or at the request of one of its organs or of one of the Specialized Organizations.

ART. 94. The program and regulations of the Specialized Conferences shall be prepared by the organs of the Council of the Organization or by the Specialized Organizations concerned; they shall be submitted to the Member Governments for consideration and transmitted to the Council for its information.

CHAPTER XV: THE SPECIALIZED ORGANIZATIONS

ART. 95. For the purposes of the present Charter, Inter-American Specialized Organizations are the intergovernmental organizations established by multi-lateral agreements and having specific functions with respect to technical matters of common interest to the American States.

ART. 96. The Council shall, for the purposes stated in Article 53, maintain a register of the Organizations that fulfill the conditions set forth in the foregoing Article.

ART. 97. The Specialized Organizations shall enjoy the fullest technical autonomy and shall take into account the recommendations of the Council, in conformity with the provisions of the present Charter.

ART. 98. The Specialized Organizations shall submit to the Council periodic reports on the progress of their work and on their annual budgets and expenses.

ART. 99. Agreements between the Council and the Specialized Organizations contemplated in paragraph c) of Article 53 may provide that such Organizations transmit their budgets to the Council for approval. Arrangements may also be made for the Pan American Union to receive the quotas of the contributing countries and distribute them in accordance with the said agreements.

ART. 100. The Specialized Organizations shall establish cooperative relations with world agencies of the same character in order to coordinate their activities. In concluding agreements with international agencies of a worldwide character, the Inter-American Specialized Organizations shall preserve their identity and their status as integral parts of the Organization of American States, even when they perform regional functions of international agencies.

ART. 101. In determining the geographic location of the Specialized Organizations the interests of all the American States shall be taken into account.

PART THREE

CHAPTER XVI: THE UNITED NATIONS

ART. 102. None of the provisions of this Charter shall be construed as impairing the rights and obligations of the Member States under the Charter of the United Nations.

CHAPTER XVII: MISCELLANEOUS PROVISIONS

ART. 103. The Organization of American States shall enjoy in the territory of each Member such legal capacity, privileges and immunities as are necessary for the exercise of its func-

tions and the accomplishment of its purposes.

ART. 104. The Representatives of the Governments on the Council of the Organization, the representatives on the organs of the Council, the personnel of their delegations, as well as the Secretary General and the Assistant Secretary General of the Organization, shall enjoy the privileges and immunities necessary for the independent performance of their duties.

ART. 105. The juridical status of the Inter-American Specialized Organizations and the privileges and immunities that should be granted to them and to their personnel, as well as to the officials of the Pan American Union shall be determined in each case through agreements between the respective organizations and the Governments concerned.

ART. 106. Correspondence of the Organization of American States, including printed matter and parcels, bearing the frank thereof, shall be carried free of charge in the mails of the Member States.

54. THE VANDENBERG RESOLUTION, 11 JUNE 1948 [1]

The establishment of the Cominform, announced on 5 October 1947, and the February 1948 *coup* by which the Communists seized control of the Czechoslovakian government quickened in the United States the fear that the European Recovery Program and the proposed "Western Union" of Britain, France and the Benelux countries would not take effect in time to deter the Soviets from moving against Western Europe. Plans for a mutual defense pact linking the United States and the "Western Union" nations, much as the United States and the Latin American nations had been united by the Rio Pact of September 1946, began to take shape in the Executive branch of the United States government. Support for so radical a departure from traditional American policy was secured from the Republican-controlled Senate in this resolution (Senate Resolution 239) introduced by Senator Vandenberg and adopted by a vote of 64 to 4.

Whereas peace with justice and the defense of human rights and fundamental freedoms require international cooperation through more effective use of the United Nations: Therefore be it

Resolved, That the Senate reaffirm the policy of the United States to achieve international peace and security through the United Nations so that armed force shall not be used except in the common interest, and that the President be advised of the sense of the Senate that this Government, by constitutional process, should particularly pursue the following objectives within the United Nations Charter:

(1) Voluntary agreement to remove the veto from all questions involving

1 *Congressional Record,* 80th Cong., 2nd   sess., XCIV (19 May 1948), p. 6053.

pacific settlements of international disputes and situations, and from the admission of new members.

(2) Progressive development of regional and other collective arrangements for individual and collective self-defense in accordance with the purposes, principles, and provisions of the Charter.

(3) Association of the United States, by constitutional process, with such regional and other collective arrangements as are based on continuous and effective self-help and mutual aid, and as affect its national security.

(4) Contributing to the maintenance of peace by making clear its determination to exercise the right of individual or collective self-defense under article 51 should any armed attack occur affecting its national security.

(5) Maximum efforts to obtain agreements to provide the United Nations with armed forces as provided by the Charter, and to obtain agreement among member nations upon universal regulation and reduction of armaments under adequate and dependable guaranty against violation.

(6) If necessary, after adequate effort toward strengthening the United Nations, review of the Charter at an appropriate time by a General Conference called under article 109 or by the General Assembly.

55. THE NORTH ATLANTIC TREATY, 4 APRIL 1949 [1]

Application of the principles of the Truman Doctrine [2] to Communist-threatened Europe took the form of a mutual defense alliance with permanent, continuously operating organs, the North Atlantic Treaty Organization or NATO. Shortly after the United States Senate adopted the Vandenberg resolution inviting the President to enter into regional arrangements for strengthening the United Nations,[3] negotiations were begun among the United States, Canada and the states of Western Europe. By the terms of this treaty twelve members of the Atlantic community organized themselves for collective self-defense in the spirit of Article 51 of the United Nations Charter.[4] Despite the establishment of Western Union among the United Kingdom, France and the Benelux countries and the Organization of American States [5] among the twenty-one republics of the Western Hemisphere, both completed in the spring of the previous year, NATO gave the United Nations its first significant accession of strength from a regional alliance. That a policy of firmness was the better answer to the Soviet threat was demonstrated a few weeks later by the lifting of the Berlin blockade.[6]

The Parties to this Treaty reaffirm their faith in the purposes and principles of the Charter of the United Nations and their desire to live in peace with all peoples and all governments.

They are determined to safeguard the freedom, common heritage and civilization of their peoples, founded on the principles of democracy, individual liberty and the rule of law.

They seek to promote stability and well-being in the North Atlantic area.

They are resolved to unite their efforts for collective defense and for the preservation of peace and security.

They therefore agree to this North Atlantic Treaty:

ART. 1. The Parties undertake, as set forth in the Charter of the United Nations, to settle any international disputes in which they may be involved by peaceful means in such a manner that international peace and security, and justice, are not endangered, and to refrain in their international relations from the threat or use of force in any manner inconsistent with the purposes of the United Nations.

ART. 2. The Parties will contribute toward the further development of peaceful and friendly international relations by strengthening their free insti-

[1] United States Statutes at Large, LXIII (1949), pp. 2242 ff.
[2] See Doc. 50.
[3] See Doc. 54.

[4] See Doc. 49. Turkey, Greece and Western Germany were subsequently added.
[5] See Doc. 53.
[6] 24 June 1948—12 May 1949.

tutions, by bringing about a better understanding of the principles upon which these institutions are founded, and by promoting conditions of stability and well-being. They will seek to eliminate conflict in their international economic policies and will encourage economic collaboration between any or all of them.

ART. 3. In order more effectively to achieve the objectives of this Treaty, the Parties, separately and jointly, by means of continuous and effective self-help and mutual aid, will maintain and develop their individual and collective capacity to resist armed attack.

ART. 4. The Parties will consult together whenever, in the opinion of any of them, the territorial integrity, political independence or security of any of the Parties is threatened.

ART. 5. The Parties agree that an armed attack against one or more of them in Europe or North America shall be considered an attack against them all; and consequently they agree that, if such an armed attack occurs, each of them, in exercise of the right of individual or collective self-defense recognized by Article 51 of the Charter of the United Nations, will assist the Party or Parties so attacked by taking forthwith, individually and in concert with the other Parties, such action as it deems necessary, including the use of armed force, to restore and maintain the security of the North Atlantic area.

Any such armed attack and all measures taken as a result thereof shall immediately be reported to the Security Council. Such measures shall be terminated when the Security Council has taken the measures necessary to restore and maintain international peace and security.

ART. 6. For the purpose of Article 5 an armed attack on one or more of the Parties is deemed to include an armed attack on the territory of any of the Parties in Europe or North America, on the Algerian departments of France, on the occupation forces of any Party in Europe, on the islands under the jurisdiction of any Party in the North Atlantic area north of the Tropic of Cancer or on the vessels or aircraft in this area of any of the Parties.

ART. 7. This Treaty does not affect, and shall not be interpreted as affecting, in any way the rights and obligations under the Charter of the Parties which are members of the United Nations, or the primary responsibility of the Security Council for the maintenance of international peace and security.

ART. 8. Each Party declares that none of the international engagements now in force between it and any other of the Parties or any third state is in conflict with the provisions of this Treaty, and undertakes not to enter into any international engagement in conflict with this Treaty.

ART. 9. The Parties hereby established a council, on which each of them shall be represented, to consider matters concerning the implementation of this Treaty. The council shall be so organized as to be able to meet promptly at any time. The council shall set up such subsidiary bodies as may be necessary; in particular it shall establish immediately a defense committee which shall recommend measures for the implementation of Articles 3 and 5.

ART. 10. The Parties may, by unanimous agreement, invite any other European state in a position to further the principles of this Treaty and to contribute to the security of the North Atlantic area to accede to this Treaty. Any state so invited may become a party to the Treaty by depositing its instrument of accession with the Government of the United States of America. The Government of the United States of America will inform each of the Parties of the deposit of each such instrument of accession.

ART. 11. This Treaty shall be ratified and its provisions carried out by the Parties in accordance with their respective constitutional processes. The instruments of ratification shall be deposited as soon as possible with the Government of the United States of America, which will notify all the other signatories of each deposit. The Treaty shall enter into force between the states which have ratified it as soon as the ratifications of the majority of the signatories, including the ratifications of Belgium, Canada, France, Luxembourg, the Netherlands, the United Kingdom and the United States, have been deposited and shall come into effect with respect to other states on the date of the deposit of their ratifications.

ART. 12. After the Treaty has been in force for ten years, or at any time thereafter, the Parties shall, if any of them so requests, consult together for the purpose of reviewing the Treaty, having regard for the factors then affecting peace and security in the North Atlantic area, including the development of universal as well as regional arrange-

ments under the Charter of the United Nations for the maintenance of international peace and security.

ART. 13. After the Treaty has been in force for twenty years, any Party may cease to be a party one year after its notice of denunciation has been given to the Government of the United States of America, which will inform the Governments of the other Parties of the deposit of each notice of denunciation.

ART. 14. This Treaty, of which the English and French texts are equally authentic, shall be deposited in the archives of the Government of the United States of America. Duly certified copies thereof will be transmitted by that Government to the Governments of the other signatories.

In witness whereof, the undersigned plenipotentiaries have signed this Treaty.

Done at Washington, the fourth day of April, 1949.

56. THE STATUTE OF THE COUNCIL OF EUROPE, 5 MAY 1949 [1]

The period which witnessed the drawing together of the Atlantic powers for common defense under the North Atlantic Treaty [2] saw the uniting of the states of Western Europe in the Council of Europe. Although, like NATO, a response to the threat from Soviet Russia, the Council of Europe is the first real achievement of the "European Movement," whose roots reach back as far as the Western State System itself. A long series of schemes for international organization remained only literary productions until, in the days of the League of Nations, Count Richard N. Coudenhove-Kalergi launched the Pan-Europe Movement in 1923 and Foreign Minister Aristide Briand, on behalf of the French Government, circulated among the other European members of the League a proposal for a European union. In 1948, following the Hague meeting organized by the International Committee of Movements of European Unity, a private body, France again took the initiative when Georges Bidault proposed that the Council of Western Union study the

problem. Out of the deliberations that followed came this Statute, which entered into force the following August.

The Governments of the Kingdom of Belgium, the Kingdom of Denmark, the French Republic, the Irish Republic, the Italian Republic, the Grand Duchy of Luxembourg, the Kingdom of the Netherlands, the Kingdom of Norway, the Kingdom of Sweden, and the United Kingdom of Great Britain and Northern Ireland;

Convinced that the pursuit of peace based upon justice and international cooperation is vital for the preservation of human society and civilization;

Reaffirming their devotion to the spiritual and moral values which are

[1] Statut de Conseil de l'Europe. Statute of the Council of Europe. Londres, 5 mai 1949. London, 5th May 1949. (Nancy, Berger—

Levrault, 1950).
[2] See Doc. 55.

the common heritage of their peoples and the true source of individual freedom, political liberty and the rule of law, principles which form the basis of all genuine democracy;

Believing that, for the maintenance and further realization of these ideals and in the interests of economic and social progress, there is need of a closer unity between all like-minded countries of Europe;

Considering that, to respond to this need and to the expressed aspirations of their peoples in this regard, it is necessary forthwith to create an organization which will bring European States into closer association;

Have in consequence decided to set up a Council of Europe consisting of a Committee of representatives of Governments and of a Consultative Assembly, and have for this purpose adopted the following Statute:—

CHAPTER I—AIM OF THE COUNCIL OF EUROPE

ART. 1. (a) The aim of the Council of Europe is to achieve a greater unity between its Members for the purpose of safeguarding and realizing the ideals and principles which are their common heritage and facilitating their economic and social progress.

(b) This aim shall be pursued through the organs of the Council by discussion of questions of common concern and by agreements and common action in economic, social, cultural, scientific, legal, and administrative matters and in the maintenance and further realization of human rights and fundamental freedoms.

(c) Participation in the Council of Europe shall not affect the collaboration of its Members in the work of the United Nations and of other international organizations or unions to which they are parties.

(d) Matters relating to National Defence do not fall within the scope of the Council of Europe.

CHAPTER II—MEMBERSHIP

ART. 2. The Members of the Council of Europe are the Parties to this Statute.

ART. 3. Every Member of the Council of Europe must accept the principles of the rule of law and of the enjoyment by all persons within its jurisdiction of human rights and fundamental freedoms, and collaborate sincerely and effectively in the realization of the aim of the Council as specified in Chapter I.

ART. 4. Any European State, which is deemed to be able and willing to fulfil the provisions of Article 3, may be invited to become a Member of the Council of Europe by the Committee of Ministers. Any State so invited shall become a Member on the deposit on its behalf with the Secretary-General of an instrument of accession to the present Statute.

ART. 5. (a) In special circumstances, a European country, which is deemed to be able and willing to fulfil the provisions of Article 3, may be invited by the Committee of Ministers to become an Associate Member of the Council of Europe. Any country so invited shall become an Associate Member on the deposit on its behalf with the Secretary-General of an instrument accepting the present Statute. An Associate Member shall be entitled to be represented in the Consultative Assembly only.

(b) The expression 'Member' in this Statute includes an Associate Member except when used in connection with representation on the Committee of Ministers.

ART. 6. Before issuing invitations under Articles 4 or 5 above, the Committee of Ministers shall determine the number of representatives on the Consultative Assembly to which the proposed Member shall be entitled and its proportionate financial contribution.

ART. 7. Any Member of the Council of Europe may withdraw by formally notifying the Secretary-General of its intention to do so. Such withdrawal shall take effect at the end of the financial year in which it is notified, if the notification is given during the first nine months of that financial year. If the notification is given in the last three months of the financial year, it shall take effect at the end of the next financial year.

ART. 8. Any Member of the Council of Europe, which has seriously violated Article 3, may be suspended from its rights of representation and requested by the Committee of Ministers to withdraw under Article 7. If such Member does not comply with this request, the Committee may decide that it has ceased to be a Member of the Council as from such date as the Committee may determine.

ART. 9. The Committee of Ministers may suspend the right of representation on the Committee and on the Consultative Assembly of a member, which has failed to fulfil its financial obligation, during such period as the obligation remains unfulfilled.

CHAPTER III—GENERAL

ART. 10. The organs of the Council of Europe are:

(i) The Committee of Ministers;

(ii) the Consultative Assembly.

Both these organs shall be served by the Secretariat of the Council of Europe.

ART. 11. The seat of the Council of Europe is at Strasbourg.

ART. 12. The official languages of the Council of Europe are English and French. The rules of procedure of the Committee of Ministers and of the Consultative Assembly shall determine in what circumstances and under what conditions other languages may be used.

CHAPTER IV—COMMITTEE OF MINISTERS

ART. 13. The Committee of Ministers is the organ which acts on behalf of the Council of Europe in accordance with Articles 15 and 16.

ART. 14. Each Member shall be entitled to one representative on the Committee of Ministers and each representative shall be entitled to one vote. Representatives on the Committee shall be the Ministers for Foreign Affairs. When a Minister for Foreign Affairs is unable to be present, or in other circumstances where it may be desirable, an alternate may be nominated to act for him, who shall, whenever possible, be a member of his Government.

ART. 15. (*a*) On the recommendation of the Consultative Assembly or on its own initiative, the Committee of Ministers shall consider the action required to further the aim of the Council of Europe, including the conclusion of conventions or agreements and the adoption by Governments of a common policy with regard to particular matters. Its conclusions shall be communicated to members by the Secretary-General.

(*b*) In appropriate cases, the conclusions of the Committee may take the form of recommendations to the Governments of Members, and the Committee may request the Governments of Members to inform it of the action taken by them with regard to such recommendations.

ART. 16. The Committee of Ministers shall, subject to the provisions of Articles 24, 28, 30, 32, 33, and 35, relating to the powers of the Consultative Assembly, decide with binding effect all matters relating to the internal organization and arrangements of the Council of Europe. For this purpose the Committee of Ministers shall adopt such financial and administrative regulations as may be necessary.

ART. 17. The Committee of Ministers may set up advisory and technical committees or commissions for such specific purposes as it may deem desirable.

ART. 18. The Committee of Ministers shall adopt its rules of procedure which shall determine amongst other things:

(i) the quorum;

(ii) the method of appointment and term of office of its President;

(iii) the procedure for the admission of items to its agenda, including the giving of notice of proposals for resolutions; and

(iv) the notifications required for the nomination of alternates under Article 14.

ART. 19. At each session of the Consultative Assembly the Committee of Ministers shall furnish the Assembly with statements of its activities, accompanied by appropriate documentation.

ART. 20. (*a*) Resolutions of the Committee of Ministers relating to the following important matters—namely:

(i) recommendations under Article 15 (*b*);

(ii) questions under Article 19;

(iii) questions under Article 21 (*a*) (i) and (*b*);

(iv) questions under Article 33;

(v) recommendations for the amendment of Articles 1 (*d*), 7, 15, 20, and 22; and

(vi) any other question which the Committee may, by a resolution passed under (*d*) below, decide should be subject to a unanimous vote on account of its importance

require the unanimous vote of the representatives casting a vote, and of a majority of the representatives entitled to sit on the Committee.

(*b*) Questions arising under the rules of procedure or under the financial and administrative regulations may be decided by a simple majority vote of the representatives entitled to sit on the Committee.

(*c*) Resolutions of the Committee under Articles 4 and 5 require a two-thirds majority of all the representatives entitled to sit on the Committee.

(*d*) All other resolutions of the Committee, including the adoption of the Budget, of rules of procedure and of financial and administrative regulations, recommendations for the amendment of articles of this Statute, other

than those mentioned in paragraph (*a*) (v) above, and deciding in case of doubt which paragraph of this Article applies, require a two-thirds majority of the representatives casting a vote and of a majority of the representatives entitled to sit on the Committee.

ART. 21. (*a*) Unless the Committee decides otherwise, meetings of the Committee of Ministers shall be held— (i) in private, and (ii) at the seat of the Council.

(*b*) The Committee shall determine what information shall be published regarding the conclusions and discussions of a meeting held in private.

(*c*) The Committee shall meet before and during the beginning of every session of the Consultative Assembly and at such other times as it may decide.

CHAPTER V—THE CONSULTATIVE ASSEMBLY

ART. 22. The Consultative Assembly is the deliberative organ of the Council of Europe. It shall debate matters within its competence under this Statute and present its conclusions, in the form of recommendations, to the Committee of Ministers.

ART. 23. (*a*) The Consultative Assembly shall discuss, and may make recommendations upon, any matter within the aim and scope of the Council of Europe as defined in Chapter I, which (i) is referred to it by the Committee of Ministers with a request for its opinion, or (ii) has been approved by the Committee for inclusion in the Agenda of the Assembly on the proposal of the latter.

(*b*) In taking decisions under (*a*), the Committee shall have regard to the work of other European inter-governmental organizations to which some or all of the Members of the Council are parties.

(*c*) The President of the Assembly shall decide, in case of doubt, whether any question raised in the course of the Session is within the Agenda of the Assembly approved under (*a*) above.

ART. 24. The Consultative Assembly may, with due regard to the provisions of Article 38 (*d*), establish committees or commissions to consider and report to it on any matter which falls within its competence under Article 23, to examine and prepare questions on its agenda and to advise on all matters of procedure.

ART. 25. (*a*) The Consultative Assembly shall consist of representatives of each Member appointed in such a manner as the Government of that Member shall decide. Each representative must be a national of the Member whom he represents, but shall not at the same time be a member of the Committee of Ministers.

(*b*) No representative shall be deprived of his position as such during a session of the Assembly without the agreement of the Assembly.

(*c*) Each representative may have a substitute who may, in the absence of the representative, sit, speak, and vote in his place. The provisions of paragraph (*a*) above apply to the appointment of substitutes.

ART. 26. The following States, on becoming Members, shall be entitled to the number of representatives given below:—Belgium 6, Denmark 4, France 18, Irish Republic 4, Italy 18, Luxembourg 3, Netherlands 6, Norway 4, Sweden 6, United Kingdom 18.

ART. 27. The conditions under which the Committee of Ministers collectively may be represented in the debates of the Consultative Assembly, or individual representatives on the Committee may address the Assembly, shall be determined by such rules of procedure on this subject as may be drawn up by the Committee after consultation with the Assembly.

ART. 28. (*a*) The Consultative Assembly shall adopt its rules of procedure and shall elect from its members its President, who shall remain in office until the next ordinary session.

(*b*) The President shall control the proceedings but shall not take part in the debate or vote. The substitute of the representative who is President may sit, speak, and vote in his place.

(*c*) The rules of procedure shall determine *inter alia*:

(i) the quorum;
(ii) the manner of the election and terms of office of the President and other officers;
(iii) the manner in which the agenda shall be drawn up and be communicated to representatives; and
(iv) The time and manner in which the names of representatives and their substitutes shall be notified.

ART. 29. Subject to the provisions of Article 30, all resolutions of the Consultative Assembly, including resolutions:

(i) embodying recommendations to the Committee of Ministers;
(ii) proposing to the Committee matters for discussion in the assembly;
(iii) establishing committees or commissions;
(iv) determining the date of commencement of its sessions;
(v) determining what majority is required for resolutions in cases not covered by (i) to (iv) above or determining cases of doubt as to what majority is required,

shall require a two-thirds majority of the representatives casting a vote.

ART. 30. On matters relating to its internal procedure, which includes the election of officers, the nomination of persons to serve on committees and commissions and the adoption of rules of procedure, resolutions of the Consultative Assembly shall be carried by such majorities as the Assembly may determine in accordance with Article 29 (v).

ART. 31. Debates on proposals to be made to the Committee of Ministers that a matter should be placed on the

Agenda of the Consultative Assembly shall be confined to an indication of the proposed subject-matter and the reasons for and against its inclusion in the Agenda.

ART. 32. The Consultative Assembly shall meet in ordinary session once a year, the date and duration of which shall be determined by the Assembly so as to avoid as far as possible overlapping with parliamentary sessions of Members and with sessions of the General Assembly of the United Nations. In no circumstances shall the duration of an ordinary session exceed one month unless both the Assembly and the Committee of Ministers concur.

ART. 33. Ordinary sessions of the Consultative Assembly shall be held at the seat of the Council unless both the Assembly and the Committee of Ministers concur that it should be held elsewhere.

ART. 34. The Committee of Ministers may convoke an extraordinary session of the Consultative Assembly at such time and place as the Committee, with the concurrence of the President of the Assembly, shall decide.

ART. 35. Unless the Consultative Assembly decides otherwise, its debates shall be conducted in public.

CHAPTER VI—THE SECRETARIAT

ART. 36. (*a*) The Secretariat shall consist of a Secretary-General, a Deputy Secretary-General and such other staff as may be required.

(*b*) The Secretary-General and Deputy Secretary-General shall be appointed by the Consultative Assembly on the recommendation of the Committee of Ministers.

(*c*) The remaining staff of the Secretariat shall be appointed by the Secretary-General, in accordance with the administrative regulations.

(*d*) No member of the Secretariat shall hold any salaried office from any Government or be a member of the Consultative Assembly or of any national legislature or engage in any oc-

cupation incompatible with his duties.

(*e*) Every member of the staff of the Secretariat shall make a solemn declaration affirming that his duty is to the Council of Europe and that he will perform his duties conscientiously, uninfluenced by any national considerations, and that he will not seek or receive instructions in connection with the performance of his duties from any Government or any authority external to the Council and will refrain from any action which might reflect on his position as an international official responsible only to the Council. In the case of the Secretary-General and the Deputy Secretary-General this declaration shall be made before the Committee, and in the case of all other members of the staff, before the Secretary-General.

(*f*) Every member shall respect the exclusively international character of the responsibilities of the Secretary-General and the staff of the Secretariat and not seek to influence them in the discharge of their responsibilities.

ART. 37. (*a*) The Secretariat shall be located at the seat of the Council.

(*b*) The Secretary-General is responsible to the Committee of Ministers for the work of the Secretariat. Amongst other things, he shall, subject to Article 38 (*d*), provide such secretarial and other assistance as the Consultative Assembly may require.

CHAPTER VII—FINANCE

ART. 38. (*a*) Each Member shall bear the expenses of its own representation in the Committee of Ministers and in the Consultative Assembly.

(*b*) The expenses of the Secretariat and all other common expenses shall be shared between all Members in such proportions as shall be determined by the Committee on the basis of the population of Members.

The contributions of an Associate Member shall be determined by the Committee.

(*c*) In accordance with the financial regulations, the Budget of the Council shall be submitted annually by the Secretary-General for adoption by the Committee.

(*d*) The Secretary-General shall refer to the Committee requests from the Assembly which involve expenditure exceeding the amount already allocated in the Budget for the Assembly and its activities.

Art. 39. The Secretary-General shall each year notify the Government of each Member of the amount of its contribution and each Member shall pay to the Secretary-General the amount of its contribution, which shall be deemed to be due on the date of its notification, not later than six months after that date.

CHAPTER VIII—PRIVILEGES AND IMMUNITIES

Art. 40. (*a*) The Council of Europe, representatives of Members and the Secretariat shall enjoy in the territories of its Members such privileges and immunities as are reasonably necessary for the fulfilment of their functions. These immunities shall include immunity for all representatives in the Consultative Assembly from arrest and all legal proceedings in the territories of all Members, in respect of words spoken and votes cast in the debates of the Assembly or its committees or commissions.

(*b*) The Members undertake as soon as possible to enter into an agreement for the purpose of fulfilling the provisions of paragraph (*a*) above. For this purpose the Committee of Ministers shall recommend to the Governments of Members the acceptance of an Agreement defining the privileges and immunities to be granted in the territories of all Members. In addition a special Agreement shall be concluded with the Government of the French Republic defining the privileges and immunities which the Council shall enjoy at its seat.

CHAPTER IX—AMENDMENTS

Art. 41. (*a*) Proposals for the amendment of this Statute may be made in the Committee of Ministers or, in the conditions provided for in Article 23, in the Consultative Assembly.

(*b*) The Committee shall recommend and cause to be embodied in a Protocol those amendments which it considers to be desirable.

(*c*) An amending Protocol shall come into force when it has been signed and ratified on behalf of two-thirds of the Members.

(*d*) Notwithstanding the provisions of the preceding paragraphs of this Article, amendments to Articles 23–35, 38, and 39 which have been approved by the Committee and by the Assembly shall come into force on the date of the certificate of the Secretary-General, transmitted to the Governments of Members, certifying that they have been so approved. This paragraph shall not operate until the conclusion of the second ordinary session of the Assembly.

CHAPTER X—FINAL PROVISIONS

Art. 42. (*a*) This Statute shall be ratified. Ratifications shall be deposited with the Government of the United Kingdom of Great Britain and Northern Ireland.

(*b*) The present Statute shall come into force as soon as seven instruments of ratification have been deposited. The Government of the United Kingdom shall transmit to all signatory Governments a certificate declaring that the Statute has entered into force, and giving the names of the Members of the Council of Europe on that date.

(*c*) Thereafter each other signatory shall become a party to this Statute as from the date of the deposit of its instrument of ratification.

In witness whereof the undersigned, being duly authorized thereto, have signed the present Statute.

Done at London, this fifth day of

May, 1949, in English and French, both texts being equally authentic, in a single copy which shall remain deposited in the archives of the Government of the United Kingdom which shall transmit certified copies to the other signatory Governments.

[*Here follow the Signatures*]

57. THE SECURITY COUNCIL'S RESOLUTION RELATIVE TO THE OUTBREAK OF HOSTILITIES IN KOREA, 25 JUNE 1950 [1]

The assault launched on 24 June 1950 by armed forces of the Soviet-sponsored authorities in northern Korea against the Republic of Korea may be regarded as the greatest crisis to face international organization since the Japanese invaded Manchuria on 18 September 1931. What was at stake was only incidently the disputed territory; the great danger was the collapse of the United Nations system as the League system had collapsed during the 1930's. Action taken under the aegis of the United Nations shows that the lesson from the League's experience had been well learned. The action began with the adoption of this resolution by the Security Council.[2]

The Security Council

Recalling the finding of the General Assembly in its resolution of 21 October 1949 that the Government of the Republic of Korea is a lawfully established government "having effective control and jurisdiction over that part of Korea where the United Nations Temporary Commission on Korea was able to observe and consult and in which the great majority of the people of Korea reside; and that this Government is based on elections which were a valid expression of the free will of the electorate of that part of Korea and which were observed by the Temporary Commission; and that this is the only such Government in Korea";

Mindful of the concern expressed by the General Assembly in its resolutions of 12 December 1948 and 21 October 1949 of the consequences which might follow unless Member States refrained from acts derogatory to the results sought to be achieved by the United Nations in bringing about the complete independence and unity of Korea; and the concern expressed that the situation described by the United Nations Commission on Korea in its report menaces the safety and well being of the Republic of Korea and of the people of Korea and might lead to open military conflict there;

Noting with grave concern the armed attack upon the Republic of Korea by forces from North Korea,

Determines that this action constitutes a breach of the peace,

I. *Calls* for the immediate cessation of hostilities; and

Calls upon the authorities of North Korea to withdraw forthwith their armed forces to the thirty-eighth parallel;

II. *Requests* the United Nations Commission on Korea

(a) To communicate its fully considered recommendations on the situation with the least possible delay;

(b) To observe the withdrawal of the North Korean forces to the thirty-eighth parallel; and

(c) To keep the Security Council informed on the execution of this resolution;

III. *Calls upon* all Members to render every assistance to the United Nations in the execution of this resolution and to refrain from giving assistance to the North Korean authorities.

---

[1] United Nations, Security Council, *Official Records,* Fifth Year, No. 15, p. 18.

[2] The Security Council was able to act because a Soviet boycott of that body since the January preceding had freed it from the veto for the time being. The vote was 9-0, with Yugoslavia abstaining.

58. THE SECURITY COUNCIL'S RESOLUTION RELATIVE TO HOSTILITIES IN KOREA, 27 JUNE 1950 [1]

On 27 June 1950 the Security Council adopted a second resolution, this one more specific than that of 25 June.[2] In the interval between the two resolutions a report from the Commission on Korea, then on the spot, stated that the evidence pointed to a calculated attack on the part of the North Korea regime and recommended more vigorous United Nations action. This 27 June recommendation of assistance to the Republic of Korea from all United Nations members was an invocation of sanctions unprecedented in the history of international organization.[3]

The Security Council,

Having determined that the armed attack upon the Republic of Korea by forces from North Korea constitutes a breach of the peace, having called for an immediate cessation of hostilities, and having called upon the authorities of North Korea to withdraw forthwith their armed forces to the 38th parallel, and having noted from the report of the United Nations Commission for Korea that the authorities in North Korea have neither ceased hostilities nor withdrawn their armed forces to the 38th parallel and that urgent military measures are required to restore international peace and security, and having noted the appeal from the Republic of Korea to the United Nations for immediate and effective steps to secure peace and security,

Recommends that the Members of the United Nations furnish such assistance to the Republic of Korea as may be necessary to repel the armed attack and to restore international peace and security in the area.

59. THE SECURITY COUNCIL'S RESOLUTION AUTHORIZING THE UNITED NATIONS' UNIFIED COMMAND, 7 July 1950 [1] *

With this action of the Security Council, the United Nations established the first "international police force" in the history of international organization. For the first time, also, the United Nations flag was authorized to be used in combat. The United Nations force, made up of contingents from sixteen states, with the United States supplying the greater part, demonstrated the feasibility of collective self-defense under the United Nations.

The Security Council,

Having determined that the armed attack upon the Republic of Korea by forces from North Korea constitutes a a breach of the peace.

Having recommended that the members of the United Nations furnish such assistance to the Republic of Korea as may be necessary to repel armed attack

and to restore international peace and security in the area,

1. *Welcomes,* the prompt and vigorous support which Governments and peoples of the United Nations have given to its resolutions of 25 and 27 June 1950 to assist the Republic of Korea in defending itself against armed attack and thus to restore international peace and security in the area;

2. *Notes* that members of the United Nations have transmitted to the United Nations offers of assistance for the Republic of Korea;

3. *Recommends* that all members providing military forces and other assistance pursuant to the aforesaid Security Council resolutions make such

[1] United Nations, Security Council, *Official Records,* Fifth Year, No. 16, p. 4.

[2] See Doc. 57.

[3] Seven Security Council members, one of whom was China, voted in favor of the resolution, with the Soviet delegate still absent and the other members abstaining.

[1] * United Nations, Security Council, Official Records, Fifth Year, No. 18, p. 8.

forces and other assistance available to a unified command under the United States;

4. *Requests* the United States to designate the commander of such forces;

5. *Authorizes* the unified command at its discretion to use the United Nations flag in the course of operations against North Korean forces concurrently with the flags of the various nations participating;

6. *Requests* the United States to provide the Security Council with reports as appropriate on the course of action taken under the unified command.

60. THE GENERAL ASSEMBLY RESOLUTION, "UNITING FOR PEACE," 3 NOVEMBER 1950 [1]

By the opening of the fifth session of the Assembly in September 1950 the handling of the Korean crisis by the Security Council, expeditious and effective in the absence of the Russians but fruitless after their return in August, had presented with dramatic force the need for the United Nations to find alternative means by which to cope with cases of aggression. The growing role of the Assembly in the settlement of disputes, the presence of the United Nations Commission on Korea in Korea at the time of the invasion and the availability nearby of United States forces for immediate action suggested the directions in which the United Nations should move. They were proposed in the so-called "Acheson Plan" submitted to the Assembly by Secretary of State Dean Acheson on 20 September 1950 and adopted, with some changes, on 3 November.

RESOLUTION A

The General Assembly,

Recognizing that the first two stated Purposes of the United Nations are:

"To maintain international peace and security, and to that end: to take effective collective measures for the prevention and removal of threats to the peace, and for the suppression of acts of aggression or other breaches of the peace, and to bring about by peaceful means, and in conformity with the principles of justice and international law, adjustment or settlement of international disputes or situations which might lead to a breach of the peace;

"To develop friendly relations among nations based on respect for the principle of equal rights and self-determination of peoples, and to take other appropriate measures to strengthen universal peace";

Reaffiming that it remains to the primary duty of all Members of the United Nations, when involved in an international dispute, to seek settlement of such a dispute by peaceful means through the procedures laid down in Chapter VI of the Charter, and recalling the successful achievements of the United Nations in this regard on a number of previous occasions,

Finding that international tension exists on a dangerous scale.

Recalling its resolution 290 (IV) entitled "Essentials of peace," which states that disregard of the Principles of the Charter of the United Nations is primarily responsible for the continuance of international tension, and desiring to contribute further to the objectives of that resolution,

Reaffirming the importance of the exercise by the Security Council of its primary responsibility for the maintenance of international peace and security, and the duty of the permanent members to seek unanimity and to exercise restraint in the use of the veto,

Reaffirming that the initiative in negotiating the agreements for armed forces provided for in Article 43 of the Charter belongs to the Security Council, and desiring to ensure that, pending the conclusion of such agreements, the United Nations has at its disposal means for maintaining international peace and security,

<hr>

[1] United Nations, General Assembly, *Offi-* *cial Records* (5th sess.), supp., No. 20, p. 10.

Conscious that failure of the Security Council to discharge its responsibilities on behalf of all the Member States, particularly those responsibilities referred to in the two preceding paragraphs, does not relieve Member States of their obligations or the United Nations of its responsibility under the Charter to maintain international peace and security,

Recognizing in particular that such failure does not deprive the General Assembly of its rights or relieve it of its responsibilities under the Charter in regard to the maintenance of international peace and security,

Recognizing that discharge by the General Assembly of its responsibilities in these respects calls for possibilities of observation which would ascertain the facts and expose aggressors; for the existence of armed forces which could be used collectively; and for the possibility of timely recommendation by the General Assembly to Members of the United Nations for collective action which, to be effective, should be prompt,

A.

1. *Resolves* that if the Security Council, because of lack of unanimity of the permanent members, fails to exercise its primary responsibility for the maintenance of international peace and security in any case where there appears to be a threat to the peace, breach of the peace, or act of aggression, the General Assembly shall consider the matter immediately with a view to making appropriate recommendations to Members for collective measures, including in the case of a breach of the peace or act of aggression the use of armed force when necessary, to maintain or restore international peace and security. If not in session at the time, the General Assembly may meet in emergency special session within twenty-four hours of the request therefor. Such emergency special session shall be called if requested by the Security Council on the vote of any seven members, or by a majority of the Members of the United Nations,

2. *Adopts* for this purpose the amendments to its rules of procedure set forth in the annex to the present resolution;

B.

3. *Establishes* a Peace Observation Commission for which the calendar years 1951 and 1952, shall be composed of fourteen Members, namely: China, Colombia, Czechoslovakia, France, India, Iraq, Israel, New Zealand, Pakistan, Sweden, the Union of Soviet Socialist Republics, the United Kingdom of Great Britain and Northern Ireland, the United States of America and Uruguay, and which could observe and report on the situation in any area where there exists international tension the continuance of which is likely to endanger the maintenance of international peace and security. Upon the invitation or with the consent of the State into whose territory the Commission would go, the General Assembly, or the Interim Committee when the Assembly is not in session, may utilize the Commission if the Security Council is not exercising the functions assigned to it by the Charter with respect to the matter in question. Decisions to utilize the Commission shall be made on the affirmative vote of two-thirds of the members present and voting. The Security Council may also utilize the Commission in accordance with its authority under the Charter;

4. *The Commission shall have* authority in its discretion to appoint sub-commisisons and to utilize the services of observers to assist it in the performance of its functions;

5. *Recommends* to all governments and authorities that they co-operate with the Commission and assist it in the performance of its functions;

6. *Requests* the Secretary-General to provide the necessary staff and facilities, utilizing, where directed by the Commission, the United Nations Panel

of Field Observers envisaged in General Assembly resolution 297 B (IV);

C.

7. *Invites* each Member of the United Nations to survey its resources in order to determine the nature and scope of the assistance it may be in a position to render in support of any recommendations of the Security Council or of the General Assembly for the restoration of international peace and security;

8. *Recommends* to the States Members of the United Nations that each Member maintain within its national armed forces elements so trained, organized and equipped that they could promptly be made available, in accordance with its constitutional processes, for service as a United Nations unit or units, upon recommendation by the Security Council or General Assembly, without prejudice to the use of such elements in exercise of the right of individual or collective self-defence recognized in Article 51 of the Charter;

9. *Invites* the Members of the United Nations to inform the Collective Measures Committee provided for in paragraph 11 as soon as possible of the measures taken in implementation of the preceding paragraph;

10. *Requests* the Secretary-General to appoint, with the approval of the Committee provided for in paragraph 11, a panel of military experts who could be made available, on request, to Member States wishing to obtain technical advice regarding the organization, training, and equipment for prompt service as United Nations units of the elements referred to in paragraph 8;

D.

11. *Establishes* a Collective Measures Committee consisting of fourteen Members, namely: Australia, Belgium, Brazil, Burma, Canada, Egypt, France, Mexico, Philippines, Turkey, the United Kingdom of Great Britain and Northern Ireland, the United States of America, Venezuela and Yugoslavia, and directs the Committee, in consultation with the Secretary-General and with such Member States as the Committee finds appropriate, to study and make a report to the Security Council and the General Assembly, not later than 1 September 1951, on methods, including those in Section C of the present resolution, which might be used to maintain and strengthen international peace and security in accordance with the Purposes and Principles of the Charter, taking account of collective self-defence and regional arrangements (Articles 51 and 52 of the Charter);

12. *Recommends* to all Member States that they co-operate with the Committee and assist it in the performance of its functions;

13. *Requests* the Secretary-General to furnish the staff and facilities necessary for the effective accomplishment of the purposes set forth in sections C and D of the present resolution;

E.

14. THE GENERAL ASSEMBLY, in adopting the proposals set forth above, is fully conscious that enduring peace will not be secured solely by collective security arrangements against breaches of international peace and acts of aggression, but that a genuine and lasting peace depends also upon the observance of all the Principles and Purposes established in the Charter of the United Nations, upon the implementation of the resolutions of the Security Council, the General Assembly and other principal organs of the United Nations intended to achieve the maintenance of international peace and security, and especially upon respect for and observance of human rights and fundamental freedoms for all and on the establishment and maintenance of conditions of economic and social well-being in all countries; and accordingly

15. *Urges* Member States to respect

fully, and to intensify, joint action, in co-operation with the United Nations, to develop and stimulate universal respect for and observance of human rights and fundamental freedoms, and to intensify individual and collective efforts to achieve conditions of economic stability and social progress, particularly through the development of underdeveloped countries and areas.

ANNEX

The rules of procedure of the General Assembly are amended in the following respects:

1. The present text of rule 8 shall become paragraph (a) of that rule, and a new paragraph (b) shall be added to read as follows:

"Emergency special sessions pursuant to resolution—(V) shall be convened within twenty-four hours of the receipt by the Secretary-General of a request for such a session from the Security Council, on the vote of any seven members thereof, or of a request from a majority of the Members of the United Nations expressed by vote in the Interim Committee or otherwise, or of the concurrence of a majority of Members as provided in rule 9."

2. The present text of rule 9 shall become paragraph (a) of that rule and a new paragraph (b) shall be added to read as follows:

"This rule shall apply also to a request by any Member for an emergency special session pursuant to resolution—(V). In such a case the Secretary-General shall communicate with other Members by the most expeditious means of communication available."

3. Rule 10 is amended by adding at the end thereof the following:

"In the case of an emergency special session convened pursuant to rule 8 (b), the Secretary-General shall notify the Members of the United Nations at least twelve hours in advance of the opening of the session."

4. Rule 16 is amended by adding at the end thereof the following:

"The provisional agenda of an emergency special session shall be communicated to the Members of the United Nations simultaneously with the communication summoning the session."

5. Rule 19 is amended by adding at the end thereof the following:

"During an emergency special session additional items concerning the matters dealt with in resolution—(V) may be added to the agenda by a two-thirds majority of the Members present and voting."

6. There is added a new rule to precede rule 65 to read as follows:

"Notwithstanding the provisions of any other rule and unless the General Assembly decides otherwise, the Assembly in case of an emergency special session, shall convene in plenary session only and proceed directly to consider the item proposed for consideration in the request for the holding of the session, without previous reference to the General Committee or to any other Committee; the President and Vice-Presidents for such emergency special sessions shall be, respectively, the Chairman of those delegations from which were elected the President and Vice-Presidents of the previous session."

RESOLUTION B

For the purpose of maintaining international peace and security, in accordance with the Charter of the United Nations, and, in particular, with Chapters V, VI and VII of the Charter,

The General Assembly

Recommends to the Security Council:

That it should take the necessary steps to ensure that the action provided for under the Charter is taken with respect to threats to the peace, breaches of the peace or acts of aggression and with respect to the peaceful settlement of disputes or situations likely to endanger the maintenance of international peace and security;

That it should devise measures for the earliest application of Articles 43, 45, 46 and 47 of the Charter of the United Nations regarding the placing of armed forces at the disposal of the Security Council by the States Members of the United Nations and the effective functioning of the Military Staff Committee.

The above dispositions should in no manner prevent the General Assembly from fulfilling its functions under resolution—(V).

RESOLUTION C

The General Assembly,

Recognizing that the primary function of the United Nations Organization is to maintain and promote peace, security and justice among all nations,

Recognizing the responsibility of all Member States to promote the cause of international peace in accordance with their obligations as provided in the Charter,

Recognizing that the Charter charges the Security Council with the primary responsibility for maintaining international peace and security,

Reaffirming the importance of unanimity among the permanent members of the Security Council on all problems which are likely to threaten world peace,

Recalling General Assembly resolution 190 (III) entitled "Appeal to the Great Powers to renew their efforts to compose their differences and establish a lasting peace,"

Recommends to the permanent members of the Security Council that:

(a) They meet and discuss, collectively or otherwise, and, if necessary, with other States concerned, all problems which are likely to threaten international peace and hamper the activities of the United Nations, with a view to their resolving fundamental differences and reaching agreement in accordance with the spirit and letter of the Charter;

(b) They advise the General Assembly and, when it is not in session, the Members of the United Nations, as soon as appropriate, of the results of their consultations.

61. ADDRESS OF HAILE SELASSIE, EMPEROR OF ETHIOPIA, 12 APRIL 1951 [1]

The Korean action of the United Nations forces was both cause and effect of a newly articulated spirit of mutual aid among nations which found expression in countless public statements of rulers and statesmen. Among the most eloquent was this address of the Emperor of Ethiopia bidding Godspeed to the Ethiopian contingent bound for the Korean front.

Soldiers.

You are to-day on the point of leaving Ethiopia on a voyage half way round the world in defense of liberty and of the principles to which all members of the United Nations stand committed.

We have personally come here in the presence of the highest officials of the Nation which is honouring you to-day and of representatives of other Nations participating in this momentous undertaking to bid you a fond farewell and God-Speed on your mission and to hand to you your Regimental Colours. These flags you will carry in valour throughout the campaign. You will, We are sure, bring them back to Your Emperor and Commander-in-Chief, to whom you have sworn allegiance, as cherished battle standards, glorified by your exploits and heroism.

You have been called upon to represent amongst the armed forces of

[1] *Address Delivered by His Imperial Majesty Haile Selassie I on April 12, 1951, on the Occasion of the Departure of the Ethi-* *opian Contingent for the United Nations Front in Korea* (Addis Ababa, Berhanena Selam Printing Press), pp. 9-11.

many friendly nations engaged in the same high endeavour, the heritage of a people that, for untold centuries, has fiercely fought to defend its freedom and independence. Everyone among you has known sacrifices and losses amongst his family, so total and bitter has been the struggle in recent years. In the dark hours when We and Our People were called upon to fight, We did not fail in Our fierce resolve, and today, thanks to that determination, Ethiopia has again resumed her rightful place amongst the United Nations. We have all earned the right to be proud of that heritage of struggle.

We must recognize, then, that every nation that fights, as we have done, for the defense and maintenance of its independence has the right to expect the honour and indeed the assistance of all freedom-loving peoples. You are departing on a long crusade in defense of that very principle for which we have so long fought—freedom, and respect for the freedom of others. With such traditions and after such sacrifices, Ethiopia would be the very first nation to recognize the imperative urgency of that call of duty towards a sister nation.

It is in yet a larger sense, Soldiers, that you are to-day leaving the Homeland to fight on distant shores. You are fighting not only for freedom as We know it in Ethiopia, and the right of each people to its freedom. You are also representing and defending in far corners of the Earth, the most sacred principle of modern international polity—the principle of collective security, with which the name of Ethiopia is imperishably associated.

It is but natural that small nations, who must so vigilantly defend their independence, should regard collective security as the cornerstone of their very existence. Their support of that principle should be instant, unhesitating and absolute. No small state, no democratic nation, no people imbued with charity towards its fellowmen, could do otherwise.

Of all the nations of the world, the name of Ethiopia has been most closely associated with that principle. Our undaunted defense of collective security at the League of Nations, Our own appeal to that august body, Our fierce and unaided struggles throughout the darkest hours preceding the last World War, the courage of our patriots, the unending sacrifices of Our families, have given to Ethiopia an imperishable place in the history of that principle in modern times.

That is why, as Sovereign Head of Ethiopia and as Commander-in-Chief of the Ethiopian Armed Forces, We did not hesitate immediately to respond to the appeal for collective assistance launched by the United Nations following the aggression in Korea.

From the first, it was evident that much time, effort and expense would be required to provide for your participation in the combined front of the United Nations forces in Korea. Foreseeing those inevitable difficulties, Ethiopia did not hesitate to provide instant assistance even before Our military forces could be brought into the battle. That is why, not only did We promise military assistance, but also immediately transmitted funds to the United Nations to help in the collective effort.

Thus it is that you are now departing to take your honoured place beside the valiant soldiers of other United Nations, Britain, France, the Netherlands, Belgium, Greece, Turkey, and others.

At this proud moment of participation in the first collective and world-wide effort for the defense of the principle of collective security, Ethiopia and Ourselves can look back with pride on the progress achieved, progress to which Ethiopia has so heavily contributed in recent years. Precisely fifteen years ago this very month, We, Your Emperor, and Commander-in-Chief, addressed from the battlefield a pressing appeal to the League of Nations for the respect and application of the principle of collective security. It was not a question, then, as now, even to hope for the application of measures of military sanction. So new then was that principle that Ethiopia could only hope for the most basic economic sanctions to restrict aggression, and urgent measures to bring to an end the use of asphyxiating gas. However, it was also in that same month, fifteen years ago to-day, that the Council of the League of Nations finally and formally declared its inability to meet these essential requirements of collective security. Undaunted by this failure, Ethiopia under Our leadership and with the courage of its patriots continued the struggle until that glorious day when, at the head of Our Troops and with the aid of British Empire heroes, We re-entered Our Capital.

To-day, it is no longer a question of asking for simple economic sanctions. Korea asks of the United Nations and receives from it collective security in the form of military assistance.

In joining to-day in these measures of collective security, We are being faithful to Ourselves and to the obligation which We conceive to be the most high and solemn duty not alone of the present hour, but of the present century. Collective security knows no bounds or distances. In participating in the measures of collective security in the Far East, We are only fulfilling our obligations towards the United Nations. Just as previously, by the sending of financial assistance, We had manifested Our sympathy towards the valiant people of China so sorely tried by natural disasters, so to-day, We deplore the new hardships which that people has been called upon to suffer as a result of the events in the Far East. Let us hope that Peace and Tranquility may soon be re-established there.

You have been fortunate, soldiers, in that each one of you has been selected thus to testify before the world to the flame of liberty and of devotion to the cause of international justice which has fired the breasts of Our patriots.

You are following the footsteps of the long line of your forefathers in proclaiming before the world the right of each nation, determined by its own efforts to save its independence and freedom, to receive as collective security the assistance of all peace-loving nations. Ethiopia could do no less to-day and still remain faithful to her traditions and to the sacrifices which We have all undergone.

Soldiers: The spirits of your ancestors, heroes of the thousand-year long struggle for the defense of Our freedom will follow you, and will strengthen your hands and hearts in the heat of battle.

Remember that you are about to pay a debt of honour for your Homeland which was liberated thanks not only to the blood of her patriots, but also to that of faithful allies, likewise members of the United Nations. Remember also that, in paying this debt, you are laying the basis for a universal system of collective security in behalf of your own Homeland as well as of all nations of the world, be they great or small, powerful or weak.

May God protect you, give you courage to acquit yourselves as heroes, and bring you back safely to your beloved Homeland.

Chapter 17

Functions: Economic and Social

62. THE GENERAL ASSEMBLY RESOLUTION ON INFORMATION UNDER ARTICLE 73E, 9 FEBRUARY 1946 [1]

In Chapter XI of the Charter, the principles underlying the trusteeship system are generalized to apply to all dependent areas. But beyond a requirement that "for information purposes" the colonial powers submit to the Secretary General reports on their administration, no machinery was set up to give effect to these principles. With the establishment of a special committee to examine the reports and make recommendations on the basis of their contents, the Assembly inaugurated practices which are slowly extending the scope of the United Nations authority with respect to dependent areas.

I. NON-SELF-GOVERNING PEOPLES

The United Nations, meeting in its first General Assembly, is keenly aware of the problems and political aspirations of the peoples who have not yet attained a full measure of self-government and who are not directly represented here.

Chapters XI, XII and XIII of the Charter recognize the problems of the non-self-governing peoples as of vital concern to the peace and general welfare of the world community.

By Chapter XI, all the Members of the United Nations which have or assume responsibilities for the administration of territories whose peoples have not yet attained a full measure of self-government recognize the principle that the interests of the inhabitants of these territories are paramount. They accept, as a sacred trust, the obligation to promote to the utmost the well-being of the inhabitants of these territories. To that end they accept certain specific obligations, including the obligation to develop self-government and to assist the inhabitants in the progressive development of their free political institutions.

By Chapters XII and XIII, the Charter provides for the establishment of an international trusteeship system, the basic objectives of which are, among others, to promote the political, economic, social and educational advancement of the inhabitants of trust territories, and to promote their progressive development towards self-government or independence.

The General Assembly regrets that the Trusteeship Council cannot be brought into being at this first part of the first session, not because of any lack of desire to do so but because, before the Trusteeship Council can be established, trusteeship agreements must be concluded.

The General Assembly holds the view that any delay in putting into effect the system of international trusteeship prevents the implementation of the principles of the trusteeship system, as declared in the Charter, and deprives the populations of such terri-

[1] United Nations, General Assembly, 1st sess., 1st part, *Official Records of the Plenary* *Meetings*, p. 376.

tories as may be brought under the trusteeship system of the opportunity of enjoying the advantages arising from the implementation of these principles.

With a view to expediting the conclusion of these agreements and the establishment of the Trusteeship Council, the Preparatory Commission recommended that the General Assembly should call on those Members of the United Nations which are now administering territories held under mandate to undertake practical steps, in concert with the other States directly concerned, for the implementation of Article 79 of the Charter.

Without waiting for the recommendation of the Preparatory Commission to be considered by the General Assembly, the Members of the United Nations administering territories held under mandate took the initiative in making declarations in regard to these territories.

Therefore
with respect to Chapter XI of the Charter, the General Assembly:

1. *Draws attention to* the fact that the obligations accepted under Chapter XI of the Charter by all Members of the United Nations are in no way contingent upon the conclusion of trusteeship agreements or upon the bringing into being of the Trusteeship Council and are, therefore, already in full force.

2. *Requests* the Secretary-General to include in his annual report on the work of the Organization, as provided for in Article 98 of the Charter, a statement summarizing such information as may have been transmitted to him by Members of the United Nations under Article 73 (*e*) of the Charter relating to economic, social and educational conditions in the territories for which they are responsible other than those to which Chapters XII and XIII apply.

with respect to Chapters XII and XIII of the Charter, the General Assembly:

3. *Welcomes* the declarations, made by certain States administering territories now held under mandate, of an intention to negotiate trusteeship agreements in respect of some of those territories and, in respect of Transjordan, to establish its independence.

4. *Invites* the States administering territories now held under mandate to undertake practical steps, in concert with the other States directly concerned, for the implementation of Article 79 of the Charter (which provides for the conclusion of agreements on the terms of trusteeship for each territory to be placed under the trusteeship system), in order to submit these agreements for approval, preferably not later than during the second part of the first session of the General Assembly.

In conclusion, the General Assembly:

5. *Expects* that the realization of the objectives of Chapters XI, XII and XIII will make possible the attainment of the political, economic, social and educational aspirations of non-self-governing peoples.

2. PROVISIONAL RULES OF PROCEDURE OF THE TRUSTEESHIP COUNCIL

The Provisional Rules of Procedure for the Trusteeship Council prepared by the Preparatory Commission (section 2 of Chapter IV of the Preparatory Commission's Report) were presented to the Fourth Committee of the Commission for consideration. On the suggestion of the Chairman, the Committee unanimously approved these Rules of Procedure at its tenth meeting on February 4.

Upon the suggestion of the Fourth Committee the General Assembly at its 27th plenary meeting on February 9, 1946, adopted the following resolution:

The General Assembly requests the Secretary-General to transmit the "Provisional rules of procedure of the Trusteeship Council" (section 2 of chapter IV of the Preparatory Commission's Report) to the Trusteeship Council as soon as it is constituted.

63. TRUSTEESHIP AGREEMENT FOR THE TERRITORY OF TANGANYIKA, 13 DECEMBER 1946 [1]

The Trusteeship system established under Chapters XII and XIII of the United Nations Charter [2] is the League of Nations Mandates system under a new name, but with modifications based upon the League experience. With few exceptions, the changes incorporated in the trusteeship system extend and strengthen the obligations assumed by the Mandatories, now called Administering Authorities, vis-à-vis the local inhabitants, on the one hand, and the organized international community on the other. Thus, the implications found in the mandates system are here developed and made explicit. A comparison of the League mandate [3] with the United Nations trust agreement for Tanganyika shows the advances made in the Charter for governing the individual territories.

Whereas the Territory known as Tanganyika has been administered in accordance with Article 22 of the Covenant of the League of Nations under a mandate conferred on His Britannic Majesty; and

Whereas Article 75 of the United Nations Charter, signed at San Francisco on 26 June 1945, provides for the establishment of an International Trusteeship System for the administration and supervision by such territories as may be placed thereunder by subsequent individual agreements; and

Whereas under Article 77 of the said Charter the International Trusteeship System may be applied to territories now held under mandate; and

Whereas His Majesty has indicated his desire to place Tanganyika under the said International Trusteeship System; and

Whereas, in accordance with Articles 75 and 77 of said Charter, the placing of a territory under the International Trusteeship System is to be effected by means of a trusteeship agreement,

Now, therefore, the General Assembly of the United Nations hereby resolves to approve the following terms of Trusteeship for Tanganyika:

ART. 1. The Territory to which this Agreement applies comprises that part of East Africa lying within the boundaries defined by article 1 of the British mandate for East Africa, and by the Anglo-Belgian Treaty of 22 November 1934, regarding the boundary between Tanganyika and Ruanda-Urundi.

ART. 2. His Majesty is hereby designated as Administering Authority for Tanganyika, the responsibility for the administration of which will be undertaken by His Majesty's Government in the United Kingdom of Great Britain and Northern Ireland.

ART. 3. The Administering Authority undertakes to administer Tanganyika in such a manner as to achieve the basic objectives of the International Trusteeship system laid down in Article 76 of the United Nations Charter. The Administering Authority further undertakes to collaborate fully with the General Assembly of the United Nations and the Trusteeship Council in the discharge of all their functions as defined in Article 87 of the United Nations Charter, and to facilitate any periodic visits to Tanganyika which they may deem necessary, at times to be agreed upon with the Administering Authority.

ART. 4. The Administering Authority shall be responsible (*a*) for the peace, order, good government and defence of Tanganyika, and (*b*) for ensuring that it shall play its part in the maintenance of international peace and security.

ART. 5. For the above-mentioned purposes and for all purposes of this Agreement, as may be necessary, the Administering Authority:

(*a*) Shall have full powers of legislation, administration, and jurisdiction in Tanganyika, subject to the provisions of the United Nations Charter and of this Agreement;

(b) Shall be entitled to constitute Tanganyika into a customs, fiscal or administrative union or federation with adjacent territories under his sovereignty or control, and to establish common services between such territories and Tanganyika where such measures are not inconsistent with the basic objectives of the International Trusteeship System and with the terms of this Agreement;

(c) And shall be entitled to establish naval, military and air bases, to erect fortifications, to station and employ his own forces in Tanganyika and to take all such other measures as are in his opinion necessary for the defence of Tanganyika and for ensuring that the territory plays its part in the maintenance of international peace and security. To this end the Administering Authority may make use of volunteer forces, facilities and assistance from Tanganyika in carrying out the obligations towards the Security Council undertaken in this regard by the Administering Authority, as well as for local defence and the maintenance of law and order within Tanganyika.

ART. 6. The Administering Authority shall promote the development of free political institutions suited to Tanganyika. To this end, the Administering Authority shall assure to the inhabitants of Tanganyika a progressively increasing share in the administrative and other services of the Territory; shall develop the participation of the inhabitants of Tanganyika in advisory and legislative bodies and in the government of the Territory, both central and local, as may be appropriate to the particular circumstances of the Territory and its peoples; and shall take all other appropriate measures with a view to the political advancement of the inhabitants of Tanganyika in accordance with Article 76 b of the United Nations Charter.

ART. 7. The Administering Authority undertakes to apply, in Tanganyika,

the provisions of any international conventions and recommendations already existing or hereafter drawn up by the United Nations or by the specialized agencies referred to in Article 57 of the Charter, which may be appropriate to the particular circumstances of the Territory and which would conduce to the achievement of the basic objectives of the International Trusteeship System.

ART. 8. In framing laws relating to the holding or transfer of land and natural resources, the Administering Authority shall take into consideration native laws and customs, and shall respect the rights and safeguard the interests, both present and future, of the native population. No native land or natural resources may be transferred, except between natives, save with the previous consent of the competent public authority. No real rights over native land or natural resources in favour of nonnatives may be created except with the same consent.

ART. 9. Subject to the provisions of article 10 of this Agreement, the Administering Authority shall take all necessary steps to ensure equal treatment in social, economic, industrial and commercial matters for all Members of the United Nations and their nationals and to this end:

(a) Shall ensure the same rights to all nationals of Members of the United Nations as to his own nationals in respect of entry into and residence in Tanganyika, freedom of transit and navigation, including freedom of transit and navigation by air, acquisition of property both movable and immovable, the protection of person and property, and the exercise of professions and trades;

(b) Shall not discriminate on grounds of nationality against nationals of any Member of the United Nations in matters relating to the grant of concessions for the development of the natural resources of Tanganyika and shall not grant concessions having the character of a general monopoly;

(c) Shall ensure equal treatment in

the administration of justice to the nationals of all Members of the United Nations.

The rights conferred by this article on nationals of Members of the United Nations apply equally to companies and associations controlled by such nationals and organized in accordance with the law of any Member of the United Nations.

ART. 10. Measures taken to give effect to article 9 of this Agreement shall be subject always to the overriding duty of the Administering Authority, in accordance with Article 76 of the United Nations Charter, to promote the political, economic, social and educational advancement of the inhabitants of Tanganyika, to carry out the other basic objectives of the International Trusteeship System, and to maintain peace, order and good government. The Administering Authority shall in particular be free:

(a) To organize essential public services and works on such terms and conditions as he thinks just;

(b) To create monopolies of a purely fiscal character in order to provide Tanganyika with the fiscal resources which seem best suited to local requirements, or otherwise to serve the interests of the inhabitants of Tanganyika;

(c) Where the interests of the economic advancement of the inhabitants of Tanganyika may require it, to establish, or permit to be established, for specific purposes, other monopolies or undertakings having in them an element of monopoly, under conditions of proper public control; provided that, in the selection of agencies to carry out the purposes of this paragraph, other than agencies controlled by the Government or those in which the Government participates, the Administering Authority shall not discriminate on grounds of nationality against Members of the United Nations or their nationals.

ART. 11. Nothing in this Agreement shall entitle any Member of the United Nations to claim for itself or for its nationals, companies and associations the benefits of article 9 of this Agreement in any respect in which it does not give to the inhabitants, companies and associations of Tanganyika equality of treatment with the nationals, companies and associations of the State which it treats most favourably.

ART. 12. The Administering Authority shall, as may be appropriate to the circumstances of Tanganyika, continue and extend a general system of elementary education designed to abolish illiteracy and to facilitate the vocational and cultural advancement of the population, child and adult, and shall similarly provide such facilities as may prove desirable and practicable, in the interests of the inhabitants, for qualified students to receive secondary and higher education, including professional training.

ART. 13. The Administering Authority shall ensure, in Tanganyika, complete freedom of conscience and, so far as is consistent with the requirements of public order and morality, freedom of religious teaching and the free exercise of all forms of worship. Subject to the provisions of article 8 of this Agreement and the local law, missionaries who are nationals of Members of the United Nations shall be free to enter Tanganyika and to travel and reside therein, to acquire and possess property, to erect religious buildings and to open schools and hospitals in the Territory. The provisions of this article shall not, however, affect the right and duty of the Administering Authority to exercise such controls as he may consider necessary for the maintenance of peace, order and good government and for the educational advancement of the inhabitants of Tanganyika, and to take all measures required for such control.

ART. 14. Subject only to the requirements of public order, the Administering Authority shall guarantee to the inhabitants of Tanganyika freedom of speech, of the press, of assembly and of petition.

ART. 15. The Administering Authority may arrange for the co-operation of Tanganyika in any regional advisory commission, regional technical organization or other voluntary association of States, any specialized international bodies, public or private, or other forms of international activity not inconsistent with the United Nations Charter.

ART. 16. The Administering Authority shall make, to the General Assembly of the United Nations, an annual report on the basis of a questionnaire drawn up by the Trusteeship Council in accordance with Article 88 of the United Nations Charter. Such reports shall include information concerning the measures taken to give effect to suggestions and recommendations of the General Assembly and the Trusteeship Council. The Administering Authority shall designate an accredited representative to be present at the sessions of the Trusteeship Council at which the reports of the Administering Authority with regard to Tanganyika are considered.

ART. 17. Nothing in this Agreement shall affect the right of the Administering Authority to propose, at any future date the amendment of this Agreement for the purpose of designating the whole or part of Tanganyika as a strategic area or for any other purpose not inconsistent with the basic objectives of the International Trusteeship System.

ART. 18. The terms of this Agreement shall not be altered or amended except as provided in Article 79 and Article 83 or 85, as the case may be, of the United Nations Charter.

ART. 19. If any dispute whatever should arise between the Administering Authority and another Member of the United Nations relating to the interpretation or application of the provisions of this Agreement, such dispute, if it cannot be settled by negotiation or other means, shall be submitted to the International Court of Justice, provided for in Chapter XIV of the United Nations Charter.

64. THE UNIVERSAL DECLARATION OF HUMAN RIGHTS, 10 DECEMBER 1948 [1]

The Charter of the United Nations commits the states members to promoting "universal respect for, and observance of, human rights and fundamental freedoms for all. . . ." (Article 55). The Declaration of Human Rights, drafted by the Commission on Human Rights under the Economic and Social Council and adopted by the Assembly 10 December 1948 at its third session,[2] may be regarded as one of the significant state papers to be drafted thus far under the auspices of the United Nations.

PREAMBLE

Whereas recognition of the inherent dignity and of the equal and inalienable rights of all members of the human family is the foundation of freedom, justice and peace in the world,

Whereas disregard and contempt for human rights have resulted in barbar-

ous acts which have outraged the conscience of mankind, and the advent of a world in which human beings shall enjoy freedom of speech and belief and freedom from fear and want has been proclaimed as the highest aspiration of the common people,

Whereas it is essential, if man is not to be compelled to have recourse, as a last resort, to rebellion against tyranny and oppression, that human rights should be protected by the rule of law,

Whereas it is essential to promote the development of friendly relations between nations,

Whereas the peoples of the United Nations have in the Charter reaffirmed their faith in fundamental human rights, in the dignity and worth of the

[1] United Nations General Assembly, *Official Records,* 3rd sess. (I), *Resolutions,* p. 71.

[2] The vote was unanimous, although there were 9 abstentions.

human person and in the equal rights of men and women and have determined to promote social progress and better standards of life in larger freedom,

Whereas Member States have pledged themselves to achieve, in co-operation with the United Nations, the promotion of universal respect for and observance of human rights and fundamental freedoms,

Whereas a common understanding of these rights and freedoms is of the greatest importance for the full realization of this pledge,

Now therefore

The General Assembly,

Proclaims this Universal Declaration of Human Rights as a common standard of achievement for all peoples and all nations, to the end that every individual and every organ of society, keeping this Declaration constantly in mind, shall strive by teaching and education to promote respect for these rights and freedoms and by progressive measures, national and international, to secure their universal and effective recognition and observance, both among the peoples of Member States themselves and among the peoples of territories under their jurisdiction.

ART. 1. All human beings are born free and equal in dignity and rights. They are endowed with reason and conscience and should act towards one another in a spirit of brotherhood.

ART. 2. Everyone is entitled to all the rights and freedoms set forth in this Declaration, without distinction of any kind, such as race, colour, sex, language, religion, political or other opinion, national or social origin, property, birth or other status.

Furthermore, no distinction shall be made on the basis of the political, jurisdictional or international status of the country or territory to which a person belongs, whether it be independent, trust, non-self-governing or under any other limitation of sovereignty.

ART. 3. Everyone has the right to life, liberty and the security of person.

ART. 4. No one shall be held in slavery or servitude; slavery and the slave trade shall be prohibited in all their forms.

ART. 5. No one shall be subjected to torture or to cruel, inhuman or degrading treatment or punishment.

ART. 6. Everyone has the right to recognition everywhere as a person before the law.

ART. 7. All are equal before the law and are entitled without any discrimination to equal protection of the law. All are entitled to equal protection against any discrimination in violation of this Declaration and against any incitement to such discrimination.

ART. 8. Everyone has the right to an effective remedy by the competent national tribunals for acts violating the fundamental rights granted him by the constitution or by law.

ART. 9. No one shall be subjected to arbitrary arrest, detention or exile.

ART. 10. Everyone is entitled in full equality to a fair and public hearing by an independent and impartial tribunal, in the determination of his rights and obligations and of any criminal charge against him.

ART. 11. *1.* Everyone charged with a penal offence has the right to be presumed innocent until proved guilty according to law in a public trial at which he has had all the guarantees necessary for his defence.

2. No one shall be held guilty of any penal offence on account of any act or omission which did not constitute a penal offence, under national or international law, at the time when it was committed. Nor shall a heavier penalty be imposed than the one that was applicable at the time the penal offence was committed.

ART. 12. No one shall be subjected to arbitrary interference with his privacy, family, home or correspondence, nor to attacks upon his honour and reputation. Everyone has the right to the protection of the law against such interference or attacks.

ART. 13. *1.* Everyone has the right to

freedom of movement and residence within the borders of each state.

2. Everyone has the right to leave any country, including his own, and to return to his country.

ART. 14. *1*. Everyone has the right to seek and to enjoy in other countries asylum from persecution.

2. This right may not be invoked in the case of prosecutions genuinely arising from non-political crimes or from acts contrary to the purposes and principles of the United Nations.

ART. 15. *1*. Everyone has the right to a nationality.

2. No one shall be arbitrarily deprived of his nationality nor denied the right to change his nationality.

ART. 16. *1*. Men and women of full age, without any limitation due to race, nationality or religion, have the right to marry and to found a family. They are entitled to equal rights as to marriage, during marriage and at its dissolution.

2. Marriage shall be entered into only with the free and full consent of the intending spouses.

3. The family is the natural and fundamental group unit of society and is entitled to protection by society and the State.

ART. 17. *1*. Everyone has the right to own property alone as well as in association with others.

2. No one shall be arbitrarily deprived of his property.

ART. 18. Everyone has the right to freedom of thought, conscience and religion; this right includes freedom to change his religion or belief, and freedom, either alone or in community with others and in public or private, to manifest his religion or belief in teaching, practice, worship and observance.

ART. 19. Everyone has the right to freedom of opinion and expression; this right includes freedom to hold opinions without interference and to seek, receive and impart information and ideas through any media and regardless of frontiers.

ART. 20. *1*. Everyone has the right to freedom of peaceful assembly and association.

2. No one may be compelled to belong to an association.

ART. 21. *1*. Everyone has the right to take part in the Government of his country, directly or through freely chosen representatives.

2. Everyone has the right of equal access to public service in his country.

3. The will of the people shall be the basis of the authority of government; this will shall be expressed in periodic and genuine elections which shall be by universal and equal suffrage and shall be held by secret vote or by equivalent free voting procedures.

ART. 22. Everyone, as a member of society, has the right to social security and is entitled to realization, through national effort and international co-operation and in accordance with the organization and resources of each State, of the economic, social and cultural rights indispensable for his dignity and the free development of his personality.

ART. 23. *1*. Everyone has the right to work, to free choice of employment, to just and favourable conditions of work and to protection against unemployment.

2. Everyone, without any discrimination, has the right to equal pay for equal work.

3. Everyone who works has the right to just and favourable remuneration insuring for himself and his family an existence worthy of human dignity, and supplemented, if necessary, by other means of social protection.

4. Everyone has the right to form and to join trade unions for the protection of his interests.

ART. 24. Everyone has the right to rest and leisure, including reasonable limitation of working hours and periodic holidays with pay.

ART. 25. *1*. Everyone has the right to a standard of living adequate for the health and well-being of himself and of his family, including food, clothing, housing and medical care and necessary social services, and the right to security in the event of unemployment, sickness, disability, widowhood, old age or other lack of livelihood in circumstances beyond his control.

2. Motherhood and childhood are entitled to special care and assistance. All children, whether born in or out of wedlock, shall enjoy the same social protection.

ART. 26. *1*. Everyone has the right to education. Education shall be free, at least in the elementary and fundamental stages. Elementary education shall be compulsory. Technical and professional education shall be made generally available and higher education shall be equally accessible to all on the basis of merit.

2. Education shall be directed to the full development of the human personality and to the strengthening of respect for human rights and fundamental freedoms. It shall promote understanding, tolerance and friendship among all nations, racial or religious groups, and shall further the activities of the United Nations for the maintenance of peace.

3. Parents have a prior right to choose the kind of education that shall be given to their children.

ART. 27. *1*. Everyone has the right freely to participate in the cultural life of the community, to enjoy the arts

and to share in scientific advancement and its benefits.

2. Everyone has the right to the protection of the moral and material interests resulting from any scientific, literary or artistic production of which he is the author.

ART. 28. Everyone is entitled to a social and international order in which the rights and freedoms set forth in this Declaration can be fully realized.

ART. 29. *1*. Everyone has duties to the community in which alone the free and full development of his personality is possible.

2. In the exercise of his rights and freedoms, everyone shall be subject only to such limitations as are determined by law solely for the purpose of securing due recognition and respect for the rights and freedoms of others and of meeting the just requirements of morality, public order and the general welfare in a democratic society.

3. These rights and freedoms may in no case be exercised contrary to the purposes and principles of the United Nations.

ART. 30. Nothing in this Declaration may be interpreted as implying for any State, group or person any right to engage in any activity or to perform any act aimed at the destruction of any of the rights and freedoms set forth herein.

Chapter 18

The United States and the United Nations

65. THE UNITED NATIONS PARTICIPATION ACT OF 1945, 20 DECEMBER 1945 [1]

The Charter of the United Nations was submitted to the Senate by President Truman in person on 2 July 1945, six days after its signature in San Francisco. On the 23rd of that month the Committee on Foreign Relations reported on it favorably, and on the 28th the Senate voted its approval 89 to 2.[2] The American instrument of ratification was deposited on 8 August.[3] Upon receipt of the Soviet instrument of ratification, the last of those required under Article 110 of the Charter, Secretary of State Byrnes signed and published the Protocol of Deposit of Ratifications [4] on 24 October, thus bringing the Charter into force. The United Nations Participation Act of 1945 provided legislative authority for executive action under the terms of the Charter.

Be it enacted by the Senate and House of Representatives of the United States of America in Congress assembled, That this Act may be cited as the "United Nations Participation Act of 1945."

SEC. 2. (a) The President, by and with the advice and consent of the Sen-

ate, shall appoint a representative and a deputy representative of the United States to the United Nations, both of whom shall have the rank and status of envoy extraordinary and ambassador plenipotentiary and shall hold office at the pleasure of the President. Such representative and deputy representative shall represent the United States in the Security Council of the United Nations and may serve ex officio as United States representative on any organ, commission, or other body of the United Nations other than specialized agencies of the United Nations, and shall perform such other functions in connection with the participation of the United States in the United Nations as the President may from time to time direct.

(b) The President, by and with the advice and consent of the Senate, shall appoint an additional deputy representative of the United States to the

[1] *United States Statutes at Large,* LIX (1945), p. 619.

[2] The uncharacteristic speed with which both the Senate of the 79th Congress and its Committee on Foreign Relations took action on the Charter contrasts remarkably with the procedure of the Senate in the 66th Congress when dealing with the League of Nations Covenant. The 1945 resolution of approval also is to be contrasted with the resolution which failed of adoption in 1920 (see Doc. 35):

"Resolved (two thirds of the Senators concurring therein), that the Senate advise and

consent to the ratification of Executive F (79th Cong., 1st sess.), the Charter of the United Nations, with the Statute of the International Court of Justice annexed thereto, formulated at the United Nations Conference on International Organization and signed at San Francisco on June 26, 1945" [*Congressional Record,* 79th Cong., 1st sess., XCI (28 July 1945), p. 8190].

[3] For the text, see *Department of State Bulletin,* XIII (12 August 1945), p. 214.

[4] For the text, see *ibid.* (28 October 1945), p. 679 f.

Security Council who shall hold office at the pleasure of the President. Such deputy representative shall represent the United States in the Security Council of the United Nations in the event of the absence or disability of both the representative and the deputy representative of the United States to the United Nations.

(c) The President, by and with the advice and consent of the Senate, shall designate from time to time to attend a specified session or specified sessions of the General Assembly of the United Nations not to exceed five representatives of the United States and such number of alternates as he may determine consistent with the rules of procedure of the General Assembly. One of the representatives shall be designated as the senior representative.

(d) The President may also appoint from time to time such other persons as he may deem necessary to represent the United States in the organs and agencies of the United Nations, but the representative of the United States in the Economic and Social Council and in the Trusteeship Council of the United Nations shall be appointed only by and with the advice and consent of the Senate, except that the President may, without the advice and consent of the Senate, designate any officer of the United States to act, without additional compensation, as the representative of the United States in either such Council (A) at any specified session thereof, where the position is vacant or in the absence or disability of the regular representative, or (B) in connection with a specified subject matter at any specified session of either such Council in lieu of the regular representative. The President may designate any officer of the Department of State, whose appointment is subject to confirmation by the Senate, to act, without additional compensation, for temporary periods as the representative of the United States in the Security Council of the United Nations in the absence or disability of the representative and deputy representatives appointed under section 2 (a) and (b) or in lieu of such representatives in connection with a specified subject matter. The advice and consent of the Senate shall be required for the appointment by the President of the representative of the United States in any commission that may be formed by the United Nations with respect to atomic energy or in any other commission of the United Nations to which the United States is entitled to appoint a representative.

(e) Nothing contained in this section shall preclude the President of the Secretary of State, at the direction of the President, from representing the United States at any meeting or session of any organ or agency of the United Nations.

(f) All persons appointed in pursuance of authority contained in this section shall receive compensation at rates determined by the President upon the basis of duties to be performed but not in excess of rates authorized by sections 411 and 412 of the Foreign Service Act of 1946 (Public Law 724, Seventy-ninth Congress) for chiefs of mission and Foreign Service officers occupying positions of equivalent importance, except that no Member of the Senate or House of Representatives or officer of the United States who is designated under subsections (c) and (d) of this section as a representative of the United States or as an alternate to attend any specified session or specified sessions of the General Assembly shall be entitled to receive such compensation.

SEC. 3. The representatives provided for in section 2 hereof, when representing the United States in the respective organs and agencies of the United Nations, shall, at all times, act in accordance with the instructions of the President transmitted by the Secretary of State unless other means of transmission is directed by the President, and such representatives shall, in accordance with such instructions, cast any and all votes under the Charter of the United Nations.

Sec. 4. The President shall, from time to time as occasion may require, but not less than once each year, make reports to the Congress of the activities of the United Nations and of the participation of the United States therein. He shall make special current reports on decisions of the Security Council to take enforcement measures under the provisions of the Charter of the United Nations, and on the participation therein under his instructions, of the representative of the United States.

Sec. 5. (a) Notwithstanding the provisions of any other law, whenever the United States is called upon by the Security Council to apply measures, which said Council has decided, pursuant to article 41 of said Charter, are to be employed to give effect to its decisions under said Charter, the President may, to the extent necessary to apply such measures, through any agency which he may designate, and under such orders, rules, and regulations as may be prescribed by him, investigate, regulate, or prohibit, in whole or in part, economic relations or rail, sea, air, postal, telegraphic, radio, and other means of communication between any foreign country or any national thereof or any person therein and the United States or any person subject to the jurisdiction thereof, or involving any property subject to the jurisdiction of the United States.

(b) Any person who willfully violates or evades or attempts to violate or evade any order, rule, or regulation issued by the President pursuant to paragraph (a) of this section shall, upon conviction, be fined not more than $10,000 or, if a natural person, be imprisoned for not more than ten years, or both; and the officer, director, or agent of any corporation who knowingly participates in such violation or evasion shall be punished by a like fine, imprisonment, or both, and any property, funds, securities, papers, or other articles or documents, or any vessel, together with her tackle, apparel, furniture, and equipment, or vehicle

or aircraft, concerned in such violation shall be forfeited to the United States.

Sec. 6. The President is authorized to negotiate a special agreement or agreements with the Security Council which shall be subject to the approval of the Congress by appropriate Act or joint resolution, providing for the numbers and types of armed forces, their degree of readiness and general location, and the nature of facilities and assistance, including rights of passage, to be made available to the Security Council on its call for the purpose of maintaining international peace and security in accordance with article 43 of said Charter. The President shall not be deemed to require the authorization of the Congress to make available to the Security Council on its call in order to take action under article 42 of said Charter and pursuant to such special agreement or agreements the armed forces, facilities, or assistance provided for therein: *Provided,* That, except as authorized in section 7 of this Act, nothing herein contained shall be construed as an authorization to the President by the Congress to make available to the Security Council for such purpose armed forces, facilities, or assistance in addition to the forces, facilities, and assistance provided for in such special agreement or agreements.

Sec. 7. (a) Notwithstanding the provisions of any other law, the President, upon the request by the United Nations for cooperative action, and to the extent that he finds that it is consistent with the national interest to comply with such request, may authorize, in support of such activities of the United Nations as are specifically directed to the peaceful settlement of disputes and not involving the employment of armed forces contemplated by chapter VII of the United Nations Charter—

(1) the detail to the United Nations, under such terms and conditions as the President shall determine, of personnel of the armed forces of the United States to serve as observers, guards, or in any noncombatant capacity, but in

no event shall more than a total of one thousand of such personnel be so detailed at any one time: *Provided,* That while so detailed, such personnel shall be considered for all purposes as acting in the line of duty, including the receipt of pay and allowances as personnel of the armed forces of the United States, credit for longevity and retirement, and all other perquisites appertaining to such duty: *Provided further,* That upon authorization or approval by the President, such personnel may accept directly from the United Nations (a) any or all of the allowances or perquisites to which they are entitled under the first proviso hereof, and (b) extraordinary expenses and perquisites incident to such detail;

(2) the furnishing of facilities, services, or other assistance and the loan of the agreed fair share of the United States of any supplies and equipment to the United Nations by the National Military Establishment, under such terms and conditions as the President shall determine;

(3) the obligation, insofar as necessary to carry out the purposes of clauses (1) and (2) of this subsection, of any funds appropriated to the National Military Establishment or any department therein, the procurement of such personnel, supplies, equipment, facilities, services, or other assistance as may be made available in accordance with the request of the United Nations, and the replacement of such items, when necessary, where they are furnished from stocks.

(b) Whenever personnel or assistance is made available pursuant to the authority contained in subsection (a) (1) and (2) of this section, the President shall require reimbursement from the United Nations for the expense thereby incurred by the United States: *Provided,* That in exceptional circumstances, or when the President finds it to be in the national interest, he may waive, in whole or in part, the requirement of such reimbursement: *Provided further,* That when any such reimbursement is made, it shall be credited, at the option of the appropriate department of the National Military Establishment, either to the appropriation, fund, or account utilized in incurring the obligation, or to an appropriate appropriation, fund, or account currently available for the purposes for which expenditures were made.

(c) In addition to the authorization of appropriations to the Department of State contained in section 8 of this Act, there is hereby authorized to be appropriated to the National Military Establishment, or any department therein, such sums as may be necessary to reimburse such Establishment or department in the event that reimbursement from the United Nations is waived in whole or in part pursuant to authority contained in subsection (b) of this section.

(d) Nothing in this Act shall authorize the disclosure of any information or knowledge in any case in which such disclosure is prohibited by any other law of the United States.

SEC. 8. There is hereby authorized to be appropriated annually to the Department of State, out of any money in the Treasury not otherwise appropriated, such sums as may be necessary for the payment by the United States of its share of the expenses of the United Nations as apportioned by the General Assembly in accordance with article 17 of the Charter, and for all necessary salaries and expenses of the representatives provided for in section 2 hereof, and of their appropriate staffs.